The Routledge Course in Modern Mandarin Chinese is a two-year undergr... students with no prior background in Chinese study. Designed to build a strong foundation in both the spoken and written language it develops all the basic skills such as pronunciation, character writing, word use, and structures, while placing strong emphasis on the development of communicative skills.

The complete course consists of Textbook level 1, Workbook level 1 – including free CDs, and Textbook level 2 and Workbook level 2 – including free CDs. All books are available separately in simplified as well as traditional characters and take the students from complete beginner to post-intermediate level.

The benefits of this course include:

– focus on the long-term retention of vocabulary, characters, and structures by reiterating structures and vocabulary throughout the book series
– carefully selected and staged introduction of characters with staged removal of Pinyin to ensure recognition and use of characters
– clear and jargon-free explanations of use and structures that are easy for students and teachers to understand
– extensive workbook exercises for homework, independent study, and classroom use focusing on all language skills and modalities including a vast inventory of carefully structured exercises focusing on listening comprehension, reading for information, and writing for communication
– an extensive inventory of classroom activities that guide students to develop communication-based speaking and listening skills
– companion website providing writing exercise sheets, a complete answers key and a teachers' manual with classroom exercises, lesson plans, quizzes, and exams
– a list of communication goals and key structures for each lesson allowing the student to assess progress
– cultural notes explaining the context of the dialogues
– language FAQs explaining aspects of Chinese language as they relate to the content and vocabulary in the lesson
– storyline following a group of students studying in China from Europe, North America, and East Asia, making the book attractive to a variety of students and facilitating the introduction of Chinese culture
– full-color text design for the simplified character textbook and carefully matched designs for the traditional and simplified books, allowing for easy cross-reference

Textbook 1 provides a paced introduction to the language by teaching from pinyin in its first 5 lessons. Characters are introduced from the sixth lesson, and this is combined with the staged removal of pinyin.

Each lesson consists of a dialogue, vocabulary lists, in-class dialogue practice, jargon-free explanations of structures, language FAQs, and notes on pronunciation, pinyin and Chinese culture.

Claudia Ross is Professor of Chinese at the College of the Holy Cross, Massachusetts. She has served as President of the Chinese Language Teachers Association and as Director of the CET Chinese Program in Beijing. Her publications include *Chinese Demystified* (2010); *The Lady in the Painting, Expanded Edition* (2008); *Modern Mandarin Chinese Grammar: A Practical Guide,* co-authored with Jing-heng Sheng Ma; *Modern Mandarin Chinese Grammar Workbook,* co-authored with Jing-heng Sheng Ma and Baozhang He (both Routledge, 2006); *Outline of Chinese Grammar* (2004); and *Traditional Chinese Tales: A Course in Intermediate Chinese* (2001).

Baozhang He is Associate Professor in Chinese at the College of the Holy Cross, Massachusetts. He has served as Director of the Chinese Language Program at Harvard University and as Head Instructor in the "Princeton in Beijing" language program. His publications include *Modern Mandarin Chinese Grammar Workbook* (Routledge, 2006), co-authored with Claudia Ross and Jing-heng Sheng Ma and *Elementary Chinese* (2006), co-authored with Pei-Chia Chen.

Pei-Chia Chen is a lecturer in Chinese at UC San Diego and has previously taught at Harvard University. Her publications include *Elementary Chinese* (2006), co-authored with Baozhang He.

Meng Yeh is Senior Lecturer in Chinese at Rice University. She has served as a Board Member of the Chinese Language Teachers Association and is a founding member of CLTA-TX. She is an AP Chinese consultant for the College Board and a certified Oral Proficiency Interviewer in Chinese for Language Testing International, ACTFL. Her publications include *Advancing in Chinese* (2010) and *Task-based Listening Workbook: Communicating in Chinese Series* (1999).

THE ROUTLEDGE COURSE IN
Modern Mandarin Chinese

Textbook Level 1: Traditional Characters

Claudia Ross
Baozhang He
Pei-Chia Chen
Meng Yeh

Routledge
Taylor & Francis Group

LONDON AND NEW YORK

First published 2010 by Routledge
270 Madison Ave, New York, NY 10016

Simultaneously published in the USA and Canada
by Routledge
2 Park Square, Milton Park, Abingdon, Oxon OX14 4RN

Routledge is an imprint of the Taylor & Francis Group, an informa business

© 2010 Claudia Ross, Baozhang He, Pei-Chia Chen, Meng Yeh

Typeset in 12/15pt Scala by Graphicraft Limited, Hong Kong
Printed by Sheridan Books, Inc.

British Library Cataloguing in Publication Data
A catalogue record for this book is available from the British Library

Library of Congress Cataloging in Publication Data
Ross, Claudia.
The Routledge course in modern Mandarin Chinese. Textbook level 1 :
Traditional characters / Claudia Ross...[et al.].
    p. cm.
Includes index.
1. Chinese language–Textbook of foreign textbooks–English. I. Title. II.
Title: Modern Mandarin Chinese.
PL1129.E5R676 2010
495.1'82421–dc22
2009038360

ISBN10: 0-415-47249-0
ISBN13: 978-0-415-47249-4 (Textbook level 1, Traditional characters)

ISBN10: 0-415-47251-2
ISBN13: 978-0-415-47251-7 (Textbook level 1, Simplified characters)

ISBN10: 0-415-47248-2
ISBN13: 978-0-415-47248-7 (Workbook level 1, Traditional characters)

ISBN10: 0-415-47252-0
ISBN13: 978-0-415-47252-4 (Workbook level 1, Simplified characters)

Acknowledgments

We thank all of the people who have been involved in the development of this course. We give a special thanks to the students in the elementary Chinese class of 2008–2009 at the College of the Holy Cross for their patience and feedback as we field tested and revised each lesson. Thanks also to Soon Suet-ching and Ko Joon Kang, foreign language assistants in Chinese at Holy Cross in the same year, for their help on many aspects of the project. We are grateful to the College of the Holy Cross for its generous support in the way of released time and resources, and to the members of the Audio-Visual Department at the College for their help in producing audio recordings that enabled field testing. We thank our editors for their guidance and for their help in keeping us on track. Last but not least, we thank our families for their ongoing support and their confidence in our work.

The stroke order charts in this book were produced with eStroke software and are included with the permission of EON Media Limited:

http://www.eon.com.hk/estroke.

Introduction

The Routledge Course in Modern Mandarin Chinese is an innovative two-year course for English-speaking learners of Chinese as a foreign language that guides students to build a strong foundation in Mandarin and prepares them for continued success in the language. The course is designed to address the five goals (the 5 *C's*) of foreign language learning highlighted by the American Council on the Teaching of Foreign Languages (ACTFL). Each *communication*-focused lesson is grounded in the *cultural* context of China, guiding students to make *comparisons* between language and social customs in the United States and the Chinese-speaking world, and providing activities that *connect* their language study to other disciplines and lead them to use Chinese in the wider *community*.

Set in China, the course introduces themes that students encounter in their first experience abroad. The themes in Level 1 include talking about *self and family, shopping and money, discussing every day activities and making plans, describing locations, giving and following directions*, and *accepting invitations and being a guest*.

Innovative Features of The Routledge Course in Modern Mandarin, Level 1

- Separate introduction of *words* and *characters*. New words are first presented in Pinyin form only, so students can focus on pronunciation, meaning, and use before learning words in their character form. The total number of new words and characters is controlled to facilitate retention. Words are introduced at a faster pace than characters so that students build a broad base of vocabulary for oral communication in their first year of study. In all, Level 1 introduces approximately 575 words and 180 characters.
- Complete replacement of Pinyin by characters. When a character is introduced, it replaces the Pinyin form in all subsequent occurrences without additional Pinyin support. Students learn to focus on the character as the primary written form of the Chinese word or syllable.
- Character literacy instruction. Once characters are introduced, each textbook and workbook lesson guides students to understand the structure of characters and to develop reading and writing strategies.
- Integration of form and function. Structures are introduced to support communication.
- "Basic to complex" introduction of grammatical structures. Students build a solid foundation in basic structures before learning more complex variations.
- Recycling. Vocabulary and structures are recycled in successive lessons to facilitate mastery.

- Ongoing focus on pronunciation. Pronunciation instruction and practice continue throughout the course.
- A comprehensive workbook with extensive information-focused and skill-focused exercises that target all aspects of each lesson.
- A Teachers' Manual with a wealth of communication-based classroom activities, project suggestions, lesson plans, and teaching tips.
- Alphabetically arranged indices for vocabulary, characters, and structures.

Textbook lessons include:

- *Communication Goals* and *Key Structures*.
- A *Dialogue*, divided into several short sections to facilitate memorization and classroom practice.
- *Dialogue Practice*, communication-based activities to practice the functions and themes introduced in the lesson. (Additional communication-based activities are provided in the Teachers' Manual.)
- *Vocabulary*, alphabetically arranged.
- *Characters*, alphabetically arranged by Pinyin (beginning in Lesson 6), and a *Stroke Order Flow Chart* (beginning in Lesson 6) that displays the radical and stroke-by-stroke formation of each new character.
- *Use and Structure Notes* with clear explanations of grammar and usage.
- *Sentence Pyramids* that illustrate the building blocks of phrases and sentences.
- *Pronunciation and Pinyin* explanations for ongoing pronunciation practice.
- *Language FAQs*, additional notes on language use addressing questions that students often ask about the language.
- *Notes on Chinese Culture* that discuss the customs and behavior associated with language use.
- An English translation of the *Dialogue*.

Workbook lessons include:

Listening and Speaking practice
- *Pronunciation and Pinyin*, including tongue twisters, poetry, transliterated names and expressions, and common sayings.
- *Structure Drills* for individual study. The Structure Drills can also be used in the classroom.
- *Listening for Information*, listening comprehension exercises built around the structures, vocabulary, and themes introduced in the lesson.

Reading and Writing practice
- *Focus on Structure*, written exercises that focus on the mastery and control of new structures at the sentence level.
- *Focus on Communication*, written exercises that focus on reading for information and on communicating information in writing.

- *Focus on Chinese Characters*: Beginning in Lesson 6, exercises that guide students to learn proper stroke order, identify common radicals, and learn characters in terms of their recurring parts. Beginning in Lesson 10, exercises that train students to "see" familiar words in authentically written Chinese texts in which spacing does not identify word boundaries, exercises that train students to read for information in texts that contain some unfamiliar characters, and exercises that train students to proofread and correct character errors within a text.

An overview of Mandarin Chinese

Mandarin and the dialects of Chinese

This course is a two-year introduction to Mandarin Chinese, the most widely spoken "dialect" in the Chinese family of languages. Other major dialects of Chinese include the Yue dialect (e.g. Cantonese), Southern Min (e.g. Taiwanese), and the Wu dialect (e.g. Shanghainese). Although they are referred to as "dialects" in Chinese, Mandarin, Cantonese, Taiwanese, and Shanghainese are as distinct from each other as Spanish is from French.

Mandarin is the national dialect in the People's Republic of China (mainland China) and in the Republic of China (Taiwan). It is also one of the four official languages of Singapore. Mandarin has a number of different names in Chinese. In mainland China it is referred to as *Putonghua* (the common language). In Taiwan it is referred to as *Guoyu* (the national language). It is also often called *Huayu* (the Chinese language).

The pronunciation of Standard Mandarin is based on the pronunciation of the city of Beijing, the capital of the People's Republic of China, but it is not exactly the same as Beijing pronunciation. The vocabulary of Standard Mandarin is drawn from a variety of dialects found in northern and southwestern China. The grammatical structure of Standard Mandarin is based on the large body of modern literary works written in vernacular Chinese.

The Chinese writing system

Chinese is written in Chinese characters, graphs that stand for units of meaning rather than pronunciation, and the same writing system is used for all dialects of Chinese. Therefore, while speakers of two different dialects cannot communicate through speech, they can understand each other perfectly when they communicate in writing. There are more than 10,000 Chinese characters in active use, and an educated reader can read 4,000 or more characters.

Characters represent meaning, but to represent pronunciation you need some kind of alphabet or *Romanization* system. The Romanization system most commonly used to represent the pronunciation of Mandarin is the *Pinyin* system. Pinyin literally means *piece the sounds together*. It is the official Romanization system in mainland China, and it is the Romanization system used by western scholars and the press when presenting Mandarin names and words. We use the Pinyin system of Romanization in this book. As you will see,

Pinyin uses the letters of the English alphabet, but the pronunciations it assigns to some of the letters are different from English.

The pronunciation of Mandarin Chinese

The basic unit of pronunciation in all Chinese dialects is the syllable. The Mandarin syllable consists of three parts: a tone, an initial consonant, and a final.

TONE	
(initial consonant)	final

Linguists further distinguish the final as consisting of a medial vowel, **i**, **u**, or **ü**, and an ending. The ending must include a vowel, and may also include a final consonant, either **n** or **ng**.

Tone			
(initial consonant)	Final		
	(medial vowel)	Ending	
		vowel	(final consonant)

The only obligatory sound in the Mandarin syllable is the vowel in the ending. Therefore, a syllable may consist of a single vowel (e.g. **a**) or it may consist of a vowel and a tone (e.g. **ā**), or a vowel and a tone followed by **n** or **ng** (e.g. **ān**), or a vowel and a tone preceded by a medial vowel (e.g. **iān**, **uén**, **üǎn**, spelled in Pinyin as **yān**, **wén**, **yuǎn**), or a vowel and a tone preceded by an initial consonant (e.g. **mā**), etc.

When we discuss and practice the pronunciation of Mandarin in this course, we talk about the structure of the syllable in terms of the three parts noted in the first table above: tone, initial consonant, and final.

Here is an overview of the three parts of the Mandarin syllable. Tones, initial consonants, and finals are discussed and practiced in more detail in the first nine lessons of the book.

Tones

Tones are changes in the pitch contour of a syllable. Tones function like consonants and vowels to determine the meaning of the syllable. Mandarin has four contour tones and a "neutral" tone. The four contour tones are normally indicated by the tone marks ˉ ´ ˇ and ` written above a vowel in the syllable. Syllables spoken in a neutral tone do not have a tone mark. Sometimes tones are indicated by the numbers 1–4 written after the syllable. When tones are indicated by numbers, the number 0 or 5 is used to indicated a neutral tone.

The tone marks indicate the pitch contour of the tones:

The first tone (¯) is a high, level tone. It starts high and remains high and level throughout the pronunciation of the syllable.
The second tone (´) is a rising tone. It starts low and rises throughout the pronunciation of the syllable.
The third tone (ˇ) is a falling-rising tone. It starts at medium range, drops to low range, and then rises.
The fourth tone (`) is a falling tone. It starts high and falls across the pronunciation of the syllable.

Initial consonants

Mandarin has 21 initial consonants. They are presented in the following table. Consonants in the same column have certain features in common. The pronunciation of consonants and the association of certain sets of consonants with certain finals is covered in detail in Lessons 1–5.

b	d	g	j	zh	z
p	t	k	q	ch	c
m	n	h	x	sh	s
f	l			r	

Finals

Here are the Mandarin finals. The pronunciation of some of the letters of the alphabet vary depending upon the final in which they occur. These variations, along with restrictions on the co-occurrence of certain initials and finals, are discussed in detail in Lessons 1–5.

Finals that begin with:	*and end with a vowel:*	*and end with n:*	*and end with ng:*	*and end with r:*
a	a, ai, ao	an	ang	
e	e, ei	en	eng	er
o	(o), ou		ong	
i	i, ia, iao, ie, iu/iou	ian, in	iang, ing, iong	
ü	ü, üe	üan, ün		
u	u, ua, uai, ui/uei, uo	uan, uen	uang, ueng	

List of abbreviations

S	subject
O	object
V	verb
AdjV	adjectival verb
ActV	action verb
VP	verb phrase
N	noun
NP	noun phrase
pron.	pronoun
prep.	preposition

Contents

Communication goals:

- Learn culturally appropriate greetings in formal situations
- Give basic information about yourself

Key structures:

- NP **shì** NP
- yes-no questions with **ma**
- negation with **bù**
- **yě** *also* + VP
- **hěn** *very* + AdjV

Communication goals:

- State your nationality and ask others about their nationalities
- Confirm that information is correct

Key structures:

- the plural form of pronouns
- follow-up questions with **ne**
- **dōu** *all, both* + VP
- **dāngrán** *of course* + VP

Communication goals:

- Greet others in the morning
- Ask about items for sale in a store
- Talk about the price of items

Key structures:

- number + classifier + N: *one bottle of water*
- specifier + classifier + N: *that bottle of water*
- the money phrase: **X kuài X máo X fēn qián**
- **hái** *in addition*
- **tài** AdjV **le** *too AdjV*

Communication goals:

- Negotiate for the price of an item
- Pay for items and get change

Key structures:

- specifier + number + classifier + N: *these/those two bottles of water*
- 哪 *which*
- AdjV 一 **diǎn** *a little more AdjV*
- 一 **bǎi** *100 and the numbers 11–999*

Communication goals:

- State your age and ask others how old they are
- Indicate dates and days of the week
- Make plans to do activities on a given date or day of the week

Key structures:

- (S) + time when + VP
- **qù** + ActV *going to do an action*
- suggestions with **ba, zěn** 麼 **yàng**, 好不好, **xíng** 不 **xíng**
- the order of information in time phrases: largest unit to smallest unit
- (time) **cái** (age) *not* (this age) *until* (this time)

Key structures:

- N **zài** location
- VV O
- **měi** (個) time **dōu** VP
- **lái** location
- A **lí** B distance
- the preposition **gěi** *for/to*

Communication goals:

- Give and follow directions by bus or train

Key structures:

- **cóng** A **dào** B 怎麼 **zǒu**?
- **zuò** vehicle
- VP₁ 還是 VP₂ (呢)
- 在 location + ActV
- **V-O V** + duration

Communication goals:

- Make and accept apologies
- Politely initiate and receive telephone calls
- Describe the location of people, places, and things

Key structures:

- 容易 + V, **nán** + V
- reference point 的 direction
- sequence with **xiān** and 再

Communication goals:

- Give and follow street directions
- Paraphrase information
- Tell someone not to do something

Key structures:

- indicating how an action with an object is performed:
    □ V + O V 得 AdjV
- after situation₁, situation₂:
    □ V₁ 了 O 以 **hòu** 就 V₂
- first, second, third: **dì** + number: **dì** 一, **dì** 二, **dì** 三
- 也就是說 *that is to say*
- 一 **zhí** + ActV *continue doing an action*
- **bié** + ActV *don't do the action*

Communication goals:

- Behave as a guest and host in a semi-formal gathering
- Give and respond to compliments

Key structures:

- V-過
- situation₁ 以前 situation₂
- 多 V 一點

Communication goals:

- Evaluate past experiences and current situations
- Talk about future plans

Key structures:

- situation₁ 的時候 situation₂
- **suī** 然 situation₁ 可是 situation₂
- 慢慢地 + VP

引言

《*Routledge* 現代漢語課程》是針對母語爲英語的學習者編寫的一套創新漢語課程。本教材爲兩年的課程，幫助學生打下堅實的漢語基礎並爲他們繼續在語言學習的成功上做好准備。教材的設計上力求全面反映全美外語教學學會(ACTFL)倡導的外語學習的五項目標(5 C's)。每一課以語言交際爲中心，以中國文化爲背景，引導學生做中美語言及社會習俗方面的對比，並提供大量的教學活動使學生把語言學習與其他專業知識的學習貫穿起來，以使他們能在更廣的範圍內使用漢語。

教材的背景是在中國，給學生介紹第一次到中國通常會遇到的情景。第一冊教材的情景包括個人和家庭，購物和錢幣，日常作息和活動計劃，地點的描述，問路，接受邀請及做客之道等。

《現代漢語課程》第一冊的創意性特點：

- "詞"、"字"分開介紹：生詞在第一次出現的時候，只以拼音的形式介紹。這樣，學生可以先把精力集中在發音、意思及用法上，然後再學漢字。生詞和漢字的數量控制在學生可以掌握的前提下。生詞的數量大于漢字的數量，目的在于使學生在第一學年打下良好的詞彙基礎，進行基本口頭交際。第一冊，介紹了大約575個詞和180個漢字。
- 漢字全部代替拼音：某一漢字一經介紹，該字的拼音形式就不再出現。學生必須學着把注意力集中在漢字上，因爲只有漢字才是漢語的詞或音節的真正書寫形式。
- 識字教學：針對每課所介紹的漢字，課本和練習本都有相應的練習幫助學生了解漢字的結構，並培養學生閱讀和書寫的策略。
- 形式和功能結合：句型結構的介紹是爲了便于交際。
- 語法結構的引進由簡到難：學生在充分掌握了簡單的語法結構後，再逐步學習較爲複雜的結構。
- 句型和生詞的重複：爲幫助學生掌握運用，第一次出現的句型和生詞在後續幾課的課文和練習中盡量重複。
- 重視發音：發音教學和練習自始至終貫穿全書。

- 綜合練習冊：練習兼顧信息溝通及語言技巧的培養，涵蓋該課的方方面面。
- 教師手冊：提供給教師大量的語言交際的課堂活動、教學建議、課程教案及教學技巧。
- 以字母順序安排的生詞、漢字及語法點的索引。

課本每一課包括的內容：

- 交際目標和重點句型。
- 對話：爲便于學生記憶和課堂練習被分爲幾小段。
- 對話練習：基于語言交際的課堂活動，練習本課所介紹的功能和情景。（教師手冊提供更多的語言交際活動。）
- 生詞：按字母順序列出。
- 漢字：按拼音字母順序排列（從第六課開始），並提供每個漢字的筆順（從第六課開始）及部首等漢字信息。
- 用法及結構注釋：簡明扼要解釋語法項目及用法。
- 句型擴展：幫助學生建造短語和句子。
- 發音和拼音：介紹發音方法，英漢發音對比，拼音書寫規則。提供持續不斷的發音正音練習。
- 語言常識問答：及時應對學生在學習時經常提出或可能遇到的問題。
- 中國文化點滴：討論與語言運用相關的習俗和行爲。
- 漢語對話的英譯。

練習冊每課包括的內容：

聽說練習
- 發音和拼音：包括繞口令、詩詞、外國人名地名的音譯和固定表達法。
- 結構操練：可以學生課外自己練習，也可以在課上使用。
- 掌握信息的聽力練習：引導學生融會貫通本課介紹的句型，生詞和主題。

讀寫練習
- 語言結構：鞏固加強學生對新句型的掌握，書寫完整正確的句子。
- 信息交際：強調閱讀理解，以書寫溝通信息。
- 漢字書寫：從第六課開始，引導學生學習正確的筆順，識別常見的部首，及熟悉漢字常用的組成部件。由于中文字與字之間的空隙並不代表詞的界線，從第十課開始，訓練學生在閱讀中去"看"學過並熟悉的詞語，訓練學生在閱讀包含有沒學過的漢字的段落中尋找信息，訓練學生在閱讀中改正錯字白字。

Lesson 1 Nǐ hǎo *Hello*

Communication goals
- Learn culturally appropriate greetings in formal situations
- Give basic information about yourself

Key structures
NP **shì** NP

yes-no questions with **ma**

negation with **bù**

yě + VP

hěn + AdjV

Dialogue

The Situation: The "new student reception" in a study-abroad program in China attended by teachers and new students. The students have come from countries around the world to continue their Chinese language study and to learn more about Chinese culture. The setting is relatively formal, and most of the students are meeting each other for the first time.

Part A

Xiǎo Zhāng:	Nǐ hǎo.
Xiǎo Gāo:	Nǐ hǎo.
Xiǎo Zhāng:	Wǒ shì xuésheng. Nǐ shì xuésheng ma?
Xiǎo Gāo:	Shì. Wǒ yě shì xuésheng.

Part B

Xiǎo Zhāng:	Tā shì xuésheng ma?
Xiǎo Gāo:	Bù shì. Tā bù shì xuésheng. Tā shì lǎoshī. Tā shì Lǐ lǎoshī.

Part C

Xiǎo Gāo:	Lǎoshī hǎo.
Lǐ lǎoshī:	Xiǎo Gāo, nǐ hǎo ma?
Xiǎo Gāo:	Wǒ hěn hǎo, xièxie.
Lǐ lǎoshī:	Zài jiàn.

Vocabulary

bù	negation	*no, not*
Gāo	family name	*(family name)*
hǎo	adjectival verb	*good*
hěn	intensifier	*very*
lǎoshī	noun	*teacher, professor*
Lǐ	family name	*(family name)*
ma	final particle	*(forms yes-no questions)*
nǐ	pronoun	*you*
nǐ hǎo	greeting	*hello (formal greeting)*
shì	stative verb	*be*
tā	pronoun	*he/him, she/her, it*
wǒ	pronoun	*I/me*
xiǎo	family name prefix	*
xièxie	conversational expression	*thank you*
xuésheng	noun	*student*
yě	adverb	*also*
zài jiàn	conversational expression	*goodbye*
Zhāng	family name	*(family name)*

Dialogue practice

Do these activities in class after mastering each part of Dialogue 1.

Dialogue 1A: Pretend you are at the new student reception. Greet a classmate and find out if he is a student. Tell him that you are also a student.

Dialogue 1B: Choose an identity, either **xuésheng** or **lǎoshī**. Greet a classmate and find out if she is a student or a teacher. Your classmate should find out if you are a student or a teacher. Repeat until you have identified at least three classmates.

Dialogue 1C: Pair up with a classmate and take turns asking how you are. When you are done, say goodbye. Repeat the conversation with at least three more classmates.

Use and structure

1.1.   Family names and addressing friends

In this lesson we are introduced to two students, Mary Girard and David James, who are "studying abroad" in China. In this book we call them **Xiǎo Gāo** and **Xiǎo Zhāng**. **Gāo** and **Zhāng** are Chinese family names (surnames) that are similar in sound to their western family names. <u>Xiǎo + family name</u> is a form of address that is often used between friends who are about the same age, and it is also a way for an older person to address a younger friend. It is the way that these two students will address each other when they become friends. In Chinese, people do not address each other with the family name alone, and **Xiǎo Gāo** and **Xiǎo Zhāng** will never call each other **Gāo** and **Zhāng**. We will learn more about names in Lesson 3.

1.2.   The Greeting **nǐ hǎo**

Nǐ hǎo is a greeting. We translate **nǐ hǎo** with the English expression *hello*, but it is more formal and more restricted in use than the greeting *hello* is in English. It can be used when meeting people for the first time in formal situations, and it is often used in business contexts, especially when answering the telephone. Students typically greet their teacher by saying **lǎoshī hǎo** *hello teacher (hello professor)* and teachers can greet a class of students by saying **xuésheng hǎo** *hello students*.

1.3.   Pronouns

Mandarin pronouns have a single form that does not change whether the pronoun is used as subject or object. **Wǒ** means *I* or *me*. **Nǐ** means *you* (subject) or *you* (object). **Tā** means *he* or *him, she* or *her*, or *it*.

	subject	object
first person	**wǒ** *I*	**wǒ** *me*
second person	**nǐ** *you*	**nǐ** *you*
third person	**tā** *he/she/it*	**tā** *him/her/it*

1.4.   Shì *be*

Shì is the verb *be* in Mandarin. It links a subject with a noun or noun phrase.

S   **V**   **N/NP**
Wǒ   **shì**   **xuésheng.**
I am (a) student.

Mandarin verbs have only one, unchanging form. Verbs do not change to mark tense or to agree with the subject. Thus, the same verb **shì** is used to indicate (I) *am*, (you) *are*, (he, she, it) *is*, *were*, and *was*.

Wǒ shì xuésheng.	*I am a student.*
Nǐ shì xuésheng ma?	*Are you a student?*
Tā shì lǎoshī.	*He/she is a teacher.*

1.5.   Word order and phrase order in the Mandarin sentence

The normal order of information in the Mandarin sentence is:

S   **V**   **O**
Tā   **shì**   **xuésheng.**
he/she   be   student
He/she is a student.

1.6.   Asking yes-no questions with **ma**

Nǐ shì xuésheng ma?
Are you a student?

Yes-no questions are questions that can be answered *yes* or *no*. Mandarin has a number of ways to form yes-no questions. The simplest way is to add the <u>final particle</u> **ma** to the end of a statement. You can think of **ma** as adding the meaning "*yes or no?*" to the sentence. The word order in statements and in yes-no questions with **ma** is the same:

S   **V**   **O**   **(ma)**
Tā   **shì**   **xuésheng.**
he/she   be   student
He/she is a student.

Tā   **shì**   **xuésheng**   **ma?**
he/she   be   student   yes or no
Is he/she a student?

1.7. Answering *yes*

There is no word for *yes* in Mandarin. When answering *yes* to a yes-no question, <u>repeat the verb</u> that is used in the question. The verb is underlined in the following example.

Q: **Nǐ <u>shì</u> xuésheng ma?**
A: **Wǒ <u>shì</u> xuésheng.**

To give the short answer *yes*, just repeat the verb:

Q: **Nǐ <u>shì</u> xuésheng ma?**
A: **<u>Shì</u>.**

1.8. Yě *also*

Yě *also* is an adverb. It always occurs before a verb or verb phrase, and never before a noun or at the end of a sentence. **Yě** occurs before negation. For more on negation, see Use and Structure note 1.9.

(S)   yě + V(P)
Wǒ   yě   shì xuésheng.
I am also a student.

1.9. Answering *no* and saying *no*

Mandarin has two words for *no*. In this lesson we learn one of them: **bù**. **Bù** negates most verbs. It occurs right before the verb or verb phrase.

Tā <u>bù</u> shì xuésheng. *She is not a student.*

If the sentence contains **yě** *also*, **yě** occurs before **bù**:

Tā <u>yě bù</u> shì xuésheng. *She is also not a student.*

To give a short answer *no*, just say **bù** + the verb:

Q: **Tā <u>shì</u> xuésheng ma?** *Is she a student?*
A: **<u>Bù shì</u>.** *No.*

We will learn the other commonly used word for *no* in Lesson 4.

1.10. Names and titles: Lǐ lǎoshī

Lǐ lǎoshī means *Teacher Li*, or, in common American usage, *Professor Li*. **Lǐ**, like **Gāo** and **Zhāng**, is a family name. **Lǎoshī** *teacher* is a title. In Mandarin, a title always follows the family name.

1.11.   Greeting vs. question: **Nǐ hǎo** and **nǐ hǎo ma?**

Nǐ hǎo *hello* is a greeting (Use and Structure note 1.2). You can respond to the greeting **nǐ hǎo** by saying **nǐ hǎo**. In contrast, **nǐ hǎo ma?** is a yes-no question, and it requires an answer. If you are all right, you respond to this question by saying **wǒ hěn hǎo** *I'm fine (I'm okay)*.

1.12.   Adjectival verbs: **Hǎo** *good*

Hǎo *good* is translated into English as an adjective, but in Mandarin it can function as the main verb in the sentence. Therefore, we call **hǎo** an <u>adjectival verb</u>. All but a few English adjectives function as adjectival verbs in Mandarin. Notice that adjectival verbs <u>do not</u> occur with the verb **shì** *be*.

Say this:	*Do not say this:*
Wǒ hěn hǎo.	⊗ Wǒ shì hěn hǎo.
I am fine.	

1.13.   Intensifier + adjectival verb: **Hěn hǎo** *very good*

Hěn *very* indicates the intensity of an adjectival verb. Therefore, we call it an <u>intensifier</u>. Words like *too, somewhat, extremely,* etc. are also intensifiers, and we will learn their Mandarin equivalents in later lessons.

Mandarin intensifiers occur right before the adjectival verb: **hěn hǎo** *very good*.

Mandarin intensifiers are always negated with **bù**.

In Mandarin, adjectival verbs are typically preceded by either an intensifier or negation. When intensity is not emphasized, the intensifier **hěn** is used. In other words, **hěn** sometimes is used to contribute the meaning *very*, and sometimes it is used in a sentence in order to satisfy the requirement that the adjectival verb has to be preceded by something. You can always translate **hěn** as *very*.

Sentence pyramids

The sentence pyramids illustrate the use of each new vocabulary item and structure introduced in the lesson. Use them to help you learn how to form phrases and sentences in Mandarin. Supply the English translation for the last line where indicated.

1. hǎo Nǐ hǎo.	*good, well* *Hello.*

2.	
xuésheng	*student*
shì xuésheng	*be a student*
Nǐ shì xuésheng.	*You are a student.*

3.	
xuésheng	*student*
shì xuésheng	*be a student*
Wǒ shì xuésheng.	*I am a student.*

4.	
shì xuésheng	*be a student*
Tā shì xuésheng.	*He/she is a student.*

5.	
ma	*(yes-no question particle)*
shì xuésheng ma?	*be a student, yes or no?*
Nǐ shì xuésheng ma?	*Are you a student?*

6.	
shì xuésheng	*be a student*
yě shì xuésheng	*also be a student*
Wǒ yě shì xuésheng.	_____

7.	
shì xuésheng	*be a student*
bù shì xuésheng	*not be a student*
Tā bù shì xuésheng.	*He/she is not a student.*

8.	
lǎoshī	*teacher*
shì lǎoshī	*be a teacher*
Tā shì lǎoshī.	_____

9.	
shì lǎoshī	*be a teacher*
shì lǎoshī ma?	*be a teacher, yes or no?*
Nǐ shì lǎoshī ma?	_____

10.	
ma	*(yes-no question particle)*
Nǐ hǎo ma?	*Are you okay?*

11.	
xièxie	*thanks, thank you*
Wǒ hěn hǎo, xièxie.	*I am fine, thanks.*

12.	
lǎoshī	*teacher*
shì lǎoshī	*be a teacher*
bù shì lǎoshī	*not be a teacher*
Wǒ bù shì lǎoshī.	_____

13.	
hǎo	*good*
Lǎoshī hǎo.	*Hello teacher. (Hello professor.)*

14.	
hǎo	*good*
Xuésheng hǎo.	*Hello students.*

15.	
Zhāng	*Zhang (family name)*
Xiǎo Zhāng	*Xiao Zhang*
shì Xiǎo Zhāng	*be Xiao Zhang*
Tā shì Xiǎo Zhāng.	_____

16.	
Gāo	*Gao (family name)*
Xiǎo Gāo	*Xiao Gao*
shì Xiǎo Gāo	*be Xiao Gao*
shì Xiǎo Gāo ma?	*be Xiao Gao, yes or no?*
Nǐ shì Xiǎo Gāo ma?	_____

17.	
Xiǎo Gāo	*Xiao Gao*
shì Xiǎo Gāo	*be Xiao Gao*
Wǒ shì Xiǎo Gāo.	*I am Xiao Gao.*
Shì. Wǒ shì Xiǎo Gāo.	*Yes. I am Xiao Gao.*

18.	
lǎoshī	*teacher, professor*
Lǐ lǎoshī	*Professor Li*
shì Lǐ lǎoshī	*be Professor Li*
Tā shì Lǐ lǎoshī.	*He is Professor Li.*

19.	
hǎo	*good*
hěn hǎo	*very good (okay)*
Tā hěn hǎo.	*She is okay.*

Pronunciation and Pinyin

Introduction to the parts of the Mandarin syllable

The Mandarin syllable can be described in terms of three parts: an initial consonant, a final, and a tone. Syllables need not begin with an initial consonant, so we put the initial consonant in parentheses here.

TONE	
(initial consonant)	final

A basic overview of the Mandarin syllable is presented at the beginning of this book. In this and the following lessons we select a group of sounds for additional practice. In this lesson we focus on the four Mandarin contour tones and on initials and finals that appear in this lesson's Chinese vocabulary.

Tones

The four contour tones

In Mandarin, tones are a feature of pronunciation like consonants and vowels, and they serve to distinguish the meaning of a syllable. Tone involves the pitch of the syllable, and contour tones are tones in which the pitch has a particular shape, for example, level, falling, or rising, across the syllable. Mandarin has four contour tones and we look at their basic forms in this lesson. In Pinyin, contour tones are usually indicated with the following tone marks written over a vowel in the syllable: ˉ ´ ˇ ` . There are also rules for the placement of tone marks over the appropriate vowel. Tones are sometimes indicated with the numbers 1–4 following the syllable, with 1 representing first tone, etc. Here are diagrams of the four contour tones of Mandarin, along with words in each tone that are introduced in Lesson 1. The diagrams indicate the pitch contour of each tone.

First tone (1st tone, level tone)

First tone starts high and remains high and level throughout the pronunciation of the syllable. It is also called a level tone.

	Gāo
	(lǎo)shī
	shēng
	tā
	Zhāng

Second tone (2nd tone, rising tone)

Second tone starts low and rises throughout the pronunciation of the syllable. It is also called a rising tone.

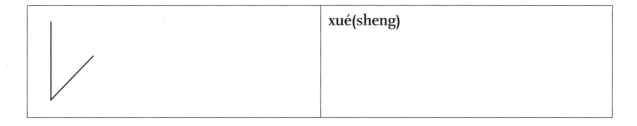

	xué(sheng)

Third tone (3rd tone, falling-rising tone)

The basic form of third tone starts at medium pitch, drops to low pitch, and then rises. It is also called a falling-rising tone.

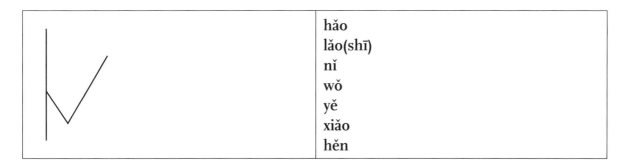

	hǎo
	lǎo(shī)
	nǐ
	wǒ
	yě
	xiǎo
	hěn

Fourth tone (4th tone, falling tone)

Fourth tone starts high and falls across the pronunciation of the syllable. It is also called a falling tone.

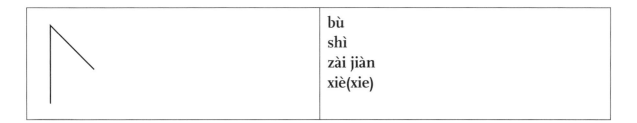

	bù
	shì
	zài jiàn
	xiè(xie)

Tone distinguishes the meaning of syllables in the same way that consonants and vowels do. Two syllables with different tones mean different things, even if the consonants and vowels are identical. Here are some examples:

mā	*mom*	**fāng**	*square*
má	*hemp*	**fáng**	*house*
mǎ	*horse*	**fǎng**	*imitate*
mà	*scold*	**fàng**	*put (something) down*

Rules for the placement of tone marks in Pinyin

The conventions of Pinyin spelling specify the location of the tone mark in the syllable. The tone mark is always placed over a vowel. To determine the vowel that receives the tone mark, apply the following rules in this order:

1. If the syllable contains only one vowel, the tone mark occurs over that vowel. Examples: **bù** *no, not*, **nǐ** *you*, **tā** *he/him, she/her, it*.
2. If the syllable contains **a** or **e**, the tone mark is placed over the **a** or the **e**. Examples: **Gāo** (*family name*), **xué(sheng)** *student*, **(nǐ) hǎo** *hello*.
3. If the final is **ou**, the tone mark occurs over the **o**. Examples (from Lessons 2–4): **dōu**, **yǒu**.
4. Otherwise, the tone mark is placed over the <u>last vowel</u> in the syllable. Examples (from Lessons 2–3): **shuō**, **guó**, **duì**.

Tone change for the word bù *no, not*

When **bù** occurs before another syllable with fourth tone, it changes to second tone (rising tone). Here is the rule that summarizes this change:

bù + 4   →   **bú** + 4
bù duì   →   **bú duì**

In this textbook we will always write **bù** in its original fourth tone.

Initial consonants

Here is a table of Mandarin initial consonants. In this lesson we focus on the highlighted groups of initial consonants.

b	d	g	j	zh	z
p	t	k	q	ch	c
m	n	h	x	sh	s
f	l			r	

When consonants are recited in Mandarin (as the alphabet is recited in English in the form of the ABC's), each group of consonants is followed by a particular "recitation" vowel. When we illustrate syllables with each consonant, the first example will be the recitation form of the consonant with its recitation vowel.

b, p, m, f

b, **p**, **m**, and **f** are pronounced similar to the way they are in English. Here are examples of Mandarin syllables that begin with **b**, **p**, **m**, and **f**.

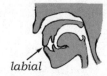

labial

b	bō, bā, bǐ, bù, bāo, bāng
p	pō, pà, pī, pǔ, pào, pàng
m	mō, mā, mǐ, mù, máo, máng
f	fō, fā, fù, fáng

d, t, n, l

d, t, n, and **l** are pronounced very similar to the way they are in English. They differ primarily in that, in Mandarin, the tongue is slightly more forward than in English during the pronunciation of the sounds. Here are examples of Mandarin syllables that begin with **d, t, n,** and **l**.

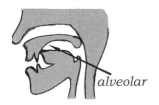

d	dē, dǎ, dì, dú, dào, dāng
t	tē, tā, tì, tǔ, tāo, táng
n	nē, nà, nǐ, nǔ, nào
l	lē, lā, lí, lù, lǎo

alveolar

Finals

Here are the finals of Mandarin as they are spelled in Pinyin. The finals introduced in Lesson 1 are highlighted.

Finals that begin with:	and end with a vowel:	and end with n:	and end with ng:	and end with r:
a	a, ai, ao	an	ang	
e	e, ei	en	eng	er
o	(o), ou		ong	
i	i, ia, iao, ie, iu/iou	ian, in	iang, ing, iong	
ü	ü, üe	üan, ün		
u	u, ua, uai, ui/uei, uo	uan, uen	uang, ueng	

Notes on pronunciation and Pinyin spelling

i

Pronunciation

- The letter **i** in Pinyin represents three different vowel sounds. In this lesson we meet two of them. When **i** follows the initial consonants **zh, ch, sh** or **r** it is pronounced with a strong *r* (or *er*) as in the English word *he<u>r</u>* or *hamm<u>er</u>*. Example: **lǎoshī**. When **i** begins a syllable or follows most other consonants it is pronounced like the English sound *ee* in words like *w<u>ee</u>k* and *sl<u>ee</u>p*. Example: **nǐ** *you*. We will learn a syllable with the third pronunciation of **i** in Lesson 3.

Spelling

- If the final begins with **i** and there is no initial consonant, **i** is spelled as **y**. Example: **yě** *also*.

ü

Pronunciation

■ The letter **ü** represents a sound that does not occur in English, a high front rounded vowel. It stands in contrast to the vowel **i** (pronounced *ee* as in *week* and *sleep*), differing from it only in the position of the lips when the vowel is pronounced. To pronounce **ü**, position your mouth to say **i** *(ee)* and then without moving anything but your lips, round your lips as if to say *oo* as in *loop*. The high front rounded vowel **ü** also occurs in French and many other languages besides Mandarin.

Spelling

■ If the final begins with **ü** and there is no initial consonant, **ü** is spelled as **yu**. We have not yet learned any words that illustrate this rule.
■ If the final begins with **ü** and the initial consonant is **j**, **q**, or **x**, **ü** is written as **u** but it is pronounced **ü**. Example: **xuésheng** *student*.

uo

Pronunciation

■ **uo** is pronounced like the syllable *aw* in the English words *awful* or *saw*.

Spelling

■ If the final is **uo** and there is no initial consonant, **uo** is spelled as **wo**. Example: **wǒ** *I/me*.
■ If the initial consonant is **b**, **p**, **m**, or **f**, the sound **uo** is spelled as **o**. Example: the recitation syllables **bo**, **po**, **mo**, **fo**. The letter **o** only occurs as a simple final following **b**, **p**, **m**, and **f**, so we place it in parentheses in the Finals table.

e

Pronunciation

■ The letter **e** occurs in eight finals and has three different pronunciations.
■ **e** is pronounced similar to the vowel in the English word *up*. Example: the recitation syllables **de**, **te**, **ne**, **le**, and the pronunciation of **e** in the final **er**.
■ **eng** rhymes with the English word *sung*. Example: **(xué)sheng** *student*.
■ **ei**, **ie**, **üe** and **en** are pronounced as the vowel in the English word *send*. Example: **yě** *also*.

Spelling

■ When **e** is preceded by the vowel **i** and **i** is not preceded by a consonant, **ie** is spelled **ye**. Example: **yě** *also*.

ian, üan

Pronunciation

- The finals **ian** and **üan** rhyme with **en** and not with **an**.

Spelling

- When **ian** is not preceded by a consonant, it is spelled **yan**. Example: **j** + **iàn** = **jiàn**, **iǎn** alone is spelled **yǎn**.
- When **üan** is not preceded by a consonant, it is spelled **yuan**. When preceded by a consonant it is spelled **uan**. Example: **j** + **üǎn** = **juǎn**, **üǎn** alone is spelled **yuǎn**.

Language FAQs (frequently asked questions)

Where are *the* and *a*?

Mandarin does not have words that are exactly equivalent to *a* and *the* in English. Do not look for translations of *a* and *the* in Mandarin.

Notes on Chinese culture

Greeting strangers

In Chinese culture, it is not common to greet people you do not know, unless you expect to interact with them in the future. People greet strangers in a business context, or in receptions such as the one in the dialogue in this lesson, since the initial contact will probably lead to future interactions. It is very uncommon to greet a stranger you pass on the street, or who you ride with in an elevator or on some form of public transportation.

Lesson 1 Dialogue in English

Part A

Xiao Zhang: Hello.
Xiao Gao: Hello.
Xiao Zhang: I am a student. Are you a student?
Xiao Gao: Yes. I am also a student.

Part B

Xiao Zhang: Is he a student?
Xiao Gao: No. He is not a student. He is a teacher. He is Professor Li.

Part C

Xiao Gao: Hello teacher.
Professor Li: Xiao Gao, how are you?
Xiao Gao: I am fine, thanks.
Professor Li: Goodbye.

Lesson 2 Nǐ shì nǎguó rén?
What country are you from?

Communication goals
- State your nationality and ask others about their nationalities
- Confirm that information is correct

Key structures
the plural form of pronouns

follow-up questions with **ne**

dōu + VP

dāngrán + VP

Dialogue

The Situation: The new student reception continues. Xiao Zhang begins a conversation with two people he has not met before, Xiao Chen and Xiao Wang. The three of them then talk with Xiao Gao, another new student, and ask about other people in the room.

Part A

Xiǎo Zhāng: Qǐng wèn, nǐmen shì Měiguó rén ma?

Xiǎo Chén: Shì. Wǒmen shì Měiguó rén, nǐ ne?

Xiǎo Zhāng: Wǒ yě shì Měiguó rén. Wǒmen dōu shì Měiguó rén.

Xiǎo Wáng (to Xiǎo Gāo):   Nǐ ne?

Xiǎo Gāo: Wǒ shì Fǎguó rén.

Part B

Xiǎo Chén: Tā shì nǎguó rén?

Xiǎo Wáng: Tā shì Yīngguó rén.

Xiǎo Chén: Tāmen yě shì Yīngguó rén, duì ma?

Xiǎo Wáng: Bú duì. Tāmen dōu shì Déguó rén.

Xiǎo Gāo: Lǎoshī shì Zhōngguó rén ma?

Xiǎo Zhāng: Dāngrán shì!

Vocabulary

Chén	family name	*(family name)*
dāngrán	adverb	*of course*
Déguó	country name	*Germany*
Déguó rén	noun phrase	*German person*
dōu	adverb	*all, both*
duì	adjectival verb	*correct*
Fǎguó	country name	*France*
Fǎguó rén	noun phrase	*French person*
guó	noun	*country*
Měiguó	country name	*America (USA)*
Měiguó rén	noun phrase	*American*
nǎguó, něiguó	question phrase	*which country*
ne	final particle	*(forms follow-up questions)*
nǐmen	pronoun	*you (plural)*
qǐng wèn	conversational expression	*may I ask, excuse me*
rén	noun	*person*
tāmen	pronoun	*they/them*
Wáng	family name	*(family name)*
wǒmen	pronoun	*we/us*
Yīngguó	country name	*Britain*
Yīngguó rén	noun	*British person*
Zhōngguó	proper noun	*China*
Zhōngguó rén	noun phrase	*Chinese person*

Country names and nationalities

Notice how the name of the nationality includes the name of the country.

country		nationality	
Déguó	*Germany*	**Déguó rén**	*German, German person*
Fǎguó	*France*	**Fǎguó rén**	*French, French person*
Měiguó	*America (USA)*	**Měiguó rén**	*American, American person*
Yīngguó	*Britain*	**Yīngguó rén**	*British, British person*
Zhōngguó	*China*	**Zhōngguó rén**	*Chinese, Chinese person*

Supplementary vocabulary: Countries of the world

Afghanistan	**Āfùhàn**	Iran	**Yīlǎng**
Argentina	**Āgēntíng**	Iraq	**Yīlākè**
Australia	**Àodàlìyà**	Ireland	**Ài'ěrlán**
Austria	**Àodìlì**	Israel	**Yǐsèliè**
Brazil	**Bāxī**	Italy	**Yìdàlì**
Canada	**Jiānádà**	Japan	**Rìběn**
Chile	**Zhìlì**	Kenya	**Kěnníyà**
Denmark	**Dānmài**	Korea (North)	**Cháoxiǎn**
Ecuador	**Èguāduō'ěr**	Korea (South)	**Hánguó**
Egypt	**Āijí**	Kuwait	**Kēwēitè**
El Salvador	**Sà'ěrwǎduō**	Lithuania	**Lìtáowǎn**
Greece	**Xīlà**	Luxembourg	**Lúsēnbǎo**
Hong Kong	**Xiānggǎng**	Mexico	**Mòxīgē**
Hungary	**Xiōngyálì**	Netherlands	**Hélán**
Iceland	**Bīngdǎo**	New Zealand	**Xīnxīlán**
India	**Yìndù**	Nicaragua	**Níjiālāguā**
Indonesia	**Yìnní**	Nigeria	**Nírìlìyà**

Norway	**Nuówēi**	Spain	**Xībānyá**
Pakistan	**Bājīsītǎn**	Sri Lanka	**Sīlǐlánkǎ**
Paraguay	**Bālāguī**	Sweden	**Ruìdiǎn**
Peru	**Bìlǔ**	Switzerland	**Ruìshì**
Philippines	**Fēilǜbīn**	Syria	**Xùlìyà**
Poland	**Bōlán**	Turkey	**Tǔ'ěrqí**
Portugal	**Pútaoyá**	Uganda	**Wūgāndá**
Romania	**Luómǎníyà**	Ukraine	**Wūkèlán**
Russia	**Éluósī**	Venezuela	**Wěinèiruìlā**
Saudi Arabia	**Shātè Ālābó**	Vietnam	**Yuènán**
Singapore	**Xīnjiāpō**		

Dialogue practice

Do these activities in class after mastering each part of Dialogue 2.

Dialogue 2A: Decide whether you are a **Zhōngguó rén**, **Yīngguó rén**, **Měiguó rén**, **Fǎguó rén**, or **Déguó rén**. Form a group of three or four students and ask each other questions until you have identified everyone's nationality. Introduce your group to the other groups in the class, using **dōu** and **yě** at least once.

Dialogue 2B: Visit another group and ask them what nationality everyone is, using the question **Tā shì nǎguó rén?** Try to guess the nationality of at least two people in the group, asking for confirmation with the expression **Duì ma?**

Use and structure

2.1. Qǐng wèn *may I ask*

Qǐng wèn is a polite way to introduce a question, and it is always followed by a question. It can be translated with the English expressions *please may I ask*, *may I ask*, or *excuse me*. Note that **qǐng wèn** can only be used when asking a question.

Qǐng wèn, nǐmen shì Měiguó rén ma?
May I ask, are you Americans?

2.2.   The plural form of pronouns

The plural form of Mandarin pronouns is the <u>singular form</u> + **men**. The same form of the pronoun is used whether the pronoun is the subject or the object in the sentence.

singular		plural	
wǒ	*I, me*	**wǒmen**	*we, us*
nǐ	*you*	**nǐmen**	*you (plural)*
tā	*he/she/it, him/her*	**tāmen**	*they, them*

2.3.   Follow-up questions with **ne**

Ne is a <u>final particle</u> that is used to ask short, follow-up questions on the current topic of conversation. This kind of question is sometimes called a <u>tag question</u>.
Ne generally occurs right after a noun or noun phrase.

Wǒmen shì Měiguó rén, nǐ ne?
We are Americans. And you? (or) What about you?

Wǒ shì xuésheng, nǐ ne?
I am a student. (And) you? (or) What about you?

Tāmen shì Yīngguó rén. Xiǎo Gāo ne?
They are British. What about Xiao Gao?

2.4.   **Nǎguó** *which country?*

In this lesson we learn how to use the expression **nǎguó** (and its alternative pronunciation **něiguó**) *which country?* to ask about nationalities.

Tā shì nǎguó rén?
What country is he from?

To answer a question with the expression **nǎguó**, replace **nǎguó** with the name of the country.

Nǐ shì <u>nǎguó</u> rén?
Where are you from? (Literally: You are <u>which-country</u> person?)

Wǒ shì <u>Fǎguó</u> rén.
I am a <u>French</u> person.

Tā shì <u>něiguó</u> rén?
Where is he from?

Tā shì <u>Yīngguó</u> rén.
He is <u>British</u>.

2.5.   Asking for confirmation: **Duì ma?** *correct? right?*

To ask for confirmation of a statement, follow the statement with the tag question **Duì ma?**

Tāmen yě shì Yīngguó rén, duì ma?
They are also British, right?

You can reply to a **Duì ma?** tag question with a short answer or a long answer.
The short answer *yes*: **Duì.**
The short answer *no*: **Bù duì.**
The long answer *yes*: **Duì. Tāmen yě shì Yīngguó rén.** *Yes. They are also British.*
The long answer *no*: **Bù duì. Tāmen bù shì Yīngguó rén.** *No. They are not British.*

2.6.   **Dōu** *all, both*

Tāmen <u>dōu</u> shì Déguó rén.
They are all/both Germans.

Dōu refers to <u>more than one</u> and is used to translate the English words *all* and *both*. **Dōu** is an adverb, and like all adverbs in Mandarin, it always occurs before a verb or verb phrase. It never occurs before a noun or noun phrase.

(S) dōu + V/VP
Wǒmen dōu shì Měiguó rén.
We are all Americans.

Tāmen dōu shì Déguó rén.
They are all Germans.

Dōu can occur before or after **bù** *no, not*. The overall meaning of a sentence changes depending upon the order of **dōu** and **bù**.

Dōu + **bù** (+ V) means *none (all are not)*.

Tāmen dōu bù shì Déguó rén.
None of them is German. (They are all not German.)

Tāmen dōu bù hěn gāo.
They are all not very tall.

Bù + **dōu** (+ V) means *not all (some are and some are not)*.

Tāmen bù dōu shì Déguó rén.
Not all of them are German. (Some are German and some are not German.)

Tāmen bù dōu hěn gāo.
They are not all tall.

2.7.   Dāngrán *of course*

Dāngrán *of course* is an adverb. It always occurs before a verb or verb phrase, and never before a noun or at the end of a sentence.

> **(S) dāngrán + V(P)**
> **Dāngrán shì!**
> *Of course (S) is.*

> **Lǎoshī dāngrán shì Zhōngguó rén.**
> *Of course the teacher is Chinese.*

> **Lǐ lǎoshī dāngrán hěn hǎo.**
> *Of course Professor Li is very good.*

Dāngrán occurs before **bù** *no, not* and before the adverbs **dōu** *all, both* and **yě** *also.*

> **Wǒ dāngrán bù shì lǎoshī.**
> *Of course I am not a teacher.*

> **Wǒmen dāngrán dōu shì xuésheng.**
> *We are all students of course.*

> **Tā dāngrán yě shì Zhōngguó rén.**
> *Of course she is also Chinese.*

2.8.   Omitting the subject and the object

In Mandarin, it is common to leave out the subject of a sentence if it is the same as the subject of the previous sentence. It is also common to leave out the object of a sentence if it is the same as the object of the previous sentence. Compare this question and answer from the dialogue. In the answer, the omitted subject and object are added in parentheses.

> Q: **Lǎoshī shì Zhōngguó rén ma?**   A: **(Lǎoshī) Dāngrán shì (Zhōngguó rén)!**
>   *Is the teacher Chinese?*   *Of course (he/she) is (Chinese).*

Sentence pyramids

The sentence pyramids illustrate the use of each new vocabulary item and structure introduced in the lesson. Use them to help you learn how to form phrases and sentences in Mandarin. Supply the English translation for the last line where indicated.

1. rén Yīngguó rén shì Yīngguó rén Wǒ shì Yīngguó rén.	*person/people* *British* *be British* *I am British.*
2. Yīngguó rén shì Yīngguó rén shì Yīngguó rén ma? Nǐmen shì Yīngguó rén ma?	*British* *be British* *be British?* *Are you (plural) British?*
3. shì xuésheng shì xuésheng ma? Nǐmen shì xuésheng ma? Qǐng wèn, nǐmen shì xuésheng ma?	*be student(s)* *be student(s)?* *Are you students?* *May I ask, are you students?*
4. rén Měiguó rén shì Měiguó rén Nǐmen shì Měiguó rén ma? Qǐng wèn, nǐmen shì Měiguó rén ma?	*person* *American person* *be American* *Are you Americans?* _____
5. Měiguó rén shì Měiguó rén Wǒmen shì Měiguó rén.	*American person* *be American* *We are Americans.*
6. ne nǐ ne? Wǒmen shì Měiguó rén, nǐ ne?	*(particle for follow-up questions)* *and you?* *We are Americans, and you?*
7. Zhōngguó rén shì Zhōngguó rén Wǒmen shì Zhōngguó rén. Wǒmen shì Zhōngguó rén, nǐ ne?	*Chinese person* *be Chinese* *We are Chinese.* _____

8.	
lǎoshī	*teacher(s)*
shì lǎoshī	*be teacher(s)*
Tāmen shì lǎoshī.	*They are teachers.*
Tāmen shì lǎoshī ma?	_____

9.	
Tāmen ne?	*What about them?*
Wǒmen shì Měiguó rén, tāmen ne?	*We are Americans. What about them?*

10.	
rén	*person*
nǎguó rén	*a person of which country*
shì nǎguó rén	*be a person of which country*
Tā shì nǎguó rén?	*What country is he from?*

11.	
duì	*correct*
duì ma?	*Correct?*
shì Fǎguó rén, duì ma?	*be French, correct?*
yě shì Fǎguó rén, duì ma?	*also be French, correct?*
Tāmen yě shì Fǎguó rén, duì ma?	_____

12.	
duì	*correct*
Bù duì.	*Not correct. (Wrong.)*

13.	
Déguó	*Germany*
Déguó rén	*German person*
shì Déguó rén	*be German person*
Tāmen shì Déguó rén.	_____

14.	
Déguó rén	*German person*
shì Déguó rén	*be German person*
dōu shì Déguó rén	*all are German*
Tāmen dōu shì Déguó rén.	*They are all German.*

15.	
lǎoshī	*teacher(s)*
shì lǎoshī	*be teacher(s)*
dōu shì lǎoshī	*all be teachers*
Tāmen dōu shì lǎoshī.	_____

16. **Zhōngguó rén** **shì Zhōngguó rén** **Lǎoshī shì Zhōngguó rén.**	*Chinese person* *be Chinese* _____
17. **duì ma?** **shì Zhōngguó rén, duì ma?** **Lǎoshī shì Zhōngguó rén, duì ma?**	*correct?* *be Chinese, correct?* _____
18. **shì** **Dāngrán shì.**	*be* *Of course (subject) is.*
19. **Zhōngguó rén** **shì Zhōngguó rén** **dāngrán shì Zhōngguó rén** **Lǎoshī dāngrán shì Zhōngguó rén.**	*Chinese person* *be Chinese* *of course be Chinese* *Of course the teacher is Chinese.*
20. **duì** **dāngrán duì** **Lǎoshī dāngrán duì.**	*correct* *of course correct* *Of course the teacher is correct.*

Pronunciation and Pinyin

Tones

Neutral tone

When a syllable does not have a contour tone, it is said to have <u>neutral tone</u>. When the tone marks ¯ ´ ˇ ` are used to indicate tone, syllables that occur in neutral tone are written with no tone mark: **wǒmen** *we/us*. When numbers are used to indicate tone, neutral tone is indicated with the number 5 or the number 0: **wo3men5** or **wo3men0**.

Syllables in neutral tone are short and unstressed. The pitch of a syllable in neutral tone depends upon the tone of the preceding syllable. This is illustrated in the following diagrams. The symbol * is used to mark the pitch of the syllable with neutral tone.

<u>First tone + neutral tone</u>: **tāmen** If the preceding syllable has first tone, the pitch of the neutral tone is slightly lower than the pitch of the preceding syllable.	
<u>Second tone + neutral tone</u>: **xuésheng** If the preceding syllable has second tone, the pitch of the neutral tone is slightly lower than the ending pitch of the preceding syllable.	
<u>Third tone + neutral tone</u>: **nǐmen** If the preceding syllable has third tone, the pitch of the neutral tone is higher than the ending pitch of the preceding syllable.	
<u>Fourth tone + neutral tone</u>: **shì de** If the preceding syllable has fourth tone, the pitch of the neutral tone is generally lower than the ending pitch of the preceding syllable.	

Particles (words like **ma** and **ne**) always have neutral tone, though **ma** is often spoken in high pitch regardless of the tone of the preceding syllable. The second syllable of certain words such as **xuésheng** *student*, **wǒmen** *we/us*, **nǐmen** *you (plural)*, and **tāmen** *they/them* always occurs in neutral tone. Dialects of Mandarin differ in the extent to which they use neutral tone. This book presents the use of neutral tone in Standard Mandarin as spoken in Beijing.

Changes in the third tone

In Lesson 1 we learned that the basic contour of the third tone is a falling-rising contour. However, it is only pronounced with the falling-rising contour when it is followed by a word in neutral tone, or when it occurs at the end of a sentence or before a pause (indicated here as #).

wǒmen   **wǒ**

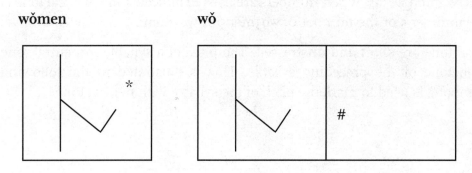

The third tone has two other contours, depending on the tone of the following syllable.

■ When a syllable in third tone occurs before another syllable in third tone, the first syllable changes its tone to second tone.

3 + 3   →   2 + 3
nǐ hǎo   →   **ní hǎo**

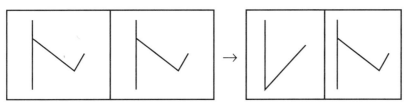

■ When a syllable in third tone occurs before a syllable in first, second, or fourth tone, it becomes a low, level tone.

3 + 1   →   **low + 1 (lǎoshī)**

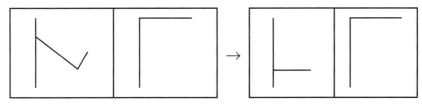

3 + 2   →   **low + 2 (nǎguó)**

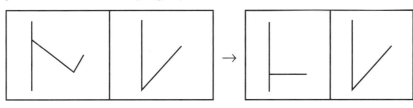

3 + 4   →   **low + 4 (nǐ shì)**

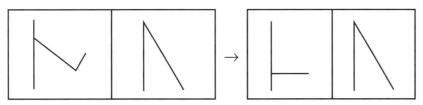

Finals

Here are the finals of Mandarin as they are spelled in Pinyin. The finals introduced in Lessons 1 and 2 are highlighted.

Finals that begin with:	and end with a vowel:	and end with **n**:	and end with **ng**:	and end with **r**:
a	a, ai, ao	an	ang	
e	e, ei	en	eng	er
o	(o), ou		ong	
i	i, ia, iao, ie, iu/iou	ian, in	iang, ing, iong	
ü	ü, üe	üan, ün		
u	u, ua, uai, ui/uei, uo	uan, uen	uang, ueng	

Notes on Pinyin spelling

Here are the rules that are relevant in spelling and pronouncing the finals introduced in Lesson 2.

ui

- Finals spelled **ui** rhyme with finals that are spelled **ei**. Examples: **duì** *correct*, **Měiguó** *America*. When **ei** is directly preceded by a consonant or if it begins a word, it is written in Pinyin as **ei**: **děi**, **měi**, **shéi**. When **ei** is preceded by a consonant + **u**, Pinyin abbreviates **uei** to **ui**: **duì** (abbreviated from **duei**), **huì** (abbreviated from **huei**), **guì** (abbreviated from **guei**). When **ei** is preceded only by **u** and no consonant, it is spelled as **wei**.

wo and uo

- As we learned in Lesson 1, when the final **uo** is not preceded by a consonant, it is spelled **wo**. If it is preceded by **b**, **p**, **m**, or **f** it is spelled **o**. Otherwise, it is spelled **uo**. Examples: **wǒ** *I/me*, **Zhōngguó** *China*

uen

- When the final **uen** is not preceded by a consonant, it is spelled **wen**. Example: **qǐng wèn** *may I ask*

Language FAQs

How do you make a noun plural?

Ordinarily, you don't. There is no singular-plural distinction in nouns. Instead, nouns have one unchanging form. As we have seen in this lesson, pronouns have singular and plural forms. The suffix **-men** that forms the plural pronoun is also used, on a <u>very</u> restricted basis, to mark nouns as plural.

Notes on Chinese culture

Qǐng wèn and formality

Qǐng wèn *may I ask* is used before requests for information from strangers or from people to whom you should show respect. For example, it can be used when asking for directions, or when inquiring about the price of items in a store, or when asking one's teacher for information. In mainland China, **qǐng wèn** is also relatively formal, and it is not frequently used in informal, everyday exchanges.

Lesson 2 Dialogue in English

Part A
Xiao Zhang: Excuse me, are you Americans?
Xiao Chen: Yes. We are Americans. What about you?
Xiao Zhang: I am also American. We are all Americans.
Xiao Wang (to Xiao Gao): What about you?
Xiao Gao: I am French.

Part B
Xiao Chen: What country is he from?
Xiao Wang: He is British.
Xiao Chen: They are also British, right?
Xiao Wang: No. They are all German.
Xiao Gao: Is the teacher Chinese?
Xiao Zhang: Of course!

Lesson 3
Nǐ jiào shénme míngzi?
What is your name?

Communication goals
- Say your name and ask people for their names
- Say what languages you can speak and ask others what languages they can speak

Key structures
V-not-V questions

the content question word **shénme** *what*

the modal verb **huì** *can*

the conjunction **hé** *and*

Dialogue

The Situation: At the new student reception, Xiao Gao and Xiao Zhang find out more about each other.

Part A

Xiǎo Zhāng: Nǐ jiào shénme míngzi?

Xiǎo Gāo: Wǒ xìng Gāo, jiào Gāo Měilì. Nǐ jiào shénme?

Xiǎo Zhāng: Wǒ xìng Zhāng, jiào Dàwéi.

Part B

Xiǎo Zhāng: Nǐ huì shuō Fǎguó huà ma?

Xiǎo Gāo: Wǒ shì Fǎguó rén, dāngrán huì shuō Fǎguó huà. Wǒ yě huì shuō Déguó huà, Rìběn huà, hé Yīngguó huà.

Xiǎo Zhāng: Zhēnde ma? Nǐ huì bù huì shuō Měiguó huà?

Xiǎo Gāo: Duìbuqǐ, wǒ bù huì. Wǒ zhǐ huì shuō Yīngguó huà.

(Xiao Gao and Xiao Zhang both laugh at this joke. To understand what is funny, see the Language FAQ section at the end of this lesson.)

Vocabulary

Dàwéi	given name	*David*
Déguó huà	noun phrase	*German language*
duìbuqǐ	conversational expression	*excuse me*
Fǎguó huà	noun phrase	*French language*
hé	conjunction	*and*
huà	noun	*speech, language*
huì	modal verb	*able to, can*
jiào	verb	*be called, call*
Měiguó huà	noun phrase	*American English*
Měilì	given name	*Marie*
míngzi	noun	*name*
Rìběn	country name	*Japan*
Rìběn huà	noun phrase	*Japanese language*
shénme	question word	*what*
shuō	verb	*speak, talk, say*
shuō huà	verb + object	*speak*
xìng	verb	*be family-named, be surnamed;*
	noun	*family name, surname*
Yīngguó huà	noun phrase	*British English*
zhēnde ma?	conversational expression	*really?*
zhǐ	adverb	*only*
Zhōngguó huà	noun phrase	*Chinese language*

Common Family Names

Bái	Huáng	Wáng
Cài	Jiāo	Wèi
Chén	Jīn	Wú
Dèng	Kǒng	Xiè
Dīng	Lǐ	Xú
Dù	Lín	Yán
Gāo	Liú	Yáng
Gù	Lù	Yè
Guō	Mǎ	Zhāng
Hé	Máo	Zhào
Hè	Sūn	Zhōu
Hú	Tāng	Zhū

Dialogue practice

Do these activities in class after mastering each part of Dialogue 3.

Dialogue 3A: Pair up with a classmate and learn each other's names. Repeat the activity with at least four other classmates.

Dialogue 3B: Prepare a list of languages that you speak. Then, pair up with a classmate and find out what languages he or she speaks. Repeat this activity with at least four other classmates.

Use and structure

3.1.   Chinese names

The parts of a Chinese name

The parts of the Chinese name are the **xìng** *family name, surname* and the **míngzi** *name*. In Chinese, the family name always occurs before a given name or title, so we do not call it the "last name."

In this lesson we use the word **xìng** as a verb meaning *be family-named* or *be surnamed*.

> **Nǐ xìng shénme?**
> Literally: *What are you family-named? (What is your family name?)*

> **Wǒ xìng Zhāng.**
> Literally: *I am family-named Zhang. (My family name is Zhang.)*

The verb **xìng** is followed by the family name alone. It is never followed by family name and given name.

> ***Say this:***
>
>   **Wǒ xìng Zhāng.** *I am family-named Zhang. (My family name is Zhang.)*
>
> ***Do not say this:***
>
>   ⊗ **Wǒ xìng Zhāng Dàwéi.** *I am family-named Zhang Dawei.*

Míngzi *name* is a noun. It can refer to the *family name + given name*, or to the given name alone.

If you ask Xiao Gao her name, she can reply with her entire name, or with her given name alone.

> Q: **Nǐ jiào shénme míngzì?**
>   *What is your name?*

> A: **Wǒ jiào Gāo Měilì.**
>   *I am called Gao Meili.*
>   or
>   **Wǒ jiào Měilì.**
>   *I am called Meili.*

Jiào must be followed by a name with more than one syllable. If your name has only one syllable, then you must say that you **jiào** *are called* your entire name, **xìng + míngzi**. When **Zhāng Dàwéi** introduces himself he can say **Wǒ jiào Dàwéi** or **Wǒ jiào Zhāng Dàwéi**. However, **Yáng Píng** (family name = **Yáng**, given name = **Píng**) can only say **Wǒ jiào Yáng Píng** and cannot say **Wǒ jiào Píng**.

In English, we say that one's name <u>is</u> Mary, or Joe, or Susan, etc. Notice that in Chinese, we use the verb **jiào** *call, be called* and say that one <u>is called</u> Mary, or Joe, or Susan, etc.

The order of information in a Chinese name

The order of information in a Chinese name is:

family name + given name

<u>xìng</u>	+ <u>míngzi</u>
Gāo	Měilì
Zhāng	Dàwéi

3.2.   **Shénme** *what* and the location of content question words in the sentence

Shénme is a <u>content question word</u> and can be translated with the English question word *what*. In English, content question words like *who, what, where, why,* and *how* occur at the beginning of the sentence. In Mandarin, the order of information in statements and in questions is the same. Content question words occur in the sentence where the answer goes.

S	+	**V**	+	**O**
Wǒ		xìng		Gāo.

I am surnamed Gao.

Nǐ	xìng	shénme?

What are you surnamed?

When answering a "**shénme**" question, replace **shénme** with the answer. Notice that the entire phrase **shénme míngzì** *what name* is replaced in the answer.

Question	Answer
Nǐ xìng <u>shénme</u>?	**Wǒ xìng <u>Gāo</u>.**
What is your family name?	*My family name is Gao.*
Nǐ jiào <u>shénme míngzì</u>?	**Wǒ jiào <u>Gāo Měilì</u>.**
What are you called?	*I am called Gao Meili.*
Tā shuō <u>shénme</u>?	**Tā shuō <u>tā shì Fǎguó rén</u>.**
What is she saying?	*She says she is French.*

3.3.   Asking for someone's name

The most common way to ask for someone's name is to say:

Nǐ jiào shénme míngzi?
or
Nǐ jiào shénme?
What is your name? or *What are you called?*

Tā jiào shénme míngzi?
What is his name? or *What is he called?*

To ask for a family name alone, say:

Nǐ xìng shénme?
What is your family name? (Literally: What are you surnamed?)

Tā xìng shénme?
What is his family name? (Literally: What is he surnamed?)

To ask for someone's entire name, say:

Nǐ xìng <u>shénme</u> jiào <u>shénme</u>?
or
Nǐ xìng <u>shénme</u> jiào <u>shénme</u> míngzi?
What is your family name and given name?
(Literally: You are family-named what and called what?)

3.4. Huì *able to, can*

Huì *able to, can* expresses learned or innate ability. It is used when you want to say that you can speak a certain language, or that you know how to write a word, or that you know how to use a computer, etc.

Wǒ <u>huì</u> shuō Déguó huà.
I can speak German.

Huì is a <u>modal verb</u>. It is part of the verb phrase and can be followed by another verb.

Xiǎo Gāo <u>huì</u> shuō Fǎguó huà.
Xiao Gao can speak French.

When a sentence contains **huì** or another modal verb, the modal verb is the verb that is used in the short answer *yes* and *no*.

Q: **Nǐ <u>huì</u> shuō Rìběn huà ma?**
   Can you speak Japanese?

A: **<u>Huì</u>.**
   Yes.

Q: **Nǐ <u>huì</u> shuō Měiguó huà ma?**
   Can you speak American English?

A: **<u>Bù huì</u>.**
   No. (I can't.)

Adverbs occur before **huì** *able to, can*.

Wǒ <u>dāngrán huì</u> shuō Fǎguó huà.
Of course I can speak French.

Wǒ <u>zhǐ huì</u> shuō Yīngguó huà.
I can only speak British English.

Wǒmen <u>dōu huì</u> shuō Zhōngguó huà.
We can all speak Chinese.

Tā <u>yě huì</u> shuō Rìběn huà.
She can also speak Japanese.

3.5.   Hé *and*

Hé *and* joins two or more pronouns, nouns, or noun phrases.

<u>Nǐmen hé tāmen</u> dōu shì Fǎguó rén.
You and they are all French.

Wǒ yě huì shuō <u>Déguó huà, Rìběn huà, hé Yīngguó huà</u>.
I can also speak German, Japanese, and British English.

<u>Zhāng Dàwéi hé Gāo Měilì</u> dōu huì shuō Zhōngguó huà.
Zhang Dawei and Gao Meili can both speak Chinese.

Hé <u>never occurs before a verb</u> and, unlike its English translation *and*, it never joins verbs, verb phrases, or sentences.

> ***Say this:***
>
> **Wǒ huì shuō Rìběn huà <u>hé</u> Yīngguó huà.**
> *I can speak Japanese and English.*
>
> ***Do not say this:***
>
> ⊗ **Wǒ huì shuō Rìběn huà <u>hé</u> huì shuō Yīngguó huà.**

3.6.   Zhēnde and zhēnde ma? *really?*

The expression **zhēnde ma?** *really?* conveys surprise on learning new information.

Xiǎo Gāo: Wǒ huì shuō Déguó huà, Rìběn huà, hé Yīngguó huà.
Xiao Gao: I can speak German, Japanese, and British English.

Xiǎo Zhāng: Zhēnde ma?
Xiao Zhang: Really?

3.7.   Verb-not-verb yes-no questions

In Lesson 1 we learned to form yes-no questions by adding the sentence final particle **ma** to the end of a statement.

Nǐ shì Yīngguó rén ma?
Are you British?

This lesson presents the <u>verb-not-verb</u> form of yes-no questions. To form verb-not-verb questions, repeat the verb, first in affirmative form, and then in negated form.

V-not-V

Nǐ <u>shì bù shì</u> Yīngguó rén?
Are you British?

Tā <u>duì bù duì</u>?
Is he correct?

If the verb phrase begins with a modal verb (see Use and Structure note 3.4), the modal verb is the verb that is repeated:

Nǐ <u>huì bù huì</u> shuō Fǎguó huà?
Can you speak French?
(Literally: *You can or cannot speak French?*)

The meanings of **ma** yes-no questions and Verb-not-verb yes-no questions are equivalent.

Nǐ <u>shì bù shì</u> Yīngguó rén?	= **Nǐ <u>shì</u> Yīngguó rén <u>ma</u>?**
Are you British?	
Ta <u>duì bù duì</u>?	= **Ta <u>duì ma</u>?**
Is he correct?	
Nǐ <u>huì bù huì</u> shuō Fǎguó huà?	= **Nǐ <u>huì</u> shuō Fǎguó huà <u>ma</u>?**
Can you speak French?	

When a sentence includes an adverb such as **yě** *also* (Use and Structure note 1.8), **dōu** *all, both* (Use and Structure note 2.6), **dāngrán** *of course* (Use and Structure note 2.7), or **zhǐ** *only* (Use and Structure note 3.9), the **ma** form of yes-no questions is used, and the verb-not-verb form is not used.

Verb-not-verb yes-no questions are answered in the same way as **ma** yes-no questions. (See Use and Structure notes 1.7 and 1.9.)

3.8. Duìbuqǐ *I'm sorry, excuse me*

Duìbuqǐ, wǒ bù huì.
I'm sorry, I can't.

Say **duìbuqǐ** when your behavior disappoints another person, or when it inconveniences him or her in some way. **Duìbuqǐ** is often followed by an explanation. Here are some situations where **duìbuqǐ** is appropriate:

- Someone asks you for information and you do not know the answer.
- Your roommate asks you to give her something but you do not have it, or you have it but cannot give it to her.
- Your friend invites you to do something with him and you are refusing the invitation.
- You bump into someone accidentally.

Duìbuqǐ can sometimes be translated by the expression *excuse me*, but it is not always equivalent to the English expression *excuse me* in its use. For example, it is not appropriate to use **duìbuqǐ** when asking a question, even though in English you may preface a question by saying *excuse me*. In Mandarin, as we have seen in Lesson 2, when asking a question, say **qǐng wèn**:

Qǐng wèn, nǐ jiào shénme míngzi?
May I ask (excuse me), what is your name?

3.9   Zhǐ *only*

Zhǐ *only* is an adverb. It occurs before a verb or verb phrase and never before a noun.

(S) zhǐ + V(P)
Wǒ zhǐ huì shuō Yīngguo huà.
I can only speak British English.

Zhǐ occurs after **dōu** *all, both* and **yě** *also*.

Wǒ yě zhǐ huì shuō Zhōngguó huà.
I can also only speak Chinese.

Wǒmen dōu zhǐ huì shuō Zhōngguó huà.
We can all only speak Chinese.

Yes-no questions involving **zhǐ** can only be formed with **ma** and never with the verb-not-verb structure.

Tā zhǐ huì shuō Yīngguó huà ma?
Can she only speak English?

To answer *yes* to a **zhǐ** question say **shì** or **duì**.

Q: **Tā zhǐ huì shuō Yīngguó huà ma?**   A: **Duì.** (or **Shì**)
   Can she only speak English?   *Yes.*

To answer *no* to a **zhǐ** question say **bù duì** or **bù shì**.

Q: **Tā zhǐ huì shuō Yīngguó huà ma?**   A: **Bù duì.** (or **Bù shì**)
   Can she only speak English?   *No.*

3.10.   Shuō *and* shuō huà *speak*

In Mandarin, verbs like **shuō** *speak* that describe actions are typically followed by an object noun. **Shuō Zhōngguó huà** means *speak Chinese*; **shuō Yīngguó huà** means *speak English*. **Shuō** typically occurs with an object. To say that someone is *speaking* in general, without saying what he or she is saying or what language he or she is speaking, say **shuō huà**:

Lǎoshī shuō huà.
The teacher is speaking.

To tell someone not to speak, say:

Bù shuō huà.
Don't speak.

To say that someone is unable to speak, say:

Tā bù huì shuō huà.
She cannot speak.

Sentence pyramids

The sentence pyramids illustrate the use of each new vocabulary item and structure introduced in the lesson. Use them to help you learn how to form phrases and sentences in Mandarin. Supply the English translation for the last line where indicated.

1.	
míngzi	*name*
shénme míngzi	*what name*
jiào shénme míngzi	*called what name*
Nǐ jiào shénme míngzi?	*What are you called?*
2.	
Měilì	*Meili*
Gāo Měilì	*Gao Meili*
jiào Gāo Měilì	*called Gao Meili*
Wǒ jiào Gāo Měilì.	*I am called Gao Meili.*
3.	
Dàwéi	*Dawei*
jiào Dàwéi	*called Dawei*
Wǒ jiào Dàwéi.	_____
4.	
Zhāng	*Zhang*
xìng Zhāng	*surnamed Zhang*
Wǒ xìng Zhāng.	*I am surnamed Zhang.* (My family name is Zhang.)
5.	
Gāo	*Gao*
xìng Gāo	*surnamed Gao*
Tā xìng Gāo.	_____

6. jiào Dàwéi xìng Zhāng jiào Dàwéi Wǒ xìng Zhāng jiào Dàwéi.	*called Dawei* *surnamed Zhang called Dawei* *My family name is Zhang and I am called Dawei.*
7. jiào Měilì xìng Gāo jiào Měilì Tā xìng Gāo jiào Měilì.	*called Meili* *surnamed Gao called Meili* _____
8. shuō huà shuō Fǎguó huà huì shuō Fǎguó huà Wǒ huì shuō Fǎguó huà.	*speak* *speak French* *can speak French* *I can speak French.*
9. shuō huà shuō Fǎguó huà huì shuō Fǎguó huà Nǐ huì shuō Fǎguó huà ma?	*speak* *speak French* *can speak French* *Can you speak French?*
10. Fǎguó huà shuō Fǎguó huà huì shuō Fǎguó huà bù huì shuō Fǎguó huà huì bù huì shuō Fǎguó huà Nǐ huì bù huì shuō Fǎguó huà?	*French* *speak French* *can speak French* *cannot speak French* *can or cannot speak French* *Can you speak French?*
11. huà shuō huà Bù shuō huà.	*speech, language* *speak* *Don't speak.*
12. Déguó huà shuō Déguó huà huì shuō Déguó huà bù huì shuō Déguó huà Wǒ bù huì shuō Déguó huà. Duìbuqǐ, wǒ bù huì shuō Déguó huà.	*German language* *speak German* *able to speak German* *not able to speak German* *I am unable to speak German.* _____

13. shuō Yīngguó huà huì shuō Yīngguó huà zhǐ huì shuō Yīngguó huà Wǒ zhǐ huì shuō Yīngguó huà.	*speak British English* *able to speak British English* *only able to speak British English* _____
14. shuō Rìběn huà huì shuō Rìběn huà huì bù huì shuō Rìběn huà Xiǎo Gāo huì bù huì shuō Rìběn huà?	*speak Japanese* *able to speak Japanese* *able or not able to speak Japanese* _____
15. Yīngguó huà hé Yīngguó huà Rìběn huà hé Yīngguó huà shuō Rìběn huà hé Yīngguó huà Tā huì shuō Rìběn huà hé Yīngguó huà.	*British English* *and British English* *Japanese and British English* *speak Japanese and British English* _____ _____
16. Déguó Déguó huà shuō Déguó huà huì shuō Déguó huà yě huì shuō Déguó huà Tā yě huì shuō Déguó huà.	*Germany* *German language* *speak German* *able to speak German* *also able to speak German* _____

17.
Rìběn huà hé Yīngguó huà
Déguó huà, Rìběn huà, hé
    Yīngguó huà
shuō Déguó huà, Rìběn huà,
    hé Yīngguó huà
huì shuō Déguó huà, Rìběn huà,
    hé Yīngguó huà
Tā huì shuō Déguó huà, Rìběn huà,
    hé Yīngguó huà.
	Japanese and British English
	German, Japanese, and British English
	
	speak German, Japanese, and British
	    English
	able to speak German, Japanese, and
	    British English
	_____
	_____

18. zhēnde zhēnde ma?	*really* *really?*

19. Měiguó huà shuō Měiguó huà huì shuō Měiguó huà huì bù huì shuō Měiguó huà Nǐ huì bù huì shuō Měiguó huà?	*American English* *speak American English* *able to speak American English* *able or not able to speak American English?*
20. shuō Měiguó huà huì shuō Měiguó huà bù huì shuō Měiguó huà Wǒ bù huì shuō Měiguó huà. Duìbuqǐ, wǒ bù huì shuō Měiguó huà.	*speak American English* *able to speak American English* *not able to speak American English* *I am not able to speak American English.* *I'm sorry, I can't speak American English.*

Pronunciation and Pinyin

Initial consonants

Here is a table of Mandarin initial consonants. In this lesson we focus on the highlighted groups of initial consonants.

b	d	g	j	zh	z
p	t	k	q	ch	c
m	n	h	x	sh	s
f	l			r	

g, k, h

The pronunciation of **g**, **k**, and **h** in Mandarin is very similar to the pronunciation of *g*, *k*, and *h* in English. In Mandarin, **h** is pronounced with more friction than *h* is in English. Here are Mandarin syllables that begin with **g**, **k**, and **h**. Some of the examples that begin with **g** and **h** are from the vocabulary introduced in Lessons 1–3.

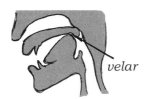
velar

g gē, gāo, gǒu, guā, guì, guó
k kē, kǎo, kǒu, kāng
h hē, hǎo, huà, huì, huó

g, **k**, and **h** are never followed by finals that begin with **i** or **ü**.

j, q, x

j is pronounced very much like the consonant *j* in the English word *jeep*. q is pronounced very much like *ch* in the English word *cheese*. x is pronounced very much like *sh* in the English word *sheep*. The difference between *jeep*, *cheese*, and *sheep* in English and j, q, and x in Mandarin is that the Mandarin sounds are all pronounced with the tongue high and flat against the roof of the mouth, and the lips spread as in a tense smile. Here are Mandarin syllables that begin with j, q, and x. Some of the examples are from the vocabulary in Lessons 1–3.

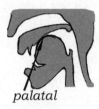

palatal

j   jī, jiào, jìng, jiù, jué, juàn

q   qī, qiáo, qǐng, qiū, què, quán

x   xī, xiǎo, xíng, xiū, xué, xuǎn

- j, q, and x are always followed by a final that begins with i or ü. i after j, q, or x is always pronounced as *ee*. Example: **(duìbu)qǐ** *excuse me*
- When a final that begins with ü follows j, q, or x, ü is written as u. Example: <u>xué</u>sheng *student*
- Like the sound *j* in the English word *jeep*, the Mandarin j is always pronounced as a hard *j*. It is NOT pronounced like the French sound (underlined here) in the English word *rou<u>g</u>e*.

Finals

Here is a table of the Mandarin finals. The finals that have been introduced in the vocabulary in Lessons 1–3 are highlighted.

Finals that begin with:	*and end with a vowel:*	*and end with n:*	*and end with ng:*	*and end with r:*
a	a, ai, ao	an	ang	
e	e, ei	en	eng	er
o	(o), ou		ong	
i	i, ia, iao, ie, iu/iou	ian, in	iang, ing, iong	
ü	ü, üe	üan, ün		
u	u, ua, uai, ui/uei, uo	uan, uen	uang, ueng	

The pronunciation of **zi** in **míngzi** *name*, introduced in Lesson 3, represents the third pronunciation of the letter i in Pinyin. There is no corresponding vowel sound in English. Listen to the recordings that accompany this textbook for its pronunciation. We will practice the three different pronunciations of the letter i in Lesson 5.

Finals that follow g, k, and h and j, q, and x

j, **q**, and **x** are always followed by finals that begin with **i** or **ü**. **g**, **k**, and **h** are <u>never</u> followed by finals that begin with **i** or **ü**. The rules of Pinyin spelling take advantage of this, and the sound **ü** is written as **u** when it follows **j**, **q**, or **x**. Keep this rule in mind when you read words in Pinyin:

- The letter **u** following **j**, **q**, or **x** is always pronounced **ü**.

Language FAQs

Saying *and*

In this lesson we learned the conjunction **hé** *and*. Mandarin has a number of words that may be translated into English with the word *and*, but they are all much more restricted than the English word *and* in the types of words and phrases that they join. In English, *and* can join almost any two words that belong to the same category: nouns (*dogs and cats*), verbs (*eat and sleep*), adjectives (*hot and cold*), adverbs (*quickly and quietly*), etc. The word **hé** can only join nouns and noun phrases. Xiao Gao can say that she can speak Japanese and British English (**Rìběn huà hé Yīngguó huà**), but she cannot use **hé** to say that she can *speak* and *read* Japanese, since *speak* and *read* are verbs.

In addition, Mandarin conjunctions such as **hé** are not used as frequently as *and* is in English. In English, when you have a list of nouns, verbs, adjectives, adverbs, etc., you must put *and* before the last item on the list. (For example: *Today I bought milk, cheese, soup, coffee, <u>and</u> bread*.) In Mandarin, it is acceptable, sometimes preferable, not to use a conjunction in a list of nouns.

Yīngguó huà and Měiguó huà

Obviously, speakers of **Yīngguó huà** *British English* and **Měiguó huà** *American English* can speak to each other without difficulty. Xiao Gao and Xiao Zhang deliberately exaggerate the differences between English as it is spoken in Britain and in the USA when they talk about being able to speak only one or the other dialect. In contrast, the Chinese so-called 'dialects' (including Mandarin, Cantonese, Shanghainese, Southern Min, Hakka, etc.) are so different from each other that speakers of different dialects cannot understand each other unless they learn each other's dialect as a foreign language.

Notes on Chinese culture

What is in a name?

There are thousands of Chinese family names, but only about 100 family names that are widely occurring. In Chinese, the expression **lǎobǎixìng**, literally, *the old 100 family names*, is used to refer to "the common man." If you do not have a Chinese family name, your Chinese teacher will probably give you one. Your name will be selected from among the most widely used Chinese family names.

Unlike family names, given names can be composed creatively, and given names are typically not selected from a fixed inventory of given names as they are in English speaking countries. There is no set translation for foreign given names in Chinese.

Traditionally, given names consist of two syllables composed with two characters. The syllables are selected from poetry, or from a Chinese saying, or they may be selected to bring good fortune, or to evoke a season or some other image. The first syllable of a two-syllable given name may be a generation name shared by all children of the same gender in the same generation of a family. Generation names mark one's place in the family. In contemporary China, given names often consist of a single syllable and are often selected for their sound and meaning. Young children are often given two-syllable baby names, such as **Bāo-bāo** and **Líng-líng** that they use until they begin to attend school.

In Chinese culture, names are not freely used, especially among strangers or casual acquaintances. People often address others by their full name (family name + given name) or by their title (doctor, teacher, chef, etc.). Chinese people never address others by their family name alone. Xiao Zhang's good friends may address him as **Xiǎo Zhāng**, but they will never address him as **Zhāng**. Only very close friends address each other by their given names alone. Even married couples may address each other by their full name

Lesson 3 Dialogue in English

Part A

Xiao Zhang: What is your name?

Xiao Gao: My family name is Gao, I'm called Gao Meili. What is your name?

Xiao Zhang: My family name is Zhang, I'm called Dawei.

Part B

Xiao Zhang: Can you speak French?

Xiao Gao: I am French, of course I can speak French. I can also speak German, Japanese, and British English.

Xiao Zhang: Really? Can you speak American English?

Xiao Gao: Sorry, I can't. I can only speak British English.

Lesson 4 Zhè shì wǒ bàba
This is my dad

Communication goals
- Introduce people to each other and respond to introductions
- List the members of your family
- Ask about other people's families

Key structures
shéi *who*

zhè *this* and nà *that*

expressing possession:

   N/pron. + **de** + N

the final particle **ba** and expressing assumptions

yǒu *have* and **méi yǒu** *not have*

Dialogue

The Situation: Xiao Chen and Xiao Wang are classmates of Xiao Zhang in a Chinese language program in China. As we learned in Lesson 2, they are all Americans. They live in a dormitory along with other international students and Chinese students. They are calling on Xiao Zhang in his dormitory room.

Part A

(Xiao Chen and Xiao Wang knock on Xiao Zhang's door.)

Xiǎo Zhāng:	Shéi?
Xiǎo Chén:	Dàwéi, shì wǒmen, Chén Míng hé Wáng Màikè.
Xiǎo Zhāng:	Xiǎo Chén, Xiǎo Wáng, qǐng jìn, qǐng jìn.
Xiǎo Chén:	Nǐ hǎo!
Xiǎo Zhāng:	Nǐmen hǎo. Zhè shì wǒ de tóngwū, Xiè Guóqiáng. Tāmen shì wǒ de tóngxué, Chén Míng hé Wáng Màikè. Tāmen dōu xué Zhōngwén.
Xiǎo Wáng:	Nǐ hǎo.
Xiǎo Xiè:	Hěn gāoxìng rènshi nǐmen.

Part B

(Xiao Chen notices a photograph on Xiao Zhang's desk.)

Xiǎo Chén: Xiǎo Zhāng, nà shì nǐ de zhàopiàn ba.

Xiǎo Zhāng: Shì. Zhè shì wǒ bàba, zhè shì wǒ māma.

Xiǎo Wáng: Tā shì shéi?

Xiǎo Zhāng: Tā shì wǒ gēge.

Xiǎo Wáng: Tā ne?

Xiǎo Zhāng: Tā shì wǒ dìdi.

Xiǎo Wáng: Xiǎo Chén, nǐ yǒu gēge dìdi ma?

Xiǎo Chén: Wǒ méi yǒu gēge dìdi, yě méi yǒu jiějie. Wǒ zhǐ yǒu mèimei.

Vocabulary

ba	final particle	*(indicates speaker's supposition)*
bàba	noun	*dad*
de	particle	*(indicates noun description)*
dìdi	noun	*younger brother*
gāoxìng	adjectival verb	*happy*
gēge	noun	*older brother*
jiějie	noun	*older sister*
māma	noun	*mom*
méi	negation adverb	*no, not (negation for **yǒu** have)*
mèimei	noun	*younger sister*
nà	demonstrative	*that*
qǐng jìn	conversational expression	*please come in*

rènshi	verb	*meet, know*
shéi	question word	*who*
tóngwū	noun	*roommate*
tóngxué	noun	*classmate*
Xiè	family name	*(family name)*
xué	verb	*study*
yǒu	stative verb	*have*
zhàopiàn	noun	*photograph*
zhè	demonstrative	*this*
Zhōngwén	noun	*Chinese language*

Family Members

male		female	
bàba	*dad*	māma	*mom*
gēge	*older brother*	jiějie	*older sister*
dìdi	*younger brother*	mèimei	*younger sister*

Dialogue practice

Do these activities in class after mastering each part of the dialogue for this lesson. Change partners so that you practice each role several times.

Dialogue 4A: Work with two other classmates. Take turns being the host, inviting the other two classmates into your home or dorm room, and introducing them to each other.

Dialogue 4B: Draw a picture of your family or bring a photo of your family to class. Work with a partner, introducing your family and asking your partner about his/her family.

Use and structure

4.1. Shéi *who?*

Shéi is the Mandarin content question word *who*. It is used to ask about the identity of nouns or pronouns in any position in the sentence.

Shéi is used to ask about the subject of the sentence:

> <u>Shéi</u> huì shuō Rìběn huà?
> *Who can speak Japanese?*

Shéi is used to ask about the object of the verb:

> Tā shì <u>shéi</u>?
> *Who is she?*

Shéi is used to ask about possession: (See Use and Structure note 4.4 below.)

> Tā shì <u>shéi</u> de tóngwū?
> *Whose roommate is he?*

In the dialogue in this lesson, Xiao Zhang uses **shéi** *who* as a one-word question *Who?* to ask who is at the door. In English we would probably say *Who's there?*

> Xiǎo Zhāng: Shéi?
> > *Who's there?*

When answering a **shéi** question, simply replace the question word with the answer.

> <u>Shéi</u> huì shuō Rìběn huà?   <u>Xiǎo Gāo</u> huì shuō Rìběn huà.
> *Who can speak Japanese?*   *Xiao Gao can speak Japanese.*
>
> Tā shì <u>shéi</u>?   →   Tā shì <u>Xiǎo Gāo</u>.
> *Who is she?*   *She is Xiao Gao.*
>
> Tā shì <u>shéi</u> de tóngwū?   Tā shì <u>wǒ</u> de tóngwū.
> *Whose roommate is he?*   *He is my roommate.*

4.2. Qǐng jìn *please come in*

Qǐng jìn is a polite way to invite someone to enter. Use it when you are inside, inviting someone else to come in. **Qǐng** is often used to make requests more polite. Recall that we have seen it in the expression **qǐng wèn** *may I ask* in Lesson 2.

4.3. Zhè *this* and nà *that*

In this lesson we learn to use the words **zhè** *this* and **nà** *that* as the subject of a sentence. **Zhè** *this* is used to refer to people or things that are close to the speaker.

<u>Zhè shì wǒ</u> de tóngwū, Xiè Guóqiáng.
This is my roommate, Xie Guoqiang.

Nà *that* is used to refer to people or things that are some distance from the speaker.

<u>Nà shì nǐ</u> de zhàopiàn ma?
Is that your photograph?

When used in this way, **zhè** *this* and **nà** *that* are called <u>demonstratives</u>. We will see another use of these words in Lesson 7.

4.4. Expressing possession and describing nouns

Expressing possession

To indicate that some noun is the possession of another noun or pronoun, say:

N/pron. de N
(possessor) (possession)
Xiǎo Zhāng de zhàopiàn
Xiao Zhang's photograph

wǒ de tóngwū
my roommate

Notice that <u>pronoun + de</u> is translated in English with possessive pronouns.

pron. + de + N

wǒ de (zhàopiàn) *my (photograph)*	**wǒmen de (zhàopiàn)** *our (photograph)*
nǐ de (zhàopiàn) *your (photograph)*	**nǐmen de (zhàopiàn)** *your (photograph)*
tā de (zhàopiàn) *his/her/its (photograph)*	**tāmen de (zhàopiàn)** *their (photograph)*

Zhè shì wǒ de tóngwū, Xiè Guóqiáng.
This is my roommate, Xie Guoqiang.

Nà shì nǐ de zhàopiàn ba.
That must be your photograph.

The particle **de** is sometimes omitted when the relationship between the pronoun and the following noun is very close. It is typically omitted when expressing family relationships.

wǒ dìdi	*my younger brother*
nǐ mèimei	*your younger sister*
wǒmen jiā	*our family*

The noun that is the possession may be omitted from the phrase when it is understood from the conversation or the text. Notice how <u>pronoun + de</u> is translated in English when the possession is omitted.

wǒ de *mine*	**wǒmen de** *ours*
nǐ de *yours*	**nǐmen de** *yours*
tā de *his/hers*	**tāmen de** *theirs*

Zhè shì wǒ de.
This is mine.

Nà shì tāmen de.
That is theirs.

Asking about possession: **shéi de** *whose*

To ask who something belongs to, use the expression **shéi de** *whose*. Remember that the question phrase occurs in the position in the sentence where the answer will occur.

Zhè shì shéi de zhàopiàn?
Whose photograph is this?

Nǐ shì shéi de tóngwū?
Whose roommate are you?

Answer a **shéi de** question with a <u>pronoun or noun + **de**</u>:

Q: **Zhè shì <u>shéi de</u> zhàopiàn?**
   Whose photograph is this?

A: **Zhè shì <u>wǒ de</u> zhàopiàn.**
   This is my photograph.

A: **Zhè shì <u>Xiǎo Zhāng de</u> zhàopiàn.**
   This is Xiao Zhang's photograph.

4.5.   Introductions and acknowledgments

Introduce others in Mandarin as you do in English, by saying "This is _____."

Zhè shì wǒ de tóngwū, Xiè Guóqiáng.
This is my roommate, Xie Guoqiang.

4.6.   Responding to introductions

When you meet someone for the first time you can say **Nǐ hǎo** (Lesson 1), or you can use the expression:

Hěn gāoxìng rènshi nǐ.
I am very happy to meet you.

If you are introduced to more than one person you can say:

Hěn gāoxìng rènshi nǐmen.
I am very happy to meet you.

Variations of this expression include:

Rènshi nǐ(men), wǒ hěn gāoxìng.
Rènshi nǐ(men) hěn gāoxìng.
I am very happy to meet you.

4.7.   Two meanings of the verb **rènshi**

The verb **rènshi** includes two different but related meanings. **Rènshi** means *meet someone for the first time*, and it means *know a person (or a place, or a Chinese character)*. It is easy to see how it can have both meanings: once you *meet* someone, you *know* them. In the expression **hěn gāoxìng rènshi nǐ**, **rènshi** can be translated as either *meet* or *know*. That is, you can think of the expression as meaning *I am happy to meet you* or *I am happy to know you*. In some sentences, only one or the other English translation of **rènshi** is possible.

4.8.   The sentence-particle **ba** and expressing assumptions

Ba is a <u>sentence-final particle</u> and always occurs at the end of the sentence. One function of **ba** is to mark the sentence as the speaker's assumption or educated guess. In the dialogue, Xiao Chen ends his sentence with **ba** because he is pretty certain that the photograph belongs to Xiao Zhang, but he does not know it for a fact.

Nà shì nǐ de zhàopiàn ba.
That is your photograph I assume. (or) *That must be your photograph.*

Notice that there is more than one way to translate the sentence into English and to express an assumption about something. We will see other functions of **ba** in later lessons.

4.9.   **Yǒu** *have* and **méi yǒu** *not have*

Yǒu means *have*, and it is used just like *have* in English when indicating one's family members or other possessions.

Wǒ yǒu mèimei.
I have younger sisters. (or) *I have a younger sister.*

Yǒu is always negated with the word **méi** and is never negated with **bù**:

Wǒ méi yǒu jiějie.
I do not have older sisters. (or) *I do not have an older sister.*

You may form yes-no questions with **yǒu** by adding **ma** at the end of the sentence.

Nǐ yǒu gēge hé dìdi ma?
Do you have older brothers and younger brothers?

The verb-not-verb form of yes-no questions with **yǒu** is **yǒu méi yǒu**.

Nǐ yǒu méi yǒu gēge hé dìdi?
Do you have older brothers and younger brothers?

Sentence pyramids

The sentence pyramids illustrate the use of each new vocabulary item and structure intro-duced in the lesson. Use them to help you learn how to form phrases and sentences in Mandarin. Supply the English translation for the last line where indicated.

1. shéi shì shéi Nǐ shì shéi?	*who* *be who* *Who are you?*
2. tóngwū wǒ de tóngwū Tā shì wǒ de tóngwū.	*roommate* *my roommate* _____
3. wǒ de tóngwū shì wǒ de tóngwū Zhè shì wǒ de tóngwū. Zhè shì wǒ de tóngwū, Xiè Guóqiáng.	*my roommate* *be my roommate* *This is my roommate.* _____
4. tóngxué wǒ de tóngxué Zhè shì wǒ de tóngxué.	*classmate* *my classmate* _____
5. zhàopiàn nǐ de zhàopiàn	*photograph* *your photograph*
6. zhàopiàn wǒ de zhàopiàn Zhè shì wǒ de zhàopiàn.	*photograph* *my photograph* _____
7. zhàopiàn shéi de zhàopiàn Zhè shì shéi de zhàopiàn?	*photograph* *whose photograph* *Whose photograph is this?* *(This is whose photograph?)*

8. nǐ de zhàopiàn shì nǐ de zhàopiàn Nà shì nǐ de zhàopiàn. Nà shì nǐ de zhàopiàn ba.	*your photograph* *be your photograph* *That is your photograph.* *That must be your photograph.*
9. mèimei tā de mèimei Zhè shì tā de mèimei. Zhè shì tā de mèimei ba.	*younger sister* *her younger sister* *This is her younger sister.*
10. māma wǒ māma Zhè shì wǒ māma.	*mom* *my mom*
11. bàba wǒ bàba Zhè shì wǒ bàba.	*dad* *my dad*
12. mèimei yǒu mèimei Tā yǒu mèimei.	*younger sister* *have younger sister*
13. gēge yǒu gēge Nǐ yǒu gēge ma?	*older brother* *have older brother*
14. nǐ de gēge rènshi nǐ de gēge Wǒ rènshi nǐ de gēge.	*your older brother* *know your older brother*
15. dìdi nǐ de dìdi Wǒ bù rènshi nǐ de dìdi.	*younger brother* *your younger brother*
16. gāoxìng hěn gāoxìng dōu hěn gāoxìng Tāmen dōu hěn gāoxìng.	*happy* *very happy* *all very happy* *They are all very happy.*

17.	
rènshi nǐ	*know you, meet you*
Hěn gāoxìng rènshi nǐ.	*(I) am very happy to know you./(I) am very happy to meet you.*

18.	
gāoxìng	*happy*
hěn gāoxìng	*very happy*
Rènshi nǐ hěn gāoxìng.	*(I) am very happy to know you./(I) am very happy to meet you.*

19.	
dìdi	*younger brother*
gēge hé dìdi	*older brother and younger brother*
yǒu gēge hé dìdi	*have older brother and younger brother*
Nǐ yǒu gēge hé dìdi ma?	_____

20.	
yǒu dìdi	*have a younger brother*
méi yǒu dìdi	*not have a younger brother*
Wǒ méi yǒu dìdi.	_____

21.	
jiějie	*older sister*
yǒu jiějie	*have older sister*
Nǐ yǒu jiějie ma?	_____

22.	
jiějie	*older sister*
yǒu jiějie	*have an older sister*
yǒu méi yǒu jiějie?	*have or not have an older sister*
Nǐ yǒu méi yǒu jiějie?	_____

23.	
gēge hé dìdi	*older brother and younger brother*
yǒu gēge hé dìdi	*have older brother and younger brother*
yǒu méi yǒu gēge hé dìdi?	*have or not have older brother and younger brother*
Nǐ yǒu méi yǒu gēge hé dìdi?	_____

24.	
Zhōngwén	*Chinese language*
xué Zhōngwén	*study Chinese language*
Wǒ xué Zhōngwén.	_____

25. Zhōngwén xué Zhōngwén Shéi xué Zhōngwén?	*Chinese language* *study Chinese language* *Who studies Chinese language?*
26. xué Zhōngwén dōu xué Zhōngwén Tāmen dōu xué Zhōngwén.	*study Chinese* *all study Chinese* _____
27. Q: Shéi? A: Shì wǒ.	*Q: Who is it?* *A: It's me.*
28. Q: Shéi? A: Chén Míng hé Wáng Màikè. A: Shì wǒmen, Chén Míng hé Wáng Màikè.	*Q: Who is it?* *A: Chen Ming and Wang Maike.* *A:* _____ _____
29. qǐng jìn Xiǎo Wáng, qǐng jìn.	*please come in* _____

Pronunciation and Pinyin

Initial consonants

Here is a table of Mandarin initial consonants. In this lesson we focus on the highlighted groups of initial consonants.

b	d	g	j	zh	z
p	t	k	q	ch	c
m	n	h	x	sh	s
f	l			r	

zh, ch, sh, r

zh, **ch**, **sh**, and **r** are pronounced with the tongue behind the alveolar ridge, the gum ridge behind the front teeth, further back in the mouth than **d**, **t**, **n**, and **l** or **j**, **q**, and **x**. The <u>blade</u> of the tongue (the top surface of the tongue near the tip) is near the roof of the mouth and the lips are rounded. The vowel **i** that is written after the consonants **zh**, **ch**, **sh**, and **r** in their recitation form is similar in pronunciation to the suffix *-er* in English with a strong *r*. The syllables **zhi**, **chi**, **shi**, and **ri** are pronounced without moving the lips.

zhi is similar in pronunciation to *Ger* in the word *German* pronounced with a strong *r*. When pronouncing words with **zh**, the tongue briefly touches the roof of the mouth.

chi is similar in pronunciation to *chur* in the word <u>church</u> when pronounced with a strong *r*. When pronouncing words with **ch**, the tongue briefly touches the roof of the mouth and the sound includes a release of air.

shi is similar in pronunciation to *shir* in the word <u>shirt</u> pronounced with a strong *r*. When saying words with **sh**, the tongue is close to the roof of the mouth but does not touch it.

ri is pronounced with the tongue slightly lower and further back than when saying **sh**. English has no sound that is similar in pronunciation to **ri**. Listen to the recordings that accompany this textbook to practice the sound.

zh, **ch**, **sh**, and **r** can occur before all finals except for those that begin with **ü** and compound and nasal finals that begin with **i**.

Here are Mandarin syllables that begin with **zh**, **ch**, **sh**, and **r**.

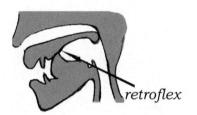

retroflex

zh	zhī, zhǐ, Zhāng, zhēn(de), Zhōng(guó)
ch	chī, Chén
sh	shī, (lǎo)shī, shì, shén(me), shuō
r	rī, Rì(běn)

z, c, s

Like the consonants **d**, **t**, **n**, and **l**, the consonants **z**, **c**, and **s** are pronounced with the tongue touching the alveolar ridge, the gum ridge behind the front teeth. English has sounds equivalent to each of **z**, **c**, and **s**, but two of the English sounds occur only at the ends of syllables and not at the beginning.

z is the sound *ds* (pronounced *dz*) in the words *car<u>ds</u>*, *ki<u>ds</u>*, and *fa<u>ds</u>*.
c is the sound *ts* in the words *ca<u>ts</u>*, *lo<u>ts</u>*, and *hi<u>ts</u>*.
s is the same as the sound *s* in English.

z, **c**, and **s** can occur before all finals except for those that begin with **ü** and compound and nasal finals that begin with **i**.

Here are Mandarin syllables that begin with **z**, **c**, and **s**. We have not yet learned any words that begin with the consonant **c**.

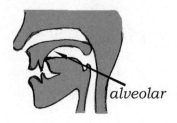

alveolar

z	zī, (míng)zi, (hái)zi, zài, zǒu
c	cī, cái, cóng, (míng)cí
s	sī, sì, sài, sòng, suǒ

Language FAQs

What is the difference between Zhōngguó huà and Zhōngwén?

Zhōngguó huà refers to the spoken language. **Zhōngwén** refers to Chinese in its spoken and written form. The spoken form of any dialect of Chinese can be referred to as **Zhōngguó huà**, though each dialect can also be referred to by its dialect name: **Guǎngdōng huà** (Cantonese), **Mǐnnán huà** (Southern Min), **Shànghǎi huà** (Shanghainese), **Kèjiā huà** (Hakka), **Pǔtōng huà** (the label for Mandarin in mainland China), **Guóyǔ** (the label for Mandarin in Taiwan), etc.

Where are *and* and *or*?

> **Nǐ yǒu gēge dìdi ma?**
> *Do you have older brothers and younger brothers?*

> **Wǒ méi yǒu gēge dìdi.**
> *I don't have older brothers or younger brothers.*

Mandarin has words for *and* and *or*, but they are not used as frequently as they are in English. When listing nouns it is acceptable to connect them with **hé**, (that is, it is acceptable to say: **wǒ méi yǒu gēge <u>hé</u> dìdi** *I don't have an older brother and a younger brother*), but it is often more common and natural sounding to express the information without **hé**. Depending upon the context, the English translation may include either *and* or *or*.

Notes on Chinese culture

Gender, relative age, and the order of kinship terms

In traditional Chinese society, gender and age determine status, with males holding a higher place in society than women, and older people holding a higher place than younger people of the same gender. When talking about members of your family or someone else's family, males of the same generation are always listed before females: **bàba māma** *father and mother*, **gēge jiějie** *older brother and older sister*. Older brothers are always mentioned before younger brothers, and older sisters are always mentioned before younger sisters: **gēge dìdi jiějie mèimei** *older brother, younger brother, older sister, younger sister*.

Lesson 4 Dialogue in English

Part A

Xiao Zhang: Who is it?

Xiao Chen: David (Dawei), it's us, Chen Ming and Wang Maike.

Xiao Zhang: Xiao Chen, Xiao Wang, come in, come in.

Xiao Chen: Hi!

Xiao Zhang: Hi. This is my roommate, Xie Guoqiang. They are my classmates, Chen Ming and Wang Maike. They both study Chinese.

Xiao Wang: Hi.

Xiao Xie: I'm very happy to meet you.

Part B

Xiao Chen: Xiao Zhang, that must be your photograph.

Xiao Zhang: Yes. This is my dad, this is my mom.

Xiao Wang: Who is he?

Xiao Zhang: He is my older brother.

Xiao Wang: And him?

Xiao Zhang: He is my younger brother.

Xiao Wang: Xiao Chen, do you have older brothers and younger brothers?

Xiao Chen: I don't have older brothers or younger brothers. I also don't have any older sisters. I only have younger sisters.

Lesson 5 Nǐ jiā yǒu jǐ gè rén?

How many people are in your family?

Communication goals
- Talk about the number of people in your family
- Recite phone numbers and ask others for their phone numbers

Key structures
numbers 1–10 and zero

number + **gè** + N

jǐ *how many?*

zěnme *how?*

describing nouns with nouns:

   N **de** N

kěyǐ *can*

asking for phone numbers with **duōshao**

gěi (someone) **dǎ diànhuà** *phone someone*

two words for *two*: **liǎng** and **èr**

Dialogue

The Situation: Xiao Zhang, Xiao Wang, Xiao Chen, and Xiao Xie continue their conversation about their families in Xiao Zhang and Xiao Xie's dorm room. Before Xiao Wang and Xiao Chen leave, they exchange cell phone numbers with Xiao Xie.

Part A

Xiǎo Wáng:	Dàwéi, nà, nǐ jiā yǒu wǔ gè rén ba.
Xiǎo Zhāng:	Duì, wǒ jiā yǒu wǔ gè rén. Xiǎo Wáng, nǐ jiā yǒu jǐ gè rén?
Xiǎo Wáng:	Wǒ jiā yǒu shí gè rén.
Xiǎo Zhāng:	Shí gè rén! Zhēnde ma?
Xiǎo Wáng:	Zhēnde. Wǒmen jiā yǒu bā gè háizi, wǔ gè nán háizi, sān gè nǚ háizi. Wǒ yǒu sì gè gēge, liǎng gè jiějie, hé yī gè mèimei.

Part B

Xiǎo Chén:	Xiǎo Xiè, nǐ jiā ne?
Xiǎo Zhāng:	Wǒ zhīdào. Xiǎo Xiè jiā yǒu sān gè rén, tā bàba, tā māma hé tā. Duì bù duì?
Xiǎo Xiè:	Duì.
Xiǎo Chén:	Nǐ zěnme zhīdào tā jiā zhǐ yǒu yī gè háizi?
Xiǎo Zhāng:	Wǒ de Zhōngguó péngyou dōu méi yǒu gēge, dìdi, yě méi yǒu jiějie, mèimei.

Part C

Xiǎo Xiè:	Xiǎo Chén, Xiǎo Wáng, wǒ de diànhuà hàomǎ shì yāo líng wǔ sì bā wǔ líng liù jiǔ èr bā, kěyǐ gěi wǒ dǎ diànhuà.
Xiǎo Chén:	Yāo líng wǔ sì bā wǔ líng liù jiǔ èr bā, duì bù duì?
Xiǎo Xiè:	Duì. Nǐmen de diànhuà hàomǎ shì duōshao?
Xiǎo Chén:	Wǒ méi yǒu shǒujī, Xiǎo Wáng yǒu. Xiǎo Wáng de hàomǎ shì yī sān èr sì bā liù qī jiǔ jiǔ líng sān.
Xiǎo Xiè:	Hǎo. Xièxiè.

Mandarin nouns are always associated with a <u>classifier</u>. See Use and Structure note 5.3. Beginning in this lesson, we will follow each noun introduced in the vocabulary list with the classifier associated with that noun. The classifier will be provided in square brackets.

Vocabulary

bā	number	*eight*
dǎ	verb	*hit*
diànhuà [gè]	noun	*telephone*
duōshao	question word	*how much, how many*
èr	number	*two*
gè (ge)	classifier	*(classifier for people and some other nouns)*
gěi	preposition	*(part of the expression gěi (someone) dǎ diànhuà)*
háizi [gè]	noun	*child*
hàomǎ [gè]	noun	*number*
jǐ	question word	*how many*

jiā [gè]	noun	*family, home*
jiǔ	number	*nine*
kěyǐ	modal verb	*can*
liǎng	number	*two*
líng	number	*zero*
liù	number	*six*
nà	pause particle	*well then*
nán	adjective	*male*
nán háizi [gè]	noun phrase	*boy (male child)*
nǚ	adjective	*female*
nǚ háizi [gè]	noun phrase	*girl (female child)*
péngyou [gè]	noun	*friend*
qī	number	*seven*
sān	number	*three*
shí	number	*ten*
shǒujī [gè]	noun	*cell phone, mobile phone*
sì	number	*four*
wǔ	number	*five*
yāo	number	*one*
yī	number	*one*
zěnme	question word	*how*
zhīdào	verb	*know*

Compound nouns

diànhuà hàomǎ	*phone number*
shǒujī hàomǎ	*cell phone number (mobile phone number)*

Fixed expressions

Nǐ de diànhuà hàomǎ shì duōshao?	*What is your phone number?*
Nǐ de shǒujī hàomǎ shì duōshao?	*What is your cell phone (mobile phone) number?*
gěi (someone) **dǎ diànhuà**	*phone (someone)*

The numbers 1–10 and zero

1	**yī**	6	**liù**
2	**èr**	7	**qī**
3	**sān**	8	**bā**
4	**sì**	9	**jiǔ**
5	**wǔ**	10	**shí**
		0	**líng**

Dialogue practice

Do these activities in class after mastering each part of the dialogue for this lesson. Change partners so that you practice each role several times.

Dialogue 5A: Interview your classmates to find out how many people there are in their families. Describe the family of one of your classmates to the entire class.

Dialogue 5B: Interview a classmate by asking one question at a time to find out if she has an older brother, an older sister, a younger brother, or a younger sister. Introduce that classmate to another classmate, saying what siblings she has and does not have.

Dialogue 5C: Exchange phone numbers with at least five of your classmates. Find out who has a cell phone and who does not. Introduce one of your classmates to the class, providing their name and phone number.

Use and structure

5.1.   Nà *well then*

When **nà** occurs at the beginning of a statement followed by a pause, it is equivalent to the English expression *well then*.

> **Nà, nǐ jiā yǒu wǔ gè rén ba.**
> *Well then, your family must have five people.*

5.2.   Yǒu *have, there is/there are*

The verb **yǒu** can sometimes be translated into English as *have* and sometimes as *there is* or *there are*. As you can see, **yǒu** in the following sentences from the dialogue can be translated either way.

> **Nǐ jiā yǒu jǐ gè rén?**
> *How many people are there in your family?*
> *How many people does your family have?*

> **Wǒ jiā yǒu wǔ gè rén.**
> *There are five people in my family.*
> *My family has five people.*

No matter how it is translated into English, **yǒu** is always negated with **méi**:

> **Tā jiā méi yǒu nǚ háizi.**
> *There are no girls in his family.*
> *His family does not have any girls.*

5.3.   The classifier **gè**: Number + **gè** + N

In Mandarin, when indicating the number of people or things, the number must be followed by a <u>classifier</u>. This lesson introduces the classifier **gè**, used when talking about the number of people, cell phones, and many other things as well.

number + gè + N

yī **gè** rén	*one person*
liǎng **gè** dìdi	*two younger brothers*
sān **gè** háizi	*three children*
sì **gè** tóngwū	*four roommates*
wǔ **gè** tóngxué	*five classmates*
liù **gè** shǒujī	*six cell phones*

Many nouns have an associated classifier, and beginning with this lesson we will present the classifier associated with the noun right after the noun, in square brackets, in the Vocabulary list. We will see in later lessons that some nouns have more than one associated classifier.

Many classifiers, including the classifier **gè**, are not translated into English. However, if the noun phrase indicates the number of nouns, the classifier must be present and <u>cannot</u> be omitted even if it is not translated into English.

The noun following the classifier can be omitted, however, if its identity is clear from context.

Wǒ jiā yǒu wǔ gè rén.   **Tā jiā yǒu sān gè (rén).**
My family has five people.   *His family has three (people).*

The classifier **gè** is normally pronounced with neutral tone.

5.4.   **Jǐ** *how much, how many*

Jǐ is a content question word and it means *how much* or *how many*. When asking about the number of people, say:

jǐ gè + N

jǐ **gè** rén	*how many people?*
jǐ **gè** háizi	*how many children?*
jǐ **gè** tóngwū	*how many roommates?*
jǐ **gè** péngyou	*how many friends?*

To answer a **jǐ** question, replace **jǐ** with a number:

Nǐ jiā yǒu jǐ gè rén?
How many people does your family have?

Wǒ jiā yǒu wǔ gè rén.
My family has five people.

Jǐ *how much, how many* is usually used when the speaker expects the answer to be a relatively small number, typically less than twenty. We will learn another way to ask *how much/how many* in Lesson 6.

5.5.   The adjectives **nán** *male* and **nǚ** *female*

Most Mandarin words that translate into adjectives in English are adjectival <u>verbs</u>. That is, they can be used to describe nouns and can also function as the main verb in the sentence. But **nán** *male* and **nǚ** *female* are adjectives, not adjectival verbs. They can only be used to describe nouns and can never be used as the main verb of the sentence.

> **nán háizi** *boy*   **nǚ háizi** *girl*
> **nán péngyǒu** *boyfriend*   **nǚ péngyou** *girlfriend*

To say that someone *is male (is a man)* or that someone *is female (is a woman)*, say:

> **Tā shì nán de.**   **Tā shì nǚ de.**
> *He is male.*   *She is female.*

5.6.   **Liǎng** and **èr**: Two words for *two*

Mandarin has two words for the number *two*, **liǎng** and **èr**. Both are introduced in this lesson. **Liǎng** is used when indicating two of something, for example, *two people, two students, two classmates*, etc. It is always followed by **gè** or another classifier.

> **Wǒ yǒu liǎng gè jiějie.**
> *I have two older sisters.*

Èr is used when the number *two* is not followed by a classifier. In this chapter, we see **èr** used when reciting a list of numbers such as numbers in a phone number.

> **Wǒ de diànhuà hàomǎ shì yāo líng wǔ sì bā wǔ líng liù jiǔ èr bā.**
> *My phone number is 105-4850-6928.*

When counting (from 1–10 for example), the number *two* is always **èr**:

> **yī èr sān sì wǔ liù qī bā jiǔ shí**
> 1   2   3   4   5   6   7   8   9   10

Here is the rule for choosing between **liǎng** and **èr**:

> 2 + classifier   → **liǎng** (classifier) (**liǎng gè**)
> 2 without classifier → **èr** (**yī èr sān**)

5.7.   **Zhīdào** *know a fact* and **rènshi** *know a person*

In Lesson 4 we learned to use the word **rènshi** when talking about *knowing people*. The verb **zhīdào** is used when saying that you *know a fact, or a piece of information.*

Xiǎo Wáng: Xiǎo Xiè, nǐ jiā yǒu jǐ gè rén?
              Xiao Xie, how many people do you have in your family?
Xiǎo Zhāng: Wǒ zhīdào. Xiǎo Xiè jiā yǒu sān gè rén.
              I know. Xiao Xie's family has three people.

The verb **zhīdào** may be followed by a statement, or by a yes-no question with **ma**.

Wǒ zhīdào tā shì xuésheng.
I know that she is a student.

Nǐ zhīdào tā de diànhuà hàomǎ ma?
Do you know his phone number?

In English, statements and questions about "knowing" are often introduced with the word *that*.

Wǒ zhīdào tā shì Měiguó rén.
I know (that) she is American.

Nǐ zhīdào tā shì Zhōngguó rén ma?
Do you know (that) he is Chinese?

Mandarin does not add a word equivalent to *that* to introduce statements or questions about knowing. Be sure to follow the Mandarin rule and not the English rule when you speak or write in Chinese.

5.8.   Describing nouns with nouns

In Lesson 4 we learned how to describe a noun with a pronoun, noun, or noun phrase to indicate possession or description (Use and Structure note 4.4). In this lesson we continue to practice describing nouns with other nouns or noun phrases.

In Mandarin, descriptions of a noun occur before the noun that is being described. We will refer to the noun that is being described as the main noun. When a noun or noun phrase describes another noun, the description may indicate possession, or it may simply provide additional information about the noun.

NP de (main) N
Xiǎo Zhāng de zhàopiàn
Xiao Zhang's photograph

Xiǎo Wáng de diànhuà hàomǎ
Xiao Wang's telephone number

Sometimes, when describing a noun with another noun or noun phrase, it is acceptable to omit **de**. For example, when referring to someone's family, **de** may be omitted:

Xiǎo Xiè de jiā   or   **Xiǎo Xiè jiā**
Xiao Xie's family   *Xiao Xie's family*

The omission of **de** is determined by the closeness of the description and the main noun and is not entirely predictable. For family members and parts of the body (for example, *my hand*) **de** can be and often is omitted. For other descriptions, include the particle **de** unless you have heard Chinese speakers use the expression without **de**.

5.9. Zěnme *how*

Zěnme is a content question word and means *how*. **Zěnme** always occurs before a verb or verb phrase.

> **(S) zěnme + V/VP**
> **Nǐ zěnme zhīdào tā jiā zhǐ yǒu yī gè háizi?**
> *How do you know that his family only has one child?*

Zěnme zhīdào? means *how do you know?* **Zěnme shuō?** means *how do you say?*

> **"Student," Zhōngwén zěnme shuō?**
> *How do you say "student" in Chinese?*

> **"Háizi" Yīngwén zěnme shuō?**
> *How do you say "háizi" in English?*

5.10.   Reciting phone numbers and two ways to say the number *one* in phone numbers

Phone numbers are recited as they are in English, as a series of numbers:

> **Wǒ de diànhuà hàomǎ shì yī líng wǔ sì bā wǔ líng liù jiǔ èr bā.**
> *My phone number is 105-4850-6928.*

In and around Beijing, when reciting phone numbers, *one* is often pronounced **yāo**.

> **Wǒ de diànhuà hàomǎ shì <u>yāo</u> líng wǔ sì bā wǔ líng liù jiǔ èr bā.**

The pronunciation **yāo** for the number *one* is also used in room numbers, addresses, and bus, train, and flight numbers. The number *one* is pronounced as **yī** and never as **yāo** when it is used in counting, and it is pronounced as **yī** and never as **yāo** when it is used in indicating the number of people, places, or things.

5.11. Líng *zero*

Líng *zero* is used when reciting phone numbers, room numbers, addresses, bus or train numbers, etc.

> **Wǒ de diànhuà hàomǎ shì yāo <u>líng</u> wǔ sì bā wǔ <u>líng</u> liù jiǔ èr bā.**
> *My phone number is 105-4850-6928.*

Ling *zero* is different from the other numbers in the way that it is used. It never occurs before **gè** or another classifier, and it is not used when saying that there are <u>no people</u> or <u>no things</u>.

Say this:	*Do not say this:*
Wǒ méi yǒu dìdi.	⊗ Wǒ yǒu líng gè dìdi.
I don't have a younger brother.	

5.12. Kěyǐ *can*

Kěyǐ *can* is used when indicating permission or acceptable behavior. It always occurs before a verb or verb phrase. When used with the expression **gěi** (someone) **dǎ diànhuà** *phone (someone)* or *give (someone) a phone call*, it occurs before **gěi**:

Nǐ kěyǐ gěi wǒ dǎ diànhuà.
You can phone me.

Kěyǐ occurs after negation and after adverbs (for example, **zhǐ** *only*, **yě** *also*, **dōu** *all, both*, and **dāngrán** *of course*):

Nǐ bù kěyǐ gěi tā dǎ diànhuà.
You cannot phone him.

Nǐ dāngrán kěyǐ gěi lǎoshī dǎ diànhuà.
Of course you can give the teacher a phone call.

Kěyǐ, like **huì** *can* (Lesson 3), is a modal verb. When a sentence contains a modal verb, the modal verb is the verb that is used in the short answer *yes* and *no*:

Q: **Wǒ kěyǐ gěi nǐ dǎ diànhuà ma?**
Can I phone you?

A: **Kěyǐ.**
(You) can.

It is also the word that is repeated in verb-not-verb questions:

Wǒ kěyǐ bù kěyǐ gěi nǐ dǎ diànhuà?
Can I phone you?

5.13. Gěi (someone) **dǎ diànhuà** *phone (someone)*

Gěi (someone) **dǎ diànhuà** means *phone (someone)* or *give (someone) a phone call*. To say that Xiao Zhang phones Xiao Xie say:

Xiǎo Zhāng gěi Xiǎo Xiè dǎ diànhuà.
Xiao Zhang phones Xiao Xie.

Learn this as a fixed expression. We will learn other uses of **gěi** in later lessons.

5.14.   Asking for phone numbers

When asking someone for his or her phone number, use the word **duōshao** and say:

Nǐ de diànhuà hàomǎ shì duōshao?
What is your phone number?

To answer the question, replace the question word with your phone number:

Wǒ de diànhuà hàomǎ shì (yāo líng wǔ sì bā wǔ líng liù jiǔ èr bā).
My phone number is (105-4850-6928).

Sentence pyramids

The sentence pyramids illustrate the use of each new vocabulary item and structure introduced in the lesson. Use them to help you learn how to form phrases and sentences in Mandarin. Supply the English translation for the last line where indicated.

1. rén yī gè rén	*person* *one person*
2. jiějie liǎng gè jiějie	*older sister* *two older sisters*
3. tóngxué sān gè tóngxué	*classmate* *three classmates*
4. lǎoshī sì gè lǎoshī	*teacher* *four teachers*
5. háizi wǔ gè háizi	*child* *five children*
6. yī gè háizi yǒu yī gè háizi zhǐ yǒu yī gè háizi Tā jiā zhǐ yǒu yī gè háizi.	*one child* *have one child* *only have one child* *His family only has one child.*

7. háizi nán háizi sì gè nán háizi Wǒ bàba māma yǒu sì gè nán háizi.	*child* *boy* *four boys* *My mom and dad have four boys.*
8. háizi nǚ háizi sān gè nǚ háizi sì gè nán háizi hé sān gè nǚ háizi Wǒ bàba māma yǒu sì gè nán háizi hé sān gè nǚ háizi.	*child* *girl* *three girls* *four boys and three girls* ———————————————— ————————————————
9. wǔ gè rén yǒu wǔ gè rén Nǐ jiā yǒu wǔ gè rén. Nǐ jiā yǒu wǔ gè rén ba. Nà, nǐ jiā yǒu wǔ gè rén ba.	*five people* *have five people* *Your family has five people.* *I guess your family has five people.* *Well then, I guess your family has* *five people.*
10. tóngxué jǐ gè tóngxué Nǐ yǒu jǐ gè tóngxué?	*classmate(s)* *how many classmates?* *How many classmates do you have?*
11. tóngxué liù gè tóngxué Wǒ yǒu liù gè tóngxué.	*classmate(s)* *six classmates* *I have six classmates.*
12. xuésheng jǐ gè xuésheng rènshi jǐ gè xuésheng Nǐ rènshi jǐ gè xuésheng?	*student(s)* *how many students?* *know how many students?* *How many students do you know?*
13. xuésheng qī gè xuésheng Wǒ rènshi qī gè xuésheng.	*student(s)* *seven students* ————————————————

14.	
háizi	*child(ren)*
bā gè háizi	*eight children*
Tā jiā yǒu bā gè háizi.	_____

15.	
péngyou	*friend*
Zhōngguó péngyou	*Chinese friends*
jiǔ gè Zhōngguó péngyou	*nine Chinese friends*
Wǒ yǒu jiǔ gè Zhōngguó péngyou.	_____

16.	
rén	*person (people)*
shí gè rén	*ten people*
yǒu shí gè rén	*have ten people*
Wǒ jiā yǒu shí gè rén.	_____

17.	
shǒujī	*cell phone (mobile phone)*
yǒu shǒujī	*have a cell phone*
Wǒ méi yǒu shǒujī.	_____

18.	
hàomǎ	*number*
shǒujī hàomǎ	*cell phone number*
wǒ de shǒujī hàomǎ	*my cell phone number*
Zhè shì wǒ de shǒujī hàomǎ.	_____

19.	
sān sì wǔ	*three, four, five*
yī èr sān sì wǔ	*one, two, three, four, five*

20.	
bā jiǔ shí	*eight, nine, ten*
liù qī bā jiǔ shí	*six, seven, eight, nine, ten*
yī èr sān sì wǔ liù qī bā jiǔ shí	_____

21.	
èr sān sì wǔ liù qī bā jiǔ	*2 3 4 5 6 7 8 9*
shì èr sān sì wǔ liù qī bā jiǔ	*is 2 3 4 5 6 7 8 9*
hàomǎ shì èr sān sì wǔ liù qī bā jiǔ	*number is 2 3 4 5 6 7 8 9*
shǒujī hàomǎ shì èr sān sì wǔ liù qī bā jiǔ	*cell phone number is 2 3 4 5 6 7 8 9*
Wǒ de shǒujī hàomǎ shì èr sān sì wǔ liù qī bā jiǔ.	_____

22.	
diànhuà	*telephone*
dǎ diànhuà	*make a phone call*
gěi wǒ dǎ diànhuà	*call me on the phone*
Wǒ de dìdi gěi wǒ dǎ diànhuà.	*My younger brother calls (called) me on the phone.*

23.	
duōshao	*how much?*
shì duōshao	*is how much?*
diànhuà hàomǎ shì duōshao	*what is ( ) phone number?*
Nǐ de diànhuà hàomǎ shì duōshao?	*What is your telephone number?*

24.	
diànhuà hàomǎ	*phone number*
tā de diànhuà hàomǎ	*his phone number*
Wǒ zhīdào tā de diànhuà hàomǎ.	*I know his phone number.*

25.	
yāo	*one (in phone numbers)*
jiǔ liù jiǔ yāo	*9 6 9 1*
èr yāo liù bā jiǔ liù jiǔ yāo	*2 1 6 8 9 6 9 1*
shì èr yāo liù bā jiǔ liù jiǔ yāo	*is 2 1 6 8 9 6 9 1*
Tā de diànhuà hàomǎ shì èr yāo liù bā jiǔ liù jiǔ yāo.	_____

26.	
zhīdào	*know*
zěnme zhīdào	*how (do you) know?*
Nǐ zěnme zhīdào?	*How do you know?*

27.	
yǒu yī gè háizi	*have one child*
zhǐ yǒu yī gè háizi	*have only one child*
tā jiā zhǐ yǒu yī gè háizi	*his family has only one child*
zhīdào tā jiā zhǐ yǒu yī gè háizi	*know his family has only one child*
Nǐ zěnme zhīdào tā jiā zhǐ yǒu yī gè háizi?	*How do you know (that) his family has only one child?*

28.	
èr sì sān wǔ	*2 4 3 5*
yāo líng líng yāo èr sì sān wǔ	*1 0 0 1 2 4 3 5*
shì yāo líng líng yāo èr sì sān wǔ	*is 1 0 0 1 2 4 3 5*
Tā de diànhuà hàomǎ shì yāo líng líng yāo èr sì sān wǔ.	_____

29. tā de diànhuà hàomǎ zěnme zhīdào tā de diànhuà hàomǎ? Nǐ zěnme zhīdào tā de diànhuà hàomǎ?	*her phone number* *how (do you) know her phone number?* —————————————— ———————————————
30. dǎ diànhuà Nǐ zěnme dǎ diànhuà?	*make a phone call* ———————————————
31. gěi wǒ dǎ diànhuà kěyǐ gěi wǒ dǎ diànhuà Nǐ kěyǐ gěi wǒ dǎ diànhuà.	*phone me* *can phone me* *You can phone me.*
32. zěnme shuō Zhōngwén zěnme shuō "Family" Zhōngwén zěnme shuō?	*how do you say?* *how do you say in Chinese?* *How do you say "family" in Chinese?*

Pronunciation and Pinyin

Tone change for **yī** *one*

When **yī** *one* occurs at the end of a phrase or sentence, it is pronounced in first tone: **yī**. When it occurs before a syllable with first, second, or third tone, it is often pronounced with fourth tone: **yì**.

yī + 1, 2, 3	→	yì + 1, 2, 3
yī zhāng	→	yì zhāng
yī píng	→	yì píng
yī běn	→	yì běn

When **yī** occurs before a syllable in fourth tone, it often changes to second tone: **yí**.

yī + 4	→	yí + 4
yīgòng	→	yígòng

Yī *one* is pronounced in second tone before the classifier **gè** whether it occurs with falling tone (**gè**) or neutral tone (**ge**): yī ge, yī gè → yí ge, yí gè.

The final **er** and finals that begin with **o**, **i**, **ü**, and **u**

Here is the table of Mandarin finals. In this lesson we focus on the final **er** and on finals that begin with **o**, **i**, **ü**, and **u**.

Finals that begin with:	and end with a vowel:	and end with **n**:	and end with **ng**:	and end with **r**:
a	a, ai, ao	an	ang	
e	e, ei	en	eng	er
o	(o), ou		ong	
i	i, ia, iao, ie, iu/iou	ian, in	iang, ing, iong	
ü	ü, üe	üan, ün		
u	u, ua, uai, ui/uei, uo	uan, uen	uang, ueng	

The final er

The final **er** occurs in a small number of words in Mandarin. It always occurs without an initial. **Er** is pronounced similar to the English word *are* when said with a strong *r*. Example: **èr** *two*

Finals that begin with o

o	(o), ou	ong

Pronunciation

- When the letter **o** begins a final (**ou**, **ong**) it is pronounced like the English sound *o* as in the words *ho̱me* or *pho̱ne*. Words with the final **ou** are close in pronunciation to the vowel in the English words *go̱* and *no̱*.
- When the letter **o** occurs in the final **uo** or follows **b**, **p**, **m**, or **f** as a simple final (**bo**, **po**, **mo**, **fo**), it is pronounced like *aw* in the English words *a̱wful* and *sa̱w*.

Restrictions

- Finals that begin with **o** cannot occur after the initials **j**, **q**, and **x**.

Finals that begin with u

u	u, ua, uai, ui/uei, uo	uan, uen	uang, ueng

Pronunciation

- Finals that begin with **u** are pronounced with rounded lips and the tongue relatively high and back in the mouth. The sound of **u** is very similar to the vowel sound in the English word *to̱ol*. In Mandarin, the lips do not move during the pronunciation of the **u** sound.

Spelling

- If a syllable that begins with **u** does not have an initial, the syllable is spelled **wu**. Example: **wǔ** *five*

Restrictions

- Finals that begin with **u** cannot occur after the initials **j**, **q**, and **x**.

Finals that begin with i

i	i, ia, iao, ie, iu/iou	ian, in	iang, ing, iong

Pronunciation

There are three pronunciations of the Pinyin letter **i**:

- When the Pinyin letter **i** follows **zh**, **ch**, **sh**, or **r** it is pronounced as a strong *r* similar to the sound of the English syllable *er* when pronounced with a strong *r*.
- When the Pinyin letter **i** follows **z**, **c**, or **s**, it is pronounced with the blade of the tongue high and flat near the roof of the mouth. English does not use this vowel sound. Listen to the recordings that accompany this book to practice the pronunciation.
- In all other instances, the Pinyin letter **i** is pronounced like the sound *ee* as in the English words *sleep* and *week*.

Spelling

- When the finals **i**, **in**, or **ing** are not preceded by an initial, they are written as **yi**. Examples: **yī, yín, yìng**
- When the final **iu** is not preceded by an initial, it is written as **you**. Example: **yǒu** *have*
- When **i** begins any other final and is not preceded by an initial, **i** is written as **y**. Examples: **yā, yào, yě, yán, yáng, yòng**

Restrictions

- Most finals that begin with **i** followed by at least one other vowel or consonant can follow **j**, **q**, or **x**, and also **n** and **l**. The final **iong** cannot follow **n** or **l**.
- The finals **iao**, **ie**, **ian**, **in**, and **ing** follow **b**, **p**, **m** (but not **f**), as well as the initials **d**, **t**, **n**, and **l**, and **j**, **q**, and **x**.
- The finals **ia**, **iu**, and **iang** can follow **n** and **l** as well as **j**, **q**, and **x**.

Finals that begin with ü

ü	ü, üe	üan, ün

Pronunciation

- **ü** is pronounced with the tongue high and flat in the mouth as when saying the sound *ee* as in the English word *sleep*, but with the lips rounded.

Spelling

- **ü** following **j**, **q**, or **x** is written as **u**. **ü** following **n** or **l** is written as **ü**. When finals that begin with **ü** occur without an initial they are written as **yu**.

Restrictions

- Finals that begin with **ü** can only follow **j**, **q**, **x**, **n**, and **l**.

Language FAQs

How many digits are there in a Chinese phone number?

In mainland China, phone numbers for landlines have eight digits. Phone numbers for cell phones (mobile phones) have eleven digits. In Taiwan, phone numbers for landlines have seven or eight digits plus a two-digit area code, and phone numbers for cell phones have ten digits. In this dialogue, the students exchange their cell phone numbers.

Notes on Chinese culture

One-child policy

In 1979, the People's Republic of China instituted a "one-child policy," restricting the number of children in most families to one. Zhang Dawei may not be aware of the one-child policy, but he has noticed its effect. Most young people in China have no siblings, no older brother or sister, and no younger brother or sister. (Twins are an exception to this of course.) China has since eased its restriction on the number of children per family, but the one-child policy led to a sharp decline in China's birthrate and the virtual disappearance of siblings in mainland China among people born after 1979.

Phone numbers and lucky numbers

The numbers six and eight are considered lucky numbers in Chinese. Six is lucky because the pronunciation **liù** is similar to the pronunciation of the word for *smooth*. The use of six implies that things will go smoothly for you. Eight is lucky because the pronunciation **bā** is similar to the pronunciation of the word for *prosperity*. The use of eight implies that you will be prosperous. In China, you are not assigned a cell phone number. Instead, you buy one from a list of available numbers. Phone numbers containing sixes and eights are more expensive than other phone numbers, and the more sixes and eights there are, the more expensive the phone number. The number four is considered an unlucky number, since the pronunciation **sì** is similar to the pronunciation of the word for *death*. Phone numbers that include the number four are less desirable (and less expensive) than other phone numbers.

Responding to expressions of thanks

In Chinese culture, if someone thanks you, you do not say *You're welcome*. Instead, the way to respond to an expression of thanks is to indicate that thanks are not necessary. Using the vocabulary that we have learned through this lesson, if someone thanks you, you can say **Bù xiè** *Don't thank me*. We will learn additional conversational expressions that can be used to respond to an expression of thanks in later lessons.

Lesson 5 Dialogue in English

Part A

Xiao Wang: David (Dawei), well then, your family must have five people.

Xiao Zhang: Yes, my family has five people. Xiao Wang, how many people does your family have?

Xiao Wang: My family has ten people.

Xiao Zhang: Ten people! Really?

Xiao Wang: Really. There are eight children in my family, five boys and three girls. I have four older brothers, two older sisters, and one younger sister.

Part B

Xiao Chen: Xiao Xie, what about your family?

Xiao Zhang: I know. Xiao Xie's family has three people, his dad, his mom, and him. Right?

Xiao Xie: Right.

Xiao Chen: How do you know his family only has one child?

Xiao Zhang: All my Chinese friends do not have older brothers or younger brothers, and they do not have older sisters or younger sisters.

Part C

Xiao Xie: Xiao Chen, Xiao Wang, my phone number is 105-4850-6928. You can give me a call.

Xiao Chen: 105-4850-6928, right?

Xiao Xie: Correct. What are your phone numbers?

Xiao Chen: I don't have a mobile phone. Xiao Wang has one. Xiao Wang's number is 132-4867-9903.

Xiao Xie: Okay. Thanks.

Lesson 6 Mǎi dōngxi
Shopping

Communication goals
- Greet others in the morning
- Ask about items for sale in a store
- Talk about the price of items

Key structures
number + classifier + N: *one bottle of water*
specifier + classifier + N: *that bottle of water*
the money phrase:
   X kuài X máo X fēn qián
hái *in addition*
tài AdjV **le** *too AdjV*

Dialogue

The Situation: Xiao Zhang is shopping at a neighborhood store for some everyday items.

Part A

Fúwùyuán: **Zǎo**。Nǐ yào mǎi shénme dōngxi？

Xiǎo Zhāng: Wǒ yào mǎi shuǐ。**一 píng shuǐ duōshao qián**？

Fúwùyuán: **一 píng shuǐ liǎng kuài 四 máo qián**，五 píng 十 kuài。

Xiǎo Zhāng: Nà，wǒ mǎi 五 píng。Kělè duōshao qián？

Fúwùyuán: 一 píng kělè yě shì liǎng kuài 四。Yào ma？

Xiǎo Zhāng: Yào。Mǎi liǎng píng。

Part B

Fúwùyuán: Nǐ **hái** yào mǎi shénme？

Xiǎo Zhāng: Wǒ hái yào mǎi bǐ。**Qiānbǐ zěnme mài？** Guì bù guì？

Fúwùyuán: Qiānbǐ hěn piányi。**六 máo 五 一 zhī**。

Xiǎo Zhāng: Duōshao qián？Qǐng 你 **zài shuō 一 cì**。

Fúwùyuán: 六 máo 五 fēn qián 一 zhī。

Xiǎo Zhāng: Hǎo，wǒ mǎi 八 zhī。Bù。Wǒ mǎi 九 zhī。

Part C

Xiǎo Zhāng:	Nǐmen mài Zhōngguó dìtú ma?
Fúwùyuán:	Mài。 Zhèi zhāng Zhōngguó dìtú 六 kuài qián。 Yào ma?
Xiǎo Zhāng:	Zhè zhāng dìtú tài xiǎo le。
Fúwùyuán:	Nèi zhāng ne? Nèi zhāng dà, yě hěn piányi。 七 kuài liǎng máo 二。 Mǎi ma?
Xiǎo Zhāng:	Mǎi。 Wǒ mǎi 一 zhāng。 Nǐmen mài zhǐ ma?
Fúwùyuán:	Duìbuqǐ, wǒmen bù mài zhǐ。

Vocabulary

bǐ [zhī]	noun	*pen, writing implement*
dà	adjectival verb	*big*
dìtú [zhāng]	noun	*map*
dōngxi [gè]	noun	*thing (concrete object)*
duōshao	question word	*how much, how many (also L5)*
fēn	classifier	*penny, cent*
fúwùyuán [gè]	noun	*clerk, service person*
guì	adjectival verb	*expensive*
hái	adverb	*in addition*
kělè [píng]	noun	*cola*
kuài	classifier	*dollar*
le	final particle	*(part of the expression **tài** adjectival verb **le** (see Use and Structure note 6.12))*

mǎi	verb	*buy*
mài	verb	*sell*
máo	classifier	*dime*
nà，nèi	specifier	*that*
piányi	adjectival verb	*cheap*
píng	classifier	*bottle*
qián	noun	*money*
qiānbǐ [zhī]	noun	*pencil*
shuǐ [píng]	noun	*water*
tài	intensifier	*too*
xiǎo	adjectival verb	*small*
yào	verb	*want*
zài shuō yí cì	conversational expression	*say it again*
zǎo	adjectival verb; greeting	*early;* *good morning*
zhāng	classifier	*(classifier for flat rectangular and square objects)* *(also L2 family name)*
zhè，zhèi	specifier	*this*
zhī	classifier	*(classifier for writing implements, e.g. pencils, pens)*
zhǐ [zhāng]	noun	*paper*

Characters

一	yī	*one*
二	èr	*two*
三	sān	*three*
四	sì	*four*
五	wǔ	*five*
六	liù	*six*
七	qī	*seven*
八	bā	*eight*
九	jiǔ	*nine*
十	shí	*ten*

Dialogue practice

Do these activities in class after mastering each part of the dialogue for this lesson. Change partners so that you practice each part several times.

Dialogue 6A: Work with a partner, taking turns being the clerk and the customer. Sell your customer some item, providing a discount for the purchase of more than one of the same item.

Dialogue 6B: Work with a partner, taking turns being the clerk and the customer. The clerk should prepare several items for sale and should decide their prices in advance. The customer should ask about the price of each item for sale and decide how many of each to buy.

Dialogue 6C: Work with a partner, taking turns being the clerk and the customer. The customer should be fussy about the items offered by the clerk, noting that they are too big, too small, or too expensive. The clerk should offer another option.

Chinese characters

Strokes and stroke order

Pinyin represents the pronunciation of Mandarin and is used in many Chinese dictionaries and computer input systems as well as in Chinese language textbooks. But Chinese texts are written in <u>Chinese characters</u>, and we begin introducing Chinese characters in this lesson. We start with the characters for the numbers 1–10 because they are among the most commonly used characters in Chinese and because they are written using a very small number of <u>strokes</u>.

All characters are composed of strokes written in a specific direction and in a specific order. Pay attention to stroke order and stroke direction as you learn each new character. The Stroke Order Flow Chart provided in each lesson, as well as exercises in each lesson on character formation and recognition, will help you to write characters correctly and to remember them more easily and efficiently.

Radicals and remainders

Every character includes a <u>radical</u>, a part of the character that is used in the organization of many Chinese dictionaries. Radicals often provide information about the meaning of a character. In this textbook, the radical for each character is presented in the Stroke Order Flow Chart in a contrasting color. As you will see in the Stroke Order Flow Chart for this lesson (over the page), sometimes a character consists of just a radical. For example, the numbers 一, 二, 八, and 十 are radicals. More often, however, the radical is only part of a character. In this lesson we will focus on learning stroke order and stroke direction. In Lesson 7 we will take a closer look at radicals.

Character size and spacing

There are many aesthetic principles associated with Chinese characters. One very important principle is that all characters in the same text (for example, all of the characters in the same sentence or paragraph or page), take up the same amount of space no matter whether they are written with one stroke or many strokes.

To help to define that space, characters are often practiced using a special kind of practice paper that is printed with squares. Notice that all of the characters on the Stroke Order Flow Chart are presented in squares.

Stroke Order Flow Chart

Here is the Stroke Order Flow Chart for the characters 1–10, indicating the order of strokes for each character. In the Stroke Order Flow Chart the radical for each character is presented in blue. The complete character is presented in the first column on the left and the total number of strokes used in writing each character is presented in the last column on the right. For the characters introduced in Lessons 6–10, the chart is followed by a discussion of the principles of stroke order as they pertain to each character.

Stroke Order Flow Chart

character:	strokes:												total strokes:
一	一												1
二	一	二											2
三	一	二	三										3
四	丨	冂	𠃌	四	四								5
五	一	丁	丙	五									4
六	丶	亠	宀	六									4
七	一	七											2
八	丿	八											2
九	丿	九											2
十	一	十											2

Principles of stroke order and stroke direction

All characters are written following the same general principles of stroke order and stroke direction. In Lessons 6–10 we introduce these principles and show how they determine the way that characters are written. Once you learn the principles, you will know how to correctly write each new character that you meet. Refer to the Stroke Order Flow Chart as you read the discussion about each character.

Lesson 6 Characters step-by-step

一	一 (**yī**) is a *horizontal stroke* and is written from left to right. It is a radical.
二	二 (**èr**) has a vertical orientation and is written from top to bottom. Each stroke is written from left to right. It is a radical.
三	三 (**sān**) has a vertical orientation and is written from top to bottom. Its radical is the character 一, which is written last.
四	四 (**sì**) is a box-shaped character with strokes inside of the box. Its radical is 囗. All boxes are written in the same way, and as you learn how to write 四 you learn all of the rules for writing box-shaped characters. The first stroke of 四 is a *vertical stroke*. It defines the left side of the box. Vertical strokes are written from top to bottom. The second stroke is a *right corner stroke*. Right corner strokes are always written from left to right and from top to bottom as a single stroke. Boxes are always filled before they are closed. After you have written the right hand corner of 四, fill in the box. The inside of 四 includes two strokes, both written from top to bottom. The stroke on the left is written first. It is a *left falling stroke*. It is written from top to bottom and falls to the left. The stroke on the right is written second. It is a *vertical curved stroke*. It starts as a vertical stroke written from top to bottom and then curves to the right. After you have filled in the box, close it with a *horizontal stroke* written from left to right. In boxes, the closing stroke is always the last stroke. Notice that although the radical for the character 四 is 囗, it is not written as a separate unit. The first two strokes of 囗 are written together, but the last stroke of 囗 is written after the two strokes on the inside of the box.

五 (**wǔ**) has a vertical orientation and is written from top to bottom. Its radical is the character 二, but as with the character 四, the strokes of the radical are not written together.

The top *horizontal stroke* of 五 is written first. It is written from left to right. The *vertical stroke* is written second. Notice that it may touch the horizontal stroke but that it does not go through it.

五 is not a box, but it includes a *right corner stroke*. Right corner strokes are always written as a single stroke.

When a character is written from top to bottom, the bottom stroke is the closing stroke. The closing stroke is always written last. In 五, this stroke is a *horizontal stroke* and it is written from left to right.

六 (**liù**) has a vertical orientation and is written from top to bottom. Its radical is 八 (**bā**) *eight*.

The first stroke of 六 is called a *dot*. A dot is always short, and it is written from left to right. It has a slightly convex, upward curve.

The second stroke of 六 is a *horizontal stroke*. It is written from left to right. The dot may touch the horizontal stroke but it does not go through.

The bottom part of 六 has a horizontal orientation and is written from left to right. The stroke on the left is a *left falling stroke*. The stroke on the right is a *long dot*.

七 (**qī**) is written in two strokes. Its radical, the character 一, is the first stroke. It is a *horizontal stroke* written from left to right.

The second stroke of 七 is a *vertical curved stroke*.

	八 (**bā**) has a horizontal orientation and is written from left to right. It is a radical. The first stroke of 八 is a *left falling stroke*. The second stroke is a *right falling stroke*.
	Notice that the top of the right falling stroke is in line with the top of the left falling stroke. When writing the character 八, the right falling stroke cannot begin to the left of the left falling stroke or below the top of the left falling stroke, because those starting points define different characters. Compare 八 with the following two characters, noting the starting point of the right falling stroke in each character: 人 (**rén**), 入 (**rù**).
	九 (**jiǔ**) has a horizontal orientation and is written from left to right. The first stroke is a *left falling stroke*. The second stroke is a *horizontal-vertical-curved stroke* with an *upward hook* at the end. That means that it begins as a horizontal stroke, turns the corner and becomes a curved stroke, and ends with a hook. It is written as one stroke from left to right and it is the radical in this character.
	十 (**shí**) is a radical and it is written in two strokes. The *horizontal stroke* is written before the *vertical stroke*.

Use and structure

6.1. **Zǎo** *good morning*

Zǎo is a very common way to greet people in the early part of the morning. As a greeting, it means *good morning*. **Zǎo** is also an adjectival verb and means *early*.

6.2. Number + classifier + noun: Saying *one bottle of water, two people*, etc.

In Mandarin, when indicating the number of nouns, you must follow the number with a <u>classifier</u>. The sequence <u>number + classifier</u> occurs before the noun:

number + classifier + N
一　　　　píng　　　shuǐ
one bottle of water

In Lesson 5 we learned to use the classifier **gè** when talking about the number of people.

一 **gè rén**	*one person*
liǎng gè xuésheng	*two students*

In this lesson we learn the classifiers **píng**, **zhāng**, and **zhī**. Classifiers are associated with particular nouns and may often contribute meaning to the noun phrase as well.

Píng means *bottle* and it is the classifier that is used when indicating the number of bottles of something.

一 **píng shuǐ**	*one bottle of water*
liǎng píng kělè	*two bottles of cola*

Zhāng is the classifier that is used when talking about flat objects that are square or rectangular in shape, for example, maps, paper, and photographs.

一 **zhāng dìtú**	*one map*
liǎng zhāng zhǐ	*two pieces of paper*

Zhī is the classifier that is used when indicating the number of pens, pencils, chalk, or any other writing implement.

九 **zhī bǐ**	*nine pens*

The classifier **gè** is used as the classifier for many nouns besides those that refer to people. For example, it is used when indicating the number of cell phones:

一 **ge shǒujī**	*one cell phone*

6.3. Duōshao *how much, how many*

In Lesson 5 we learned the word **duōshao** in the expression

Nǐ de diànhuà hàomǎ shì duōshao?
What is your phone number?

In this lesson we learn how to use the word **duōshao** as a content question word meaning *how much, how many*. The content question word **duōshao** occurs right before a noun and it asks *how much* or *how many* of the noun. It can be used to ask about the quantity of any noun.

duōshao rén?	*how many people?*
duōshao xuésheng?	*how many students?*
duōshao dìtú?	*how many maps?*
duōshao shuǐ?	*how much water?*
duōshao qián?	*how much money?*

6.4. Prices

To state the price of an item, say:

item (**shì**) price
一 **píng shuǐ (shì) liǎng kuài** 四 **máo qián**。
One bottle of water is ¥ *2.4.*

To ask the price of an item, you can say:

item (**shì**) **duōshao qián**?
一 **píng shuǐ duōshao qián**?
How much is one bottle of water?

If you know that the price of an item is a relatively small number of dollars, you may ask:

item (**shì**) **jǐ kuài qián**?
一 **zhāng dìtú (shì) jǐ kuài qián**?
How many dollars is one map? (How many dollars does a map cost?)

If you know that the price of an item is somewhere between ten cents and ninety cents you can ask:

item (**shì**) **jǐ máo qián**?
一 **zhī qiānbǐ jǐ máo qián**?
How many dimes is a pencil?

If you know that the price of an item is between one cent and nine cents, you can ask:

item (shì) **jǐ fēn qián**?
五 **zhāng zhǐ jǐ fēn qián**?
How many cents is a piece of paper?

(See note 6.6 for more about money phrases in Mandarin.)

Shì *be* is usually omitted if the sentence does not contain negation or an adverb. **Shì** *be* <u>must</u> be included in negated sentences or when the sentence includes an adverb. Negation and adverbs occur before **shì**.

一 **píng shuǐ bù shì liǎng kuài** 四 **máo qián**。
One bottle of water is not ¥ *2.40.*

一 **píng shuǐ zhǐ shì liǎng kuài** 一 **máo liǎng fēn qián**。
One bottle of water is only ¥ *2.12.*

To ask how something is sold, see note 6.8.

To state the cost <u>per</u> item see note 6.9.

6.5.   Duōshao and jǐ compared

Duōshao and **jǐ** are both question words that mean *how much, how many,* but they differ in use and meaning.

Use

Jǐ must be followed by a classifier (Use and Structure note 5.4). **Duōshao** can occur right before a noun and is typically not followed by a classifier.

jǐ + classifier + N	duōshao + N	
jǐ ge rén?	**duōshao rén**?	*how many people?*
jǐ zhāng dìtú?	**duōshao dìtú**?	*how many maps?*

Meaning

Jǐ and **duōshao** differ in the quantity that they refer to. **Jǐ** refers to a relatively small quantity of items or a relatively small number. It is used when the expected answer is relatively small, typically under ten or twenty. **Duōshao** is used when the expected answer is a big number, or if the speaker does not have any expectations about the number of items. For example, if you want to know how many bottles of water your friend drinks each day, you would ask the question with **jǐ**: **jǐ píng shuǐ**? In contrast, if you want to know the price of your friend's new car, you would ask the question with **duōshao**: **duōshao qián**?

6.6.   The money phrase

A complete money phrase with **kuài** *dollar,* **máo** *dime* and **fēn** *cents* is expressed as follows:

number + **kuài**		number + **máo**		number + **fēn**		**qián**
	dollars		*dimes*		*cents*	*money*
liǎng	**kuài**	四	**máo**	五	**fēn**	**qián**
two	*dollar*	*four*	*dime*	*five*	*cent*	*money*

two dollars and forty-five cents

十	**kuài**	五	**máo**	九	**fēn**	**qián**
ten	*dollar*	*five*	*dime*	*nine*	*cent*	*money*

ten dollars and fifty-nine cents

Taiwan does not use the units **máo** and **fēn**, and a complete money phrase is expressed as

number + kuài	**qián**
dollars	*money*
七 **kuài**	**qián**

seven dollars

Kuài *dollar,* **máo** *dime,* and **fēn** *cent* are <u>always</u> preceded by a number or the question word **jǐ** *how much, how many.*

The word **qián** *money* is a noun, and it is the main noun in a money phrase. It is often omitted from the money phrase, since the presence of **kuài** *dollar*, **máo** *dime*, and **fēn** *cent* make it clear that the expression is about money.

七 **kuài** 四 **máo qián**   →   七 **kuài** 四 **máo**
seven dollars and forty cents

七 **kuài qián**   →   七 **kuài**
seven dollars

If **qián** is omitted, **máo** or **fēn** may also be omitted if it is the last classifier in the money phrase.

七 **kuài** 四 **máo**   →   七 **kuài** 四
七 **kuài** 四 **máo** 五 **fēn**   →   七 **kuài** 四 **máo** 五

In China, prices are often written using Arabic numerals preceded by the Chinese dollar sign ￥, and that is the convention we will use in this book.

￥1.50   一 **kuài** 五 **máo qián**
￥3.70   三 **kuài** 七 **máo qián**
￥10.20   十 **kuài liǎng máo qián**

Notice that the position after the decimal point can include either one or two digits. If the second number (the "cents" number) is zero, it can be omitted.

￥1.50   =   ￥1.50 or ￥1.5
￥3.70   =   ￥3.70 or ￥3.7
￥10.20   =   ￥10.20 or ￥10.2

In the Chinese money phrase, the largest number of cents is nine.

Ten cents is expressed as *one dime*: 一 **máo**, *twenty cents* as *two dimes*: **liǎng máo**, *thirty cents* is expressed as *three dimes*: 三 **máo**, *forty-five cents* is expressed as *four dimes five cents*: 四 **máo** 五 **fēn**, etc.

The words **kuài** *(Chinese) dollar*, **máo** *(Chinese) dime*, and **fēn** *(Chinese) cent* that are introduced in this lesson are the words that are used to refer to money in everyday speech in mainland China. Mandarin has another set of words for *dollar* and *dime* that are used in formal or literary contexts.

6.7.   Hái *in addition, also*

Hái *in addition, also* is an adverb and it occurs at the beginning of the verb phrase, before the verb or modal verb if there is one. In this lesson we learn to use **hái** to indicate additional actions, or actions that you *also* do. When talking about additional actions in the future, **hái** typically occurs before **yào** *want*. Depending upon the overall sentence, **hái** can be translated as *in addition, also, still*, or *(what) else*.

Nǐ hái yào mǎi shénme?
What else do you want to buy?

Wǒ hái yào mǎi 三 píng shuǐ。
I also want to buy three bottles of water.

We will learn additional meanings of **hái** in later lessons.

6.8. Zěnme mài? *how is it sold?*

We learned the word **zěnme** *how* in Lesson 5. **Zěnme mài** is used when you are asking *how* something is sold. **Zěnme** *how* always goes before the verb or verb phrase.

Qiānbǐ zěnme mài?
How are pencils sold?

6.9. Cost per item

To state the cost per item, state the item and the price, followed by the phrase 一 classifier. 一 classifier can be translated into English as *each*, *apiece*, or *for one*.

item + price + 一 classifier
Qiānbǐ 六 máo qián 一 zhī。
Pencils (are) sixty cents apiece.

If the item is understood from the context, it can be omitted. The classifier cannot be omitted.

liǎng kuài qián 一 zhī
two dollars each (two dollars a pen)

三 kuài（qián）一 zhāng
three dollars each (three dollars a sheet)

Negation of this kind of phrase is as follows. Notice that when negated, the phrase must contain the verb **shì**. (See note 6.4.)

Qiānbǐ bù shì 六 máo qián 一 zhī。
Pencils are not sixty cents apiece.

6.10. Zài shuō 一 cì *say it again*

To request that someone say something again, say:

（Qǐng nǐ）zài shuō 一 cì。
(Please) say (it) again.

6.11. Saying *this (pencil)* and *that (person)*

In Lesson 4 we learned how to use the words **zhè** *this* and **nà** *that* as the subject of the sentence. We called this the <u>demonstrative</u> use of **zhè** and **nà** since, in this use, **zhè** and **nà** are used to point to some noun. (See Use and Structure note 4.3.)

Zhè shì wǒ de tóngwū, Xiè Guóqiáng。
This is my roommate, Xie Guoqiang.

Nà shì tā de zhàopiàn。
That is her photograph.

In this lesson we learn to use **zhè** and **nà**, and their alternative pronunciations **zhèi** and **nèi**, when specifying a particular person, place, or thing as when saying *this pencil* or *that person*. In this function **zhè/zhèi** and **nà/nèi** are called <u>specifiers</u>. When used as specifiers, **zhè/zhèi** and **nà/nèi** always occur <u>before a classifier</u>.

To say *this* (person, place or thing), say:

zhè/zhèi + classifier + N
zhèi   zhī   qiānbǐ
this pencil

To say *that* (person, place or thing), say:

nà/nèi + classifier + N
nà   gè   rén
that person

Noun phrases with specifiers can occur as the subject or the object of the sentence:

<u>**Zhèi zhāng Zhōngguó dìtú**</u> 六 **kuài qián。**
This map of China is six dollars.

Wǒ yào mǎi <u>**nà píng shuǐ**</u>**。**
I want to buy that bottle of water.

Two pronunciations for the specifiers *this* and *that*

The basic pronunciations of the specifiers that mean *this* and *that* are **zhè** and **nà**. We will see in Lesson 7 that specifiers may be followed by a number. The pronunciations **zhèi** and **nèi** were originally a contraction of **zhè** and **nà** followed by the number **yī**:

zhè yī → **zhèi**   *this one*
nà yī → **nèi**   *that one*

Nowadays, for many speakers, the choice of one or the other pronunciation is simply a matter of individual preference. Some speakers use them interchangeably, and some speakers use the pronunciations **zhèi** and **nèi** only when talking about one item.

We will see in Lesson 7 that the specifier that means *this* is written with the same character whether it is pronounced **zhè** or **zhèi**, and the specifier that means *that* is written with the same character whether it is pronounced **nà** or **nèi**.

6.12 Tài AdjV **le** *too AdjV*

Tài *too*, like **hěn** *very*, precedes adjectival verbs. When **tài** is used, the adjectival verb is often followed by the particle **le**. **Le** does not contribute any meaning to the phrase **tài AdjV le**.

Zhè zhāng dìtú tài xiǎo le。
This map is too small.

Sentence pyramids

The sentence pyramids illustrate the use of each new vocabulary item and structure introduced in the lesson. Use them to help you learn how to form phrases and sentences in Mandarin. Supply the English translation for the last line where indicated.

1. shénme mǎi shénme Nǐ yào mǎi shénme?	*what* *buy what* *What do you want to buy?*
2. dōngxi shénme dōngxi mǎi shénme dōngxi Nǐ yào mǎi shénme dōngxi?	*thing (item)* *what thing?* *buy what thing?* _____
3. dōngxi shénme dōngxi shì shénme dōngxi? Zhè shì shénme dōngxi?	*thing* *what thing* *is what thing?* _____
4. Zǎo。 Zǎo。Nǐ yào mǎi shénme?	*Good morning.* _____
5. shuǐ 一 píng shuǐ	*water* *one bottle of water*

6.	
一 píng shuǐ	*one bottle of water*
mǎi 一 píng shuǐ	*buy one bottle of water*
yào mǎi 一 píng shuǐ	*want to buy one bottle of water*
Wǒ yào mǎi 一 píng shuǐ。	_____

7.	
mǎi shénme	*buy what*
yào mǎi shénme?	*want to buy what*
hái yào mǎi shénme?	*also want to buy what*
Nǐ hái yào mǎi shénme?	*What else do you want to buy?*
	(You also want to buy what?)

8.	
bǐ	*pen (writing implement)*
mǎi bǐ	*buy pen*
yào mǎi bǐ	*want to buy pen*
hái yào mǎi bǐ	*in addition want to buy pen*
Wǒ hái yào mǎi bǐ。	_____

9.	
bǐ	*pen (writing implement)*
一 zhī bǐ	*one pen*

10.	
qiānbǐ	*pencil*
八 zhī qiānbǐ	*eight pencils*
mǎi 八 zhī qiānbǐ	*buy eight pencils*
Wǒ yào mǎi 八 zhī qiānbǐ。	_____

11.	
Wǒ yào mǎi 八 zhī qiānbǐ。	*I want to buy eight pencils.*
Wǒ yào mǎi 八 zhī。	*I want to buy eight.*
Yào mǎi 八 zhī。	*(I) want to buy eight.*

12.	
mài	*sell*
zěnme mài?	*how sold?*
Qiānbǐ zěnme mài?	*How are pencils sold?*

13.	
guì bù guì?	*expensive or not expensive?*
Qiānbǐ guì bù guì?	_____

14. piányi hěn piányi Qiānbǐ hěn piányi。	*cheap* *very cheap* _____
15. qián duōshao qián？ Kělè duōshao qián？	*money* *how much money?* *How much is cola?*
16. máo 六 máo	*dime* *sixty cents*
17. qián 六 máo qián	*money* *sixty cents*
18. 六 máo qián 一 zhī qiānbǐ 六 máo qián。	*sixty cents* *One pencil is sixty cents.*
19. jǐ máo qián？ 一 zhī qiānbǐ jǐ máo qián？	*how many dimes?* *How much is one pencil?* *(How many dimes does one pencil cost?)*
20. 一 zhī 六 máo 一 zhī。	*one (pencil)* *Sixty cents each.*
21. kuài liǎng kuài	*dollar* *two dollars*
22. qián liǎng kuài qián	*money* *two dollars*
23. dìtú 一 zhāng dìtú	*map* *one map*
24. jǐ kuài qián？ 一 zhāng dìtú jǐ kuài qián？	*how many dollars?* _____

25.	
四 máo	*forty cents*
liǎng kuài 四 máo	*two dollars and forty cents*

26.	
qián	*money*
五 fēn qián	*five cents*
六 máo 五 fēn qián	*sixty-five cents*
Qiānbǐ 六 máo 五 fēn qián。	_____

27.	
一 píng	*one bottle*
四 máo 一 píng	*forty cents a bottle*
liǎng kuài 四 máo 一 píng	*two dollars and forty cents a bottle*
Kělè liǎng kuài 四 máo 一 píng。	*Cola is ￥2.40 a bottle.*

28.	
liǎng kuài 四 máo qián	*two dollars and forty cents*
liǎng kuài 四 máo	*two dollars and forty cents*
liǎng kuài 四	*two dollars forty*

29.	
guì	*expensive*
tài guì le	*too expensive*

30.	
Zhōngguó dìtú	*map of China*
mài Zhōngguó dìtú	*sell maps of China*
Nǐmen mài Zhōngguó dìtú ma？	_____

31.	
xiǎo	*small*
tài xiǎo le	*too small*
Zhè zhāng dìtú tài xiǎo le。	*This map is too small.*

32.	
dà	*big*
tài dà le	*too big*
Nà píng shuǐ tài dà le。	*That bottle of water is too big.*

33.	
dǎ diànhuà	*make a phone call*
gěi wǒ dǎ diànhuà	*make a phone call to me*
Qǐng gěi wǒ dǎ diànhuà。	*Please phone me.*

34.	
七 kuài 二	*seven dollars twenty*
dìtú 七 kuài 二	*maps (are) seven dollars twenty*
一 zhāng dìtú 七 kuài 二。	
35.	
qián	*money*
duōshao qián？	*how much money?*
十 zhāng zhǐ duōshao qián？	*Ten sheets of paper are how much money?*
36.	
qián	*money*
liǎng fēn qián	*two cents*
七 máo liǎng fēn qián	*seventy-two cents*
十 zhāng zhǐ 七 máo liǎng fēn qián。	*Ten sheets of paper are seventy-two cents.*
37.	
七 máo 二	*seventy-two cents*
十 zhāng zhǐ 七 máo 二	*Ten pieces of paper is seventy-two cents.*
38.	
一 zhāng	*one (sheet)*
七 máo 二 一 zhāng	*seventy-two cents a sheet*
39.	
一 cì	*once*
shuō 一 cì	*say once*
zài shuō 一 cì	*again say once*
Qǐng nǐ zài shuō 一 cì。	*Please say (it) again.*

Language FAQs

More about 二 and liǎng

Liǎng *two* must be followed by a classifier. When no classifier follows, 二 is used. When indicating the price of maps, the clerk can say:

> 一 **zhāng Zhōngguó dìtú** 七 **kuài liǎng máo qián**。
>
> or 一 **zhāng Zhōngguó dìtú** 七 **kuài** 二。
> *One map is* ￥7.2.

Because **liǎng** cannot be used without a following classifier, the clerk cannot say:

> ⊗ 一 **zhāng Zhōngguó dìtú** 七 **kuài liǎng**。

Nowadays in Beijing, in informal speech, many people also use 二 when there <u>is</u> a following classifier. As a result, sentences like this one are becoming acceptable in <u>casual</u> speech.

> 一 **zhāng Zhōngguó dìtú** 七 **kuài** 二 **máo qián**。
> *One map is* ￥7.2.

Does English have classifiers?

Yes. When talking about the number of people or pencils or maps, the number goes right before the noun: *one person, two pencils, three maps.* But when talking about the number of things like water or bread, you cannot put the number right in front of the noun. You need to include another word after the number: *one <u>bottle</u> of water, two <u>cups</u> of water, three <u>slices</u> of bread.* In English, only mass nouns like water and bread require classifiers. In Mandarin, all nouns require classifiers.

Adjectival verbs and comparisons

Adjectival verbs often imply comparisons. We see this in Part C of the dialogue, when Xiao Zhang and the clerk are discussing maps.

Xiǎo Zhāng:	**Zhè zhāng dìtú tài xiǎo le**。
	This map is too small.
Fúwùyuán:	**Nèi zhāng ne? Nèi zhāng dà, yě hěn piányi**。
	How about that map? That map is big(ger), and also very cheap.

Notes on Chinese culture

Early morning activities

For many Chinese people, life begins early. Especially when the weather is warm, many city people head to the parks at sunrise to join in such early morning activities as folk dancing, opera, martial arts, badminton, aerobics, and calligraphy.

Lesson 6 Dialogue in English

Part A

Clerk:	Good morning. What would you like to buy?
Xiao Zhang:	I want to buy water. How much is one bottle of water?
Clerk:	One bottle of water is two dollars and forty cents. Five bottles are ten dollars.
Xiao Zhang:	Well then, I'll buy five bottles. How much is cola?
Clerk:	A bottle of cola is also two dollars and forty cents. Do you want some?
Xiao Zhang:	Yes. I'll buy two bottles.

Part B

Clerk:	What else do you want to buy?
Xiao Zhang:	I also want to buy some pens (something to write with). How are pencils sold? Are they expensive?
Clerk:	Pencils are very cheap, sixty-five cents each.
Xiao Zhang:	How much money? Can you please say it again?
Clerk:	Sixty-five cents each.
Xiao Zhang:	Okay. I'll buy eight. No. I'll buy nine.

Part C

Xiao Zhang:	Do you sell maps of China?
Clerk:	Yes. This map of China is six dollars. Do you want it?
Xiao Zhang:	This map is too small.
Clerk:	How about that map? That map is big(ger), and it is also very cheap. It is seven twenty-two. Do you want to buy it?
Xiao Zhang:	Yes. I will buy one. Do you sell paper?
Clerk:	Sorry, we don't sell paper.

Lesson 7
一 gòng duōshao qián?
How much is it altogether?

Communication goals
- Negotiate for the price of an item
- Pay for items and get change

Key structures
specifier + number + classifier + N:
   these/those two bottles of water
哪 *which*
AdjV 一 **diǎn** *a little more AdjV*
一 **bǎi** *100 and the numbers 11–999*

Dialogue

The Situation: Xiao Zhang continues his shopping in a neighborhood store and negotiates with the clerk over the price of some items.

Part A

Xiǎo Zhāng:	那個 běnzi duōshao qián？
Fúwùyuán:	哪個 **běnzi**？
Xiǎo Zhāng:	那個 Hàn zì liànxí běn。
Fúwùyuán:	這個 Hàn zì liànxí běn 六 kuài 八一 běn。Nǐ yào 幾 běn？
Xiǎo Zhāng:	Mǎi 兩 běn kěyǐ **piányi 一 diǎn** 嗎？
Fúwùyuán:	Kěyǐ。兩 běn kěyǐ mài **十二** kuài。Yào 嗎？
Xiǎo Zhāng:	Yào。

Part B

Fúwùyuán:	Nǐ hái xiǎng mǎi 甚麼？
Xiǎo Zhāng:	Wǒ hái yào mǎi **一 niánjí** 的 **Zhōngwén shū**。
Fúwùyuán:	**這兩 běn shū** shì 一 niánjí 的 Zhōngwén shū。
Xiǎo Zhāng:	Duōshao qián？
Fúwùyuán:	三十五 kuài。
Xiǎo Zhāng:	Hǎo。

Part C

Xiǎo Zhāng:	一 gòng duōshao qián？
Fúwùyuán:	Shū 三十五 kuài，九 zhī qiānbǐ 五 kuài 八 máo 五，Zhōngguó dìtú 七 kuài 二，五 píng shuǐ 十 kuài，兩 píng kělè 四 kuài 八，兩個 liànxí běn 十二 kuài。一 gòng 七十四 kuài 八 máo 五 fēn qián。
Xiǎo Zhāng:	Gěi nǐ 一 bǎi kuài。
Fúwùyuán:	Zhǎo nǐ 二十五 kuài 一 máo 五 fēn qián。
Xiǎo Zhāng:	Hǎo。Zài jiàn。
Fúwùyuán:	Zài jiàn。

Vocabulary

bǎi		number	*hundred*
běn		classifier	*(classifier for books)*
běnzi [gè, běn]		noun	*notebook*
gěi		verb	*give*
Hàn zì [gè]		noun phrase	*Chinese character*
liànxí		verb	*practice*
liànxí běn [gè]		noun	*notebook*
niánjí		noun	*year in school, grade*
shū [běn]		noun	*book*
xiǎng		noun	*think (about), plan (to), want (to)*
yīdiǎn	一 diǎn	quantifier	*a little*
yīgòng	一 gòng	adverb	*altogether*
yī niánjí	一 niánjí	noun phrase	*first-year level*
zhǎo [qián]		verb	*make (change)*
zì [gè]		noun	*character (Chinese character)*

Numbers 11–20

11	十一	shíyī	16	十六	shíliù
12	十二	shí'èr	17	十七	shíqī
13	十三	shísān	18	十八	shíbā
14	十四	shísì	19	十九	shíjiǔ
15	十五	shíwǔ	20	二十	èrshí

Numbers 20–90

20	二十	èrshí	60	六十	liùshí
30	三十	sānshí	70	七十	qīshí
40	四十	sìshí	80	八十	bāshí
50	五十	wǔshí	90	九十	jiǔshí

Numbers 100–999

100	一 bǎi	yī bǎi	605	六 bǎi líng 五	liù bǎi líng wǔ
200	兩 bǎi	liǎng bǎi	708	七 bǎi líng 八	qī bǎi líng bā
300	三 bǎi	sān bǎi	810	八 bǎi 一十	bā bǎi yīshí
400	四 bǎi	sì bǎi	965	九 bǎi 六十五	jiǔ bǎi liùshí wǔ
500	五 bǎi	wǔ bǎi	999	九 bǎi 九十九	jiǔ bǎi jiǔshí jiǔ

Characters

的	de	*(marks noun description)*	
個	gè	*(classifier for people and some other nouns)*	
幾	jǐ	*how many, how much*	
兩	liǎng	*two (of something)*	
嗎	ma	*(yes-no question)*	
麼	me	*	甚麼 **(shénme)** *what?*
哪	nǎ, něi	*which*	
那	nà, nèi	*that*	
人	rén	*person*	
甚	shén	*	甚麼 **(shénme)** *what?*
這	zhè, zhèi	*this*	

Stroke Order Flow Chart

character:	strokes:												total strokes:
的	′	亻	竹	白	白	白′	的	的					8
個	ノ	亻	亻	们	佪	個	個	個	個				10
幾	ﺀ	幺	幺	幺′	丝	丝	絲	絲	絲	幾	幾	幾	12
兩	一	厂	厅	雨	雨	雨	兩	兩					8
嗎	′	口	口	叮	叱	叱	吓	咡	嗎	嗎	嗎	嗎	13
麼	、	亠	广	广	庐	庐	庐	庐	庶	麻	麻	麼 麼 麼	14
哪	｜	口	口	叨	叨	叨	明	明′	哪′	哪			10
那	ᄀ	彐	彐	月	月′	那′	那						7
人	ノ	人											2
甚	一	十	廿	廿	甘	其	其	其	甚				9
這	、	亠	亠	言	言	言	言	′言	讠	讠	這		11

Dialogue practice

Do these activities in class after mastering the dialogue for this lesson. Change partners so that you practice each part several times.

Dialogue 7A: Work with a partner, taking turns being the clerk and the customer. The customer should ask the price of several items and try to get the clerk to lower the price on the purchase of more than one item. After the purchases are completed, switch roles.

Dialogue 7B: Work with a partner, taking turns being the clerk and the customer. Customer: Ask the clerk the price of *those two books*, *those three notebooks*, and *those five maps*. Clerk: Reply with the price of *these two books*, *these three notebooks*, and *these five maps*. (Feel free to change the number and the type of item in your own dialogues.) Switch roles when all of the questions are answered.

Dialogue 7C: Work with a partner, taking turns being the clerk and the customer. Purchase several items, figure out the total, pay for the bill, and make change. Switch roles after paying the bill.

Use and structure

7.1. 哪 (nǎ) *which?*

In Lesson 2 we learned the question word 哪 (**nǎ**) *which* in the phrase 哪 **guó** *which country* (Use and Structure note 2.4).

Nǐ shì 哪 **guó** 人？
Where are you from?

In this lesson we learn to use 哪 *which* to ask about the identity of other nouns. Like the specifiers 這 *this, these* and 那 *that, those,* 哪 never occurs directly before a noun. It always occurs before a classifier, or before a number + classifier.

哪 + **classifier** + **N**
哪個 **běnzi**？
Which notebook?

哪兩 **zhāng dìtú**？
Which two maps?

Like the specifiers 這 *this, these* and 那 *that, those,* 哪 has an alternative pronunciation: **něi**. As with **zhèi** and **nèi**, the pronunciation **něi** was originally the contraction of **nǎ yī**.

<u>**Něi zhāng dìtú**</u>？
Which map?

Nowadays, the choice of **nǎ** or **něi** is largely one of individual preference.

7.2. AdjV 一 **diǎn** *a little more AdjV*

To say *a little more adjectival verb,* say:

AdjV 一 **diǎn**
Kěyǐ piányi 一 **diǎn** 嗎？
Can it be a little cheaper?

Any adjectival verb can occur before 一 **diǎn**:

guì 一 **diǎn**   *a little more expensive*
hǎo 一 **diǎn**   *a little better*

7.3.   11–99

The numbers 11–19 are formed by 十 *(10)* followed by the numbers 一 *(1)* through 九 *(9)*:

11	十一	16	十六
12	十二	17	十七
13	十三	18	十八
14	十四	19	十九
15	十五		

The "round" numbers 20–90 are formed as follows:

20	二十	60	六十
30	三十	70	七十
40	四十	80	八十
50	五十	90	九十

The numbers 21–99 are formed by the appropriate round number 十 *(10)* through 九十 *(90)* followed by the numbers 一 *(1)* through 九 *(9)*.

21	二十一	65	六十五
32	三十二	78	七十八
43	四十三	86	八十六
54	五十四	99	九十九

Notice that the Arabic numbers 21, 32, 43, etc. are written using two digits, but the Chinese numbers are written using three characters (二十一, 三十二, 四十三, etc.). Don't forget to include the 十 when you write these numbers.

In number expressions involving the number two, such as 十二 *(12)*, 二十 *(20)*, 二十二 *(22)*, 三十二 *(32)*, etc., *two* is always written as 二 and is pronounced as **èr**.

7.4.   Niánjí *year in school, grade*

一 **niánjí** refers to the first year of a course or program that takes multiple years to complete. The first year of a Chinese language program is **Zhōngwén** 一 **niánjí**. Notice that the title of the program (e.g. **Zhōngwén** *Chinese*) is stated before the level. 一 **niánjí** also refers to the first year of high school or college. The second year is 二 **niánjí**. What do you think that the third year is called? To ask *which level*, use the question word 幾 and ask 幾 **niánjí**?

7.5.   Describing nouns with noun phrases

The phrase 一 **niánjí** 的 **Zhōngwén shū** is a noun phrase in which the main noun, **Zhōngwén shū** *Chinese book* is described by the noun phrase 一 **niánjí**.

NP 的 **(main) N**
一 **niánjí** 的 **Zhōngwén shū**
first-year Chinese book

As when describing nouns with pronouns or with nouns, the main noun occurs after the description. See Use and Structure notes 4.4 and 5.8.

7.6.   Saying *these two pencils* and *those three people*

In Lesson 6 (Use and Structure note 6.11) we learned to use the specifiers 這 and 那 to say things like *this pencil* and *that notebook*. We learned that in these structures, 這 and 那 must be followed by a classifier, and that the order of information in the phrase is:

specifier + classifier + N

這	zhī	qiānbǐ

this pencil

那	個	běnzi

that notebook

To add a number to this noun phrase to say things such as *these two pencils* and *those three notebooks*, present the information in this order:

specifier + number + classifier + N

這	兩	zhī	qiānbǐ

these two pencils

那	三	個	běnzi

those three notebooks

Noun phrases that include specifier and number can occur as the subject or the object of a sentence:

這兩 **běn shū shì niánjí** 的 **Zhōngwén shū**。
These two books are first-year Chinese books.

Wǒ yào mǎi 那兩 **zhāng dìtú**。
I want to buy those two maps.

7.7.   一 gòng *altogether*: 一 gòng duōshao qián?

一 **gòng** *altogether* is an adverb, and it normally occurs before the verb or modal verb of the sentence. Notice that in English, the word *altogether* can occur at the beginning or end of the sentence. Be careful to follow Chinese word order and not English word order when using 一 **gòng** and other adverbs.

那個 **lǎoshī** 一 **gòng yǒu** 四十五個 **xuésheng**。
That teacher has forty-five students altogether.

Wǒ 一 **gòng rènshi** 六個人。
Altogether, I know six people.

When talking about prices, 一 **gòng** usually occurs directly before the price.

一 **gòng** 七十七 **kuài** 四 **máo qián**。
Altogether it is ￥77.4.

When asking about prices, 一 **gòng** occurs before the question phrase **duōshao qián**.

> 一 **gòng duōshao qián**?
> *How much money is it altogether?*

Shì *be* may be used when stating the price of some objects. When it is present, 一 **gòng** occurs right before **shì**.

> 那四個 **běnzi** 一 **gòng (shì)** 兩 **kuài qián**。
> *Those four notebooks are two dollars altogether.*

7.8. Gěi *give*

In Lesson 5 we learned the word **gěi** as part of the fixed expression **gěi** (someone) **dǎ diànhuà** *phone (someone)*. In this lesson we learn to use the word **gěi** as the verb *give*.

> **Gěi nǐ** 八十。
> *I'm giving you ¥80.*

7.9. 一 bǎi *100* and the numbers *100–999*

The word for *hundred* is **bǎi**. **Bǎi** is always preceded by a number: *100* is 一 **bǎi**, *200* is 兩 **bǎi**, *300* is 三 **bǎi**, etc. The numbers *101–999* are formed by stating the number of hundreds (**bǎi**), tens (十) and ones as follows:

	hundreds (bǎi)	tens (十)	ones
123	一 **bǎi**	二十	三
212	兩 **bǎi**	一十	二
468	四 **bǎi**	六十	八
750	七 **bǎi**	五十	
999	九 **bǎi**	九十	九

Notice that when the number expression includes hundreds, the numbers 11–19 in the tens column are expressed with 一 **yī** as 一十一 **yīshí yī**, 一十二 **yīshí èr**, 一十三 **yīshí sān**, etc. If a number has hundreds and ones but no tens, the word **líng** *zero* is used between the hundreds and the ones:

602	六 **bǎi líng** 二
801	八 **bǎi líng** 一

7.10. Zhǎo *make change*

When giving change, a clerk may say:

> **Zhǎo nǐ** (三十 **kuài** 四 **máo qián**)。
> *I'm giving you (¥30.4) in change.*

Sentence pyramids

The sentence pyramids illustrate the use of each new vocabulary item and structure introduced in the lesson. Use them to help you learn how to form phrases and sentences in Mandarin. Supply the English translation for the last line where indicated.

I. **běnzi** 那個 **běnzi**	*notebook* *that notebook*
2. **běnzi** 哪個 **běnzi** **Nǐ yào mǎi** 哪個 **běnzi**?	*notebook* *which notebook?* *Which notebook do you want to buy?*
3. **hǎo** 哪 **běn shū hǎo**?	*good* *Which book is good?*
4. **liànxí běn** **Hàn zì liànxí běn** 那個 **Hàn zì liànxí běn**	*practice book* *Chinese character practice book* _____
5. 一 **běn** 六 **kuài** 八一 **běn** **Liànxí běn** 六 **kuài** 八一 **běn**。 那個 **liànxí běn** 六 **kuài** 八一 **běn**。	*one volume* *six dollars and eighty cents a volume* *Practice books are six dollars and eighty cents each.* *Those practice notebooks are six dollars and eighty cents each.*
6. 一 **diǎn** **piányi** 一 **diǎn** **kěyǐ piányi** 一 **diǎn** 嗎? **Mǎi** 兩 **běn kěyǐ piányi** 一 **diǎn** 嗎?	*a little* *a little cheaper* *can it be a little cheaper?* *If I buy two (books) can it be a little cheaper?*
7. **mǎi** 甚麼? **xiǎng mǎi** 甚麼? **hái xiǎng mǎi** 甚麼? **Nǐ hái xiǎng mǎi** 甚麼?	*buy what?* *want to buy what?* *still want to buy what?* *What else do you want to buy?*

8.	
shū	*book*
Zhōngwén shū	*Chinese book*
一 niánjí 的 Zhōngwén shū	*first-year Chinese book*

9.	
一 niánjí 的 Zhōngwén shū	*first-year Chinese book*
mǎi 一 niánjí 的 Zhōngwén shū	*buy first-year Chinese book*
yào mǎi 一 niánjí 的 Zhōngwén shū	*want to buy first-year Chinese book*
hái yào mǎi 一 niánjí 的 Zhōngwén shū	*in addition want to buy first-year Chinese book*
Wǒ hái yào mǎi 一 niánjí 的 Zhōngwén shū。	*I also want to buy a first-year Chinese book.*

10.	
shū	*book*
兩 běn shū	*two books*
這兩 běn shū	*these two books*

11.	
duōshao qián?	*how much money?*
shuǐ duōshao qián?	*water is how much money?*
三 píng shuǐ duōshao qián?	*three bottles of water are how much?*
那三 píng shuǐ duōshao qián?	_____

12.	
Zhōngwén shū	*Chinese books*
一 niánjí 的 Zhōngwén shū	*first-year Chinese books*
這兩 běn shū shì 一 niánjí 的 Zhōngwén shū。	*These two books are first-year Chinese books.*

13.	
duōshao qián?	*how much money?*
一 gòng duōshao qián?	*altogether how much money?*
這兩 běn shū 一 gòng duōshao qián。	*How much are these two books altogether?*

14.	
五 kuài qián	*five dollars*
三十五 kuài qián	*thirty-five dollars*
一 gòng 三十五 kuài qián	*altogether thirty-five dollars*
這兩 běn shū 一 gòng 三十五 kuài qián。	_____

15. 一 **bǎi kuài** **Gěi nǐ** 一 **bǎi kuài**。	￥100 *(I) give you ￥100.*
16. 四 **máo qián** 三十 **kuài** 四 **máo qián** **Zhǎo nǐ** 三十 **kuài** 四 **máo qián**。	*forty cents* *thirty dollars and forty cents* *I am giving you thirty dollars and forty* *cents in change.*

Chinese characters

Radicals

In this lesson we take a closer look at radicals. Every character has a radical. Sometimes the radical is the character. For example, for the characters 一 (**yī**) *one,* 二 (**èr**) *two,* and 十 (**shí**) *ten* introduced in Lesson 6, the character is also the radical. In most cases, however, the radical is some part of the character. For example, in the characters 嗎 (**ma**) and 哪 (**nǎ**) introduced in this lesson, the radical is 口, which means 'mouth,' and is the radical for many characters whose meanings have to do with language.

There are about two hundred radicals but there are many thousands of characters. That means that many characters share the same radical.

The spatial orientation of characters

The strokes of a character may form a single unit, or they may form two or more parts. The characters in Lesson 6 all consist of a single unit. Many of the characters introduced in Lesson 7, however, consist of two parts, and these parts have a distinctive spatial orientation. For example, the characters 那, 這, 的, and 嗎 each consist of two parts arranged in a horizontal, left-to-right orientation.

When the parts of a character are arranged in a horizontal left-to-right orientation, the part on the left is often, but not always, the radical. For example, in the character 那, the radical is the part on the right. When the parts of a character have horizontal orientation, the part on the left is usually, but not always, the part that is written first. Notice that in the character 這, the part that is written first is on the right. When characters have a vertical orientation, the part on the top is always written first.

The spacing of characters and words

We learned in Lesson 6 that when writing Chinese characters, each character takes the same amount of space on a page. In this lesson we learn additional things about writing texts in Chinese characters:

- When words are written with two or more characters, each character is written in its own box, equally spaced from the other character or characters in the word:

甚	麼

- Each punctuation mark is written in its own box. Punctuation marks are not written inside the space of another character.

這	**shì**	**nǐ**	的	，	**duì**	嗎	？

- Words do not have spaces around them as they do in English written texts, and there is nothing in a written text to indicate the boundaries of words.

八	十	六	。

Lesson 7   Characters step-by-step

的 (**de**) has a horizontal orientation and is written from left to right. Its radical is on the left and is written first. The radical consists of five strokes. The first stroke is a *left falling stroke*. The second stroke is a *vertical stroke*. The third stroke is a *right corner stroke*.

The fourth stroke is a left-to-right *horizontal stroke* that fills in the box. The fifth stroke is a left-to-right *horizontal stroke* that closes the box.

白 白

The right side of 的 is written in three strokes. The first stroke is a *left falling stroke*. The second stroke is a *right corner stroke* that ends in a *left-facing hook*. The third stroke is a *dot*.

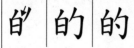

個 (**gè**) has a horizontal orientation and is written from left to right. The left part of 個, 亻, is its radical. The radical 亻 is called the *person* radical and it appears in characters in two different forms. When it is its own character it is written 人 (see page 127). As a radical it may be written as 人 or as 亻. When it is written as 亻 as in the character 個, its first stroke is a *left falling stroke*. Its second stroke is a *vertical stroke* that begins at the midpoint of the falling stroke.

The right half of 個 is a box with the strokes that form 古 inside.

When writing a box, always follow this order: *write the first two strokes of the box, fill in the box,* and then *close the box.* The first stroke of a box is always the left side: a *vertical stroke* written from top to bottom. The second stroke is a *right corner stroke.* The corner stroke ends with a *left facing hook.*

The inside of the box in the character 個, 古, is written in five strokes. The first stroke is a *horizontal stroke* written from left to right. The second stroke is a *vertical stroke* written from top to bottom.

The remaining strokes of 古 form a box: a *vertical stroke*, a *right corner stroke*, and a *horizontal stroke* at the bottom of the box that serves as the closing stroke and closes the box.

The last stroke of 個 is a *horizontal stroke* written from left to right that closes the large box.

幾 (**jǐ**) *how many* has a vertical orientation and is written from top to bottom. The top part consists of two identical parts. The part on the left is written first. It begins with a *left falling stroke* that turns into a *horizontal line* going from left to right. This sequence is written as a single stroke.

It is followed by the same stroke directly below it. The sequence ends with a *dot*. A dot is a short stroke that falls, usually from left to right, with an outward, convex curve.

This three-stroke sequence is repeated to the right.

It is underscored by a *horizontal stroke* written from left to right.

The next stroke is a *left falling stroke* that begins at the midpoint of the first of the pair of 幺 parts. It is followed by a *dot* that begins at the midpoint of the left falling stroke and falls to the right.

The next stroke is a *right falling slanting stroke* that begins between the pair of 幺. It ends with a *right upwards facing hook*. It is intersected by a *left falling stroke* below the horizontal line that is written from right to left. The last stroke is a *dot* that begins at the top of the left falling stroke. It is written from left to right.

兩 (**liǎng**) is written from top to bottom. The first stroke is a *horizontal stroke* written from left to right. The second and third strokes form a box that is open at the bottom. The fourth stroke is a *vertical stroke* that begins at the midpoint of the top horizontal line and divides the open box in two.

Each of the open sections of the box gets an identical sequence of strokes, a *left falling stroke* followed by a *dot* that begins above the starting point of the falling stroke and falls to the right.

 嗎 (ma) has a horizontal orientation and consists of two parts. The left part of the character is the radical 口 and it is written first. 口 (pronounced **kǒu**) means *mouth* and is often called the "mouth" radical. It is shaped like a small box. We have already seen that Chinese characters with a box shape are written in three strokes:

丶　冂　口

The right part of the character 嗎 (**ma**) is written in ten strokes. The first stroke is a *horizontal stroke* written from left to right. The second stroke is a *vertical stroke* written from top to bottom that begins at the left side of the horizontal stroke.

口ー　口厂

The next two strokes are *horizontal strokes* written below the top horizontal stroke. They are shorter than the top horizontal stroke and do not go through the vertical stroke on the left.

口F　口E

The fifth stroke is a *vertical stroke* that intersects the shorter horizontal strokes. It may touch the top horizontal stroke but it does not go through it.

口耳

The next stroke is a *horizontal stroke that turns into a vertical stroke* that slants to the left and ends with an *upward facing hook*. This is written as a single stroke.

The last four strokes are *dots*. The first dot is a *left falling dot*.

嗎

The remaining dots are *right falling dots*.

嗎 | 嗎 | 嗎

麼 (**me**), the second character in the word 甚麼 (**shénme**) *what*, has a vertical orientation and is written in fourteen strokes. The first stroke is a *dot*. The second stroke is a *horizontal stroke* written from left to right. The top of the dot is centered over the horizontal stroke.

亠

The third stroke is a *left falling stroke*. It begins on the right side of the horizontal stroke.

广

As you can see, there are two levels within the enclosure formed by the first three strokes. The top level includes two nearly identical shapes written side by side, from left to right. They are each written in four strokes. The shape on the left is written with a *horizontal stroke*, a *vertical stroke*, a *left falling stroke*, and a *right falling stroke*.

庐 | 庁 | 庄 | 床

The shape on the right is written with a *horizontal stroke* a *vertical stroke*, a *left falling stroke*, and a *right falling stroke* with a rightward curve and an upward hook.

庐 | 庍 | 庥 | 麻

The last part of the character is centered below the "almost twins" and is written in three strokes: a *left falling stroke* that turns to the right, another *left falling stroke* that turns to the right, and a *dot*.

幺 | 幺 | 幺

It lies within the enclosure made by the first three strokes.

麼 | 麼 | 麼

哪	哪 (**nǎ**) has a horizontal orientation and is written from left to right. It consists of the radical 口 on the left and the character 那 on the right. 口 is written first. See the character 嗎 above for instructions on writing 口. See the character 那 below for instructions on writing 那.
那	那 (**nà**) consists of two parts and is written from left to right. The first part is written in four strokes. The first stroke is a *right corner stroke* that ends in a *left upward hook*. コ The second and third strokes are short *horizontal strokes*. ヨ The fourth stroke is a *left falling stroke* that is written through the two horizontal strokes. 尹 The right side of 那 (**nà**) is its radical. It is written in three strokes. The first stroke is a *horizontal-left falling stroke*. ㄱ
	The second stroke is a *curved stroke* that ends in a *left facing hook*. 乀 The third stroke is a *vertical stroke*. 阝
人	人 (**rén**) is written in two strokes. The first stroke is a *left falling stroke*. The second stroke is a *right falling stroke* that begins slightly below the top of the first stroke. 人 rén is also a radical. In some characters, the radical 人 is written 人, but in most characters in which it is the radical, it is written 亻.
甚	甚 (**shén**), the first character in the word 甚麼 (**shénme**) *what*, has a vertical orientation and is written in nine strokes. The first stroke is a *horizontal stroke* that is written from left to right toward the top of the space that the character will occupy. The second and third strokes are the *vertical strokes*, written from top to bottom, that intersect the horizontal stroke. 

The next three strokes are *horizontal strokes* written from left to right. The first two strokes are written between the vertical lines. They may touch the lines but they do not go through. The third stroke is written below the vertical lines. It touches the bottom of the vertical lines and serves to close off the space above.

其 ｜ 甘 ｜ 其

The next two strokes are a *left falling stroke* and a *vertical stroke* that turns to the right and becomes a *curved stroke*.

其 ｜ 其

The last stroke begins as a *vertical stroke* that turns to the right and becomes a *horizontal stroke*.

甚

The character 這 (**zhè**) has a horizontal orientation and consists of two parts. The radical of this character, 辶, is always written last, so in the character 這, 言 is written first.

言 has a vertical orientation and is written from top to bottom in seven strokes. The first stroke is a *dot*. The second stroke is a *horizontal stroke* written from left to right. The next two strokes are *horizontal strokes* that are shorter than the first horizontal stroke.

丶 ｜ 亠 ｜ 亠 ｜ 言

The next three strokes form a box, just like the radical 口. 口 is not the radical in this character, but its shape is used in the character. See 嗎 on page 125 for instructions on writing 口.

言 ｜ 言 ｜ 言

The radical 辶 is written last and it is written in four strokes. The first stroke is a *dot*.

The second stroke is a *horizontal stroke* that turns into a *left falling stroke*.

The third stroke is a *curved stroke*.

The fourth stroke is a *right falling stroke* that continues below and beyond 言 on the right side of the character.

Language FAQs

What is the difference between xiǎng and yào?

Xiǎng and **yào** overlap in meaning, but they are not identical. You can use either **xiǎng** or **yào** when saying that you *want to do* something or *plan to do* something.

> **Nǐ xiǎng mǎi** 甚麼? *What do you want to buy?*
> **Wǒ yào mǎi** 一個 **běnzi**。 *I want to buy a notebook.*

To say that you are *thinking about* something, use **xiǎng**.

> **Wǒ xiǎng wǒ** 的 **nán péngyou**。
> *I am thinking about my boyfriend.*

To express your opinion or to ask someone's opinion, use **xiǎng**.

> **Nǐ xiǎng** 那個 **běnzi guì bù guì**?
> *Do you think that notebook is expensive?*

To say that you *want an object*, use **yào**.

> **Wǒ yào** 那個 **běnzi**。
> *I want that notebook.*

Notes on Chinese culture

Can you make it cheaper?

It is common to expect a discount in small, privately owned stores in China, and Xiao Zhang is behaving appropriately when he asks if he can get a discount when purchasing more than one notebook. Chain stores may have special sale prices for certain items that they advertise, but clerks are not able to give discounts for items that are not on sale.

Lesson 7 Dialogue in English

Part A

Xiao Zhang:	How much is that notebook?
Clerk:	Which notebook?
Xiao Zhang:	That Chinese character practice notebook.
Clerk:	This Chinese character practice notebook is ¥6.8 for one. How many do you want?
Xiao Zhang:	If I buy two, can you make it a little cheaper?
Clerk:	I can. I can sell two for ¥12. Do you want them?
Xiao Zhang:	Yes.

Part B

Clerk:	What else are you thinking of buying?
Xiao Zhang:	I also want to buy a first-year Chinese book.
Clerk:	These two books are first-year Chinese books.
Xiao Zhang:	How much are they?
Clerk:	¥35.
Xiao Zhang:	Okay.

Part C

Xiao Zhang:	How much is it altogether?
Clerk:	The books are ¥35, nine pencils are ¥5.85, the Chinese map is ¥7.2, five bottles of water are ¥10, two bottles of cola are ¥4.8, two practice notebooks are ¥12. Altogether it's ¥74.85.
Xiao Zhang:	I'm giving you ¥100.
Clerk:	Here is ¥25.15 in change.
Xiao Zhang:	Okay. Goodbye.
Clerk:	Goodbye.

Lesson 8 Shēngri kuàilè!
Happy birthday!

Communication goals
- State your age and ask others how old they are
- Indicate dates and days of the week
- Make plans to do activities on a given date or day of the week

Key structures

(S) + time when + VP

qù + ActV *going to do an action*

suggestions with **ba**, **zěn** 麼 **yàng**, 好不好, **xíng** 不 **xíng**

the order of information in time phrases:

    largest unit to smallest unit

(time) **cái** (age) *not* (this age) *until* (this time)

Dialogue

The Situation: Xiao Gao and her Chinese roommate Xiao Ye are having a conversation in their dorm room. Xiao Gao has been in China for almost three months and is looking forward to her birthday.

Part A

Xiǎo Gāo: Jīntiān 是幾 yuè 幾 hào？

Xiǎo Yè: Jīntiān 是十一 yuè 九 hào。

Xiǎo Gāo: 十一 yuè 十二 hào 是我的 shēngri。

Xiǎo Yè: 是嗎？Shēngri kuàilè！你 jīnnián duō dà？

Xiǎo Gāo: 我 jīnnián 二十 suì。你也是二十 suì 嗎？

Xiǎo Yè: 不。我 jīnnián 十九 suì，míngnián cái 二十 suì。

Part B

Xiǎo Yè: 十一 yuè 十二 hào 是 xīngqī 幾？

Xiǎo Gāo: 十一 yuè 十二 hào 是 xīngqī 四。

Xiǎo Yè: 那，我 xīngqī 四 wǎnshang qǐng 你 chī wǎnfàn，hē píjiǔ，zěn 麼 yàng？

Xiǎo Gāo: Tài 好 le。Xièxie 你 qǐng 我 chī fàn！ *(Xiao Gao looks at the calendar....)* Zāogāo！Xīngqī 四 wǎnshang 不 xíng。我 xīngqī 五 yǒu 一個 kǎoshì。

Part C

Xiǎo Yè: Xīngqī 五 wǎnshang 呢？我們也 kěyǐ qù chàng kǎlā OK，zěn 麼 yàng？

Xiǎo Gāo: Chàng gē 嗎？我不 huì chàng gē！我 zhǐ xǐhuan tīng yīnyuè。我們 qù tiào wǔ ba。

Xiǎo Yè: 你不 huì chàng gēr。我不 huì tiào wǔ。這 yàng，這個 xīngqī 五我們 chàng kǎlā OK，我 jiāo 你 chàng gēr。Xià 個 xīngqītiān 我們 qù tiào wǔ，你 jiāo 我 tiào wǔ，好不好？

Xiǎo Gāo: 好。我們也 qǐng Xiǎo Zhāng hé Xiǎo Mǎ ba。他們很 xǐhuan chàng gē。

Xiǎo Yè: Xíng。我 míngtiān gěi 他們 dǎ diànhuà。

Vocabulary

ba	final particle	*(used for making suggestions)*
cái	adverb	*not until, (later than expected)*
chàng	verb	*sing*
chàng gē, chàng gēr	verb + object	*sing songs*
chī	verb	*eat*
chī fàn	verb + object	*eat (eat food, eat rice)*
duō dà	question phrase	*how old*
fàn	noun	*rice, food*
gē, gēr	noun	*song*
hào	classifier	*date of the month*
hē	verb	*drink*
hē jiǔ	verb + object	*drink alcohol*

jiāo		verb	*teach*
jīnnián		noun	*this year*
jīntiān		noun	*today*
jiǔ [píng]		noun	*wine, alcohol*
kǎlā OK		noun	*karaoke*
kǎoshì [gè]		noun	*test*
kuàilè		adjectival verb	*happy*
Mǎ		family name	*(family name)* *(literally: horse)*
míngnián		noun	*next year*
míngtiān		noun	*tomorrow*
nián		classifier	*year*
píjiǔ [píng]		noun	*beer*
qǐng		verb	*invite*
qù		verb	*go*
shēngri [gè]		noun	*birthday*
shēngri kuàilè		conversational expression	*happy birthday*
shíyī yuè	十一 yuè	noun	*November*
suì		classifier	*years of age*
tài hǎo le	tài 好 le	conversational expression	*great, terrific*
tiān		classifier	*day*
tiào		verb	*jump, dance*
tiào wǔ		verb + object	*dance*

tīng		verb	*listen (to)*
tīng yīnyuè		verb + object	*listen to music*
wǎnfàn		noun	*dinner*
wǎnshang [gè]		noun	*evening, night*
wǔ		*	*dance*
xià		specifier	*next (used with certain time expressions)*
xǐhuan		stative verb	*like*
xíng		adjectival verb	*okay, be acceptable*
xīngqī [gè]		noun	*week*
xīngqīsì	**xīngqī 四**	noun	*Thursday*
xīngqītiān		noun	*Sunday*
xīngqīwǔ	**xīngqī 五**	noun	*Friday*
Yè		family name	*(family name)*
yīnyuè		noun	*music*
yuè [gè]		noun	*month*
zāogāo		conversational expression	*oh no!*
zěnmeyàng	**zěn 麼 yàng**	question phrase	*how about it? okay?*
zhè yàng	**這 yàng**	noun phrase	*in this way, how about this*

Verb-object phrases with action verbs

(Use and Structure note 8.13)

chàng gē	*sing songs*	→	*sing*
chī fàn	*eat rice*	→	*eat*
hē jiǔ	*drink alcohol*	→	*drink*
shuō huà (L3)	*speak talk*	→	*speak*
tiào wǔ	*dance dances*	→	*dance*
tīng yīnyuè	*listen to music*		

The days of the week

(Use and Structure note 8.9)

xīngqīyī	**xīngqī** 一	*Monday*
xīngqī'èr	**xīngqī** 二	*Tuesday*
xīngqīsān	**xīngqī** 三	*Wednesday*
xīngqīsì	**xīngqī** 四	*Thursday*
xīngqīwǔ	**xīngqī** 五	*Friday*
xīngqīliù	**xīngqī** 六	*Saturday*
xīngqītiān		*Sunday*

The months of the year

(Use and Structure note 8.2)

yī yuè	一 yuè	*January*
èr yuè	二 yuè	*February*
sān yuè	三 yuè	*March*
sì yuè	四 yuè	*April*
wǔ yuè	五 yuè	*May*
liù yuè	六 yuè	*June*
qī yuè	七 yuè	*July*
bā yuè	八 yuè	*August*
jiǔ yuè	九 yuè	*September*
shí yuè	十 yuè	*October*
shíyī yuè	十一 yuè	*November*
shí'èr yuè	十二 yuè	*December*

Characters

不	bù	*no (negation)*	
好	hǎo	*good, well*	
很	hěn	*very*	
們	men	*(plural suffix for pronouns)*	我們 (**wǒmen**) *we, us*
			你們 (**nǐmen**) *you*
			他們 (**tāmen**) *they, them*

呢	ne	(final particle/follow-up questions)	
你	nǐ	you	你們 (**nǐmen**) *you*
是	shì	be	
她	tā	she	她們 (**tāmen**) *they, them (female)*
他	tā	he	他們 (**tāmen**) *they, them*
我	wǒ	I, me	我們 (**wǒmen**) *we, us*
也	yě	also	

Stroke Order Flow Chart

character:	strokes:											total strokes:
不	一	丁	不	不								4
好	く	乡	女	好	奵	好						6
很	ノ	ク	彳	彳	彴	徂	徂	很	很			9
們	ノ	亻	亻	们	們	們	們	們	們	們		10
呢	丶	口	口	叮	叮	吲	听	呢				8
你	ノ	亻	亻	亇	伫	你	你					7
是	丶	口	日	日	旦	旱	旱	是	是			9
她	く	乡	女	如	妁	她						6
他	ノ	亻	亻	仲	他							5
我	丿	二	千	手	扎	我	我					7
也	一	乜	也									3

Dialogue practice

Do these activities in class after mastering each part of the dialogue for this lesson. Change partners so that you practice each role several times.

Dialogue 8A: *Paired activity.* Work with one other classmate. Take turns asking each other the date of your birthday and your age. Introduce your partner to one other student, telling her your partner's birthday and age.

Dialogue 8B: *Whole class activity, small group, or paired activity.* Using a calendar for the current month, take turns with your classmates stating a date and asking what day of the week it is. For example, you can ask: 十一 **yuè** 十二 **hào** 是 **xīngqī** 幾？ or you can point to a day and say: **Jīntiān** 是 **xīngqī** 三，**míngtiān** 是 **xīngqī** 幾？

Dialogue 8C: *Paired activity.* Think of an activity that you want to do with your partner this Friday. Your partner will think of a different activity. Negotiate with your partner until you agree on plans to do your activities on two separate dates. Report your arrangements to the class.

Use and structure

8.1. Counting days, weeks, months, and years

Days

To count days or to indicate the number of days, say:

number + tiān
一 **tiān**, 兩 **tiān**, 三 **tiān**
one day, two days, three days

Weeks

To count weeks or to indicate the number of weeks, use the classifier 個 and say:

number + 個 + xīngqī
一個 **xīngqī**, 兩個 **xīngqī**, 三個 **xīngqī**
one week, two weeks, three weeks

Months

To count months or to indicate the number of months, use the classifier 個 and say:

number + 個 + yuè
一個 **yuè**, 兩個 **yuè**, 三個 **yuè**
one month, two months, three months

Years

To count years or to indicate the number of years, say:

number + nián
一 **nián**, 兩 **nián**, 三 **nián**
one year, two years, three years

Notice that although the words **tiān** *day* and **nián** *year* translate into English as nouns, in Mandarin they function as classifiers. That is, like classifiers, and unlike nouns, they occur right after a number.

Tiān *day* occurs as part of the words **jīntiān** *today* and **míngtiān** *tomorrow*, and **nián** *year* occurs as part of the words **jīnnián** *this year* and **míngnián** *next year*. **Nián** also occurs in the word (一) **niánjí** *(first) year level* introduced in Lesson 7.

8.2 The months of the year

The names of the months are formed by:

number + yuè
一 **yuè** *January*, 二 **yuè** *February*, 三 **yuè** *March*

Compare the way that months are named and the way that they are counted.

names of months		number of months	
一 **yuè**	*January*	一個 **yuè**	*one month*
二 **yuè**	*February*	兩個 **yuè**	*two months*
三 **yuè**	*March*	三個 **yuè**	*three months*

To ask what month it is, use the question word 幾 and ask 幾 **yuè** *what (number) month?*

8.3. The dates of the month

The dates of the month are formed by:

number + hào
一 **hào** *the first (day of the month)*
二 **hào** *the second (day of the month)*
三 **hào** *the third (day of the month)*

To ask what date it is, use the question word 幾 and ask 幾 **hào** *what date?*

Compare the difference between the word **hào** and the word **tiān** *day* when talking about days and dates. **Hào** is used when indicating the date. **Tiān** is used when indicating the number of days.

names of dates	number of days
一 **hào** *the first (day of the month)*	一 **tiān** *one day*
二 **hào** *the second (day of the month)*	兩 **tiān** *two days*
三 **hào** *the third (day of the month)*	三 **tiān** *three days*

8.4. Month and date

Month and date are stated in the same order as in English:

month	+	date	
十一 **yuè**		九 **hào**	*November 9ᵗʰ*
四 **yuè**		一 **hào**	*April 1ˢᵗ*

To ask *what month and date* it is, put the two questions together and say:

幾 **yuè** 幾 **hào**?

To ask what month and date it is <u>today</u>, say:

Jīntiān (是) 幾 **yuè** 幾 **hào**?

8.5. 是嗎? *is that so?*

是嗎? means *is that so?* 是嗎? is often used to acknowledge information that someone has just given you.

Xiǎo Gāo: 十一 **yuè** 十二 **hào** 是我的 **shēngri**。
Xiǎo Yè: 是嗎?

是嗎? is similar in meaning to the expression **zhēn** 的 (嗎?) *really?* that we learned in Lesson 3.

8.6. Age

Stating age

Age is indicated as:

number + suì
我二十 **suì**。
I am 20 years old.

Notice that **suì**, like **tiān** *day* and **nián** *year*, occurs right after a number.

In informal speech, **suì** may be omitted when the number is more than ten and it is clear from the context that the number refers to *years of age*.

他 **jīnnián** 二十三。
He is 23 this year.

Asking about age

To ask someone's age, use the question phrase **duō dà** *how old*:

Q: **Nǐ duō dà?** *How old are you?*   A: (我)二十二 (**suì**)。 *(I'm)* 22.

When speaking to a child, you can also use the question word 幾 and say:

Q: 你幾 **suì**? *How old are you?*   A: (我)十 **suì**。 *(I'm)* 10.

Remember that 幾 is used when asking about relatively small numbers (Use and Structure notes 5.4 and 6.5).

8.7.   Omitting the verb 是

是 *be* links two noun phrases. We learned in Lesson 6 that 是 is often omitted when the information that would follow 是 is a price. (Use and Structure note 6.4) 是 is also omitted when the information that would follow it is a date or someone's age.

with 是	without 是
Jīntiān 是幾 **yuè** 幾 **hào**?	**Jīntiān** 幾 **yuè** 幾 **hào**?
What month and date is it today?	*What month and date is it today?*
(What is today's date?)	*(What is today's date?)*
Jīntiān 是十 **yuè** 九 **hào**。	**Jīntiān** 十 **yuè** 九 **hào**。
Today is October 9th.	*Today is October 9th.*
我 **jīnnián** 是二十 **suì**。	我 **jīnnián** 二十 **suì**。
I am 20 years old this year.	*I am 20 years old this year.*

If the sentence is negated, or if it includes an adverb, 是 must occur and may not be omitted:

Say this:	***Do not say this:***
Jīntiān 不是十 **yuè** 九 **hào**。	⊗ **Jīntiān** 不十 **yuè** 九 **hào**。
Today is not October 9th.	
我 **jīnnián** 不是二十 **suì**。	⊗ 我 **jīnnián** 不二十 **suì**。
I am not 20 years old this year.	
我也是二十 **suì le**。	⊗ 我也二十 **suì le**。
I am also 20 years old.	

8.8.   Time + **cái** + age *not (this age) until (this time)*

Cái indicates that something happens later than expected. In this dialogue, **cái** is used to indicate that Xiao Ye turns 20 later than Xiao Gao assumes.

Xiǎo Gāo: 我 **jīnnián** 二十 **suì**。你也是 二十 **suì** 嗎?
     I am 20 this year. Are you also 20?

Xiǎo Yè: 不。我 **jīnnián** 十九 **suì**,**míngnián cái** 二十 **suì**。
     No. I'm 19 this year. I won't be 20 until next year.

When **cái** contributes the meaning *later than expected*, it can often be translated with the English expression *not until*. Notice that the Chinese expression does not involve negation.

In this lesson, we will practice using **cái** to indicate that someone turns a certain age later than others expect. We will practice using **cái** in other contexts in Lesson 9.

8.9. The days of the week

The days of the week are presented in the vocabulary section of this lesson. They are formed by the noun **xīngqī** *week* followed by a number: Monday is **xīngqī** 一, Tuesday is **xīngqī** 二, etc. Sunday is **xīngqītiān**. Chinese calendars begin the week with **xīngqī** 一 *Monday* and not with **xīngqītiān** *Sunday*.

Asking about the day of the week

To ask what day of the week it is, use the question word 幾 and ask **xīngqī** 幾？

十一 **yuè** 十二 **hào** 是 **xīngqī** 幾？
November 12th is what day of the week? (What day of the week is November 12th?)

Jīntiān 是 **xīngqī** 幾？
What day of the week is it today?

8.10. The order of information in a time phrase

In Chinese, time is always recited from the <u>largest</u> unit to the <u>smallest</u> unit.

When giving a calendar date or asking about a calendar date, the month is always stated first and the date is always stated second.

二 **yuè**   五 **hào**
February   5th

When talking about a part of the day (for example *morning, midday, evening*), state the day first and the part of the day second.

xīngqī 四   **wǎnshang**
Thursday   *evening*

xià 個 **xīngqī** 四 **wǎnshang**
next Thursday   *evening*

When talking about a part of the year (for example *September, November*), state the year first and the part of the year second.

jīnnián   九 **yuè**
this year   September   →   *September of this year*

8.11. The time when a situation occurs

To indicate the <u>time when</u> a situation occurs, state the time phrase before the verb phrase as follows:

S + time when   +   VP

我 <u>xīngqī 四 wǎnshang</u>   qǐng 你 chī fàn，zěn 麼 yàng？
How about if I treat you to dinner on Thursday night?

If you want to emphasize the <u>time when</u> a situation occurs, state the time phrase first as follows:

time when   +   S   +   VP

<u>這個 xīngqī 五</u>   我們   <u>chàng kǎ lā OK</u>。
This Friday we will sing karaoke.

8.12.   Qǐng *invite*

The basic meaning of **qǐng** is *invite*. In Chinese culture, when you invite someone to do something, you also pay the bill. Therefore, **qǐng** (someone) **chī fàn** can be translated into English as either *invite (someone) to eat*, or *treat (someone) to a meal*, or *buy (someone) a meal*.

我 xīngqī 四 wǎnshang qǐng 你 chī wǎnfàn，hē píjiǔ，zěn 麼 yàng？
Let me treat you to dinner and beer this Thursday night, okay?

When talking about inviting someone to eat or drink something, always use the word **qǐng** *invite*. Do not use the word **mǎi** *buy*.

Say this:	*Do not say this:*
我 qǐng 你 chī fàn，zěn 麼 yàng？	⊗ 我 mǎi nǐ fàn，zěn 麼 yàng？
How about if I treat you to a meal?	

8.13.   Action verbs and action verb phrases

Some actions that are expressed with a single verb in English are expressed with a verb and an object in Mandarin. We have already learned one such action in Lesson 3: **shuō huà** *speak* (Use and Structure note 3.10). In this lesson we learn several more action verb phrases. The object in each of the following verb phrases is underlined.

English	Mandarin
eat	**chī <u>fàn</u>** (*eat <u>rice</u>*)
sing	**chàng <u>gē</u>** (*sing <u>a song</u>*)
dance	**tiào <u>wǔ</u>** (*dance <u>a dance</u>*)

In these Mandarin verb phrases, **fàn**, **gē**, and **wǔ** stand for the general type of thing that you can *eat*, *sing*, or *dance*. When talking about something more specific, you replace the <u>general noun</u> with the <u>more specific noun</u>.

general noun	specific noun
chī <u>fàn</u>	**chī <u>Zhōngguó fàn</u>**
eat	*eat <u>Chinese food</u>*

chàng gē	chàng kǎlā OK
sing	*sing karaoke*
tiào wǔ	tiào bālěi wǔ
dance	*dance ballet*

Some textbooks write the Pinyin form of expressions like **shuō huà** *speak*, **chī fàn** *eat*, **chàng gē** *sing*, and **tiào wǔ** *dance* as single words without a space between the verb and the object. We keep a space between the verb and the object to remind you that the general object can be replaced by a more specific object.

More about action verbs and general objects

chī fàn *eat*
Sometimes, the object noun in an action verb phrase has a more general meaning when it occurs with the action verb than it does in other contexts. For example, in the verb phrase **chī fàn**, the word **fàn** means *food*, but in other contexts it means *rice*. If someone said they didn't like **fàn** or if they had to buy **fàn** they would be referring to *rice*. But if someone invites you to **chī fàn** they are inviting you to a meal, and that meal need not include rice.

tiào wǔ *dance*
Sometimes the object noun does not always occur freely outside of the action verb phrase.

For example, in the phrase **tiào wǔ**, the word **wǔ** does not normally occur by itself to mean *dance* but is usually used with another word or phrase. When a part of an expression cannot occur on its own, we mark it with a following asterisk (*) in the vocabulary list.

We will learn more about action verb phrases in Lesson 9, including how to ask the question *what are you doing?*

8.14. Making suggestions with **zěn** 麼 **yàng**, 好不好 and **xíng** 不 **xíng**

In this lesson we learn four expressions that can be used when making a suggestion: **zěn** 麼 **yàng**, 好不好 (or 好嗎), **xíng** 不 **xíng** (or **xíng** 嗎), and **ba**. All occur at the end of a statement. **Zěn** 麼 **yàng**, 好不好, and **xíng** 不 **xíng** are tag questions that follow a statement. They ask for feedback from the listener and are equivalent to the English expressions *okay?* or *how about it?*

> 我 **xīngqī** 四 **wǎnshang qǐng** 你 **chī fàn**, **zěn** 麼 **yàng**?
> *How about if I treat you to dinner on Thursday night?*

> 你 **jiāo** 我 **tiào wǔ**, 好不好?
> *You teach me how to dance, okay?*

> **Xīngqī** 四 **wǎnshang xíng** 不 **xíng**?
> *How about Thursday night?*

You can reply *"okay"* to a suggestion with **zěn** 麼 **yàng**, 好不好, or **xíng** 不 **xíng** by saying 好, **xíng**, or **kěyǐ**. You can indicate that you cannot or do not want to go along with a suggestion by saying 不好, 不 **xíng**, or 不 **kěyǐ**.

See note 8.15 for more about **xíng**, and see note 8.17 for the sentence final particle **ba**.

8.15.   Xíng *okay*

Xíng is another way to indicate that a suggestion is acceptable or *okay*. It is commonly used in and around the city of Beijing. Although its meaning sometimes overlaps with 好 *good*, it has a much more restricted use than 好. It is used as a reply to suggestions, but is not otherwise used to describe something as being "good," and it is never preceded by an intensifier. That is, you cannot say ⊗ 很 **xíng**.

To say that some suggestion is acceptable, say **xíng** *okay*:

> **Xiǎo Zhāng：**   我們 **qù chī fàn ba**。 *Let's go eat.*
> **Xiǎo Xiè：**   **Xíng**。 *Okay.*

To say that some suggestion is not acceptable, say 不 **xíng** *not okay*:

> **Xīngqī** 四 **wǎnshang** 不 **xíng**。
> *Thursday night is not okay.*

To ask if something is acceptable to the person you are speaking with, say **xíng** 嗎？ or **xíng** 不 **xíng**？

> **Xīngqī** 四 **wǎnshang xíng** 不 **xíng**？
> *Is Thursday night okay?*

8.16.   Going to do an action: Qù + ActV

In this lesson we learn to use the verb **qù** *go* + an action verb to indicate *"go"* do an action.

> 我們 **qù chàng kǎlā OK，zěn** 麼 **yàng**？
> *How about if we go sing karaoke?*

8.17.   Making suggestions with the sentence-final particle ba

To say *let's (do an action)*, end the sentence with the sentence-final particle **ba**.

> 我們 **qù tiào wǔ ba**。
> *Let's go dancing.*

> 我們也 **qǐng Xiǎo Zhāng hé Xiǎo Mǎ ba**。
> *Let's also invite Xiao Zhang and Xiao Ma.*

When the subject of the suggestion is 你 *you*, <u>你 VP **ba**</u> can be translated into English in either of the following ways:

你 **jiào** 我 **chàng gē ba**!
Teach me to sing!
or
Why don't you teach me to sing!

In Lesson 4 (Use and Structure note 4.8) we learned the use of the sentence-final particle **ba** to indicate a speaker's assumption. When a sentence ends with **ba**, the content of the sentence and the context in which it is used will make it clear whether **ba** is used to indicate an assumption or a suggestion. Normally, only one or the other interpretation of **ba** makes sense in any situation. For example, if Xiao Gao says to Xiao Zhang 你是 **xuésheng ba** the sentence cannot be interpreted as a suggestion. It can only be interpreted as an assumption: *you must be a student*. Similarly, if Xiao Gao says to Xiao Ye 我們 **qù chàng gē ba** it can only be interpreted as a suggestion: *let's go singing*.

8.18. The retroflex suffix **-r**: **chàng gēr** vs. **chàng gē**

Speakers of the Beijing dialect of Mandarin add the suffix -**r** to the end of many words. In this lesson, we see -**r** used as the suffix on the noun **gē** *song*. The suffix -**r** does not change the meaning of a word. When -**r** is added to a word that ends with a vowel, -**r** simply occurs at the end of the word. In this course we will introduce the use of the -**r** suffix on a number of commonly used words so that you can hear the pronunciation of the suffix and learn how -**r** is used. The pronunciation of Beijing Mandarin is more complicated than the addition of an -**r** suffix at the end of a few words. If you have the opportunity to live in Beijing for study or work, you will easily hear the difference between Beijing Mandarin and Standard Mandarin.

8.19. *This week* and *next week*, *this month* and *next month*

To say *this week*, or *this day of the week*, or *this month* say:

這個 **xīngqī**	這個 **xīngqī(tiān)**	這個 **yuè**
this week	*this (Sun)day*	*this month*

The phrase *next week*, *next day of the week*, or *next month* is expressed with the word **xià** *below*:

xià 個 **xīngqī**	**xià** 個 **xīngqī(tiān)**	**xià** 個 **yuè**
next week	*next (Sun)day*	*next month*

Xià 個 **xīngqī** literally means *the week below*, **xià** 個 **xīngqī(tiān)** means *the (Sun)day below* and **xià** 個 **yuè** means *the month below*. In the expressions **xià** 個 **xīngqi** *next week* and **xià** 個 **xīngqī(tiān)** *next (Sun)day*, the classifier 個 can be omitted.

8.20. 他 **tā** *he/him*, 她 **tā** *she/her*

As we have already learned, in its spoken form, the third person pronoun **tā** is neutral in terms of gender and is used for *he/him*, *she/her*, and *it*. Chinese reflects gender in the Chinese characters for the third person pronoun, however. In this lesson we learn the character 他, pronounced **tā**, for *he/him* and the character 她, also pronounced **tā**, for *she/her*. 他 is the character used in the plural 他們 **tāmen** *they, them* when the group includes all males or males and females. It can also be used when referring to animals or inanimate objects. Chinese has another character for *it*, also pronounced **tā**, that refers specifically to animals and inanimate objects.

Sentence pyramids

The sentence pyramids illustrate the use of each new vocabulary item and structure introduced in the lesson. Use them to help you learn how to form phrases and sentences in Mandarin. Supply the English translation for the last line where indicated.

1. kǎoshì yǒu kǎoshì yǒu Zhōngwén kǎoshì 我 yǒu Zhōngwén kǎoshì。	*test* *have a test* *have a Chinese test* _____
2. kǎoshì Zhōngwén kǎoshì yǒu Zhōngwén kǎoshì jīntiān yǒu Zhōngwén kǎoshì 我 jīntiān yǒu Zhōngwén kǎoshì。	*test* *Chinese test* *have a Chinese test* *have a Chinese test today* _____
3. 甚麼？ chī 甚麼？ 你 chī 甚麼？	*what* *eating what* _____
4. fàn Zhōngguó fàn 我 chī Zhōngguó fàn。	*rice, food* *Chinese food* _____

5. chī fàn qǐng 你 chī fàn 我 xiǎng qǐng 你 chī fàn。	*eat* *invite you to eat* *I'd like to invite you to eat.*
6. zěn 麼 yàng chī Zhōngguó fàn，zěn 麼 yàng？ 我們 jīntiān chī Zhōngguó fàn， zěn 麼 yàng？	*how about it? (okay?)* *eat Chinese food, okay?* *How about if we eat Chinese food today?*

7.
Tài 好 le！
Xiǎo Zhāng： 我 jīntiān wǎnshang
  qǐng 你 chī fàn。
Xiǎo Xiè： Tài 好 le！
	Terrific!
	Xiao Zhang: I'm inviting you to
	  dinner tonight.
	Xiao Xie: Terrific!

8. yǒu kǎoshì xīngqī 五 yǒu kǎoshì xīngqī 五 yǒu kǎoshì 嗎？ 你 xīngqī 五 yǒu kǎoshì 嗎？	*have a test* *have a test on Friday* *have a test on Friday?* _____
9. Zhōngwén kǎoshì yǒu Zhōngwén kǎoshì 我 míngtiān yǒu Zhōngwén kǎoshì。 Zāogāo！我 míngtiān yǒu Zhōngwén kǎoshì。	*Chinese test* *have a Chinese test* *I have a Chinese test tomorrow.* *Oh no! I have a Chinese test tomorrow.*
10. yīnyuè tīng yīnyuè xǐhuan tīng yīnyuè zhǐ xǐhuan tīng yīnyuè 我 zhǐ xǐhuan tīng yīnyuè。	*music* *listen to music* *like to listen to music* *only like to listen to music* _____
11. gē chàng gē 我們 xīngqī 五 chàng gē 我們 xīngqī 五 chàng gē，好不好？	*song(s)* *sing (songs)* *we sing on Friday* *Let's sing on Friday, okay?*

12. gěi 他 dǎ diànhuà míngtiān gěi 他 dǎ diànhuà 我 míngtiān gěi 他 dǎ diànhuà。	*phone him* *phone him tomorrow* _____
13. wǔ tiào wǔ xǐhuan tiào wǔ 很 xǐhuan tiào wǔ 她很 xǐhuan tiào wǔ。	*dance* *(to) dance* *like to dance* *likes to dance very much* *She really likes to dance.*
14. 是嗎? Xiǎo Gāo: 她很 xǐhuan tiào wǔ。 Xiǎo Yè: 是嗎?	*Is that so?* *Xiao Gao: She likes dancing a lot.* *Xiao Ye: _____*
15. tiào wǔ qù tiào wǔ 我 xiǎng qù tiào wǔ。	*dancing* *go dancing* _____
16. ba qù tiào wǔ ba Xiǎo Zhāng: 我們 qù tiào wǔ ba。 Xiǎo Yè: Tài 好 le!	*(suggestion)* *go dancing (suggestion)* *Xiao Zhang: Let's go dancing.* *Xiao Ye: _____*
17. yǒu kǎoshì méi yǒu kǎoshì míngtiān méi yǒu kǎoshì 我們 míngtiān méi yǒu kǎoshì。	*have a test* *do not have a test* *do not have a test tomorrow* _____
18. duō dà 你 duō dà?	*how old* _____
19. suì 十八 suì 我十八 suì。 我十八 suì。你呢?	*years of age* *18 years old* *I am 18 years old.* _____

20. 二十 **suì** 是二十 **suì** 也是二十 **suì** 我也是二十 **suì**。	*20 years old* *be 20 years old* *also be 20 years old* _____
21. 二十 **suì** **cái** 二十 **suì** **míngnián cái** 二十 **suì** 我 **míngnián cái** 二十 **suì**。	*20 years old* *only then will be 20 years old* *won't be 20 until next year* *I won't be 20 until next year.*
22. **hào** 幾 **hào**？ **Jīntiān** 幾 **hào**？	*(date)* *what date?* *What is today's date?*
23. **yuè** 幾 **yuè**？ 幾 **yuè** 幾 **hào**？ **Jīntiān** 幾 **yuè** 幾 **hào**？	*month* *which month?* *which month and date?* *What is today's (month and) date?*
24. **shēngri** 你的 **shēngri** 你的 **shēngri** 是幾 **yuè** 幾 **hào**？	*birthday* *your birthday* _____
25. 十二 **hào** 十一 **yuè** 十二 **hào** 是十一 **yuè** 十二 **hào** 我的 **shēngri** 是十一 **yuè** 十二 **hào**。	*the 12th day of the month* *November 12th* *is November 12th* _____
26. **kǎlā OK** **chàng kǎlā OK** **qù chàng kǎlā OK** **xiǎng qù chàng kǎlā OK** 我 **xiǎng qù chàng kǎlā OK**。	*karaoke* *sing karaoke* *go sing karaoke* *want to go sing karaoke* _____
27. **qù tiào wǔ** **xīngqītiān qù tiào wǔ** 我們 **xīngqītiān qù tiào wǔ**。 我們 **xīngqītiān qù tiào wǔ**， 　**zěn** 麼 **yàng**？	*go dancing* *go dancing on Sunday* *We go dancing on Sunday.* _____

28.	
tīng yīnyuè	*listen to music*
qù tīng yīnyuè	*go listen to music*
xīngqītiān qù tīng yīnyuè	*go listen to music on Sunday*
xià xīngqītiān qù tīng yīnyuè	*go listen to music next Sunday*
Xiǎo Gāo： 我們 **xià xīngqītiān qù tīng yīnyuè ba**。	*Xiao Gao: Let's go listen to music next Sunday.*
Xiǎo Yè：Xíng。	*Xiao Ye: Okay.*
29.	
chàng gēr	*sing*
jiāo 你 **chàng gēr**	*teach you to sing*
我 **jiāo** 你 **chàng gēr**。	_____
30.	
我 **jiāo** 你 **chàng gē**。	*I will teach you to sing.*
這 **yàng**，我 **jiāo** 你 **chàng gē**。	*How about this, I teach to sing.*
這 **yàng**，我 **jiāo** 你 **chàng gē**，好不好。	_____

Chinese characters

Be a character sleuth!

Characters are composed of strokes, and strokes are often grouped in <u>recurring parts</u>, units that occur in other characters. When you learn a new character, be a <u>character sleuth</u>. Look for parts that you have already learned in other characters. Use these recurring parts to help you to learn the new characters, and to review the "old" ones.

In Lessons 7 and 8 we learn several characters with recurring parts. Take a close look at the characters in each of the following lines and identify the recurring parts.

Characters that share a recurring part	*The recurring part is:*
哪，嗎，呢	口
那，哪	那
你，他，們	亻
也，他，她	也
好，她	女

Find each of these characters in the Stroke Order Flow Charts in Lessons 7 and 8. You will see that sometimes the recurring part is the radical of the character, but sometimes it is not. For example, the recurring part 口 is the radical in the characters 哪, 嗎, and 呢, but the recurring part 也 is not the radical in the characters 他 and 她.

Lesson 8 Characters step-by-step

不 (**bù**) has a vertical orientation and is written from top to bottom.

The first stroke is a *horizontal stroke*. It is the radical in this character.

The remaining strokes are written from left to right. The *left falling stroke* is written before the *vertical stroke*. The last stroke is a *long dot* and is written with a slight outward curve.

好 (**hǎo**) has a horizontal orientation and consists of two parts.

The left part, 女, is the radical and it is written first. It is written in three strokes.

The first stroke is a *left-right falling stroke*. That is, it starts falling left and then changes direction and falls right.

The second stroke is a *left falling stroke*. Notice that it has a slight downward curve.

The last stroke is a left-to-right *horizontal stroke*. Notice where it meets the left falling stroke.

The right part of 好, 子, is written in 3 strokes.

The first stroke is a *horizontal-left falling stroke.*

The second stroke is a *vertical stroke* with a *left hook.*

The third stroke is a *horizontal stroke*. Notice that it crosses the vertical stroke near the top.

很 **(hěn)** has a horizontal orientation and consists of two parts written from left to right. Notice that the two parts of the character are the same height.

The left part of the character is the radical 彳. It has a vertical orientation and is written from top to bottom. The order of strokes is: *left falling stroke, left falling stroke, vertical stroke.*

The right part of the character occurs in many characters. It is neither entirely vertical nor horizontal in orientation.

The first stroke is a *right hand corner* stroke. It is a single stroke that starts as a horizontal stroke and then becomes a vertical stroke.

The second stroke is the stroke inside the right hand corner. It is a *horizontal stroke* written from left to right.

The third stroke is the bottom stroke. It is a *horizontal stroke* written from left to right.

The fourth stroke is a *vertical stroke* that ends with a small *upward hook* that slants to the right.

The fifth stroke is a *left falling stroke*.

很

The sixth stroke is a *right falling stroke*. It starts from the center and falls to the right. Notice that the previous left falling stroke meets it at about the midpoint.

很

 們 **(men)** has a horizontal orientation and is written from left to right. The left part of 們 is the radical 亻, the same radical used in the character 個, and it is written first in two strokes.

丿　亻

The right part of 們 is written from left to right in eight strokes. The first stroke is a *vertical stroke* written from top to bottom. The second stroke is a *right corner stroke*. Notice that these strokes form a box with a short right side. The third stroke is a *horizontal stroke* that fills in the box. The fourth stroke is a *horizontal stroke* that closes the box.

亻　伊　伊　伊

The next four strokes also form a box, but this box has a short left side. The first stroke is the short *vertical stroke*. The next stroke is a *right corner stroke*. Notice that it is about as long as the long stroke to the left, and that it ends with a hook. The next stroke is the *horizontal stroke* that fills in the box. The last stroke is the *horizontal stroke* that closes the box.

伊　們　們　們

呢 呢 (**ne**) has a horizontal orientation and is written from left to right.

The left part of 呢 is the mouth radical 口 and it is written first. It is the same radical as in the character 嗎 (**ma**) introduced in lesson 7.

The right side of 呢 consists of two parts. The top is written first in three strokes in this order: a *right hand corner stroke*, a *horizontal stroke*, and a *left falling stroke*.

The bottom half is written in two strokes. The first stroke is a *left falling stroke*. The second stroke is a stroke that starts vertical, curves to the right, and ends with a hook. In Chinese this is called a *vertical-curved-hooked stroke*. It is written as a single stroke. Notice that the curve is relatively flat on the bottom.

你 你 (**nǐ**) has a horizontal orientation and is written in two parts from left to right.

The first part of 你 is the radical 亻. It is the same radical used in the characters 個 and 們.

The second part of 你 has vertical orientation and consists of two parts.

The part on the top is written in two strokes, a *left falling stroke* and a *horizontal stroke* with a *left downward hook*, written in that order. Notice that the horizontal stroke meets the falling stroke just below its midpoint. The two strokes may touch but the horizontal stroke does not go through the falling stroke.

The second part is symmetrical. The center is written first and the sides are written afterwards. The first stroke is a *vertical stroke* with a *left hook*. The remaining strokes are a *left falling stroke* and a *right falling stroke*.

是 (shì) has a vertical orientation and is written from top to bottom.

The top of 是 is the radical 曰. It is a box with a horizontal stroke inside.

Boxes are always written in the same way. The *left vertical stroke* is written first, and the *right corner stroke* is written second.

丨 口

If the inside of the box contains one or more strokes, they are written next. The last stroke of the box is a left-to-right *horizontal stroke* that closes the box.

日 日

The bottom half of 是 is written in 5 strokes. It is written from top to bottom and from left to right.

The first stroke is a *horizontal stroke.*

The second stroke is a *vertical stroke* that starts at the midpoint of the horizontal stroke. It does not go through the top of the horizontal stroke.

The third stroke is a *horizontal stroke* written from the midpoint of the vertical stroke to the right. It does not go through the left side of the vertical line.

The fourth stroke is a *left falling stroke.* It begins about halfway between the start of the horizontal stroke and the vertical stroke.

The fifth stroke is a *right falling stroke.* Notice that it begins just below the top of the left falling stroke and extends the entire width of the character.

她 (tā) has a horizontal orientation. It consists of two parts and is written from left to right.

The left part is the radical 女. 女 means *female,* and that is why it is used as the radical in this character. (Compare 她 with 他.) We have already learned how to write 女 as the left part of the character 好.

The right part of 她 is the character 也 (yě). We will see how to write it below.

	他 (**tā**) consists of two parts. It has a horizontal orientation and is written from left to right.
	The left part of 他 is the radical 亻. We have already seen how to write it: it is the radical for 們 (**men**) and 你 (**nǐ**).
	The right part is the character 也 (**yě**).
	我 (**wǒ**) consists of one part and is written in seven strokes from top to bottom and left to right.
	The first stroke is a *left falling stroke* written from right to left.
	The second stroke is a *horizontal* stroke and is written from left to right.
	The third stroke is a *vertical stroke* with an *upward left hook*.

The fourth stroke is an *upward slanting stroke*. It is written from left to right. Notice that it goes through the vertical stroke. Do not confuse an upward slanting stroke with a left falling stroke. They are written in opposite directions and do not look the same. A falling stroke is concave. That is, it has a slight downward curve like the base of a spoon. An upward slanting stroke is slightly convex. That is, it has a slight upward curve.

The fifth stroke is a *right slanted stroke* with a *right upward hook*. It is written from top to bottom.

The sixth stroke is a *left falling stroke*. It goes through the vertical stroke.

The last stroke is a *dot*. It is written from left to right and has a slight upward curve.

我

Notice that the strokes of the radical 戈 in the character 我 are not written consecutively. Instead, the radical is merged into the character. Also notice that this radical occurs on the right side of the character.

也 (**yě**) consists of a single part and is written in 3 strokes.

The first stroke is an *upward slanting horizontal stroke* with a *bottom, left-facing hook.*

The second stroke is a *vertical stroke.*

The third stroke is a *vertical-curved stroke* with an *upward hook.* It is the radical.

Language FAQs

Which part of the sentence indicates present and future tense?

Unlike English and many other languages, Chinese does not have grammatical structures that mark a sentence as past, present, or future. Instead, when time is relevant, Mandarin uses words or phrases to signal the time. For example, words like **jīntiān** *today* and **jīnnián** *this year* indicate that a sentence is talking about present time. Words and phrases such as **yào** *want*, **xiǎng** *think about, plan*, and **xià** 個 **xīngqī** *next week* refer to future time. Mandarin sentences are often <u>unmarked</u> for time. That is, they need not include words or particles that indicate time or tense. When a sentence is unmarked for time, the context of the sentence will let you know if it refers to the past, present, or future time, or if it is simply stating a situation that is generally true.

Why is suì *years of age* a classifier?

We call **suì** a classifier because it can occur directly after a number, and it cannot be preceded by a classifier. That is, you say:

兩 **suì** *2 years old*, 十八 **suì** *18 years old*, 六十 **suì** *60 years old*
and not

⊗ 兩 個 **suì**, ⊗ 十八 個 **suì**, ⊗ 六十 個 **suì**

Suì is one of a small number of classifiers in Mandarin that has noun-like meaning and is not followed by an associated noun. We have already learned two other words like **suì**: **tiān** *day* and **nián** *year*.

What kind of word is kǎlā OK *karaoke*?

Kǎlā OK is a loan word from Japanese. The Japanese word that Mandarin borrowed is "karaoke." In Japanese, "kara" means *empty*; and "oke" is a shortened form of a word that Japanese borrowed from English: *orchestra*. In Japanese, "karaoke" means *empty orchestra*. Karaoke is a very popular form of entertainment in China. When it is written in Chinese, **kǎlā** is written in Chinese characters, and "ok" is written as **ok**, or it is written using capital letters as **OK**.

Notes on Chinese culture

When is your birthday?

In traditional Chinese culture, birthdays are not individual events celebrated on the anniversary of one's birth date. Instead, everyone celebrates their birthday at the start of the Chinese New Year holiday. (The traditional Chinese year is based on a lunar calendar, and the New Year usually falls between the end of January and the middle of February.) In Chinese culture, noodles are a traditional birthday food, because noodles symbolize long life. However, it is now common in Chinese cities to celebrate birthdays on one's birth date, and to celebrate it with a birthday cake.

How old are you this year?

In traditional Chinese culture, everyone's age increases at the start of the Chinese New Year. Therefore, it is common to ask how old you are *this year* (你 **jīnnián duō dà**?) rather than how old you <u>will</u> be on your birthday. In the traditional Chinese system, you are 1 year old at birth. At the Chinese New Year you add another year. Therefore, a child born on January 1, before the start of the Chinese New Year, would be considered to be 2 years old at the Chinese New Year, one month after he or she was born.

Qǐng *invite* and the obligations of the host

In Chinese culture, when you invite someone to do something, you assume the obligations of the host. That is, you make the arrangements, and you pay the bill. Therefore, you can translate the sentence 我 **xiǎng qǐng** 你 **chī fàn** as *I want to <u>invite</u> you to eat*, or *I want to <u>treat</u> you to eat*, or *I want to <u>buy</u> you dinner*. When students go out in groups, they often each pay their own share, but for working adults, splitting the bill is not very common. Within a group of friends or close acquaintances, members take turns assuming the role of host, usually in a friendly, competitive way. Taking turns being the host and the guest is one of the ways that defines friendships in Chinese culture.

In the expression chī fàn, why does the word fàn mean *food*?

In traditional Chinese culture, rice is the most important part of a meal, and everything else is considered an accompaniment to the rice. In this way, rice is symbolic of the meal, and to eat a meal is to **chī fàn** *eat rice*.

Lesson 8 Dialogue in English

Part A

Xiao Gao:	What's today's date?
Xiao Ye:	Today is November 9th.
Xiao Gao:	November 12th is my birthday.
Xiao Ye:	Really? Happy birthday! How old are you this year?
Xiao Gao:	I'm 20 this year. Are you also 20?
Xiao Ye:	No. I'm 19 this year. I won't be 20 until next year.

Part B

Xiao Ye:	What day of the week is November 12th?
Xiao Gao:	November 12th is a Thursday.
Xiao Ye:	Well then, I'll treat you to dinner and beer on Thursday night, okay?
Xiao Gao:	Terrific! Thanks for inviting me to eat. (Xiao Gao looks at the calendar....) Oh no! Thursday night is not good (for me). I have a test on Friday.

Part C

Xiao Ye:	What about Friday night then? We can also go sing karaoke, okay?
Xiao Gao:	Go singing? I can't sing! I only like to listen to music. Let's go dancing.
Xiao Ye:	You can't sing, I can't dance. How about this. This Friday we sing karaoke and I teach you to sing. Next Sunday we go dancing and you teach me to dance, okay?
Xiao Gao:	Okay. Let's also invite Xiao Zhang and Xiao Ma. They like to sing a lot. *(They really like to sing.)*
Xiao Ye:	Okay. I'll call them tomorrow.

Lesson 9 你 zài zuò 甚麼?
What are you doing right now?

Communication goals
- Talk about clock time
- Describe daily routines
- Talk about actions that you are doing right now
- Talk about things you must do and things you are not allowed to do
- Make plans for the future

Key structures

zài + ActV

你 zuò 甚麼?

(time) + cái + ActV *not until* (action happens later than expected)

jiù + ActV (action happens sooner than expected)

obligations and prohibitions: děi *must* and 不可以 *not allowed to*

sentence le for new information

Dialogue

The Situation: Xiao Xie goes to the library to study, sees his roommate Xiao Zhang, and begins a conversation with him.

Part A

小謝:　小張，你 **zài zuò** 甚麼？

小張:　我 zài **xuéxí** 中文。我明 tiān shàngwǔ 有 Zhōngwén kǎoshì。

小謝:　你明 tiān shàngwǔ 有 kǎoshì，zěnme xiànzài **cái** fùxí？

小張:　我 jīntiān 中 wǔ 有 diànnǎo kè 的 kǎoshì，xiàwǔ 有 kè。五 diǎn zhōng **cái** xià kè。Xiànzài 幾 **diǎn zhōng**？

小謝:　Xiànzài 十 **diǎn zhōng le**。

Part B

小張:　十 diǎn zhōng! Tài wǎn le。我 xiànzài **děi** huí sùshè le。

小謝:　你 huí sùshè zuò 甚麼？你 **有 shì** 嗎？

小張:　我 xiǎng **jīntiān wǎnshang 十 diǎn bàn shuì jiào**。

小謝:　十 diǎn bàn **jiù** shuì jiào，tài 早 le ba!

小張:　我明 tiān 早 shang 八 diǎn zhōng jiù **kǎo shì**。我 děi 六 diǎn zhōng **起 chuáng**，六 diǎn 一 kè **xǐ zǎo**，六 diǎn bàn **chī** 早 **fàn**，七 diǎn **fùxí gōngkè、liànxí Hàn zì**，七 diǎn 四十分 qù **shàng kè**。

小謝:　你可以 jīntiān wǎnshang xǐ zǎo，明 tiān，wǎn 一 diǎn **起** chuáng。

小張:　我不 **xǐhuan** wǎnshang xǐ zǎo。我 xiànzài jiù huí sùshè le。

Part C

(librarian): 這是 **túshūguǎn**。你們 **zhǐ** 可以 **kàn shū**，**xuéxí**，不可以說話。

小張： 對不起。小謝，再見。

小謝： 好，好，再見。

Vocabulary

bàn		number	*half*
chuáng [gè]		noun	*bed* (起 **chuáng**)
děi		modal verb	*must*
diǎn		classifier	*dot, o'clock* (一 **diǎn zhōng**)
diànnǎo [gè]		noun	*computer*
fēn	分	classifier	*minute* (L6, *penny, cent*)
fùxí		verb	*review*
gōngkè		noun	*class work, course work*
huí		verb	*return to a location*
jiù		adverb	*(sooner than expected)*
kàn		verb	*read* (**kàn shū**), *see* (**kàn péngyou** *see friends*), *look at*
kàn shū		verb + object	*read*
kǎo		verb	*(take a test)*
kǎo shì		verb + object	*take a test*
kè		noun	*class*
kè		classifier	*quarter*
le		final particle	*(new information, change)*
qǐ	起	verb	*get up, rise up* (起 **chuáng**)

qǐ chuáng	起 chuáng	verb + object	*get out of bed, wake up*
shàng			*attend (school or class), go up*
shàng kè		verb	*go to class*
shàngwǔ		noun	*morning*
shì		*	*work (*有 shì*)*
shuì		verb	*sleep*
shuì jiào		verb + object	*sleep*
sùshè [gè]		noun	*dormitory*
túshūguǎn [gè]		noun	*library*
wǎn		adjectival verb	*late*
xǐ		verb	*wash (*xǐ zǎo*)*
xǐ zǎo		verb + object	*bathe*
xià kè		verb + object	*get out of class*
xiànzài		time word	*now*
xiàwǔ		noun	*afternoon*
xuéxí		verb	*study*
yǒu shì	有 shì	verb phrase	*have something to do, be busy*
yǒu shì ma?	有 shì 嗎?	conversational expression	*What's up?*
zài		adverb	*(indicates an action in progress)*
zǎofàn	早 fàn	noun	*breakfast (L6, 早 early)*
zǎoshang	早 shang	noun	*morning*
zhōng		*	*(part of clock time expression, e.g. 一 diǎn zhōng)*
zhōngwǔ	中 wǔ	noun	*noon*
zuò		verb	*do (*zuò 甚麼*)*

Verb-object phrases with action verbs

chàng gē		*sing*
chī fàn		*eat*
hē jiǔ		*drink (alcohol)*
kàn shū		*read*
kǎo shì		*take a test*
shuì jiào		*sleep*
shuō huà	說話	*speak*
tiào wǔ		*dance*
xǐ zǎo		*bathe*

Characters

對	duì	*correct*	對不起 (**duìbuqǐ**) *excuse me*
分	fēn	*minute, cent, penny*	
話	huà	*speech, language*	說話 (**shuō huà**) *speak, talk*
			中 guó 話 (**Zhōngguó huà**) *Chinese language*
			dǎ diàn 話 (**dǎ diànhuà**) *make a phonecall*
見	jiàn	*see*	再見 (**zài jiàn**) *goodbye*
可	kě	*	可以 (**kěyǐ**) *can (permission)*
明	míng	*	明 tiān (**míngtiān**) *tomorrow*
			明 nián (**míngnián**) *next year*

起	qǐ	*	對不起 (**duìbuqǐ**) *excuse me*
			起 **chuáng** (**qǐ chuáng**) *get up, get out of bed*
說	shuō	*speak, talk, say*	說話 (**shuō huà**) *speak, talk*
文	wén	*	中文 (**Zhōngwén**) *Chinese language*
小	xiǎo	*little, small (family name prefix)*	小張 (**Xiǎo Zhāng**) *Xiao Zhang*
謝	xiè	*thank, (family name)*	謝謝 (**xièxie**) *thank you*
以	yǐ	*	可以 (**kěyǐ**) *can (permission)*
有	yǒu	*have, there is/there are*	
再	zài	*again*	再見 (**zài jiàn**) *goodbye*
早	zǎo	*early*	早 **fàn** (**zǎofàn**) *breakfast*
			早 (**zǎo**) *good morning (greeting)*
張	zhāng	*sheet (classifier), (family name)*	
中	zhōng	*middle*	中文 (**Zhōngwén**) *Chinese language*
			中 **guó** 話 (**Zhōngguó huà**) *Chinese language*

Stroke Order Flow Chart

character: **strokes:** **total strokes:**

														total
對	丶	丷	丷	业	业	业	业	业	业	业	對	對		14
分	丿	八	分	分										4
話	丶	二	三	言	言	言	言	計	訐	訐	話	話		13
見	丨	冂	月	月	目	貝	見							7
可	一	丁	河	百	可									5
明	丨	冂	日	日	明	明	明	明						8
起	一	十	土	丰	丰	走	走	起	起	起				10
説	丶	二	三	言	言	言	言	訂	訂	詥	詥	詥	説	14
文	丶	一	亠	文										4
小	亅	小	小											3
謝	丶	二	三	三	言	言	言	訂	訂	訏	訏	訏	訏	
	謝	謝	謝											17
以	丨	丩	以	以	以									5
有	一	大	才	有	有	有								6
再	一	丆	冂	再	再	再								6
早	丶	口	日	日	旦	早								6
張	丁	弓	弓	弓	弘	弘	弘	張	張	張				11
中	丶	冂	口	中										4

Dialogue practice

Do these activities in class after mastering each part of the dialogue for this lesson. Change partners so that you practice each role several times.

Dialogue 9A: *Activity 1, Charades.* Select one of the actions that we have learned through Lesson 9 and act it out in front of the class. Ask your classmates: 我 **zài zuò** 甚麼？Have them identify your action in a complete sentence. For example: 你 **zài chī fàn，duì** 不 **duì**？

Activity 2. Take turns asking and telling your classmates what time it is.

Dialogue 9B: *Activity 1 (Paired Activity).* Make a list of the things you do in the morning (evening) and the time you do them. Find a partner and ask him what he does in the morning (evening), and then find out what time he does each of these activities.

Activity 2. Write down an early wake-up time, dinner time, and bedtime, and an explanation for each one. Find a partner and ask her what time she is going to wake up, eat dinner, or go to sleep tomorrow. Say that the time is too early, and listen to her explanation. Then change roles and repeat the activity.

Dialogue 9C: Work with your classmates to make a list of all of the things that you cannot do in the library (or in Chinese class, or in the dormitory). Then, explain the rules in Chinese beginning with 這是 **túshūguǎn** or 這是中文 **kè**.

Use and structure

9.1.   Ongoing actions: **Zài** + ActV

Zài indicates that a situation is ongoing at the time of speaking, or was/will be ongoing at the point of reference, either in the past or the future. In this lesson we learn to use **zài** with verbs that refer to actions. To emphasize that an action is ongoing right now, say:

zài + ActV
我 **zài fùxí Fǎ** 文。
I am studying French right now.

To ask what someone is doing right now, say:

你 **zài zuò** 甚麼？
What are you doing right now?

To ask if someone is doing a specific action now, ask:

你 **zài xuéxí** 中文嗎？
Are you studying Chinese right now?

To emphasize that some action was ongoing at some time in the past, include a time expression that refers to past time.

我 **zuótiān wǎnshang zài fùxí gōngkè**。
I was reviewing my course work last night.

To emphasize that some action will be ongoing at some time in the future, add a time expression that refers to future time:

明 **tiān** 早 **shang** 八 **diǎn** 我 **zài kǎo shì**。
Tomorrow at 8 a.m. I'll be taking a test.

9.2. 你 **zuò** 甚麼? *What are you doing?*

To ask what someone is doing, or what someone does (for a living), say:

你 **zuò** 甚麼？
What are you doing?

你 **bàba zuò** 甚麼？
What does your father do?

To ask what someone is doing <u>right now</u> (Use and Structure note 9.1), say:

你 **zài zuò** 甚麼？
What are you doing right now?

To answer the question, replace **zuò** 甚麼 with the <u>entire action</u>. Do not repeat **zuò** in the answer.

Question	Answer
你 <u>**jīntiān wǎnshang** xiǎng</u> **zuò** 甚麼？	我 **xiǎng** <u>**qù kàn péngyou**</u>。
What do you want to do tonight?	*I want to go see friends.*
你 **bàba zuò** 甚麼？	他是 **lǎoshī**。
What does your father do?	*He is a teacher.*

9.3. **Xuéxí** *study* and **xué** *study* compared

Xuéxí and **xué** can both be translated by the English verb *study*, but they are not used in the same way. **Xuéxí** can be used more broadly than **xué**. It can be followed by the subject area that you are studying, and it can be used to say that you are "studying" without specifying what it is that you are studying. **Xué** must be followed by the subject area that you are studying: **xué Zhōngwén** *study Chinese*, **xué Yīngwén** *study English*, etc. You cannot use **xué** when you want to simply say that you are "studying."

	xuéxí		**xué**
Say this:	我 zài xuéxí 中文。	*or this:*	我 zài xué 中文。
	I am studying Chinese.		*I am studying Chinese.*
Say this:	我 zài xuéxí。	*Don't say this:*	⊗ 我 zài xué。
	I am studying.		

9.4.   Saying that an action occurs later than expected: Time **cái** ActV

In Lesson 8 we learned to use the adverb **cái** to say that someone turns a certain age later than expected (Use and Structure note 8.8). In this lesson we expand this use of **cái** to other actions. To say an action occurs later than expected, say:

> **time + cái + ActV**

The most literal way to translate **cái** sentences, the way that follows the order of information in Chinese, is with the expression *only then*:

> 我五 **diǎn zhōng cái xià kè**。
> *It was 5 o'clock and only then I got out of class.*

> 我 **zuótiān wǎnshang** 九 **diǎn cái chī fàn**。
> *Last night at 9 o'clock only then I ate.*

As you can see, translations with *only then* are not very natural sounding in English. A more natural sounding way to convey the meaning of **cái** sentences is with the expression *not until*, or *no action until (time)*.

> 我五 **diǎn zhōng cái xià kè**。
> *I did <u>not</u> get out of class <u>until</u> 5 o'clock.*

> 我 **zuótiān wǎnshang** 九 **diǎn cái chī fàn**。
> *I did <u>not</u> eat last night <u>until</u> 9 o'clock.*

> (你) **zěnme xiànzài cái fùxí**?
> *How come you have <u>not</u> studied <u>until</u> now?*

Mandarin sentences with **cái** and English sentences with *not until* correspond in meaning but are very different in form. Study these differences in these pairs of sentences.

time + cái + ActV	=	*no ActV until time*
我五 **diǎn zhōng cái xià kè**。	=	*I didn't <u>get out of class</u> until 5 o'clock.*
我 **zuótiān wǎnshang** 九 **diǎn cái chī fàn**。	=	*Last night I didn't <u>eat</u> until 9 o'clock.*

9.5.   Clock time

Time on the hour

To indicate time on the hour, say:

(number) diǎn zhōng

一 **diǎn zhōng**	*1 o'clock*
兩 **diǎn zhōng**	*2 o'clock*
三 **diǎn zhōng**	*3 o'clock*
十 **diǎn zhōng**	*10 o'clock*
十二 **diǎn zhōng**	*12 o'clock*

The word **diǎn** cannot be omitted from the clock time expression. However, the word **zhōng** can be omitted and it often is. The clock time expression means the same thing whether **zhōng** is present or omitted.

一 **diǎn zhōng**	=	一 **diǎn**	*1 o'clock*
兩 **diǎn zhōng**	=	兩 **diǎn**	*2 o'clock*
三 **diǎn zhōng**	=	三 **diǎn**	*3 o'clock*
十 **diǎn zhōng**	=	十 **diǎn**	*10 o'clock*

Clock time in hours and minutes

To recite clock time in hours and minutes, use the words **diǎn** and 分 (**fēn**) *minutes* as follows. Notice that the word for minute, **fēn**, is the same as the word for *cent* and is written with the same character, 分.

(number) diǎn (number) 分

一 **diǎn** 二十分	*1:20*	*(twenty minutes after 1)*
十一 **diǎn** 三十五分	*11:35*	*(thirty-five minutes after 11)*
十二 **diǎn** 五分	*12:05*	*(five minutes after 12)*

When the number of minutes is expressed in two syllables (that is, when it is more than ten minutes after the hour), 分 may be omitted.

一 **diǎn** 二十分	or	一 **diǎn** 二十	*1:20*
十一 **diǎn** 三十五分	or	十一 **diǎn** 三十五	*11:35*

When the number of minutes after the hour is between one and ten, minutes may be expressed as:

líng + number of minutes

八 **diǎn líng** 六分	*8:06*
七 **diǎn líng** 四分	*7:04*

Notice that **líng** *zero* adds a syllable to the "minutes" expression, so 分 can be omitted.

十二 **diǎn líng** 五分	or	十二 **diǎn líng** 五	*12:05*
兩 **diǎn líng sān** 分	or	兩 **diǎn líng sān**	*2:03*

Half past the hour

To say half past the hour, use the word **bàn** *half* and say:

number + diǎn bàn

一 **diǎn bàn**   *1:30*   *half past one*   三 **diǎn bàn**   *3:30*   *half past three*
兩 **diǎn bàn**   *2:30*   *half past two*   十 **diǎn bàn**   *10:30*   *half past ten*

A quarter past the hour

To say a quarter past the hour, use the word **kè** and say:

number + diǎn 一 kè

四 **diǎn** 一 **kè**   *4:15*   *a quarter past four*
五 **diǎn** 一 **kè**   *5:15*   *a quarter past five*
六 **diǎn** 一 **kè**   *6:15*   *a quarter past six*

Kè means a *cut*, and you can think of it as talking about cutting the clock in four quarters like four large pieces of pie. One quarter of the clock is 一 **kè**. As noted above, *half* of the clock is expressed as **bàn**. 三 **kè** means *three quarters* of the clock (45 minutes past the hour).

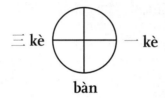

The expression 三 **kè** *three quarters* of the clock (45 minutes) is not often used in conversational speech, though it is sometimes used in formal announcements of time. In ordinary conversation, 45 minutes past the hour is expressed as:

number + diǎn 四十五(分)

六 **diǎn** 四十五   =   六 **diǎn** 三 **kè**   *6:45*
十二 **diǎn** 四十五   =   十二 **diǎn** 三 **kè**   *12:45*

Asking what time it is

To ask what time it is, say:

幾 **diǎn zhōng**？

To ask what time it is, <u>now</u>, say:

<u>Xiànzài</u> 幾 **diǎn zhōng**？

9.6.   New information with sentence-final **le**

Mandarin speakers often indicate that information is new in some way by ending a sentence with the sentence-final particle **le**.

Xiànzài 十 **diǎn zhōng le**。
It's now 10 o'clock.

There are many ways that information may be <u>new</u>. It can be something that has just happened, or something that the speaker thinks the listener does not know, or it can be some change from a previous situation that the listener was familiar with. Sentence-final **le** presents information from the speaker's perspective, and as long as the speaker thinks that some information is new for the listener, the speaker can end the sentence with **le**. Sentence-final **le** is never required by grammar, and the same information can be presented with or without **le**.

9.7. Obligation with **děi** *must* and prohibitions with 不可以 *cannot*

Mandarin has a number of words that can be used to indicate that you <u>must</u> do something. In this lesson we learn the word **děi** *must*. **Děi** is a <u>modal verb</u>. It occurs at the beginning of the verb phrase, usually right before the verb.

> 我 **xiànzài děi huí sùshè**。
> *I have to go back to the dormitory now.*

To say that you <u>cannot</u> do something, say 不可以 + action. Do not say 不 **děi**.

> 這是 **túshūguǎn**。你 **zhǐ** 可以 **kàn shū**，不可以說話。
> *This is the library. You are only allowed to read, you can't talk.*

9.8. 有 **shì** *have something to do, be busy*

有 **shì** means *have something to do* and the question 你有 **shì** 嗎？ is a common way to ask someone if she is busy.

> 你有 **shì** 嗎？
> *Do you have something to do?*

To respond to this question saying that you are not busy, say: 我 **méi** (有) **shì**。

有 **shì** 嗎？ is also used like the informal English question, *What's up?* It can be used when someone calls you on the phone or approaches you with a question or request.

9.9. Doing an action at a time and planning to do an action at a time: **Xiǎng** + time when + ActV

In Lesson 8 we learned that the <u>time when</u> a situation occurs always goes <u>before</u> the situation (Use and Structure note 8.11). In this lesson we practice this pattern using clock time.

> **time when + situation**
> 我明 **tiān** 早 **shang** 八 **diǎn zhōng jiù kǎo shì**。
> *I'm taking a test tomorrow morning at 8 a.m.*

When talking about *planning* to do an action at some time, or *thinking about* doing an action at some time, state the verb that refers to *planning* or *thinking about* (**xiǎng** or **yào**) before the time:

xiǎng + time when + ActV

我 xiǎng jīntiān wǎnshang 十 diǎn bàn shuì jiào。

I want to go to sleep tonight at 10:30.

Say this:	*Do not say this:*
我 xiǎng jīntiān wǎnshang 十 diǎn bàn shuì jiào。	⊗ 我十 diǎn bàn xiǎng jīntiān wǎnshang shuì jiào。
I want to go to sleep tonight at 10:30.	

9.10.   Jiù + ActV: The action occurs earlier than expected

The adverb **jiù** can be used to indicate that some action occurs earlier than the speaker expects it to occur. **Jiù** conveys this meaning when the sentence takes the following form:

time when + jiù + ActV

十 diǎn bàn jiù shuì jiào，tài 早 le！

Going to sleep at 10:30 is too early!

When **jiù** is used in this way, it often does not get translated into English.

Notice that **jiù** conveys the opposite meaning of the adverb **cái** discussed in Use and Structure note 9.4. **Jiù** indicates that some action happens earlier than expected. **Cái** indicates that some action happens later than expected.

time jiù ActV	**time cái ActV**
他十 diǎn bàn jiù shuì jiào。	他十 diǎn bàn cái shuì jiào。
He goes to sleep (as early as) 10:30.	*He doesn't go to sleep until 10:30.*

Remember that **jiù** and **cái**, like all adverbs, always occur before the verb phrase.

9.11.   Action verbs and their objects, continued

In previous lessons we learned the following action verbs + objects that refer to general actions: 說話 *speak, talk*, **chàng gē** *sing*, **chī fàn** *eat*, **hē jiǔ** *drink (alcohol)*, and **tiào wǔ** *dance*.

In this lesson we learn additional action verb phrases that can be used to talk about doing general actions. In each of the phrases, the object is not translated into English.

kàn shū	*read*
kǎo shì	*take a test*
shuì jiào	*sleep*
xǐ zǎo	*bathe*

As with 說話 *speak talk*, **chàng gē** *sing*, **chī fàn** *eat*, **hē jiǔ** *drink (alcohol)*, and **tiào wǔ** *dance*, the objects in **kàn shū** *read* and **kǎo shì** *take a test* can be replaced with a more specific noun. For example, if you want to say that you are planning to read, you say:

我 xiǎng kàn <u>shū</u>。

But if you want to say that you are planning to read a <u>Japanese</u> book you say:

我 **xiǎng kàn** 一 **běn Rì** 文 **shū**。

If you want to say that you have to take a test tomorrow you say:

我明 **tiān kǎo shì**。

But if you want to say that you have a <u>French</u> test tomorrow you say:

我明 **tiān kǎo Fǎ** 文。

Notice that you omit **shì** in the answer and do not say **kǎo Fǎ** 文 **shì**.

This lesson also introduces three additional verb + object phrases that have idiomatic meanings: 起 **chuáng** *get out of bed*, **shàng kè** *attend class, go to class* and **xià kè** *get out of class*. 起 **chuáng** literally means *rise up from the bed*. **Shàng kè** literally means *go up to class*. The verb **shàng** is also used as the verb when saying *attend school, attend high school, attend college*, etc. **Xià kè** literally means *go down from class*. We will learn other uses of **shàng** and **xià** in later lessons.

9.12. Stating a series of actions with serial verbs

When stating a series of actions, simply state the actions one after another without any connecting words:

七 **diǎn fùxí gōngkè**、**liànxí Hàn zì**
at 7 o'clock review class work and practice Chinese characters

When actions are stated in a series in this way, they are sometimes referred to as <u>serial verbs</u>. Notice that when writing a list, Chinese uses a special comma. See Use and Structure note 9.13.

9.13. The "list" comma

Written Chinese uses a special list comma "、" to separate items in a list of things or activities:

七 **diǎn fùxí gōngkè**、**liànxí Hàn zì**
at 7 o'clock review class work and practice Chinese characters

這是 **túshūguǎn**。你們 **zhǐ** 可以 **kàn shū**、**xuéxí**，不可以說話。
This is the library. You can only read and study, you can't talk.

Sentence pyramids

The sentence pyramids illustrate the use of each new vocabulary item and structure introduced in the lesson. Use them to help you learn how to form phrases and sentences in Mandarin. Supply the English translation for the last line where indicated.

1. 甚麼？ **zuò** 甚麼？ 明 **tiān wǎnshang zuò** 甚麼？ 你明 **tiān wǎnshang zuò** 甚麼？	*what?* *do what?* *tomorrow night do what?* *What are you doing tomorrow night?*
2. **tiào wǔ** **qù tiào wǔ** 明 **tiān wǎnshang qù tiào wǔ** 我明 **tiān wǎnshang qù tiào wǔ**。	*dance* *go dancing* *tomorrow night go dancing* _____
3. **zuò** 甚麼？ **zài zuò** 甚麼？ 你 **zài zuò** 甚麼？	*do what?* *doing what right now?* _____
4. 中文 **xuéxí** 中文 **zài xuéxí** 中文 我 **zài xuéxí** 中文。	*Chinese* *study Chinese* *studying Chinese* _____
5. 甚麼？ **zuò** 甚麼？ 你 **xiǎng zuò** 甚麼？	*what* *do what* *What do you want to do?*
6. **jiā** **huí jiā** 我 **xiǎng huí jiā**。	*home* *return home (go home)* _____
7. **fùxí** 中文 **děi fùxí** 中文 我 **děi fùxí** 中文。	*review Chinese* *must review Chinese* _____

8.	
kǎo shì	*take a test*
shàngwǔ kǎo shì	*take a test in the morning*
明 tiān shàngwǔ kǎo shì	*take a test tomorrow morning*
我明 tiān shàngwǔ kǎo shì。	_____

9.	
kè	*class*
shàng kè	*attend class (go to class)*
xīngqī 六 shàng kè	*go to class on Saturday*
你 xīngqī 六 shàng kè 嗎？	_____

10.	
kè	*class*
shàng kè	*go to class*
幾 diǎn shàng kè？	*go to class at what time?*
早 shang 幾 diǎn shàng kè？	*go to class at what time in the morning?*
你早 shang 幾 diǎn shàng kè？	_____

11.	
zhōng	*(clock)*
九 diǎn zhōng	*9 o'clock*
Xiànzài 九 diǎn zhōng。	*It is now 9 o'clock.*

12.	
kè	*class*
diànnǎo kè	*computer class*
shàng diànnǎo kè	*go to computer class*
九 diǎn zhōng shàng diànnǎo kè	*go to computer class at 9 o'clock*
我九 diǎn zhōng shàng diànnǎo kè。	_____

13.	
gōngkè	*course work*
fùxí gōngkè	*review course work*
幾 diǎn zhōng fùxí gōngkè？	*review course work at what time?*
你幾 diǎn zhōng fùxí gōngkè？	_____

14.	
早 fàn	*breakfast*
chī 早 fàn	*eat breakfast*
幾 diǎn zhōng chī 早 fàn？	*eat breakfast at what time?*
你幾 diǎn zhōng chī 早 fàn？	_____

15.	
chī 早 fàn	*eat breakfast*
七 diǎn bàn chī 早 fàn	*eat breakfast at 7:30*
我七 diǎn bàn chī 早 fàn。	_____

16. kè 一 kè 五 diǎn 一 kè Xiànzài 五 diǎn 一 kè。	*(quarter)* *one quarter (15 minutes past)* *5:15*
17. sùshè huí sùshè 四 diǎn zhōng huí sùshè xiàwǔ 四 diǎn zhōng huí sùshè 我 xiàwǔ 四 diǎn zhōng huí sùshè。	*dormitory* *return to the dormitory* *return to the dormitory at 4 o'clock* *return to the dormitory at 4 o'clock in the afternoon*
18. huí sùshè jiù huí sùshè 我 xiànzài jiù huí sùshè le。	*return to the dormitory* *return to the dormitory* *I'm going back to the dormitory now.*
19. huí sùshè cái huí sùshè 十一 diǎn bàn cái huí sùshè 她 wǎnshang 十一 diǎn bàn cái huí sùshè。	*return to the dormitory* *only then returned to the dormitory* *didn't return to the dormitory until 11:30* *She didn't return to the dormitory until 11:30 at night.*
20. túshūguǎn 是 túshūguǎn 這是 túshūguǎn。	*library* *is the library* *This is the library.*
21. 說話 可以說話 不可以說話。 這是 túshūguǎn，不可以說話。	*talk* *can talk* *can't talk*
22. hē jiǔ 可以 hē jiǔ cái 可以 hē jiǔ 美國人二十一 suì cái 可以 hē jiǔ。	*drink alcohol* *can drink alcohol* *only then can drink alcohol* *Americans can't drink alcohol until they are 21 years old.*

23.	
shū	*book*
kàn shū	*read (books)*
我 hěn xǐhuan kàn shū。	*I really like to read.*

24.	
péngyou	*friend(s)*
kàn péngyou	*see friends*
qù kàn péngyou	*go see friends*
jīntiān wǎnshang qù kàn péngyou	*go see friends tonight*
xiǎng jīntiān wǎnshang qù kàn péngyou	*want to go see friends tonight*
我 xiǎng jīntiān wǎnshang qù kàn péngyou。	_____
	_____

25.	
分	*minute*
十分	*10 minutes*
十一 diǎn 十分	*11:10*
Xiànzài 十一 diǎn 十分。	_____

26.	
shuì jiào	*go to sleep*
幾 diǎn zhōng shuì jiào？	*go to sleep at what time?*
wǎnshang 幾 diǎn zhōng shuì jiào？	*go to sleep what time at night?*
你 wǎnshang 幾 diǎn zhōng shuì jiào？	_____

27.	
五分	*5 minutes*
líng 五分	*05 minutes*
十二 diǎn líng 五分	*12:05*

28.	
shuì jiào	*go to sleep*
十二 diǎn líng 五分 shuì jiào	*go to sleep at 12:05*
我 十二 diǎn líng 五分 shuì jiào。	_____

29.	
wǎn	*late*
tài wǎn le	*too late*
十二 diǎn shuì jiào tài wǎn le。	_____

30. chuáng 起 chuáng 六 diǎn 一 kè 起 chuáng 她早 shang 六 diǎn 一 kè 起 chuáng。	*bed* *get out of bed* *get out of bed at 6:15* _____

31.
起 chuáng
jiù 起 chuáng
六 diǎn 一 kè jiù 起 chuáng
她早 shang 六 diǎn 一 kè jiù 起
  chuáng。
	get out of bed
	get out of bed
	get out of bed as early as 6:15
	She gets up as early as 6:15 in the
	  morning. (speaker thinks it is early)

32. xǐ zǎo 六 diǎn bàn xǐ zǎo 我早 shang 六 diǎn bàn xǐ zǎo。	*bathe* *bathe at 6:30* _____

33.
liànxí Hàn zì
fùxí gōngkè、liànxí Hàn zì
 	
七 diǎn zhōng fùxí gōngkè、liànxí
  Hàn zì
我 xiǎng 七 diǎn zhōng fùxí
  gōngkè、liànxí Hàn zì。
	practice Chinese characters
	review course work (and) practice
	  Chinese characters
	at 7 o'clock review course work (and)
	  practice Chinese characters
	_____
	_____

34. shì 有 shì 有 shì 嗎？ jīntiān wǎnshang 有 shì 嗎？ 你 jīntiān wǎnshang 有 shì 嗎？	*matter* *have something to do* *have something to do?* *have something to do tonight?* _____
35. 有 shì méi 有 shì jīntiān wǎnshang méi 有 shì 我 jīntiān wǎnshang méi 有 shì。	*have something to do* *not have anything to do* *tonight not have anything to do*
36. 小張：對不起。 小謝：Méi shì。	*Xiao Zhang: Excuse me.* *Xiao Xie: No problem.*

Focus on pronunciation

Sentence stress

Every sentence in Mandarin has at least one syllable that receives greater stress than the other syllables. We call this kind of stress <u>sentence stress</u>. The syllable that receives sentence stress is recited louder or longer than the other syllables in the sentence. The stressed syllable is always a syllable that has a full tone. Syllables that occur in neutral tone are never stressed. Sometimes the location of sentence stress is predictable. In this lesson we focus on sentence stress in several predictable contexts.

Stress in subject + verb + object sentences

In simple subject + verb + object sentences, the sentence stress falls on the object of the verb. If the object contains more than one syllable, stress occurs on the last syllable that has a full tone. If the last syllable of the object is spoken in neutral tone, sentence stress occurs on the next to the last syllable. In these sentences from the dialogue, the syllable that receives stress and the verbs are underlined.

我 zài <u>fùxí</u> 法<u>文</u>。   *I am reviewing French.*
我 děi <u>huí sùshè</u> le。   *I have to return to the dormitory.*
我明 tiān 早 shang <u>kǎo shì</u>。   *Tomorrow morning I'll take a test.*

In the following sentence, the last syllable of the object is spoken in neutral tone, so stress occurs on the next to last syllable.

她<u>是</u>你的 <u>mèi</u>mei 嗎？   *Is she your younger sister?*

Stress and the recitation of calendar time

When reciting the date and month, the stress is on the last syllable of the last number in the phrase. If the phrase includes the day of the week, the stress is on the number of the day of the week.

Jīntiān <u>yī</u> hào。
Today is the first day of the month.

Xiànzài <u>sān</u>yuè。
It is March.

Jīntiān sìyuè <u>yī</u> hào。
Today is April 1st.

Jīntiān shí<u>yī</u> hào。
Today is the 11th.

Jīntiān shì xīngqī<u>yī</u>。
Today is Monday.

Stress and the recitation of clock time

When reciting clock time, the stress is on **diǎn** *o'clock*, 分 *minute*, or **zhōng** *(o')clock*, whichever is the last word in the time phrase.

> **Xiànzài sān <u>diǎn</u>**。
> *It's now 3 o'clock.*

> **Xiànzài sān diǎn wǔ** 分。
> *It's now 3:05.*

> **Xiànzài sān diǎn <u>zhōng</u>**。
> *It's now 3 o'clock.*

If the time phrase includes **bàn** *half past*, 一 **kè** *a quarter past*, or 三 **kè** *three quarters past*, the stress is on **bàn** or **kè**.

> 兩 **diǎn <u>bàn</u>**   *2:30*
> 三 **diǎn** 一 **<u>kè</u>**   *3:15*
> 五 **diǎn** 三 **<u>kè</u>**   *5:45*

Chinese characters

Be a character sleuth!

Take a close look at the new characters in this lesson. They include characters with recurring parts that we have already learned, and characters with recurring parts that we will see many times in the lessons ahead.

What part of the character 明 have we seen in an earlier lesson? What other new character in this lesson has this same recurring part? The recurring part is 日, and it serves as the radical in the characters 明 and 早. Many radicals convey a general meaning that is shared by characters for which it is the radical. The radical 日 is the "sun" radical, and characters for which it is the radical often have something to do with the sun or with some part of the day. The character 明 when used alone means *bright*. 明 is part of the word 明 **tiān** *tomorrow*. The character 早 means *early* and it is part of the word 早 **shang** *morning*.

The radical 言 serves as the radical for many characters. It is called the "language" radical. Which characters introduced in this lesson include the radical 言? What do these characters mean, and what do they have to do with "language"?

Lesson 9 Characters step-by-step

對 (**duì**) *correct* has a horizontal orientation and is written from left to right.

The left side is written first in eleven strokes, from top to bottom. The first two strokes are the *vertical strokes* at the top center of the character. The first stroke is shorter than the second.

The next two strokes are a *dot* to the left and a *left falling stroke* to the right of the vertical strokes.

The top part of the character is "closed" with a *horizontal stroke* written below it. Like all horizontal strokes, it is written from left to right.

The next two strokes are a *dot* on the left and a *left falling stroke* on the right.

Below them are two *horizontal strokes* of about equal length, and a *vertical stroke* that begins just below the top horizontal stroke. Notice that the vertical stroke can touch the top horizontal stroke but it does not go through it.

The last stroke on the left side of 對 is a *horizontal stroke*. It is the closing stroke in this part of the character and is written below the end of the vertical stroke. It may touch the vertical stroke but it does not go through it.

The right half of 對, 寸, is the radical in this character. It is written in three strokes. The first stroke is a *horizontal stroke*. The second stroke is a *vertical stroke* that ends in a *left upward hook*. The last stroke is a *dot*.

寸 serves as the radical in many characters and we will see it again.

分 (**fēn**) has a vertical orientation. The top is written first: a *left falling stroke* and then a *right falling stroke*.

The bottom half of 分 is the radical. The *right corner stroke* ending in a *hook* is written first. The *left falling stroke* is written second.

話 (**huà**) *speech* has a horizontal orientation and consists of two parts. The left side of 話 is the radical 言 . It is used in many characters that refer to language, and it is often called the "language" radical. It consists of seven strokes. The first stroke is a *dot* written from left to right with a slightly outward curve. The second stroke is a *horizontal stroke*.

The next two strokes are *horizontal strokes*. They are of equal length and are shorter than the first horizontal stroke.

The next three strokes form a box. Review the discussion of the character 嗎 in lesson 7 for directions on how to write a box.

The right side of 話 is also a character in the word for *tongue*. It is written in six strokes. The first stroke is a *left falling stroke*. It is written from right to left. The second stroke is a *horizontal stroke* written from left to right.

The third stroke is a *vertical stroke*. It may touch the top stroke, but it does not go through it.

The last three strokes form a box.

The character 見 (**jiàn**), part of the phrase 再見 *goodbye, see you again*, is also a radical. It has a vertical orientation and is written from top to bottom in seven strokes. The first stroke is a *vertical stroke* written from top to bottom. The second stroke is a *right corner stroke*. Together they form an open box.

The next three strokes are *horizontal strokes*. The first two horizontal strokes are written inside of the box. They may touch the sides of the box but they do not go through them. The last horizontal stroke is the closing stroke of the box.

The last two strokes are a *left falling stroke* and a *vertical-curved stroke* that ends with an *upward hook*.

可 (**kě**) has a vertical orientation and is written in five strokes. The first stroke is a *horizontal stroke* written at the top. The next three strokes form a box, the radical in this character.

The last stroke is a *vertical stroke*. It ends with a *left-facing hook*.

明 明 (**míng**) has a horizontal orientation and is written in eight strokes. The radical 日 is on the left and it is written first, in four strokes. The first stroke is a *vertical stroke* written from top to bottom. The second stroke is a *right corner stroke*. The third stroke is a *horizontal stroke* written inside of the enclosure formed by the previous strokes. The horizontal stroke may touch the lines of the enclosure, but it does not go through. The fourth stroke is the closing stroke, a *horizontal stroke* written from left to right that closes the enclosure and makes it a box.

The right side of 明 is also written in four strokes. The first stroke is a *left falling stroke*. The second stroke is a *right corner stroke* with a *left-facing hook*. The last two strokes are *horizontal strokes* written inside the enclosure formed by the first two strokes. They may touch the strokes that form the enclosure, but they do not go through.

起 起 (**qǐ**), part of the word 对不起 *excuse me*, and the phrase 起 **chuáng** *get out of bed*, has a horizontal orientation and has two parts. The part on the left is the radical 走 and it is written first.

走 has a vertical orientation and is written from top to bottom. The first stroke is a short *horizontal stroke*. The second stroke is a *vertical stroke* that goes through the horizontal stroke. The third stroke is a longer *horizontal stroke*. It can touch the vertical stroke but it does not go through it.

The bottom part of 走 is written in four strokes. The first stroke is a *vertical stroke*. The second stroke is a *horizontal stroke* that begins on the right side of the vertical stroke. It does not go through the vertical stroke.

The third stroke is a *left falling stroke*.

The last stroke is a *right falling stroke*. It begins just below the top of the left falling stroke and it touches the bottom of the vertical stroke. Notice that it extends far enough to the right so that the remainder of the character 起 can be written on top of it.

The right side of 起 is written in three strokes. The first stroke is a *right corner stroke*. The second stroke is a *horizontal stroke* written from left to right.

起 | 起

The last stroke is a *vertical-curved stroke* that ends with an *upward hook*.

起

說 (**shuō**) *say, speak,* has a horizontal orientation and is written from left to right. The left side of 說 is the language radical 言. It is the same radical used in the character 話 (**huà**) and is written in the same way.

The right side of 說 consists of seven strokes. It is written from top to bottom, and from left to right. The first stroke is a *dot* written from left to right. The second stroke is a *left falling stroke* written from right to left.

言 | 言

The next three strokes form a box.

訁 | 訁 | 訁

The last two strokes are a *left falling stroke* followed by a *vertical-curved stroke* with an *upward hook*. They are the same strokes as the last two strokes in the character 見.

說 | 說

文 (**wén**) is a radical and is written in four strokes. The first stroke is a *dot*. The second stroke is a *horizontal stroke* written from left to right.

The third stroke is a *left falling stroke*. The last stroke is a *right falling stroke*.

小 (**xiǎo**) *small, little* is a radical. It is a symmetrical character in which the center is written first. The first stroke is a *vertical stroke* with a *left upward hook*.

The second stroke is a *left falling dot*. The third stroke is a *right falling dot*.

謝 (**xiè**) *thank (also, a family name)*, is written with seventeen strokes. Seventeen strokes may seem like a lot, but if you look carefully at 謝 you will see that it consists of three pieces, and we have already learned how to write two of them. The first piece is the language radical 言 . It is the same radical used in the characters 說 (**shuō**) and 話 (**huà**), and is written in the same way.

The next piece is written in seven strokes. It is written from top to bottom and from left to right. The first stroke is the *left falling stroke* at the top.

言′

The second and third strokes form an open box: a *vertical stroke* followed by a *right corner stroke*. Notice that in this character, the right hand corner stroke extends below the vertical stroke and ends in a *left-facing hook*, and that is longer than the language radical.

訂 訂

The fourth and fifth strokes fill in the box. They are *horizontal strokes* written from left to right. They do not go through the sides of the box.

訽 | 訽

The six stroke closes the box. It is a *horizontal stroke* written from left to right.

訽

The seventh stroke is a *left falling stroke* written from right to left. Notice that it begins at the bottom right hand corner of the box.

訽

The last piece of 謝 is 寸. It is the right half of the character 對 (**duì**) and we learned how to write it earlier.

訽 | 謝 | 謝

以 (**yǐ**) is the second character in the word 可以 (**kěyǐ**) *can*. It is written from left to right in five strokes. The first stroke is a *vertical stroke*. The second stroke is an *upward stroke*. It begins at the bottom of the vertical stroke. These two pieces are sometimes considered a single stroke.

丨 | 丄

The third stroke is a *dot*. It is written from left to right.

以

The fourth stroke is a *left falling stroke*. Notice that it begins a bit higher than the previous dot. The fifth stroke is a *long dot*, written from left to right, with a slight upward curve.

以 | 以

有 (**yǒu**) *have*, has a vertical orientation and it is written in six strokes. The first stroke is a *horizontal stroke* written from left to right. The second stroke is a *left falling stroke* that falls through the horizontal stroke.

一 | 有

The remaining four strokes form the radical of 有, 月.

	The first stroke of 月 is a *vertical stroke*. It begins around the mid-point of the previous stroke. The next stroke is a *right corner stroke* that ends in a *left-facing upward hook*. The last two strokes are *horizontal strokes*. They may touch the strokes on the sides but they do not go through them. 有 有
	再 (**zài**) *again*, has a vertical orientation and it is written in six strokes. The first stroke of 再 is the *horizontal stroke* on top. The next two strokes form the radical 冂: a *vertical stroke* and a *right corner stroke* that ends with a *left upward-facing hook*. ⼀ 冂 冂 The next stroke is a short *horizontal stroke* written inside of 冂. It is shorter than the horizontal stroke that begins the character. 冃 The next stroke is a *vertical stroke* that ends at around the midpoint of 冂. The last stroke is a long *horizontal stroke* written from left to right. It begins outside of the left side of 冂 and goes through it and out the right side. It is the longest horizontal stroke in the character. 再 再
	早 (**zǎo**) has a horizontal orientation and is written in six strokes. It consists of two parts. The top part, 日, is the radical. It is the same radical that occurs in the character 明. It is written as follows: 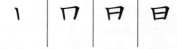 The last two strokes of 早 are writen like the number 十, a *horizontal stroke* followed by a *vertical stroke*. Notice that the vertical stroke can touch the bottom of 日 but it does not go through it.

張

張 (**zhāng**) (*classifier, family name*) is written from left to right and consists of two pieces. The left piece is the radical 弓. It is written in three strokes. The first stroke is a *right corner stroke*.

⁊

The second stroke is a *horizontal stroke* written from left to right.

⁊

The third stroke is written from top to bottom. It begins as a *vertical stroke*, turns into a *right corner stroke*, and ends with a *left-facing hook*.

弓

The right half of 張 is written in eight strokes from top to bottom. The first stroke is a *horizontal stroke*. It is followed by a *vertical stroke* that begins at the left side of the horizontal stroke. The next two strokes are *horizontal strokes* that begin to the right of the vertical stroke. They may touch the vertical stroke but they do not go through it.

弓ˉ ⎮ 弓⌐ ⎮ 弓F ⎮ 弓F

The next stroke is a longer *horizontal stroke*. It begins below and to the left of the vertical stroke and is written from left to right so that it extends beyond the horizontal strokes above.

弡

The next stroke is a *vertical stroke* that ends with a *right upward hook*. It is written below the horizontal stroke and begins slightly to the left of the vertical stroke above.

張

The last two strokes are a short *left falling stroke* written just under the bottom horizontal line, and a *right falling stroke* that falls under the left falling stroke. Notice that the left falling stroke is located at about the midpoint of the right falling stroke.

張 ⎮ 張

中 (**zhōng**) *middle* is a box with a vertical stroke through the center. Like all boxes, it is written in three strokes.

The *vertical stroke* is the radical and it is written last.

Language FAQs

Same pronunciation, different meanings

The syllable **zǎo** in the verb + object phrase **xǐ zǎo** *bathe* and the syllable **zǎo** (早) in the noun **zǎofàn** *breakfast* are <u>homophones</u>, syllables that are pronounced the same but have different meanings. The syllable **shì** in the phrases 有 **shì** *have something to do* and **kǎo shì** *take a test* are also homophones. They have the same pronunciation but different meanings. All languages have homophones. In English, the words <u>pear</u> *a type of fruit*, <u>pair</u> *two of something*, and <u>pare</u> *peel with a knife* are homophones. Notice that in English, although homophones have the same pronunciation, they may be spelled differently. In Mandarin, homophones always have the same Pinyin spelling, but since they have different meanings, they are written with different characters.

Word families and Chinese characters

In Mandarin, almost all syllables have a meaning, and when a syllable is part of a word or phrase, it usually brings its meaning with it. Words that share the same syllable/meaning are part of the same <u>word family</u>. Notice the word family that we now have involving the word 早 (**zǎo**) *early*.

zǎo ⟶	*early*	(Lesson 6)
↘	*good morning*	(Lesson 6)
zǎoshang	*morning*	(Lesson 9)
zǎofàn	*breakfast*	(Lesson 9)

All of the syllables that are part of the same word family are always written with the same character. Therefore, the syllable **zǎo** in **zǎo** *early, good morning*, **zǎoshang** *morning*, and **zǎofàn** *breakfast*, is written as 早: 早, 早 **shang**, 早 **fàn**. Not all words that have the same pronunciation are written with the same character. Usually, syllables have to have a common meaning as well as a shared pronunciation in order to be written with the same character. For example, the syllable **zǎo** in the verb + object phrase **xǐ zǎo** *bathe*, does not overlap in meaning with 早 *early*, and it is written with a different character. See also the previous Language FAQ on homophones and Chinese characters.

Syllables that are part of the same word family are written with the same character, but occasionally a single character may have more than one meaning, or more than one pronunciation. We will learn examples of these kinds of characters in later lessons.

What is the difference between shàngwǔ and 早 shang?

Shàngwǔ refers to any time in the morning before noon. It can be used to express *a.m.*:

> **jīntiān shàngwǔ** 十 **diǎn zhōng**   *this morning at 10 a.m.*

早 **shang** refers to the early part of the morning. It can be used when talking about times up until around 9 a.m.:

> 明 **tiān** 早 **shang** 六 **diǎn bàn**   *6:30 tomorrow morning*

The meanings of 說

The verb 說 includes the meanings of *say* and *speak* in English. In the phrase 說 話, and also when 說 is followed by the name of a language, 說 is translated as *speak*:

說話	*speak*
Lǎoshī zài 說話。	*The teacher is speaking.*
說中文，說 **Yīng**文	*speak Chinese, speak English*
我 **huì** 說中文。	*I can speak Chinese.*

In the expression 再說 (一 **cì**), or when asking what someone is saying, or when introducing what someone is saying, 說 is translated as *say*:

> **Qǐng** 你再說 (一 **cì**)。
> *Please say it again.*

▶

她說甚麼？
What is she saying? (What did she say?)

她說這是 **túshūguǎn**，你不可以說話。
She said this is the library. You are not allowed to talk.

Kǎoshì *a test* and kǎo shì *to take a test*

In Mandarin, words or phrases can function as members of different grammatical categories. For example, **kǎoshì** functions as a noun (*test*) when it is used in phrases such as 一個 **kǎoshì** *one test* and 我有 **kǎoshì** *I have a test*. It functions as a verb + object phrase (*take a test*) in sentences such as: 我們明 **tiān** 早 **shang** 八 **diǎn kǎo shì**。 *We will take a test tomorrow at 8 a.m.* In this book, we leave a space between the verb and its object when we write words in Pinyin so that you will remember to replace the object with a more specific object when appropriate.

Notes on Chinese culture

The rhythm of the Chinese day

Cultures differ in the time of day that people tend to do certain actions. For example, people from France, Spain, and Italy like to eat dinner relatively late in the evening while Chinese and Americans prefer to eat dinner much earlier, usually between 5 and 7 p.m. The preferred time of day for bathing differs from culture to culture as well. In this lesson we see that Xiao Zhang is typical of many Americans in preferring to bathe in the morning. Xiao Xie, his Chinese roommate, expresses the Chinese preference for bathing at night.

Lesson 9 Dialogue in English

Part A

Xiao Xie: Xiao Zhang, what are you doing?

Xiao Zhang: I'm studying Chinese. I have a Chinese test tomorrow morning.

Xiao Xie: You have a test tomorrow morning, how come you are only now getting around to reviewing?

Xiao Zhang: I had a computer test at noon today, and I had classes this afternoon. I didn't get out of class until 5 o'clock. What time is it now?

Xiao Xie: It's 10 o'clock now.

Part B

Xiao Zhang: 10 o'clock! That's too late! I have to go back to the dorm right now.

Xiao Xie: Why are you going back to the dorm? Do you have something you have to do?

Xiao Zhang: I was planning to go to sleep tonight at 10:30.

Xiao Xie: Going to sleep at 10:30, that's too early!

Xiao Zhang: I have the test tomorrow morning at 8 a.m. I have to get up at 6, take a shower at 6:15, eat breakfast at 6:30, review the lesson and practice Chinese characters at 7, and get on my way to class at 7:40.

Xiao Xie: You can take a shower tonight and get up a little later tomorrow.

Xiao Zhang: I don't like to bathe at night. I'm going back to the dorm now.

Part C

(librarian):   This is the library. You can only read and study. You can't talk.

Xiao Zhang: Sorry. Xiao Xie, see you tomorrow.

Xiao Xie: Okay, okay, see you later.

Lesson 10 你 juéde zuótiān 的 kǎoshì 怎麼 yàng? *What did you think of yesterday's test?*

Communication goals
- Express your opinion and ask others for their opinions
- Talk about how actions are performed
- Talk about things you have done and things you have not yet done

Key structures
AdjV 的 NP

V **de** AdjV

VP 了, V 了 O, **yǐjing** VP 了, **gāng** V

hái, 沒 VP, **hái** 沒 VP

situation₁ 可是 situation₂

gēn NP 一起

kuài time 了

Dialogue

The Situation: It is early Friday afternoon. Xiao Zhang and Xiao Gao see each other in the hallway of a classroom building and begin a conversation.

Part A

小 Gāo: 你 **juéde** zuótiān 的中文 **kǎoshì** 怎麼 yàng?

小張: 我 juéde 很 nán。

小 Gāo: 我也 juéde 很 nán。**Shàng** 個 **xīngqī** 的 kǎoshì 很 **róngyì**,**可是** zuótiān 的 kǎoshì fēicháng **nán**。

小張: 你 **kǎo de** 怎麼 yàng?

小 Gāo: 我 **xiě de** 很 **màn**。**Hái** 有,我 **wàng** 了幾個 zì。當然 kǎo de 不好。 你 **kǎo de** 怎麼 yàng?

小張: 我 kǎo de 也不好。我 zuótiān 晚 shang shuì de tài 少。我 xiě de kuài, **可是有的 yǔfǎ** 我不 dǒng,**有的 zì** 我不會 xiě。

Part B

小張: **Xiànzài kuài** 一 diǎn **了**。你吃 **wǔ** 飯了沒有?

小 Gāo: **Yǐjing** 吃了。你呢?

小張: 我 **gāng** xià kè,**hái** 沒吃呢。我 gēn 小 Yè yào **去**那個 **xīn** 的 **kāfēiguǎn** 吃飯。你 **yào** 不 **yào gēn** 我們一起去?

小 Gāo: 好,你們去吃飯,我可以去 **hē** 一 **bēi chá**。

Vocabulary

bēi		classifier	*cup*
chá [bēi]		noun	*tea*
de		particle	*(indicates verb description)*
dǒng		verb	*understand*
duō		adjectival verb	*many, a lot*
fēicháng		intensifier	*extremely*
gāng		adverb	*just now*
gēn		preposition; conjunction	*with; and*
gēn NP 一 qǐ	**gēn NP 一起**	prepositional phrase	*together with NP*
hái yǒu	**hái 有**	adverb	*in addition, furthermore*
jǐ	**幾**	quantifier	*several*
juéde		verb	*think, hold an opinion*
kāfēi [bēi]		noun	*coffee*
kāfēiguǎn		noun	*coffee shop*
kěshì	**可是**	conjunction	*but*
kuài		adjectival verb	*fast, soon*
le	**了**	particle, verb suffix	*(completed action)*
màn		adjectival verb	*slow*

nán		adjectival verb	*difficult*
róngyì		adjectival verb	*easy*
shǎo	少	adjectival verb	*few, little in number*
wàng		verb	*forget*
wǔfàn	wǔ 飯	noun	*lunch*
xiě		verb	*write*
xīn		adjectival verb	*new*
yǐjing		adverb	*already*
yǒu de	有的	noun description phrase	*some*
yǔfǎ		noun	*grammar*
zuótiān		noun	*yesterday*

Time words: yesterday, today, tomorrow

zuótiān *yesterday*   **jīntiān** *today*   明 **tiān** *tomorrow*

Characters

吃	chī	eat	吃飯 (**chī fàn**) *eat*
當	dāng	*	當然 (**dāngrán**) *of course*
都	dōu	all, both	
多	duō	many, more	多少 (**duōshao**) *how much, how many*
飯	fàn	rice	吃飯 (**chī fàn**) *eat*
會	huì	can, able to	
老	lǎo	old	老師 (**lǎoshī**) *teacher*
了	le	*(sentence final particle: new information, change, completion)*	
沒	méi	negation	
去	qù	go	
然	rán	*	當然 (**dāngrán**) *of course*
少	shǎo	few, less	多少 (**duōshao**) *how much, how many*
生	shēng	*	學生 (**xuésheng**) *student*
師	shī	*	老師 (**lǎoshī**) *teacher*
晚	wǎn	late	晚 **shang** (**wǎnshang**) *evening*
			晚飯 (**wǎnfàn**) *dinner*
學	xué	study	學生 (**xuésheng**) *student*
怎	zěn	*	怎麼 (**zěnme**) *how*
			怎麼 **yàng** (**zěnmeyàng**) *what about it?*

Stroke Order Flow Chart

character:	strokes:													total strokes:
吃	丶	冂	口	叮	吖	吃								6
當	丨	丩	丷	少	屮	尚	尚	尚	當	常	常	當	當	13
都	一	十	土	耂	耂	者	者	者	者	都	都			11
多	丿	夕	夕	多	多	多								6
飯	丿	𠂊	𠂤	𠂤	𠂤	𠂤	食	食	飤	飰	飯	飯		12
會	丿	人	𠆢	𠆢	今	侖	侖	侖	侖	曾	曾	曾	會	13
老	一	十	土	耂	耂	老								6
了	𠃌	了												2
沒	丶	丷	氵	氿	汋	汐	沒							7
去	一	十	土	去	去									5
然	丿	夕	夕	夕	夕	外	狀	狀	狀	然	然	然		12
少	丨	小	小	少										4
生	丿	𠂉	仁	牛	生									5
師	丿	亻	𠂤	𠂤	自	自	師	師	師	師				10
晚	丨	冂	日	日	日'	日'	晧	晧	晚	晚	晚			11
學	丶	𡭔	彡	𡭴	𡭴	臼	臼	𦥑	𦥑	𦥑	𦥑	與	與	
	學	學												16
怎	丿	𠂉	仁	乍	乍	作	怎	怎	怎					9

Dialogue practice

Do these activities in class after mastering the dialogue for this lesson. Change partners so that you practice each part several times.

Dialogue 10A: Pair up with a classmate and ask him what he thought about last night's homework or a recent test. Add your opinion after he tells you his.

Dialogue 10B: *Part 1.* Make a list of everyday activities in your life such as eating breakfast, lunch, or dinner, preparing for class, going to Chinese class, etc., and pair up with a classmate to ask each other whether you have already done these activities today. Report on your findings to the class.

Part 2. For an activity that your classmate has not yet done, make a suggestion to go some place to do it. For example, if your classmate has not prepared for class, tell her to go to the library to prepare.

Use and structure

10.1. Juéde *in (my) opinion, feel, think*

The verb **juéde** is used to express opinions and to ask others for their opinions.

你 **juéde zuótiān** 的 **kǎoshì** 怎麼 **yàng**?
What did you think about yesterday's test?

我 **juéde** 很 **nán**。
I thought it was very difficult.

Juéde is not preceded by negation. In English, you can say that you <u>don't think</u> that yesterday's test was difficult, but in Mandarin you say:

我 **juéde zuótiān** 的 **kǎoshì** 不 **nán**。
I think that yesterday's test was not difficult.

In English you can say that you <u>don't think</u> that cell phones are expensive, but in Mandarin you say:

我 **juéde shǒujī** 不 **guì**。
I think that cell phones are not expensive.

10.2. Adjectival verbs as main verbs

Adjectival verbs like **nán** *difficult*, **róngyì** *easy*, **guì** *expensive*, **piányi** *cheap*, 多 *many, a lot*, and 少 *few, little in number*, may serve as the main verb in the Mandarin sentence. When they do, the order of information in the sentence is <u>S + V</u>. Remember that since **nán** *difficult*, **róngyì** *easy*, **guì** *expensive*, **piányi** *cheap*, 多 *many, a lot*, and 少 *few, little in number* are adjectival <u>verbs</u>, these sentences do not include the verb 是.

S + V
Shàng 個 **xīngqī** 的 **kǎoshì** 很 <u>**róngyì**</u>。
Last week's test was very easy.

Zuótiān 的 **kǎoshì** fēicháng <u>**nán**</u>。
Yesterday's test was really hard.

那 **běn shū** 很 <u>**guì**</u>。
That book is very expensive.

Qiānbǐ 很 <u>**piányi**</u>。
Pencils are very cheap.

Notice that when the adjectival verb is 多 *many, a lot*, or 少 *few*, English and Mandarin presents the information in the sentence in very different ways.

S + V
人很<u>多</u>。
There are a lot of people.

學中文的人很多。
There are a lot of people studying Chinese.

人很<u>少</u>。
There are few people.

Adjectival verbs and comparisons

When adjectival verbs occur as the predicate of the sentence, they can sometimes be used to make comparisons. For example, if I ask you which is more difficult, French or German, you could answer:

Dé 文 **nán**。 *German is harder.*

If I ask you which is cheaper, pencils or pens, you could answer:

Qiānbǐ piányi。 *Pencils are cheaper.*

When used to indicate a comparison, adjectival verbs are not preceded by 很 or another intensifier.

10.3. *Last (week), last (month):* **Shàng** 個 **(xīngqī), shàng** 個 **(yuè)**

In Lesson 8 we learned how to say *next week* and *next month* with the expressions **xià** 個 **xīngqī** and **xià** 個 **yuè**. To say *last week* and *last month* use the expressions **shàng** 個 **xīngqī** and **shàng** 個 **yuè**:

> **Shàng** 個 **xīngqī** 的 **kǎoshì róngyì**，可是 **zuótiān** 的 **kǎoshì fēicháng nán**。
> *Last week's test was easy, but yesterday's test was extremely hard.*

We learned in Lesson 9 that **shàng** also means *attend* or *go up*. **Shàng** 個 **xīngqī** and **shàng** 個 **yuè** refer to the week or month <u>above</u> this one. **Xià** 個 **xīngqī** and **xià** 個 **yuè** refer to the week or month <u>below</u> this one.

10.4. 可是 *but*

可是 *but* joins sentences or verb phrases and indicates some kind of contrast between them. 可是 occurs before an entire sentence or before a verb phrase.

> **Shàng** 個 **xīngqī** 的 **kǎoshì** 很 **róngyì**，可是 **zuótiān** 的 **kǎoshì fēicháng nán**。
> *Last week's test was very easy, but yesterday's test was extremely hard.*

> 我 **xiě de kuài**，可是有的 **zì** 我不會 **xiě**。
> *I wrote quickly, but I could not write some of the characters.*

10.5. Talking about how actions are performed: **Xiě de** 很 **màn**，**kǎo de** 不好

Describing how an action is performed

To describe how an action is performed, use the following structure:

> **ActV de AdjV**
> **xiě de** (很) **màn**
> *write slowly*

or

> **ActV de** 不 **AdjV**
> **xiě de** 不好
> *didn't write well* (literally: *wrote not well*)

Notice that negation occurs before the adjectival verb and not before the action verb. The negation of <u>ActV **de** AdjV</u> is <u>ActV **de** 不 AdjV</u>:

Say This:	*Say This:*	*Do not say this:*
我 **kǎo de** 很好。	我 **kǎo de** 不好。	⊗ 我不 **kǎo de** 好。
I did well on the test.	*I did poorly on the test.*	
(I "examed" well.)	(I "examed" poorly.)	

Additional examples:

我 **xiě de** 很 **màn**。
I wrote very slowly.

我 **zuótiān** 晚 **shang shuì de tài** 少。
Last night I slept too little.

我 **kǎo de** 不好。
I did poorly on the exam. (I "examed" poorly.)

Asking how an action is performed

To ask how an action is performed, say:

(S) V de 怎麼 **yàng**?
你 **kǎo de** 怎麼 **yàng**?
How did you do on the test? (How did you test?)

To ask whether an action was performed in a specific way, say:

(S) V de AdjV 不 **AdjV**?
你 **kǎo de** 好不好?
Did you do well on the test?

你吃 **de** 多不多?
Did you eat a lot?

Note: Completed action 了 (Use and Structure note 10.7) is not used when describing how an action is performed, even if the action is completed.

Say this:	*Do not say this:*
我 **xiě de** 很 **màn**。	⊗ 我 **xiě** 了 **de** 很 **màn**。
I wrote (I write) slowly.	

10.6.   Hái 有 *in addition*

To introduce additional information, start your sentence with **hái** 有 *in addition*.

Hái 有，我 **wàng** 了幾個 **zì**。
In addition, I forgot several characters.

10.7.   Completed action: ActV + 了

Mandarin does not have grammatical structures that indicate past, present, and future tense the way that English and many European languages do. In Mandarin, the distinction that is signaled in the grammar is that an action is <u>complete</u>. Completion is signaled with the particle 了 (**le**), either <u>after the action verb</u>, or <u>after the action verb + object</u>. In this lesson we learn some general rules about the location of 了 in the verb + object phrase. We will continue to learn more about the use of 了 to indicate completed action in later lessons.

了 follows the action verb (V 了 O)

- when the object of the action verb includes a number:

    V 了 [number + classifier + O]

    我 **hē** 了一 **bēi kāfēi**。

    I drank a cup of coffee.

- when the object of an action verb refers to something specific such as <u>this</u> object or <u>that</u> object:

    V 了 [這/那 + classifier + O]

    我 **mǎi** 了那 **běn shū**。

    I bought that book.

- when the object includes a description:

    V 了 [description 的 O]

    我 **mǎi** 了 **Wáng** 老師的 **shū**。

    I bought Professor Wang's book.

- when the verb refers to an action that is completed as soon as it is performed:

    V 了 O

    我 **wàng** 了幾個 **zì**。

    I forgot several characters.

了 follows verb + object (V O 了)

- when the phrase describes a general event such as eating, bathing, reading, studying, etc.

    我 **zuótiān kàn shū** 了。

    I read yesterday.

- when the object has no meaning outside of the phrase (e.g. **xǐ zǎo** *bathe* and **shuì jiào** *sleep*):

    我 **zuótiān** 晚 **shang xǐ zǎo** 了。

    I bathed last night.

    他 **zuótiān** 晚 **shang** 十一 **diǎn zhōng shuì jiào** 了。

    Last night he went to sleep at 11 o'clock.

- when the object of the verb stands for some category of things rather than for something specific or definite:

    我六 **diǎn zhōng** 吃飯了。

    I ate at 6 o'clock.

Some nouns can be interpreted as either specific or general depending upon the context of the sentence or on the speaker. As a result, the same verb + object sequence may include 了 after the verb or after the object.

我 jīntiān 早 shang yǐjing hē 了 kāfēi。
我 jīntiān 早 shang yǐjing hē kāfēi 了。
I have already drunk coffee this morning.

Variations like these characterize the placement and use of 了 to indicate completion. The use of 了 in a sentence to signal a completed action is not obligatory, and the position of 了 after the verb or after the object of the verb is subject to the context of the sentence and speaker perception of the event.

Two fixed rules about the use of 了

- 了 only indicates a completed action when it follows an <u>action</u> verb. If the verb in the sentence is not an action verb, for example, if it is an adjectival verb like **róngyì** *easy*, or a stative verb like **xǐhuan** *like*, or a modal verb like 會 *can*, then 了 cannot be understood as indicating completed action. Instead it must be understood as indicating <u>new information</u> (Use and Structure note 9.6). To indicate that some <u>non-action</u> was true in the past (for example, a test <u>was</u> easy, you <u>used to</u> like German food, or you <u>couldn't</u> talk in the library), you can add a time word to indicate the time (See Lesson 10 Language FAQs).
- Completed action 了 can only be used if an action has occurred. 了 cannot be used when talking about actions that did not occur. For example, you do not use 了 when saying that you <u>have not eaten</u> lunch today.

To ask whether an action has happened see note 10.11. To say that an action did not happen or has not happened yet, see note 10.14.

10.8. 幾 *several, a few*

In Lesson 5 we learned the question word 幾 *how much, how many*.

你 jiā 有幾個人?
How many people are there in your family?

幾 may also mean *several, a few*.

我 wàng 了幾個 zì。
I forgot several characters.

The context will make it clear whether 幾 should be translated as *how many* or as *several*. 幾 usually has the question meaning (*how much, how many*) when it occurs in questions:

你 jiā 有幾個人?

幾 usually has the meaning *several, a few* when it occurs in statements:

我 **hái qǐng** 了幾個 **péngyou**。
I've also invited several friends.

10.9.   有的 *NP: some NP*

To indicate *some* or *some of the*, say:

有的 **NP**
有的 **yǔfǎ** *some of the grammar*
有的 **zì** *some of the characters*

有的 NP always occurs before the verb of the sentence. When the noun phrase is the subject of the sentence, 有的 NP occurs in the normal subject position, since the subject normally occurs before the verb:

有的學生學中文，有的學生學 **Rì** 文。
Some students study Chinese, some students study Japanese.

When 有的 NP is the object of the verb, 有的 NP occurs at the beginning of the sentence, before the verb, and often before the subject and time phrase if there is one.

有的 **yǔfǎ** 我 **bù dǒng**，有的 **zì** 我不會 **xiě**。
I didn't understand some of the grammar, I couldn't write some of the characters.

有的 NP implies a comparison with other nouns or noun phrases. For example, when Xiao Gao says 有的 **yǔfǎ** 我 **bù dǒng** she implies that there was some grammar that she <u>did</u> understand.

When the object occurs before the verb we say that the object is <u>topicalized</u>.

10.10.   **Kuài** (time) 了 *it will soon be (time)*

<u>**Kuài** (time) 了</u> indicates that it will *soon* be that time. <u>**Kuài** (time) 了</u> can be translated into English as *almost*.

Xiànzài kuài 一 **diǎn** 了。
It is almost 1 o'clock.

10.11.   Asking whether an action has happened: 你吃 **wǔ** 飯了沒有? *Have you eaten lunch?*

To ask whether an action has happened, ask a yes-no question. The yes-no question can be a 嗎 question:

V 了 (**O**) 嗎?
你吃 **wǔ** 飯了嗎?
Have you eaten lunch?

Or, the yes-no question can take the following verb-not-verb form:

V 了 **(O)** 沒有?
你吃 **wǔ** 飯了沒有?
Have you eaten lunch?

To answer a question about whether an action has happened with a simple *yes*, say **V** 了.

Q: 你吃 **wǔ** 飯了嗎?　　　or　　　Q: 你吃 **wǔ** 飯了沒有?
Have you eaten lunch?

A: 吃了。
Yes. (I have eaten it.)

To answer a question about whether an action has happened with a simple *no*, say 沒有.

Q: 你吃 **wǔ** 飯了嗎?　　　or　　　Q: 你吃 **wǔ** 飯了沒有?
Have you eaten lunch?

A: 沒有。
No. (I have not.)

To answer a question about whether or not something has happened with a *not yet*, say **hái** 沒有.

Q: 你吃 **wǔ** 飯了嗎?　　　or　　　Q: 你吃 **wǔ** 飯了沒有?
Have you eaten lunch?

A: **Hái** 沒有。
Not yet.

See Use and Structure note 10.14 for more about saying that a situation has not happened or has not happened yet.

10.12. **Yǐjing** V 了 *the situation has already happened*

The adverb **yǐjing** *already* may occur before the verb phrase to emphasize that an action has already been completed or that some situation has already come about.

(S) yǐjing V (O) 了
我 **yǐjing** 吃 (**wǔ** 飯) 了。
I've already eaten dinner.

When the verb phrase consists of 是 + age or 是 + time, 是 is usually omitted, and **yǐjing** occurs right before the age or time (Use and Structure note 8.7).

我 **yǐjing** (是) 二十 **suì** 了。
I'm already 20 years old.

Xiànzài yǐjing (是) 一 **diǎn** 了。
It's already 1 o'clock.

10.13.   Gāng ActV *the action has just happened*

To say that you have just done an action or that something has just happened, state the adverb **gāng** before the action verb and say:

gāng ActV (O)
我 **gāng xià kè**。
I have just gotten out of class.

Even though **gāng** refers to completed actions, sentences with **gāng** often do not include 了.

10.14.   Saying that an action has not happened or has not happened yet: 沒 ActV, **hái** 沒 ActV 呢

To say that an action did not happen or has not happened, say:

(S) 沒 + ActV (O)
我沒吃 **wǔ** 飯。
I didn't eat lunch.
I have not eaten lunch.

Do not use 了 when stating that an action did not or has not happened.

Say this: ***Do not say this:***
我沒吃 **wǔ** 飯。   ⊗ 我沒吃了 **wǔ** 飯。
I didn't eat lunch.

To say that an action has not happened yet, say:

(S) hái 沒 + ActV (呢)
我 **hái** 沒吃 **wǔ** 飯呢。
I have not eaten lunch yet.

10.15.   不 and 沒 compared

沒 has two functions. As we learned in Lesson 4, 沒 negates the verb 有 *have, exist* (Use and Structure note 4.9):

我沒有 **gēge**。   *I don't have an older brother.*

We learn in this lesson that 沒 is also the form of negation that is used when saying that some action did not occur in the past.

我沒吃 **wǔ** 飯。
I didn't eat lunch.

When used with action verbs, 沒 and 不 say different things about the action:

■ 沒 + ActV
indicates that an action did not occur.

- 不 + ActV

indicates that an action <u>is not happening now</u>, or <u>does not happen</u>.

Compare the meanings of the following sentences with 沒 and 不.

不 + ActV (+ O)	沒 + ActV (+ O)
我不吃 **wǔ** 飯。	我沒吃 **wǔ** 飯。
I don't eat lunch.	*I didn't eat lunch.*
我不 **hē kāfēi**。	我沒 **hē kāfēi**。
I don't drink coffee.	*I didn't drink coffee.*
我不 **kàn shū**。	我沒 **kàn shū**。
I don't read.	*I didn't read.*

Remember that when describing how actions are performed, negation is always 不.

我考 **de** 不好。
I didn't do well on the test.

(See Use and Structure note 10.5).

10.16.　去 location: Go to a location

In Lesson 8 we learned that <u>去</u> *go* + ActV means *go do an action*. In this lesson we learn that <u>去</u> *go* + location means *go to a location*.

我 **gēn** 小 **Yě yào** 去那個 **xīn** 的 **kāfēiguǎn** 吃飯。
I'm going to that new coffee shop with Xiao Ye.

10.17.　Describing nouns with adjectival verbs: AdjV 的 N

When an adjectival verb describes a noun, the adjectival verb, followed by the particle 的, occurs <u>before</u> the noun that is being described, the main noun:

AdjV 的 (main) N
<u>**xīn**</u>　的 **kāfēi guǎn**
new coffee shop

Recall that when nouns or pronouns are used to describe a noun, they also occur before the noun that is being described.

我的 **tóngwū**
my roommate

<u>小 **Wáng**</u> 的 **hàomǎ**
Xiao Wang's number

<u>一 **niánjí**</u> 的中文 **shū**
first-year Chinese book

When the description is an adjectival verb, there are some important variations in the pattern.

- Adjectival verbs usually do not occur alone, but are either preceded by an intensifier (*very, extremely*, etc.) or 不.

  fēicháng nán 的 **kǎoshì**   *an extremely difficult test*
  不 **guì** 的 **shǒujī**   *an inexpensive cell phone*

  When no special emphasis is intended, the intensifier 很 is used before the adjectival verb.

  很 **guì** 的 **shǒujī**   *an expensive cell phone*
  很 **piányi** 的 **běnzi**   *a cheap notebook*

- As is the case when nouns and pronouns describe nouns, 的 is sometimes omitted from the description phrase. Here are some general rules that explain the presence and absence of 的.

  的 is generally present if the adjectival verb is more than one syllable long, or if the adjectival verb is preceded by an intensifier.

  很 **piányi** 的 **shū**   *a very cheap book*
  很 **guì** 的 **shǒujī**   *an expensive cell phone*

  的 is often omitted if the adjectival verb + noun together form a commonly used expression. For example, the expression for *good child* typically does not include 的.

  好 **háizi**   *good child*

  Notice that this expression also does not include an intensifier. If an intensifier is used, 的 is usually present. However, if the adjectival verb is 多 *a lot/many*, 的 is omitted:

  很多 **zì**   *a lot of characters*

10.18. Describing nouns with more than one description phrase

We have already learned several types of phrases that can be used to describe a (main) noun:

[pron. 的] + (main) N: 他的 **diànnǎo**
(Use and Structure note 4.4)   *his computer*

[N 的] + (main) N: 老师的 **diànnǎo**
(Use and Structure note 5.8)   *the teacher's computer*

[number + classifier] + (main) N: 一個 **kāfēiguǎn**
(Use and Structure note 6.2)   *one coffee shop*

[specifier + classifier] + (main) N: 那個 **kāfēiguǎn**
(Use and Structure note 6.11)   *coffee shop*

[specifier + number + classifier] + (main) N: 那兩個 **kāfēiguǎn**
(Use and Structure note 7.6)   *those two coffee shops*

[AdjV 的] + (main) N:　　　　　　　　**xīn 的 kāfēiguǎn**
(Use and Structure note 10.17)　　　　*new coffee shop*

Notice that descriptions involving specifiers and/or numbers always end in a <u>classifier</u>. All other descriptions end in 的.

In this lesson we see that a noun can be described by more than one description at the same time. When describing a noun with more than one description, state the descriptions one at a time before the main noun. The main noun occurs once, following the descriptions:

[description₁]	[description₂]	...	(main) N
[那個]	[xīn 的]		kāfēiguǎn
that	*new*		*coffee shop*

Here are additional examples of nouns described by more than one description.

這三 **běn**	**xīn** 的	中文 **shū**	
these three	*new*	*Chinese books*	

那兩個	很 **guì** 的	**diànnǎo**	
those two	*very expensive*	*computers*	

那兩個	很 **guì** 的	**Rìběn** 的	**diànnǎo**
those two	*very expensive*	*Japanese*	*computers*

10.19.　Gēn NP (一起) *with NP*

Gēn *with* is a preposition. Like prepositions in English, **gēn** always occurs before a noun phrase:

gēn 小 **Yè**　*with Xiao Ye*

The preposition and its following noun phrase form a <u>prepositional phrase</u>.

In Mandarin, the prepositional phrase usually occurs before the <u>verb</u> that it is associated with:

我 **gēn** 小 **Yè yào** 去那個 **xīn** 的 **kāfēiguǎn**。
I am going to that new coffee shop with Xiao Ye.

Notice that in English, the prepositional phrase occurs <u>after</u> the verb phrase.

When saying that you are doing an activity together with someone else, you can add the expression 一起 after the noun phrase and say:

gēn NP 一起 VP
你 **yào** 不 **yào gēn** 我們一起去?
Would you like to go with us?

Gēn has a wider use than the phrase **gēn** NP 一起. It can be used to translate the English preposition *with* and is also equivalent in use to the conjunction **hé** *and*.

Sentence pyramids

The sentence pyramids illustrate the use of each new vocabulary item and structure introduced in the lesson. Use them to help you learn how to form phrases and sentences in Mandarin. Supply the English translation for the last line where indicated.

1.
怎麼 yàng?
kǎoshì 怎麼 yàng?
zuótiān 的 kǎoshì 怎麼 yàng?
你 juéde zuótiān 的 kǎoshì 怎麼 yàng?

how was it?
how was the test?
how was yesterday's test?
What did you think about yesterday's test?

2.
nán
很 nán
我 juéde 很 nán。

difficult
very difficult
I thought it was very difficult.

3.
róngyì
kǎoshì 很 róngyì
Shàng 個 xīngqī 的 kǎoshì 很 róngyì。

easy
the test is very easy
Last week's test was very easy.

4.
nán
fēicháng nán
zuótiān 的 kǎoshì fēicháng nán
Shàng 個 xīngqī 的 kǎoshì 很 róngyì,
  可是 zuótiān 的 kǎoshì fēicháng nán。

difficult
extremely difficult
yesterday's test was extremely difficult
Last week's test was easy, but yesterday's
  test was extremely difficult.

5.
màn
很 màn
xiě de 很 màn
我 xiě de 很 màn。

slow
very slow
write very slowly
I write very slowly.

6.
yǔfǎ
fùxí yǔfǎ
xiǎng fùxí yǔfǎ
jīntiān 晚 shang xiǎng fùxí yǔfǎ
我 jīntiān 晚 shang xiǎng fùxí yǔfǎ。

grammar
review grammar
plan to review grammar
plan to review grammar tonight
I plan to review grammar tonight.

7.	
nán	*difficult*
nán 不 **nán**？	*difficult?*
中文 **yǔfǎ nán** 不 **nán**？	*Is Chinese grammar difficult?*
你 **juéde** 中文 **yǔfǎ nán** 不 **nán**？	*Do you think that Chinese grammar is difficult?*

8.	
不 **nán**	*not difficult*
juéde 不 **nán**	*think it is not difficult*
我 **juéde** 中文 **yǔfǎ** 不 **nán**。	_____

9.	
怎麼 **yàng**？	*how about it?*
kǎo de 怎麼 **yàng**？	*how did (you) (do on the) test?*
你 **kǎo de** 怎麼 **yàng**？	*How did you do on the test?*

10.	
不好	*not well*
kǎo de 不好	*did poorly on the test (tested not well)*
當然 **kǎo de** 不好	*of course did poorly on the test*
我當然 **kǎo de** 不好。	_____

11.	
少	*few, little in number*
tài 少	*too few, too little*
shuì de tài 少	*slept too little*
我 **zuótiān** 晚 **shang shuì de tài** 少。	*I slept too little last night.*

12.	
幾個 **zì**	*several characters*
wàng 了幾個 **zì**	*forgot several characters*
我 **wàng** 了幾個 **zì**。	_____

13.	
xiě	*write*
會 **xiě**	*can write*
不會 **xiě**	*cannot write*
有的 **zì** 我不會 **xiě**。	*Some characters I could not write. (I could not write some of the characters.)*

14. 不會 xiě 有的 zì 我不會 xiě 可是有的 zì 我不會 xiě 我 xiě de kuài，可是有的 zì 我不會 xiě。	*unable to write* *I was unable to write some of the characters* *but I was unable to write some of the characters* *I wrote quickly, but I was unable to write some of the characters.*
15. 他的 míngzì wàng 了他的 míngzì 我 wàng 了他的 míngzì。	*his name* *forgot his name* *I forgot his name.*
16. 中文 dǒng 中文 dǒng 不 dǒng 中文？ 你 dǒng 不 dǒng 中文？	*Chinese* *understand Chinese* *understand Chinese?* *Do you understand Chinese?*
17. kuài tài kuài 說 de tài kuài 你說 de tài kuài。我不 dǒng。	*fast* *too fast* *speak too fast* *You speak too fast. I don't understand.*
18. rènshi 不 rènshi 有的 zì 我不 rènshi。	*know, recognize* *not recognize* *Some characters I don't recognize.* *(I don't know some of the characters.)*
19. tài màn xiě de tài màn 我 xiě de tài màn。 我 xiě de tài màn。Hái 有，有的 zì 我不 rènshi。	*too slow* *write too slowly* *I wrote too slowly.* *I wrote too slowly. Also, I didn't know some of the characters.*
20. kāfēi 一 bēi kāfēi hē 一 bēi kāfēi 我 xiǎng hē 一 bēi kāfēi。	*coffee* *one cup of coffee* *drink a cup of coffee*

21. **chá** 幾 **bēi chá** **hē** 了 幾 **bēi chá** 我 **jīntiān hē** 了 幾 **bēi chá**。	*tea* *several cups of tea* *drank several cups of tea* *I drank several cups of tea today.*
22. **wǔ** 飯 吃 **wǔ** 飯 吃 **wǔ** 飯 了 你 吃 **wǔ** 飯 了 嗎？	*lunch* *eat lunch* *ate lunch* *Have you eaten lunch?*
23. 沒有 吃 了 沒有？ 吃 了 **wǔ** 飯 沒有？ 你 吃 了 **wǔ** 飯 沒有？	*not* *ate or not?* *ate lunch or not?* *Have you eaten lunch?*
24. 吃 了 **yǐjing** 吃 了 我 **yǐjing** 吃 了。	*ate* *already ate* _____
25. **shuì jiào** **yǐjing shuì jiào** 了 我 的 **tóngwū yǐjing shuì jiào** 了。	*sleep* *already sleeping* *My roommate is already sleeping.*
26. **tīng yīnyuè** **gēn** 我 的 **tóngwū** 一起 **tīng yīnyuè** 我 **zuótiān gēn** 我 的 **tóngwū** 一起 **tīng** 　**yīnyuè** 了。	*listen to music* *listen to music with my roommate* *Yesterday I listened to music with my* 　*roommate.*
27. **xià kè** **gāng xià kè** 我 **gāng xià kè**。	*get out of class* *just got out of class* _____
28. 吃 沒 吃 **hái** 沒 吃 呢 我 **hái** 沒 吃 呢。	*eat* *didn't eat* *haven't eaten yet* *I haven't eaten yet.*

29.	
沒吃	*haven't eaten*
hái 沒吃呢	*haven't eaten yet*
我 **gāng xià kè**，**hái** 沒吃呢。	_____

30.	
學 **xí** 中文	*study Chinese*
沒學 **xí** 中文	*didn't study Chinese*
hái 沒學 **xí** 中文呢	*haven't studied Chinese yet*
我 **jīntiān hái** 沒學 **xí** 中文呢。	_____

31.	
kāfēiguǎn	*coffee shop*
xīn 的 **kāfēiguǎn**	*new coffee shop*
那個 **xīn** 的 **kāfēiguǎn**	_____

32.	
guì	*expensive*
zhēn guì	*really expensive*
kāfēiguǎn zhēn guì	*coffee shop is really expensive*
那個 **kāfēiguǎn zhēn guì**。	*That coffee shop is really expensive.*

33.	
xīn 的 **kāfēiguǎn**	*new coffee shop*
那個 **xīn** 的 **kāfēiguǎn**	*that new coffee shop*
去那個 **xīn** 的 **kāfēiguǎn**	*go to that new coffee shop*
去那個 **xīn** 的 **kāfēiguǎn**， 　**xíng** 不 **xíng**？	*go to that new coffee shop, okay?*
我們去那個 **xīn** 的 **kāfēiguǎn**， 　**xíng** 不 **xíng**？	_____

34.	
那個 **xīn** 的 **kāfēiguǎn**	*that new coffee shop*
去那個 **xīn** 的 **kāfēiguǎn**	*go to that new coffee shop*
gēn 我一起去那個 **xīn** 的 **kāfēiguǎn**	*go to that new coffee shop with me*
Gēn 我一起去那個 **xīn** 的 **kāfēiguǎn**， 　**xíng** 不 **xíng**？	*Go to that new coffee shop with me,* 　*okay?*

35.	
一 **diǎn**	*1 o'clock*
kuài 一 **diǎn** 了	*almost 1 o'clock*
Xiàn 在 **kuài** 一 **diǎn** 了。	_____

Focus on pronunciation

Sentence stress in questions and answers

Sentence stress in yes-no questions

嗎 questions

In 嗎 questions, 嗎 has neutral tone, and sentence stress is usually on the syllable right before 嗎. In the answer, sentence stress falls on the verb.

> Q: **Nǐ xué Zhōngwén ma**。
> A: **Wǒ <u>xué</u> Zhōngwén**。

V-not-V questions

In V-not-V questions, sentence stress is on the last syllable of the question that has a full tone. If the last syllable has neutral tone, the stress falls on the syllable before it. In the answer, sentence stress falls on the verb.

> Q: **Nǐ xué bù xué Zhōng<u>wén</u>**?
> A: **Wǒ <u>xué</u> Zhōngwén**。

Stress in content questions

In content questions, the first syllable of the question word receives sentence stress. In the answer, the word that replaces the question word receives sentence stress.

> Q: **Nǐ xìng <u>shén</u>me**?
> A: **Wǒ xìng <u>Lǐ</u>**。
> Q: **Nǐ shì <u>nǎ</u>guó rén**?
> A: **Wǒ shì <u>Zhōng</u>guó rén**。

Chinese characters

Be a character sleuth!

Another good reason to look for recurring parts in characters is that recurring parts sometimes indicate that characters have related pronunciations. The characters 小 (**xiǎo**) *small, little* and 少 (**shǎo**) *few* have in common the radical 小, and they also have similar pronunciations. Recurring parts may indicate similar pronunciations even when the recurring part is not the radical. We have already learned two pairs of characters which share recurring parts that are not the radical and which have identical pronunciations: 那 (**nà**) *that* and 哪 (**nǎ**) *which*, and 他 (**tā**) *he, him* and 她 (**tā**) *she, her*. A recurring part does not necessarily indicate similar pronunciations, however. For example, 也 is pronounced very differently from 他 and 她.

Lesson 10 Characters step-by-step

 吃 (chī) *eat* has a horizontal orientation and is written from left to right. The left part of 吃 is the radical 口. We have seen it in several characters that we have already learned. It is written in three strokes.

丨   冂   口

The right side of 吃 is written in three strokes. The first stroke is a *left falling stroke*. The second stroke is a *horizontal stroke*.

口丿   口ㄥ

The third stoke begins as a *horizontal stroke*, falls to the left, continues as a *curved stroke*, and ends with an *upward hook*.

吃

當 (dāng) has a vertical orientation and is written in thirteen strokes. The top part of 當 is written in three strokes. The first stroke is the central stroke and it is a *vertical stroke*. The second stroke is the stroke on the left side. It is a *right falling dot*. The third stroke is the stroke on the right. It is a *left falling stroke*.

丨   ⺌   ⺌

The next part of 當 is written in two strokes: a *dot*, followed by a *horizontal stroke* with a *downward hook*.

The third part of 當 is a box.

Below the box is another box with the character 十 inside. Remember to fill in the box before closing the box.

都 (**dōu**) has a horizontal orientation and is written in eleven stokes. The left part is written first. It is written from top to bottom and it consists of two parts. The first stroke is a *horizontal stroke*, the second stroke is a *vertical stroke*, the third stroke is a *horizontal stroke* that completes the top half. Notice that it may touch the vertical stroke but it does not go through it.

The next stroke is a *left falling stroke* that goes through the bottom horizontal stroke.

者

The remaining four strokes are a box with a *horizontal stroke* inside. The last stroke of the box is the closing stroke.

才　者　者　者

The right side of 都 is the radical 阝. It is written in three strokes.

The first stroke is a *horizontal stroke* with an upward slant that turns into a *left falling stroke*.

The second stroke is a *curved stroke* with an *upward hook*.

都

The third stroke is a *vertical stroke*.

都

Note: There are two radicals with this shape. One is written on the left side of a character, and one is written on the right.

多 (**duō**) has a vertical orientation and is written in six strokes. The top part of the character is the radical and is written in three strokes. The first stroke is a *left falling stroke*. The second stroke is a left to right *horizontal stroke* the turns into a *left falling stroke*.

The third stroke is a *right falling dot*.

The bottom half of 多 is identical to the top half. It is aligned with the top so that if a vertical line were written straight through the character it would divide the character in half.

 飯 (**fàn**) has a horizontal orientation and is written in twelve stokes. The left side is the radical and it is written first. The first stroke is a *left falling stroke*. The next two strokes are *dots*.

The next stroke is a *right corner stroke*.

The next two strokes are *horizontal strokes*. The first is written from left to right inside of the right corner. The second is written from left to right, ending at the bottom of the right corner stroke.

The next stroke is a *vertical stroke* that turns into a *rising stroke*. It is followed by a *dot*.

The right side of 飯 is written in four strokes. The first stroke is a *left falling stroke*. The second stroke is a longer *left falling stroke*.

	The third stroke is a *horizontal stroke* that turns into a *left falling stroke*. The last stroke is a *right falling dot*.
	會 (**huì**) has a vertical orientation and is written in thirteen strokes. The first stroke is a *left falling stroke*. The second stroke is a *right falling stroke* that begins just below the top of the previous stroke. The next stroke is a *horizontal stroke* centered below the top two strokes. It does not go through the top two strokes. The next two strokes are a *vertical stroke* and a *right corner stroke* written inside of the two strokes but below the horizontal stroke. Together they form an open box. The next stroke is a *vertical stroke* written from the top center of the open box. It is the same height as the sides of the box and it divides the box into two sections. The next strokes are a *dot* written in the left section of the open box, a *left falling stroke* written in the right section of the open box, and a *horizontal stroke* that closes the box.  The remaining four strokes form the radical 日 that we have seen in the characters 是, 早, and 明, and that we will see in the character 晚. 

老	老 (lǎo) is a radical. It has a vertical orientation and is written in six strokes. The first four strokes are written in the same way as the first four strokes in the left part of 都. The fifth stroke is a *left falling stroke*. The sixth stroke begins as a *vertical stroke* and turns into a *curved stroke* that ends in an *upward hook*.
了	了 (le) has a vertical orientation and is written in two strokes. The first stroke begins as a slightly rising *horizontal stroke* and turns into a *left falling stroke*. The second stroke is a *horizontal stroke* that ends with a *left-facing upward hook*.
沒	沒 (méi) has a horizontal orientation and is written in seven strokes. The left side of the character is the radical 氵 and it is written first. 氵 is written in three strokes from top to bottom. The first stroke is a *right falling dot*. The second stroke is also a *right falling dot*. The third stroke is an *upward stroke*. It starts at the bottom and is written upwards, moving from left to right. The right side of 沒 consists of two pieces and is written from top to bottom. The top is written in two strokes, a *left falling stroke*, followed by a *right corner stroke* that ends in an *upward, left hook*.  The bottom piece is written in two strokes, a *horizontal stroke* that turns into a *left falling stroke*, and a *right falling stroke*.

去 (**qù**) has a vertical orientation and is written in five strokes. The first stroke is a *horizontal stroke*. The second stroke is a *vertical stroke*. The third stroke is a *horizontal stroke*, longer than the first one, that runs under the vertical stroke.

The next two strokes form the radical. They are a *left falling stroke* that turns into a *rising stroke*, and a *right falling dot*.

去 | 去

然 (**rán**) has a vertical orientation and is written in twelve strokes. The top half of 然 has two parts written from left to right in eight strokes. The left half is written in four strokes. The first stroke is a *right falling stroke*, the second stroke starts as a left-to-right *horizontal stroke* and turns into a *right falling stroke*. Within the enclosure formed by the first two strokes are two *right falling dots*.

ノ | ク | 夕 | 夕

The second part of the top half of 然 also has four strokes. The first stroke is a *horizontal stroke*. The second stroke is a *left falling stroke*. The third stroke is a *right falling stroke*, and the last stroke is a *dot* written over and to the right of the horizontal stroke.

歹 | 犲 | 犰 | 犾

The last four strokes of 然 are dots and together they form the radical. The first dot is *a left falling dot*. The last three are *right falling dots*.

然 | 然 | 然 | 然

少 (**shǎo**) is written in four strokes. The first four strokes form the radical, the character 小 that we learned in Lesson 9.

亅 | 刂 | 小

The last stroke is a *left falling stroke*. It begins around the midpoint of the right dot and it falls below the radical and past the left dot.

生 (**shēng**) is a radical. It has a vertical orientation and is written in five strokes. The first stroke is a *left falling stroke*. The second stroke is a *horizontal stroke*.

It begins just above the midpoint of the left falling stroke.

The third stroke is also a *horizontal stroke*.

仁

The fourth stroke is a *vertical stroke*. The last stroke is the *horizontal stroke* that closes the character. Notices that it may touch the vertical stroke but it does not go through it.

牛 | 生

師 (**shī**) has a horizontal orientation and is written in ten strokes. The left side is written first. The first two strokes are a *left falling stroke* followed by a *vertical stroke* that begins at about the endpoint of the falling stroke.

The next four strokes form a pair of small boxes along the vertical stroke. They are written from top to bottom as a *right corner stroke* followed by a *horizontal stroke* that closes the first box, and a *right corner stroke* followed by a *horizontal stroke* that closes the second box.

The right side is written in four strokes. The first stroke is a *horizontal stroke*.

The remaining three strokes form the radical, 巾. It is written with a *vertical stroke*, a *right corner stroke* that ends with a *left facing hook*, and a *vertical stroke* that goes through the center of the right corner stroke. Notice that the final vertical stroke may touch the horizontal stroke above it but it does not go through it.

晚 (**wǎn**) has a horizontal orientation and is written in eleven strokes. The radical is on the left and is written first in four strokes. The first stroke is a *vertical stroke.* The second strong is a *right corner stroke.* The third stroke is a *horizontal stroke* written about halfway down and inside of the enclosure made by the first two strokes. It may touch the lines that form the enclosure but it does not go through them.

The last stroke is the closing stroke, a *horizontal stroke* written from left to right.

日

The right side of 晚 has a vertical orientation and is written in seven strokes. The first stroke is a *left falling stroke.* The second stroke is a *horizontal stroke* that turns into a *left falling stroke.* These two strokes form the same shape as the first two strokes of the character 然 above.

The next three strokes form a rectangular box.

The next stroke is a *left falling stroke* that starts inside the box and falls to the left.

The last stroke is a *vertical stroke* with a *curve to the right* that ends in an *upward facing hook.*

學 (**xué**) has a vertical orientation and is written in three parts from top to bottom in sixteen strokes. The first strokes form the pair of "x's" in the center of the top part of the character. Each "x" is written as a *left falling stroke* followed by a *dot.*

The next strokes form the enclosure for the x's. The left side is written first: a *left falling stroke*, a *vertical stroke,* and two short *horizontal strokes* that begin on the right side of the horizontal stroke.

The right side is written next in three strokes: a *horizontal stroke* that turns into a *vertical stroke,* and two short *horizontal strokes* that begin inside of the enclosure and end at the right vertical stroke.

The top part of 學 is followed by a two-stroke section: a *dot* followed by a *horizontal stroke* that ends with a *left downward hook.* Notice that the horizontal stroke starts below the top of the dot.

The third part of 學 is the radical 子 and it is written in three strokes. The first two strokes are written the same way as 了. The third stroke is a *horizontal stroke* that crosses at the intersection of the two previous strokes.

怎 (**zěn**) has a vertical orientation and is written in nine strokes. The top part of 怎 is written in five strokes. The first two strokes are a *left falling stroke* followed by a *horizontal stroke.*

The remaining three strokes are a *vertical stroke* and two *horizontal strokes* that begin on the right side of the vertical stroke. Notice that the last horizontal stroke starts before the bottom of the vertical stroke.

The second part of 怎 is the radical 心. It is written in four strokes, a *dot,* a *reclining curved stroke* that ends with an *upward hook,* a *dot* inside the curve, and a *dot* outside the curve.

Language FAQs

Why doesn't completed action 了 occur with V de AdjV "manner" descriptions?

Verb descriptions expressed with the pattern V **de** AdjV focus on how the action is performed (well, poorly, quickly, slowly, etc.). Completed action 了 focuses on the completion of an action. The meanings focus on different things and the structures cannot be combined. In Mandarin, you can either say that an action was completed or that it was performed in a particular way.

How can you tell whether 了 indicates a new situation or completion?

Look at what 了 follows. If 了 directly follows an action verb, it indicates completion. If 了 follows the entire sentence (minus the final particle) it indicates that the situation is new in some way. If 了 follows an action verb and also occurs at the end of a sentence, it may be indicating both completion and a new situation, and you must decide which meanings make sense in the context of the sentence. Remember also that the inclusion of 了 is optional, reflecting the speaker's perspective about a situation, and speakers need not include 了 even if an action is completed or a situation is new.

Two particles pronounced "de"

We have now learned two particles that are pronounced **de**. They have different functions and are written with different Chinese characters. We have already learned that the particle **de** that is used to indicate noun description is written 的. The particle **de** introduced in this lesson to indicate how an action is performed is written with a different character. We will learn it in a later lesson.

Signalling time without grammatical tense

Because Mandarin does not have grammatical structures that indicate past, present, and future tense, Mandarin sentences are often <u>unmarked</u> for time. When the time of a situation is relevant or important to communicate, the time is expressed with time words such as **zuótiān** *yesterday*, **jīntiān** *today*, and 明 **tiān** *tomorrow*, or with words and phrases like *previously* or *in the future* that indicate the time of a situation. Remember that words and phrases that indicate the <u>time when</u> a situation takes place are always stated <u>before</u> the verb phrase.

我 **zuótiān** 有中文 **kǎoshì**。
I had a Chinese test yesterday.

Notes on Chinese culture

More about expressing past months and future months

Languages often express time with words and phrases that refer to location. In Mandarin, weeks and months that have occurred before this week/this month are expressed with the word **shàng** *above*, and weeks and months that will occur after this week/this month are expressed with the word **xià** *below*. In other words, for weeks and months, Chinese describes the past as "above" us and the future as "below" us.

TIME

(Past)	shàng 個 xīngqī，shàng 個 yuè	*last week, last month*
(Present)	這個 xīngqī，這個 yuè	*this week, this month*
(Future)	xià 個 xīngqī，xià 個 yuè	*next week, next month*

Lesson 10 Dialogue in English

Part A

Xiao Gao:	What did you think about yesterday's test?
Xiao Zhang:	I thought it was very difficult.
Xiao Gao:	I also thought it was difficult. Last week's test was very easy, but yesterday's test was extremely difficult.
Xiao Zhang:	How did you do?
Xiao Gao:	I wrote very slowly. Also, I forgot some characters. Of course I did poorly on the test. How did you do?
Xiao Zhang:	I also didn't do well. I slept too little last night. I wrote quickly, but I didn't understand some of the grammar, and I couldn't write some of the characters.

Part B

Xiao Zhang:	It's almost one o'clock. Have you eaten lunch?
Xiao Gao:	I've already eaten. What about you?
Xiao Zhang:	I just got out of class, I haven't eaten yet. I'm going with Xiao Ye to that new coffee shop to eat. Do you want to come with us?
Xiao Gao:	Okay. You two can (go to) eat lunch, I can (go and) drink a cup of tea.

Lesson 11 Lái我家吃飯
Come to my house for dinner

Communication goals
- Talk about the location of people, places, and things in terms of compass directions
- Talk about the distance between places

Key structures
N **zài** location
VV O
měi (個) time **dōu** VP
lái location
A **lí** B distance
the preposition **gěi** *for/to*

Dialogue

The Situation: It is Wednesday night, and Xiao Xie and Xiao Zhang are in their dorm room talking. Xiao Xie often goes home on Sunday to have dinner with his family, and he is planning to invite Xiao Zhang to come to his home for dinner.

Part A

小謝： 你這個星期天做甚麼，**máng** 不 **máng**？

小張： 這個星期天我沒 **shì**，**jiù** **xiǎng** **上上** **wǎng**、**看看** **diànshì**。

小謝： 那，星期天 **lái** 我家吃飯，怎麼樣？

小張： 星期天甚麼 **shíhou**？我 **měi** 個星期天 **xiàwǔ** **都** **gěi** 我 **māma** **dǎ diàn** 話。

小謝： 星期天晚上六點半怎麼樣？

小張： 可以。你還 **xiǎng** 請誰？

小謝： 我還 **xiǎng** 請土 **Màikè**，**Gāo Měilì**，當然還有你的女 **péngyou** **Yè Yǒu** 文。

小張： 太好了！

小謝： **對了**。**Gāo Měilì** 有男 **péngyou** 嗎？

小張： 不 **zhīdào**。我 **bāng** 你 **wènwen**。

Part B

小張:　你家 **lí** 這兒有多 **yuǎn**？

小謝:　不 **yuǎn**。我家 **lí** 這兒只有五 **lǐ lù**。我 **gěi** 你 **huà** 一張 **dìtú**。你看，這兒是 **shì** 中 **xīn**，**fēijīchǎng** 在 **běibiān**，**huǒchē zhàn** 在 **dōngbiān**，**Dōng Shān gōngyuán** 在 **dōngběi biān**，學 **xiào** 在 **nánbiān**，我家在 **xībiān**，**lí** 中 **shān shūdiàn** 很 **jìn**。

小張:　你家 **lí Běi Hú** 也很 **jìn**，對不對？**Běi Hú** 在哪兒？

小謝:　**Běi Hú** 在這兒，在 **xīběi biān**，**lí** 我家只有半 **lǐ lù**。

běibiān

Běi Hú	fēijīchǎng	Dōngshān gōngyuán
我家		
	shì 中 xīn	huǒchē zhàn
中 shān shūdiàn		
	學 xiào	

xībiān dōngbiān

nánbiān

Vocabulary

bāng	verb	*help*
běi	*	*north*
běibiān	noun	*north side*
diànshì [gè]	noun	*television*
dōng	*	*east*
dōngbiān	noun	*east side*

duì le	對了	conversational expression	*by the way*
duō yuǎn		question phrase	*how far*
fēijī		noun	*airplane*
fēijīchǎng [gè]		noun	*airport*
gěi		preposition	*for, to*
gōngyuán [gè]		noun	*park*
hú		noun	*lake*
huà		verb	*draw*
huǒchē [gè]		noun	*train*
huǒchē zhàn [gè]		noun phrase	*train station*
jìn		adjectival verb	*near, close by*
jiù		adverb	*only*
lái		verb	*come*
lí		preposition	*separated from*
lǐ		classifier	*Chinese mile*
lù		noun	*road, street*
máng		adjectival verb	*busy*
měi		quantifier	*every*
nán		*	*south*
nánbiān		noun	*south side*
nǎr	哪兒	question word	*where*
nàr	那兒	noun	*there*
shān [gè]		noun	*mountain*
shàng wǎng	上 **wǎng**	verb + object	*use internet, go online*

shénme shíhou	甚麼 **shíhou**	question phrase	*what time*
shì		*	*city*
shíhou		noun	*time*
shì zhōngxīn [gè]	**shì** 中 **xīn**	noun phrase	*city center, center of the city, downtown*
shūdiàn [gè]		noun	*bookstore*
wǎng		noun	*web, internet*
wèn		verb	*ask*
xī		*	*west*
xīběi (biān)		noun	*northwest (side)*
xībiān		noun	*west side*
xuéxiào [gè]	學 **xiào**	noun	*school*
Yǒuwén	**Yǒu** 文	given name	*(given name)*
yuǎn		adjectival verb	*far*
zài	在	verb	*be located at*
zhàn [gè]		noun	*station, (bus or train) stop*
zhèr	這兒	noun	*here*
Zhōngshān	中 **shān**	given name	*Sun Yatsen (see notes on Chinese culture)*
zhōngxīn [gè]	中 **xīn**	noun	*center*

Characters

半	bàn	*half*	
點	diǎn	*dot*	一點 **(yīdiǎn)** *a little*
			(三)點 zhōng **((sān) diǎn zhōng)** *(3) o'clock*
兒	ér, r	*	**chàng gē** 兒 **(chàng gēr)** *sing songs*
			這兒 **(zhèr)** *here*
還	hái	*in addition*	
家	jiā	*family, home*	
看	kàn	*see, look at, visit, read*	看 **shū (kàn shū)** *read*
			看 **diànshì (kàn diànshì)** *watch television*
			看 **péngyou (kàn péngyou)** *see friends*
男	nán	*male*	男 **háizi (nán háizi)** *boy*
			男 **péngyou (nán péngyou)** *boyfriend*
女	nǚ	*female*	女 **háizi (nǚ háizi)** *girl*
			女 **péngyou (nǚ péngyou)** *girlfriend*
期	qī	*	星期 **(xīngqī)** *week*
請	qǐng	*invite, "please"*	請 **wèn (qǐng wèn)** *may I ask*
			請 **jìn (qǐng jìn)** *please come in*
上	shàng	*last (week, month) above*	上個星期 **(shàng gè xīngqī)** *last week*
			晚上 **(wǎnshang)** *evening*
			早上 **(zǎoshang)** *morning*
			上 **kè (shàng kè)** *go to class*

誰	shéi	who	
太	tài	too	
天	tiān	day, heaven	星期天 (**xīngqītiān**) *Sunday*
王	Wáng	(family name)	
星	xīng	star	星期 (**xīngqī**) *week*
樣	yàng	*	怎麼樣 (**zěnmeyàng**) *what about it?*
			這樣 (**zhèyàng**) *this way*
在	zài	located at; (ongoing action)	
只	zhǐ	only	
做	zuò	do	

Stroke Order Flow Chart

character: strokes: **total strokes:**

半	丶	⺍	⳦	兰	半									5
點	丨	冂	冃	冊	曱	四	甲	里	黒	黑	黑	黑	點	
	黑	點	點											17
兒	丿	仃	仃	臼	臼	臼	臼	兒						8
還	丶	冂	冂	四	四	罒	睪	罘	罟	罘	睘	睘	睘	
	睘	還	還											17
家	丶	丷	宀	宀	宀	宁	穷	家	家					10
看	一	二	三	手	手	看	看	看						9
男	丨	冂	日	田	田	甼	男							7
女	人	女	女											3

期	一	十	卄	丗	甘	其	其	其	期	期	期	期		12
請	丶	亠	二	三	言	言	言	訁	訂	詰	請	請	請	15
請	請													15
上	丨	卜	上											3
誰	丶	亠	二	三	言	言	言	訁	訃	訃	誰	誰	誰	
誰	誰													15
太	一	ナ	大	太										4
天	一	二	天	天										4
王	一	二	干	王										4
星	丶	冂	日	日	尸	旦	昌	星	星					9
樣	一	十	才	木	术	术	样	样	样	样	样	様	様	
樣	様													15
在	一	ナ	才	右	存	在								6
只	丶	冂	口	尸	只									5
做	丿	亻	亻	仁	付	估	估	做	做	做				11

Dialogue practice

Do these activities in class after mastering the dialogue for this lesson. Change partners so that you practice each part several times.

Dialogue 11A: Pair up with a classmate and take turns inviting each other to do something. The guest should find out who else is coming and ask about the time of the event. Negotiate a time that is convenient for both of you.

Dialogue 11B: Draw a simple map indicating the location of your home and the distance between your home and other places on the map. Pair up with a classmate and take turns asking each other where your homes are located, and how far your homes are from other places.

Use and structure

11.1.   Jiù + V *only (V)*

In Lesson 9 we learned that the adverb **jiù** can be used to indicate that an action occurs earlier than the speaker expects (Use and Structure note 9.10). **Jiù** can also mean *only, just*. In this function, it is equivalent in meaning to 只 *only, just*.

這個星期天我沒 **shì**，**jiù xiǎng** 上上 **wǎng**、看看 **diànshì**。
I don't have anything to do this Sunday. I am just planning to use the internet and watch a little television.

11.2.   Do an action for a short time: 上上 **wǎng**, 看看 **diànshì**

To indicate that an action is performed for a short period of time and in a casual way, repeat the action verb:

這個星期天我沒 **shì**，**jiù xiǎng** 上上 **wǎng**、看看 **diànshì**。
I don't have anything to do this Sunday. I am just planning to use the internet and watch a little television.

Notice that it is only the verb that is repeated. If the verb takes an object, the object occurs only once. If the verb is a two-syllable verb, the entire two syllables are repeated:

她星期天 **fùxí fùxí gōngkè**、**liànxí liànxí Hàn zì**，也上上 **wǎng**。
Every Sunday she reviews her lessons, practices Chinese characters, and uses the internet.

11.3.   Lái + location *come to a location*

In Lesson 10 we learned how to use the verb 去 *go* to say *go to a location* (Use and Structure note 10.16). In this lesson we learn the word **lái** *come*. To say *come to a location* say:

lái + location
lái 我家
come to my home

To say *come, go,* or *return* to a place to do some action, the order of information is as in English:

lái/去/huí location + ActV
星期天 **lái** 我家吃飯，怎麼樣？
Come to my home to eat on Sunday, okay?

我 **xiǎng** 去 **túshūguǎn** 看 **shū**。
I'm planning to go to the library to read.

我 **xiǎng huí sùshè shuì jiào**。
I want to go back to the dorm to sleep.

11.4.   Měi (個) time 都 VP *do an action every (time)*

To say that someone does an action *every day, week, month, year*, etc., say:

(S) měi (個) time 都 VP

If the time expression is counted with the classifier 個, say **méi 個 time**. This includes 星期 *week*, **yuè** *month*, and days of the week.

我 **měi** 個星期天 **xiàwǔ** 都 **gěi** 我 **māma dǎ diàn** 話。
I call my mother every Sunday afternoon.

他們 **měi** 個星期都有中文 **kǎoshì**。
They have a Chinese test every week.

我的 **tóngwū měi** 個 **yuè** 都 **huí** 家。
My roommate goes home every month.

Remember that the time expressions 天 *day* and **nián** *year* do not occur with a classifier. To say *every day*, say **měi** 天. To say *every year*, say **měi nián**:

我 **měi** 天都 **gēn péngyou** 一起去 **kāfēiguǎn hē kāfēi**。
Every day I go with my friends to a coffee shop to drink coffee.

他 **měi nián** 都 **mǎi xīn** 的 **diànnǎo**。
He buys a new computer every year.

11.5.   對了 *by the way…*

The expression 對了 can be used to add information that the speaker thinks the listener would like to know, or to ask a question that has been on the speaker's mind. When used in this way it can often be translated with the English expression *by the way*.

對了。**Gāo Měilì** 有男朋友嗎？
By the way, does Gao Meili have a boyfriend?

11.6.   Distance

When talking about the distance between location A and location B use the word **lí** *separated from* in this pattern:

A lí B distance
A is separated from B (by distance)

Stating distance

When stating the distance between A and B say:

> **A lí B** (有) **distance**
> 我家 **lí** 這兒(有)五 **lǐ lù**。
> *My house is five miles from here.*

有 is optional unless the sentence includes an adverb. For example, when the adverb 只 *only* occurs in the sentence, the verb 有 must occur:

> 我家 **lí** 這兒只有五 **lǐ lù**。
> *My house is only five miles from here.*

The traditional measure of distance in China is the **lǐ**, sometimes translated as *mile* and sometimes as *Chinese mile*. A **lǐ** is approximately ¹/₃ of a British or American mile. **Lǐ** is a classifier and directly follows the number. It is often followed by the noun **lù** *road*. **Lù** does not get translated in this phrase.

> 五 **lǐ lù**   *five miles*

Saying that A is *close to* or *far from* B

To say that A is close to B, say:

> **A lí B** 很 **jìn**。
> 我家 **lí** 中 **shān shūdiàn** 很 **jìn**。
> *My house is very close to Zhongshan Bookstore.*

To say that A is not close to B, say:

> **A lí B** 不 **jìn**。
> 我家 **lí** 中 **shān shūdiàn** 不 **jìn**。
> *My house is not very close to Zhongshan Bookstore.*

To say that A is far from B, say:

> **A lí B** 很 **yuǎn**。
> 我家 **lí** 那兒很 **yuǎn**。
> *My house is very far from there.*

To say that A is not far from B, say:

> **A lí B** 不 **yuǎn**。
> 我家 **lí** 這兒不 **yuǎn**。
> *My house is not far from here.*

Asking about distance

To ask how far A is from B, ask:

A lí B (有)多 **yuǎn**?
你家 **lí** 這兒(有)多 **yuǎn**?
How far is your house from here?

To ask whether A is far from B, ask:

A lí B yuǎn 嗎?   or   **A lí B yuǎn** 不 **yuǎn**?

To ask whether A is close to B, ask:

A lí B jìn 嗎?
你家 **lí Běi Hú** 很 **jìn** 嗎?
Is your house near North Lake?

11.7.   這兒 *here*, 那兒 *there*, and 哪兒 *where*

這兒 *here* refers to locations that are near to the speaker.

這兒是 **shì** 中 **xīn**。 *Here is the center of the city.*

那兒 *there* refers to locations that are not close to the speaker.

學生 **sùshè zài** 那兒。
The student dormitories are there.

哪兒 means *where*.

Q: **Běi Hú** 在哪兒?   *Where is North Lake?*
A: **Běi Hú** 在這兒。   *North Lake is here.*

11.8.   **Gěi** as a preposition *to, for*

We have learned the word **gěi** as the verb *give* and in the expression **gěi** (someone) **dǎ diànhuà** *phone (someone)*. In this lesson we learn to use the word **gěi** as a preposition meaning *to* or *for (someone)*.

我 **gěi** 你 **huà** 一張 **dìtú**。
I'll draw a map for you.

Like the preposition **gēn** *with* introduced in Lesson 10, when used as a preposition, **gěi** is followed by a noun or noun phrase to form a prepositional phrase:

gěi 你   *for you*

As noted in Lesson 10, the prepositional phrase usually occurs before the verb phrase with which it is associated, while in English, prepositional phrases usually occur after the verb.

gěi 你 **huà** 一張 **dìtú**
draw a map for you

Gěi goes before the person who receives or benefits from the action of the verb. The translation of **gěi** into English as *for* or *to* depends upon the verb. Here are some examples:

gěi (someone) **huà** 一張 **dìtú**	*draw a map for someone*
gěi (someone) **mǎi dōngxi**	*buy something for someone*
gěi (someone) **xiě** "email"	*write an email to someone*

11.9.   Pointing out the location of people, places, and things: 這兒是 *here is*

The expression 這兒是 *here is/here are* can be used to point out the location of people, places, and things. In Part B of the dialogue, 小謝 uses the expression while pointing to the center of the city.

這兒是 **shì** 中 **xīn**。
Here is the center of the city.

11.10.   Compass directions

In Mandarin, compass directions are recited as:

dōng nán xī běi	or as	**dōng xī nán běi**
east south west north		*east west south north*

Dōng, **nán**, **xī**, and **běi** do not occur as free words but must be combined with another syllable. When they are followed by the suffix **biān** *side* they become free words. There is often no need to translate **biān** into English.

dōngbiān	*(the) east (side)*
nánbiān	*(the) south (side)*
xībiān	*(the) west (side)*
běibiān	*(the) north (side)*

Dōng, **nán**, **xī**, and **běi** also become free words when they are paired together to say *northeast*, *northwest*, *southeast*, and *southwest*:

dōngnán (biān)	*southeast*	**xīnán (biān)**	*southwest*
dōngběi (biān)	*northeast*	**xīběi (biān)**	*northwest*

Dōngběi *northeast* usually occurs with an ending, however, because the word **dōngběi** without an ending is the Chinese name for the province of Manchuria.

> **Fēijīchǎng** 在 **běibiān，huǒchē zhàn** 在 **dōngbiān，Dōng Shān gōngyuán** 在 **dōngběi biān，**學 **xiào** 在 **nánbiān，**我家在 **xībiān。**
> *The airport is in the north, the train station is in the east, East Mountain Park is in the northeast, the school is in the south, my home is in the west.*

Here is a chart of the Mandarin compass direction words:

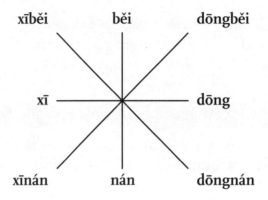

A number of other suffixes also occur with direction words. We do not include them in this book, but you will encounter them as you continue your study of Chinese. Your teacher may prefer to use one of these other suffixes when talking about directions.

11.11. Location with the verb 在

To indicate the location of some noun, that is, some person, place, or thing, use the verb 在 *be located in/at/on* and say:

> **N** 在 **location**
> 我在 **huǒchē zhàn。**   *I am at the train station.*

The location may be a direction or a place.

> **Gōngyuán** 在 **běibiān。**   *The park is (located) in the north.*
> 她在 **jiā。**   *She is (located) at home.*

11.12. 半 *half* with numbers: 半 **lǐ lù** *half a mile*

In Lesson 9 we learned to use the word 半 *half* when talking about clock time (Use and Structure note 9.5). In this lesson we learn to use 半 *half* in any number expression.

Half of something

When saying *half* of some noun, 半 occurs directly <u>before</u> the classifier:

半 **+ classifier (+ N)**
半 **lǐ lù** *half a mile*
半 **ge yuè** *half a month*
半 **běn shū** *half a book*

Remember that in Mandarin, the words **nián** *year* and 天 *day* function as classifiers. Therefore, they are directly preceded by 半:

半 **nián** *half a year*
半天 *half a day*

(The expression 半天 also means *a long time*.)

Běi Hú lí 我家只有半 **lǐ lù**。
North Lake is only half a mile from my house.

Some number and a half

When saying *some number and a half*, 半 goes <u>after</u> the classifier.

number + classifier + 半

Time nouns follow 半:

number + classifier + 半 **+ N**
一個半 **yuè** *one and a half months*
三個半星期 *three and a half weeks*

Since the time words **nián** *year* and 天 *day* function as classifiers, not nouns, they precede 半.

一 **nián** 半 *1½ years*
兩天半 *2½ days*

The word **suì** *years of age* is also a classifier and precedes 半.

一 **suì** 半 *1½ years old*

For nouns that are not time words, some speakers follow <u>number + classifier + 半</u> by <u>的 + N</u>, or they omit the noun altogether.

五 **lǐ** 半 **lù**   or   五 **lǐ** 半的 **lù**   *5½ miles*
一 **ping** 半 **shuǐ** or   一 **ping** 半的 **shuǐ**   *1½ bottles of water*

Sentence pyramids

*The sentence pyramids illustrate the use of each new vocabulary item and structure intro-
duced in the lesson. Use them to help you learn how to form phrases and sentences in Mandarin.
Supply the English translation for the last line where indicated.*

1.	
máng	*busy*
máng 不 **máng**	*busy or not*
你 **jīn** 天 **máng** 不 **máng**？	*Are you busy today?*
2.	
wǎng	*web, internet*
上 **wǎng**	*use the internet*
都上 **wǎng**	*always use the internet*
我 **měi** 天都上 **wǎng**。	*I use the internet every day.*
3.	
diànshì	*television*
看 **diànshì**	*watch television*
xiǎng 看 **diànshì**	*plan to watch television*
jīn 天晚上 **xiǎng** 看 **diànshì**	*tonight plan to watch television*
我們 **jīn** 天晚上 **xiǎng** 看 **diànshì**。	_____
4.	
看看 **diànshì**	*watch a little television*
上上 **wǎng**、看看 **diànshì**	*use the internet, watch a little television*
xiǎng 上上 **wǎng**、看看 **diànshì**	*plan to use the internet, watch a little television*
jiù xiǎng 上上 **wǎng**、看看 **diànshì**	*only plan to use the internet and watch a little television*
我星期天 **jiù xiǎng** 上上 **wǎng**、看看 **diànshì**。	*On Sunday I only plan to use the internet and watch a little television.*
5.	
吃飯	*eat*
lái 我家吃飯	*come to my house to eat*
Lái 我家吃飯，怎麼樣？	*Come to my house to eat, okay?*
星期天 **lái** 我家吃飯，怎麼樣？	_____
6.	
去你家	*go to your house*
甚麼 **shíhou** 去你家？	*what time go to your house?*
星期天甚麼 **shíhou** 去你家？	*What time should (I) go to your house on Sunday?*

7. **diànshì** 看 **diànshì** 都看 **diànshì** **měi** 個星期天都看 **diànshì** 我 **měi** 個星期天都看 **diànshì**。	*television* *watch television* *always watch television* *every Sunday I always watch television* _____
8. **gěi** 我 **māma dǎ diàn** 話 都 **gěi** 我 **māma dǎ diàn** 話 星期天都 **gěi** 我 **māma dǎ diàn** 話 **měi** 個星期天都 **gěi** 我 **māma dǎ** 　　**diàn** 話 我 **měi** 個星期天都 **gěi** 我 **māma dǎ** 　　**diàn** 話。	*phone my mom* *always phone my mom* *Sunday always phone my mom* *every Sunday always phone my mom* _____
9. **dìtú** 一張 **dìtú** **huà** 一張 **dìtú** **gěi** 你 **huà** 一張 **dìtú** 我 **gěi** 你 **huà** 一張 **dìtú**。	*map* *one map* *draw a map* *draw a map for you* *I'll draw a map for you.*
10. **shuǐ** 幾 **píng shuǐ** **mǎi** 了幾 **píng shuǐ** **gěi** 我 **tóngwū mǎi** 了幾 **píng shuǐ** 我 **gěi** 我 **tóngwū mǎi** 了幾 **píng shuǐ**。	*water* *several bottles of water* *bought a few bottles of water* *bought a few bottles of water for my* 　　*roommate* _____
11. **péngyou** 男 **péngyou** 有男 **péngyou** 有男 **péngyou** 嗎？ 她有男 **péngyou** 嗎？ 對了。她有男 **péngyou** 嗎？	*friend* *boyfriend* *have a boyfriend* *have a boyfriend?* *Does she have a boyfriend?* *By the way, does she have a boyfriend?*
12. 有多 **yuǎn**？ **lí** 這兒有多 **yuǎn**？ 你家 **lí** 這兒有多 **yuǎn**？	*how far?* *how far from here?* *How far is your house from here?*

13. 有多 **yuǎn**？ **lí sùshè** 有多 **yuǎn**？ **Túshūguǎn lí sùshè** 有多 **yuǎn**？	*how far?* *how far from the dormitory?*
14. 五 **lǐ lù** 有五 **lǐ lù** **lí** 這兒有五 **lǐ lù** 我家 **lí** 這兒有五 **lǐ lù**。	*five miles* *(there are) five miles* *five miles from here* *My house is five miles from here.*
15. 幾 **lǐ lù**？ **lí** 這兒有幾 **lǐ lù**？ 你家 **lí** 這兒有幾 **lǐ lù**？	*how many miles?* *how many miles from here?* *How many miles is your house from here?*
16. 五 **lǐ lù** 有五 **lǐ lù** 只有五 **lǐ lù** 我家 **lí** 這兒只有五 **lǐ lù**。	*five miles* *(there are) five miles* *(there are) only five miles* *My house is only five miles from here.*
17. **yuǎn** 嗎？ **lí** 這兒 **yuǎn** 嗎？ 你家 **lí** 這兒 **yuǎn** 嗎？	*far?* *is it far from here?* *Is your house far from here?*
18. **yuǎn** 不 **yuǎn**？ **lí sùshè yuǎn** 不 **yuǎn**？ **Túshūguǎn lí sùshè yuǎn** 不 **yuǎn**？	*far (or not far)?* *far from the dormitory?* *Is the library far from the dormitory?*
19. 不 **yuǎn** **lí** 這兒不 **yuǎn** **Shūdiàn lí** 這兒不 **yuǎn**。	*not far* *not far from here* *The bookstore is not far from here.*
20. **shì** 中 **xīn** 這兒是 **shì** 中 **xīn**。 你看，這兒是 **shì** 中 **xīn**。	*the center of the city* *Here is the center of the city.* *Look, here is the center of the city.*

21.	
běibiān	*north side*
在 **běibiān**	*on the north side (in the north, to the north)*
Gōngyuán 在 **běibiān**。	*The park is on the north side (in the north, to the north).*
你看，**gōngyuán** 在 **běibiān**。	_____
22.	
nánbiān	*south side*
在 **nánbiān**	*on the south side (in the south, to the south)*
Huǒchē zhàn 在 **nánbiān**。	*The train station is on the south side (in the south, to the south).*
23.	
dōngbiān	*east side*
在 **dōngbiān**	*on the east side (in the east, to the east)*
學 **xiào** 在 **dōngbiān**。	_____
24.	
xībiān	*west side*
在 **xībiān**	*on the west side (in the west, to the west)*
我家在 **xībiān**。	_____
25.	
jìn	*close, near*
很 **jìn**	*very close*
lí shūdiàn 很 **jìn**	*very close to the bookstore*
lí 中 **shān shūdiàn** 很 **jìn**	*very close to Zhongshan bookstore*
我家 **lí** 中 **shān shūdiàn** 很 **jìn**。	_____
26.	
對不對？	*right?*
很 **jìn**，對不對？	*very near, right?*
也很 **jìn**，對不對？	*also very near, right?*
lí Běi Hú 也很 **jìn**，對不對？	*also very near to North Lake, right?*
你家 **lí Běi Hú** 也很 **jìn**，對不對？	*Your home is also very near to North Lake, right?*
27.	
哪兒？	*where?*
在哪兒？	*be located where?*
hú 在哪兒？	*where is the lake?*
Běi Hú 在哪兒？	*Where is North Lake?*
請 **wèn**，**Běi Hú** 在哪兒？	_____

28.	
這兒	*here*
在這兒	*be located here*
Běi Hú 在這兒。	*North Lake is here.*

29.	
jìn	*close*
很 **jìn**	*very close*
lí shān 很 **jìn**	*very close to the mountain*
Hú lí shān 很 **jìn**。	*The lake is very close to the mountain.*

30.	
xīběi biān	*northwest side*
在 **xīběi biān**	*on the northwest side*
Běi Hú 在 **xīběi biān**。	

31.	
在哪兒？	*where?*
fēijīchǎng 在哪兒？	*Where is the airport?*
Wèn 他 **fēijīchǎng** 在哪兒。	*Ask him where the airport is.*
請你 **wèn** 他 **fēijīchǎng** 在哪兒。	*Please ask him where the airport is.*

32.	
那兒	*there*
在那兒	*located there*
Fēijīchǎng 在那兒。	*The airport is there.*

33.	
wèn	*ask*
bāng 你 **wèn**	*help you to ask*
我 **bāng** 你 **wèn**。	*I'll help you to ask.*

34.	
diànnǎo	*computer*
mǎi diànnǎo	*buy (a) computer*
bāng 你 **mǎi diànnǎo**	*help you buy a computer*
我可以 **bāng** 你 **mǎi diànnǎo**。	*I can help you buy a computer.*

35.	
半 **lǐ lù**	*half a mile*
有半 **lǐ lù**	*is (has) half a mile*
只有半 **lǐ lù**	*is (has) only half a mile*
lí 我家只有半 **lǐ lù**	*is only half a mile from my home*
Běi Hú lí 我家只有半 **lǐ lù**。	

Language FAQs

Why does 家 mean both *family* and *home*?

In traditional Chinese society, a family stayed in the same village, town, or city for generations. One's *home* was the place where one's *family* lived, now, and in the past. Therefore, the word 家 (**jiā**) refers to both the people in the family and the place where the family resides. The character 家 is based on the structure of traditional homes in southern China. The top of the character 家, 宀, is a roof. The bottom part of the character is an early form of the character for *pig*, now written in traditional form as 豬. That is, a good home includes a roof for shelter and food for the family.

Why do the compass direction words dōng, nán, xī, and běi require the suffix biān in order to be used as free words?

Most Mandarin words are two syllables in length, and the language seems to prefer the two-syllable length for words. Many one-syllable units like **dōng**, **nán**, **xī**, and **běi** are bound forms. That is, they cannot be used on their own as free words even though they have meanings that can stand on their own. The suffix **biān** contributes the meaning of side when it joins with **dōng**, **nán**, **xī**, and **běi**, but the meaning that it contributes is much less important than the extra syllable, making **dōng**, **nán**, **xī**, and **běi** into two-syllable words.

Notes on Chinese culture

Compass directions and traditional spatial orientation

In traditional Chinese culture, the points of the compass are an important part of architectural design. Therefore, it is common to give directions in terms of the points of the compass. The orientation of buildings and streets according to the compass are part of the practice of **fēngshuǐ**, a word often translated into English as *geomancy*.

Who is 中 shān (Zhōngshān)

In China, many streets, parks, and other public places include the name 中 **shān**. 中 **shān** is the given name of **Sūn Zhōngshān** (*Sun Yatsen*), the first president of the Republic of China and widely considered to be the father of modern China.

Lesson 11 Dialogue in English

Part A

Xiao Xie: What are you doing this Sunday? Are you busy?

Xiao Zhang: I don't have anything to do this Sunday. I'm just planning to use the internet and watch a little television.

Xiao Xie: Well then, how about coming to my home to eat on Sunday?

Xiao Zhang: What time on Sunday? Every Sunday afternoon I phone my mom.

Xiao Xie: How about Sunday night at 6:30?

Xiao Zhang: That works. Who else are you planning to invite?

Xiao Xie: I'm also planning to invite Wang Maike, Gao Meili, and of course your girlfriend, Ye Youwen.

Xiao Zhang: Great!

Xiao Xie: By the way, does Gao Meili have a boyfriend?

Xiao Zhang: I don't know. I'll help you ask.

Part B

Xiao Zhang: How far is your house from here?

Xiao Xie: Not far. My house is only five miles from here. I'll draw a map for you. Look, here is the city center. The airport is in the north, the train station is in the east, East Mountain Park is in the northeast, the school is in the south, my house is in the west, very near to Zhongshan Bookstore.

Xiao Zhang: Your home is also close to North Lake, right? Where is North Lake?

Xiao Xie: North Lake is here, on the northwest side of the city, only a half mile from my house.

Lesson 12 Cóng 我的 sùshè dào 你家怎麼 zǒu?
How do I get to your house from my dorm?

Communication goals
- Give and follow directions by bus or train

Key structures

cóng A dào B 怎麼 zǒu?

zuò vehicle

VP₁ 還是 VP₂ (呢)

在 location + ActV

V-O V + duration

Dialogue

The Situation: Xiao Xie has invited Xiao Zhang to his home for dinner on Sunday. He has drawn a map for Xiao Zhang to show him where his home is located and is now giving Xiao Zhang directions to get there from the dormitory.

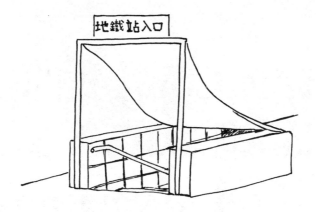

Part A

小張： **Cóng** 我的 **sùshè dào** 你家怎麼 **zǒu**？

小謝： 你想 **zuò dìtiě** 還是想 **zuò gōnggòng qìchē** 呢？

小張： 我 **zuò dìtiě**。

小謝： 好。你在大學的 **dìtiě zhàn** 上 **chē**，上六號 **xiàn**，去 **shì** 中 **xīn**。

小張： **Zuò** 幾 **zhàn**？

小謝： **Zuò** 三 **zhàn**。在圖書館 **zhàn** 下 **chē**，**huàn** 九號 **xiàn**，**wǎng xī zǒu**。**Zuò** 四 **zhàn**。在中 **huá lù** 下 **chē**。在那兒有一個電 **yǐngyuàn**、一個書 **diàn**、還有一個日本飯館。

小張： **Cóng sùshè dào** 你家 **zuò chē yào zuò** 多 **cháng shíjiān**？

小謝： 你 **děi zuò chà** 不多一個 **zhōngtóu**。

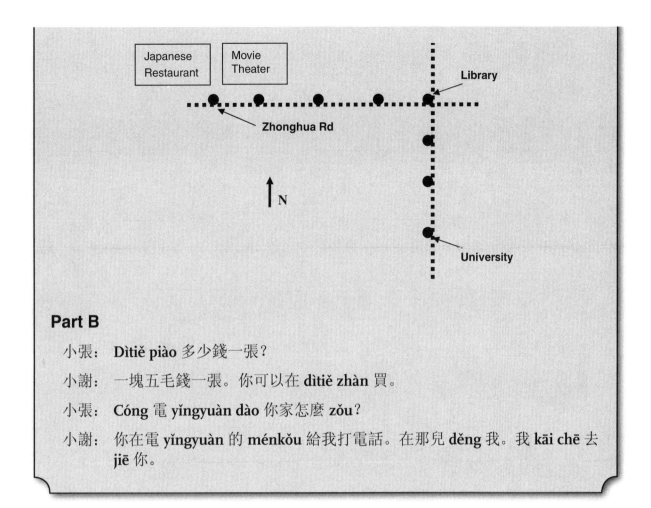

Part B

小張：　**Dìtiě piào** 多少錢一張？

小謝：　一塊五毛錢一張。你可以在 **dìtiě zhàn** 買。

小張：　**Cóng** 電 **yǐngyuàn dào** 你家怎麼 **zǒu**？

小謝：　你在電 **yǐngyuàn** 的 **ménkǒu** 給我打電話。在那兒 **děng** 我。我 **kāi chē** 去 **jiē** 你。

Vocabulary

chàbuduō	**chà** 不多	adjectival verb	*almost*
chē [**gè**]		noun	*car, vehicle*
cóng		preposition	*from*
dào		preposition	*to*
dàxué [**gè**]	大學	noun	*college*
děng		verb	*wait*
diànyǐng [**gè**]	電 **yǐng**	noun	*movie*

diànyǐngyuàn [gè]	電 yǐngyuàn	noun	*movie theater*
dìtiě [gè]		noun	*subway*
duō cháng shíjiān	多 cháng shíjiān	question phrase	*how much time, how long*
fànguǎn [gè]	飯館	noun	*restaurant*
gōnggòng qìchē [gè]		noun	*(public) bus*
háishi	還是	conjunction	*or*
hào	號	classifier	*number (for buses and trains)*
	號 mǎ (hàomǎ)		*(telephone) number*
huàn		verb	*change (one thing for another)*
jiē		verb	*fetch someone*
kāi		verb	*drive*
kāi chē		verb + object	*drive a car*
kǒu		noun	*mouth*
mén [gè]		noun	*door, gate*
ménkǒu [gè]		noun	*doorway (the mouth of the door)*
piào [zhāng]		noun	*ticket*
qìchē [gè]		noun	*car (with an engine)*
shàng	上	verb	*go up, get on*
shíjiān		noun	*time*
wǎng		preposition	*toward*
xià	下	verb	*go down, get off*

xiàn		noun	*line (train line, subway line)*
zài	在	preposition	*at, in, on*
Zhōnghuá	中 **huá**	proper name	*China*
zhōngtóu [gè]		noun	*hour*
zǒu		verb	*go*
zuò		verb	*sit, ride, or "take" a form of transportation*

Characters

本 **běn**	*(classifier: volume)*		日本 (**Rìběn**) *Japan*
			一本書 (**yī běn shū**) *one book*
打 **dǎ**	*hit*		打電話 (**dǎ diànhuà**) *make a phone call*
大 **dà**	*big*		大學 (**dàxué**) *college*
電 **diàn**	*electricity*		電話 (**diànhuà**) *telephone*
			電 **yǐng** (**diànyǐng**) *movie*
			電 **yǐngyuàn** (**diànyǐngyuàn**) *movie theater*
給 **gěi**	*give; for, to*		給他打電話 (**gěi tā dǎ diànhuà**) *phone him*
館 **guǎn**	*		圖書館 (**túshūguǎn**) *library*
			飯館 (**fànguǎn**) *restaurant*
			kāfēi 館 (**kāfēiguǎn**) *coffee shop*

號	hào	number	號 mǎ (hàomǎ) (phone) number
			幾 yuè 幾號 (jǐyuè jǐhào) what month and what date?
就	jiù	precisely, only, (sooner than expected)	
塊	kuài	dollar	一塊錢 (yī kuài qián) one dollar
買	mǎi	buy	
毛	máo	dime	兩毛錢 (liǎng máo qián) twenty cents
錢	qián	money	一塊錢 (yī kuài qián) one dollar
日	rì	*	日本 (Rìběn) Japan
書	shū	book	圖書館 (túshūguǎn) library
			kàn 書 (kàn shū) read books, read
圖	tú	*	圖書館 (túshūguǎn) library
			dì 圖 (dìtú) map
下	xià	next, go down, get off	下個星期 (xià gè xīngqī) next week
			下 chē (xià chē) get out of the vehicle
			下 kè (xià kè) get out of class
想	xiǎng	think, want, plan to	

Stroke Order Flow Chart

character:	strokes:												total strokes:
本	一	十	才	木	本								5
打	一	十	扌	扩	打								5
大	一	ナ	大										3
電	一	厂	戶	示	雨	雨	雨	雨	雫	雨	雨	電	13
給	ㄥ	纟	纟	纟	纟	糸	糸	給	給	給	給		12
館	ノ	𠆢	𠂊	今	今	今	食	食	食	飠	館	館	
	館	館											16
號	丶	口	口	吊	号	号'	号ゲ	虷	虒	號	號	號	13
就	丶	亠	亠	吉	古	亨	京	京	京	尤	就	就	12
塊	一	十	土	圹	圹	坭	坭	坤	坤	塊	塊	塊	13
買	丶	口	四	四	四	罒	買	買	胃	買	買	買	12
毛	一	二	三	毛									4
錢	ノ	𠆢	𠂉	乍	午	牟	余	金	釒	鈛	錢	錢	錢	
	錢	錢											16
日	丨	冂	日	日									4
書	㇆	𠃌	彐	彐	聿	聿	書	書	書	書			10
圖	丨	冂	冂	門	門	冏	冏	圄	圖	圖	圖	圖	14
下	一	丁	下										3
想	一	十	才	木	和	相	相	相	相	想	想	想	13

Dialogue practice

Do these activities in class after mastering the dialogue for this lesson. Change partners so that you practice each part several times.

Dialogue 12A: *Activity 1.* Pair up with a classmate and give him a choice of two things to do, two things to eat, or two things to study. Your classmate should tell you which he would prefer.

Activity 2. Draw a simple map indicating the route from your school to some destination by bus or train. Pair up with a classmate and take turns asking each other how to get to the destination from school and explaining the process.

Dialogue 12B: Prepare a list of prices for train tickets, subway tickets, bus tickets, and movie tickets. Indicate where each kind of ticket can be bought. Pair up with a classmate and take turns asking about the price of train, subway, bus, and movie tickets, and the locations where they can be purchased.

Use and structure

12.1. Prepositions: **Cóng** *from*, **dào** *to*, 在 *at, in, on*, and **wǎng** *toward*

In this lesson we learn four more Mandarin prepositions: **cóng** *from*, **dào** *to*, 在 *at, in, on*, and **wǎng** *toward*.

Remember that prepositions are always followed by a noun or noun phrase. The preposition and the following noun or noun phrase form a prepositional phrase (PP).

prep. + NP = PP	
cóng 我的 **sùshè**	*from my dormitory*
dào 你家	*to your house*
在 **chēzhàn**	*at the station*
wǎng běi	*toward the north*

In Mandarin, the prepositional phrase generally occurs <u>before</u> the verb phrase. In English, the prepositional phrase usually occurs <u>after</u> the verb phrase.

PP	**+**	**VP**	
cóng 我家		**lái**	*from my home come (come from my home)*
dào 你家		去	*to your home go (go to your home)*
在 **chēzhàn**		上六號 **xiàn**	*at the station get on the number 6 line*
wǎng běi		**zǒu**	*toward the north go (go north)*

If **cóng** and **dào** occur in the same sentence, the **cóng** prepositional phrase always occurs before the **dào** prepositional phrase.

> **Cóng** 我的 **sùshè dào** 你家怎麼 **zǒu**？
> *How do I go from my dormitory to your home?*

Negation and adverbs occur before the prepositional phrase.

> 他們都 **dào** 圖書館去看書。
> *They are all going to the library to read.*

> 我不在 **sùshè** 吃飯。
> *I don't eat at the dorm.*

The prepositions **dào** and **gěi** can both be translated into English with the word *to*, but in Mandarin, the meanings of **dào** and **gěi** are distinct. **Dào** is used when talking about movement to some location. **Gěi** is used when talking about doing something to or for someone.

12.2. Movement from one location to another

Asking how to go from one location to another

To ask how to go from one location to another use the prepositions **cóng** and **dào** and say:

> **cóng (location A) dào (location B)** 怎麼 **zǒu**？
> **Cóng** 我的 **sùshè dào** 你家怎麼 **zǒu**？
> *How do I go from my dormitory to your home?*

> **Cóng** 電 **yǐngyuàn dào** 你家怎麼 **zǒu?**
> *How do I go from the movie theater to your home?*

You can omit either the **cóng** *from* phrase or the **dào** *to* phrase if it is understood from the context:

> **Cóng** 我的 **sùshè** 怎麼 **zǒu**？   *How do I go from my dormitory?*
> **Dào** 你家怎麼 **zǒu**？   *How do I go to your home?*

Saying *go to a location*: **dào** location 去 and *come to a location*: **dào** location **lái**

In Lessons 10 and 11 we learned how to say *go to a location* and *come to a location* using the verbs 去 *go* and **lái** *come* (Use and Structure notes 10.16 and 11.3).

> 我們去那個 **xīn** 的 **kāfēi** 館，怎麼樣？
> *How about if we go to that new coffee shop?*

> 星期天晚上 **lái** 我家吃飯，怎麼樣？
> *Come to my house to eat on Sunday night, okay?*

You can also talk about *going to a location* with **dào** *to* and 去 *go* in the following pattern:

> **dào location** 去
> 我想 <u>**dào** 書 **diàn**</u> 去。
> *I want to go to the bookstore.*

You can talk about *coming to a location* with **dào** *to* and **lái** *come* in the following pattern:

> **dào location lái**
> 請 <u>**dào** 我家 **lái**</u>。
> *Please come to my house.*

The pattern **dào** <u>location</u> 去 is equivalent in meaning to the pattern <u>去 location</u>:

> 我想 **dào** 書 **diàn** 去。 = 我想<u>去書 **diàn**</u>。
> *I want to go to the bookstore.*

The pattern **dào** <u>location</u> **lái** is equivalent in meaning to the pattern <u>**lái** location</u>:

> 請 **dào** 我家 **lái**。 = 請 <u>**lái** 我家</u>。
> *Please come to my house.*

When talking about a completed action, 了 occurs after the verb 去 *go* or **lái** *come*, and never after the preposition **dào** *to*.

Say this:	***Do not say this:***
我 **zuó** 天 **dào** 圖書館去了。	⊗ 我 **zuó** 天 **dào** 了圖書館去。
Yesterday I went to the library.	

Talking about going toward a location or going in a compass direction

To talk about going *toward* a location or going in a compass direction, use the preposition **wǎng** *toward* with the verb **zǒu** *go*:

> **Cóng** 電 **yǐngyuàn dào** 我家 <u>**wǎng běi zǒu**</u>。
> *From the movie theater to my home go (toward the) north.*

12.3.   Alternatives: VP₁ 還是 VP₂ (呢) *VP₁ or VP₂*

Asking someone to choose between two alternatives

When asking someone to choose between two alternatives use 還是 and say:

> **VP**₁ 還是 **VP**₂ (呢)
> 你想 <u>**zuò dìtiě**</u> 還是想 <u>**zuò gōnggòng qìchē**</u> 呢？
> *Would you like to go by subway or by bus?*

Questions with 還是 are often called <u>split-choice questions</u>, since the question presents two choices. Split-choice questions often end with the sentence final particle 呢. 呢 serves to soften the tone of the question.

When the verb in the second alternative is 是, the alternative is expressed as:

是 **NP₁** 還是 **NP₂**
你是學生還是老師?
Are you a student or a teacher?
(Not: 你是學生還是<u>是</u>老師?)

Replying to a 還是 question

When replying to a 還是 question, state the alternative that you prefer.

Q: 你想 **zuò dìtiě** 還是想 **zuò gōnggòng qìchē** 呢?
Would you like to go by subway or by bus?

A: 我 <u>**zuò dìtiě**</u>。
I'll go by subway.

12.4.   Riding a vehicle as a passenger: **Zuò chē**

In Mandarin, to indicate that you are a passenger on a vehicle, you use the verb **zuò** *sit*. Notice that this use of **zuò** is often expressed in English as *take*.

你想 **zuò dìtiě** 還是想 **zuò gōnggòng qìchē** 呢?
Would you rather take the subway or the bus?

To indicate the number of stops you ride on a bus or train, say:

zuò (number) zhàn
Zuò 三 **zhàn**。   *Ride for three stops.*

To ask how many stops to take a bus or train, ask:

Zuò 幾 **zhàn**?   *How many stops do I go? (Literally: Sit for how many stops?)*

To say that you are taking a form of transportation to a location, state the means of transportation before the action of going, coming, or returning:

means of transportation + 去**/lái/huí location**
or
means of transportation + 到 **location** 去**/lái**
你可以 **zuò dìtiě** 去電 **yǐngyuàn**。
You can take the subway to the movie theater.

他們 **zuò fēijī dào** 中 **guó lái**。
They are coming to China by plane.

我們 **zuò gōnggòng qìchē huí** 家了。
We took the bus home.

To say that you are driving a car, bus, or train, use the verb **kāi** and say **kāi chē** (**kāi gōnggòng qìchē, kāi huǒchē**). See also Use and Structure notes 12.6 and 12.7.

12.5.   Doing an action at a location: 在 location ActV

To talk about doing an action at a location, use the preposition 在 *at, in, on* and say:

在 **location ActV**
在圖書館 **zhàn** 下 **chē**
at Library Station get off the train

你可以在 **dìtiě zhàn** 買 **piào**。
You can buy tickets at the subway station. (You can at the subway station buy tickets)

Notice that in Mandarin, if you are talking about doing an action <u>here</u> or <u>there</u> you must use the preposition 在 along with the word 這兒 *here* or 那兒 *there*:

你可以<u>在這兒</u>買 **piào**。
You can buy tickets here.

你<u>在那兒</u>上六號 **xiàn**。
Get on the number 6 line there.

When talking about doing an action at a given place and time, the order of information is:

time when + location
我 **zuó** 天晚上在一個日本飯館吃飯了。
Last night I ate dinner at a Japanese restaurant.

12.6.   上 **chē** *get on the vehicle*, 下 **chē** *get off the vehicle*

To say that you are getting on a vehicle (a subway, a bus, a car, a bicycle, an airplane, etc.) use the verb 上 and say 上 **chē** *get on the vehicle.*

你在那兒上六號 **chē**。   *Get on the number 6 train there.*

To say that you are getting off a vehicle, use the verb 下 and say 下 **chē** *get off the vehicle.*

在中 **huá lù** 下 **chē**。   *Get off the train at Zhonghua Road.*

Say "下 **chē**" if you are riding a crowded bus or train and want to let others know that you are planning to get off.

We have already learned the words 上 and 下 in other expressions:

上個 **yuè**	*last month*	下個 **yuè**	*next month*
上個星期	*last week*	下個星期	*next week*
上 **kè**	*go to class*	下 **kè**	*get out of class*
晚上	*evening*	早上	*morning*

12.7. Train and bus numbers

Bus and train numbers are formed by <u>number + 號</u>. When the number two precedes 號 it is always 二: 二號.

The names of bus lines usually end with **chē** *car* or **gōnggòng qìchē** *bus*: 五號 **chē** *the number 5 bus*, 三號 **gōnggòng qìchē** *the number 3 bus*.

The names of subway lines usually end with the word **xiàn** *line*: 一號 **xiàn** *the number 1 line*, 八號 **xiàn** *the number 8 line*.

12.8. Changing train or bus lines

To talk about changing train or bus lines, use the word **huàn** *change* and say **huàn chē** *change cars/changes busses*, **huàn xiàn** *change lines*, **huàn** 八號 **xiàn** *change to the number 8 line*.

在圖書館 **zhàn** 下 **chē**，**huàn** 九號 **xiàn**。
Get off at Library Station and change to line 9.

12.9. Something exists at a location: 在 location 有 N or 有 N 在 location

To indicate that something exists at a location say:

在 **location** 有 **N**   or   有 **N** 在 **location**
在那兒有一個電 **yǐngyuàn**。   有一個電 **yǐngyuàn** 在那兒。
There is a movie theater there.   *There is a movie theater there.*
(At that location there is a movie theater.)

When indicating location, if 在 is the first word of the sentence, it may be omitted.

在那兒有一個電 **yǐngyuàn**。   =   那兒有一個電 **yǐngyuàn**。
There is a movie theater there.

在大學的 **ménkǒu** 有 **dìtiě zhàn**。 =   大學的 **ménkǒu** 有 **dìtiě zhàn**。
At the entrance to the university there is a subway station.

12.10. The duration of a situation: (V + O) V + duration

Stating the duration of a situation

Stating duration without including the object of the verb
To indicate the duration of a situation, that is, to say how long a situation occurs, follow the verb with the duration expression.

V + duration
你 **děi zuò** 一個 **zhōngtóu**。
You have to ride for an hour.

When talking about the duration of completed actions, 了 follows the verb.

我 **zuó**天晚上 **shuì** 了八個 **zhōngtóu**。
Last night I slept for eight hours.

The adverb **chà** 不多 *almost* comes right before the duration expression.

你 **děi zuò chà** 不多一個 **zhōngtóu**。
You have to ride for about an hour.

To say that you have done an action for a long period of time, say 很 **cháng shíjiān**.

我 **děng** 了很 **cháng shíjiān**。
I waited for a long time.

Stating duration and including the object of the verb
When indicating the duration of an action, if you include the object of the verb, you must state the verb twice, first followed by the object, and then followed by the duration phrase:

V + O   **V + duration**
你 **zuò dìtiě**   **zuò** 一個 **zhōngtóu**。
You ride the subway for an hour.

You may think of "verb + object" as the topic of the sentence, something like *As for riding the subway, you ride for an hour.* See also the Lesson 12 Language FAQs.

Notice that if 了 is used, it follows the <u>second</u> occurrence of the verb.

我 **zuó**天晚上 **shuì jiào** <u>**shuì** 了</u> 八個 **zhōngtóu**。
Last night I slept for eight hours.

我 **zuò dìtiě** <u>**zuò** 了</u> **chà** 不多一個 **zhōngtóu**。
I rode the subway for almost an hour.

Asking about the duration of situations

To ask how long a situation occurs, use the question phrase 多 **cháng shíjiān** *how long* after the verb.

(V + O) V 多 **cháng shíjiān**
Zuò dìtiě yào zuò 多 **cháng shíjiān**?
How long do you have to ride the train?

你 **shuì jiào shuì** 了多 **cháng shíjiān**?
How long did you sleep?

Time expressions that indicate duration

Here are time expressions that are commonly used to indicate duration. Notice that when talking about the number of minutes that an action occurs for, the phrase to use is number + 分 + **zhōng**.

分	*minute*	**zuò** 十五分 **zhōng**	*sat (rode) for 15 minutes*
zhōngtóu	*hour*	**shuì** 了八個 **zhōngtóu**	*slept for 8 hours*
天	*day*	**xiǎng** 了一天	*thought (about something) for a day*
星期	*week*	**fùxí** 了一個星期	*reviewed for a week*
yuè	*month*	學了六個 **yuè**	*studied for 6 months*
nián	*year*	學中文學了一 **nián**	*studied Chinese for a year*

Sentence pyramids

The sentence pyramids illustrate the use of each new vocabulary item and structure introduced in the lesson. Use them to help you learn how to form phrases and sentences in Mandarin. Supply the English translation for the last line where indicated.

I. **zǒu** 怎麼 **zǒu**？ **Dào** 你家怎麼 **zǒu**？	*go* *how do you go?* *How do you go to your home?*
2. 怎麼 **zǒu**？ **Dào** 你家怎麼 **zǒu**？ **Cóng** 我的 **sùshè dào** 你家怎麼 **zǒu**？	*How do you go?* *How do you go to your home?* *How do you go from my dormitory to your home?*
3. 怎麼 **zǒu**？ **Dào** 你家怎麼 **zǒu**？ **Cóng** 電 **yǐngyuàn dào** 你家怎麼 **zǒu**？	*How do you go?* *How do you go to your home?* _____ _____
4. **gōnggòng qìchē** **zuò gōnggòng qìchē** 想 **zuò gōnggòng qìchē** 我想 **zuò gōnggòng qìchē**。	*(public) bus* *take the bus* *plan to take the bus*

5. **gōnggòng qìchē** **zuò gōnggòng qìchē** 還是 **zuò gōnggòng qìchē** 你 **zuò dìtiě** 還是 **zuò gōnggòng** 　　**qìchē**?	*bus* *take the bus* *or take the bus* *Will you take the subway or the bus?*
6. 吃中 **guó** 飯 還是吃中 **guó** 飯 吃日本飯還是吃中 **guó** 飯? 你想吃日本飯還是吃中 **guó** 飯呢?	*eat Chinese food* *or eat Chinese food* *eat Japanese food or Chinese food?* _____
7. **piányi** 很 **piányi** **Dìtiě piào** 很 **piányi**。	*cheap* *very cheap* *Subway tickets are very cheap.*
8. **zhàn** **dìtiě zhàn** 有 **dìtiě zhàn** 在大學的 **ménkǒu** 有 **dìtiě zhàn**。	*station* *subway station* *there is a subway station* *At the entrance to the college there is* 　　*a subway station.*
9. 上 **chē** 在那兒上 **chē** 你在那兒上 **chē**。	*get on the car* *get on the car (train) there* *Get on the train there.*
10. 六號 **xiàn** 上六號 **xiàn** 在那兒上六號 **xiàn** 你在那兒上六號 **xiàn**。	*number 6 train* *get on the number 6 train* *get on the number 6 train there* _____
11. **shì** 中 **xīn** 去 **shì** 中 **xīn** 在那兒上六號 **xiàn**，去 **shì** 中**xīn**。 你在那兒上六號 **xiàn**，去 **shì** 　　中 **xīn**。	*the center of the city* *go to the center of the city* *get on the number 6 train there and go* 　　*to the center of the city* _____ _____

12. **zǒu** Wǎng xī zǒu。	*go* *Go west.*
13. **zhàn** 幾 **zhàn**? Zuò 幾 **zhàn**?	*stops (stations)* *how many stops?* *Take (the vehicle) for how many stops?*
14. **zhàn** 三 **zhàn** Zuò 三 **zhàn**。	*stops (stations)* *three stops* _____
15. **chē** 下 **chē** 在圖書館 **zhàn** 下 **chē**。	*car (vehicle)* *get off the vehicle* *Get off (the vehicle) at Library Station.*
16. **xiàn** 九號 **xiàn** Huàn 九號 **xiàn**。	*(train) line* *number 9 train line* *Change for the number 9 train line.*
17. **zhōngtóu** 一個 **zhōngtóu** **zuò** 一個 **zhōngtóu** **zuò chà** 不多一個 **zhōngtóu** 你 **děi zuò chà** 不多一個 **zhōngtóu**。	*hour* *one hour* *sit (ride) for an hour* *sit (ride) for almost an hour* *You have to sit (ride) for almost an hour.*
18. **shíjiān** 多 **cháng shíjiān** **zuò** 多 **cháng shíjiān**? Zuò chē zuò 多 **cháng shíjiān**?	*time* *how long?* *sit (ride) for how long?* *How long do you ride the train?*
19. 兩個 **zhōngtóu** 兩個半 **zhōngtóu** 看了兩個半 **zhōngtóu** 看電 **yǐng** 看了兩個半 **zhōngtóu** 我 **zuó** 天看電 **yǐng** 看了兩個半 **zhōngtóu**。	*two hours* *two and a half hours* *watched for two and a half hours* *watched movies for two and a half hours* *Yesterday I watched movies for two and a half hours.*

20. 下 **chē** 在中 **huá lù** 下 **chē**。	*get off the vehicle* *Get off at Zhonghua Road.*
21. 電 **yǐngyuàn** 一個電 **yǐngyuàn** 有一個電 **yǐngyuàn** 那兒有一個電 **yǐngyuàn**。 在那兒有一個電 **yǐngyuàn**。	*movie theater* *a movie theater* *there is a movie theater* *There is a movie theater there.* *There is a movie theater there.*
22. 飯館 日本飯館 有一個日本飯館 在那兒有一個日本飯館。	*restaurant* *Japanese restaurant* *there is a Japanese restaurant* *There is a Japanese restaurant there.*
23. 一張 多少錢一張？ **Dìtiě piào** 多少錢一張？	*one (ticket)* *how much money for one (ticket)?* *How much does a subway ticket cost?*
24. 一張 五毛錢一張 一塊五毛錢一張	*one (ticket)* *fifty cents for one ticket* *A subway ticket is ￥1.5.*
25. 買 在 **dìtiě zhàn** 買 你可以在 **dìtiě zhàn** 買。	*buy* *buy at the subway station* *You can buy (one) at the subway station.*
26. **děng** 我 在那兒 **děng** 我。	*wait for me* *Wait for me there.*
27. **jiē** 你 我去 **jiē** 你。	*get you* *I will go and get you.*
28. **jiē** 你 去 **jiē** 你 **kāi chē** 去 **jiē** 你 我可以 **kāi chē** 去 **jiē** 你。	*get you (pick you up)* *go and get you* *drive over and get you* *I can drive over and get you.*

Language FAQs

What is the difference between 去 *go* and zǒu *go?*

去 refers to movement that ends at some destination.

> 我想去書 **diàn**。
> *I want to go to the bookstore.*

Zǒu is used when talking about going <u>toward</u> (but not <u>to</u>) some place, or movement in some compass direction.

> **Wǎng** 書 **diàn zǒu**。
> *Go toward the bookstore.*

> **Wǎng běi zǒu**。
> *Go north.*

Zǒu is also used when asking about the <u>process</u> of going from place to place.

> **Cóng** 電 **yǐngyuàn dào** 你家怎麼 **zǒu**？
> *How do you go from the movie theater to your home?*

How can 在 be a verb and a preposition?

In Lesson 11 we learned how to use 在 as a verb (Use and Structure note 11.11).

> **Gōngyuán** 在 **běibiān**。 *The park is (located) in the north.*

In this lesson we learn to use 在 as a preposition (Use and Structure note 12.5).

> 在 **chēzhàn** 上六號 **xiàn**。 *At the station, get on the number 6 line.*

Mandarin words do not include any features that mark their grammatical function. Therefore, some Mandarin words can be used in more than one way, and 在 is one of those words. In any given sentence, 在 only has only one grammatical function, and the overall structure of the sentence makes it clear how 在 is being used. If 在 is followed by a noun phrase and a verb phrase, it is being used as a preposition that indicates the location where some action takes place (在 **chēzhàn** 上六號 **xiàn** *get on the number 6 line at the station*), or the location where something exists (在那兒 有一個電 **yǐngyuàn** *there is a movie theater there*). If 在 is followed only by a noun phrase and not a verb phrase, it is being used as a verb indicating the location of some noun (**gōngyuán** 在 **běibiān** *the park is in the north*).

Why do you repeat the verb in duration expressions?

Generally speaking, Mandarin verbs are followed by <u>only one</u> piece of information at a time. If the verb is followed by two pieces of information, for example, an object and a phrase that indicates duration, the verb is stated twice. In later lessons we will learn additional structures involving <u>verb + object verb + additional information</u>.

Notes on Chinese culture

What is the difference between 中 guó and 中 huá?

Both words refer to China, but they are not interchangeable in the expressions in which they occur. 中 **huá** is used in the official name for the People's Republic of China ("mainland China": 中 **huá Rénmín Gònghéguó**) and the Republic of China ("Taiwan": 中 **huá Mínguó**). **Huá** is generally used to refer to ethnicity rather than citizenship. Thus, the expression **Huá** 人 refers to people of Chinese descent, regardless of their citizenship or residence. In contrast, the expression 中 **guó** 人 refers to Chinese people from China.

Getting a guest: 我去 jiē 你

Jiē means to pick up a person from some location and bring her someplace. When guests come to visit, it is polite to "**jiē**" them and bring them to your home or to the place where you will be gathering. Most cultures have certain rituals associated with receiving a guest, and we will learn other vocabulary and rituals associated with the behavior of guest and host in the following lessons.

Lesson 12 Dialogue in English

Part A

Xiao Zhang:	How do I go from my dormitory to your home?
Xiao Xie:	Do you want to go by subway or by bus?
Xiao Zhang:	I'll go by subway.
Xiao Xie:	Okay. Get on the train at the college subway station. Get on Line 6 and go to the city center.
Xiao Zhang:	How many stops do I ride?
Xiao Xie:	Take it for three stops. Get off at Library Station, change to the number 9 line, and go west. Go for four stops. Get off at Zhonghua Road. There is a movie theater there, a bookstore, and also a Japanese restaurant.
Xiao Zhang:	How long do I have to ride from the dorm to your house?
Xiao Xie:	You have to ride for about an hour.

Part B

Xiao Zhang:	How much is a subway ticket?
Xiao Xie:	¥1.50 a ticket. You can buy one at the subway station.
Xiao Zhang:	How do I go from the movie theater to your home?
Xiao Xie:	Phone me at the entrance to the movie theater. Wait for me there. I'll drive over to get you.

Lesson 13 我家很容易找
My home is easy to find

Communication goals
- Make and accept apologies
- Politely initiate and receive telephone calls
- Describe the location of people, places, and things

Key structures
容易 + V, **nán** + V

reference point 的 direction

sequence with **xiān** and 再

Dialogue

The Situation: Xiao Zhang has arrived at the subway station near to Xiao Xie's house and is phoning Xiao Xie to let him know.

Part A

小謝：　Wéi？

小張：　請問，小謝在嗎？

小謝：　我就是。Nín 是哪 wèi？

小張：　是我，小張。我現在在中 huá 路車 zhàn。

Part B

小謝：　對不起，bié 的 kè 人已經到了。我不 néng 去 jiē 你了。Zhēn 不好 yìsi。

小張：　沒 guānxi。

小謝：　我 gàosu 你怎麼走。我家很容易找。

小張：　好。

Part C

小謝： 你在車 zhàn 的 lǐbiān 還是在車 zhàn 的 wàibiān？

小張： 我在 wàibiān。

小謝： 車 zhàn wài 有一個日本飯館，門上有 "東京" 兩個 zì。你看見了嗎？

小張： 看見了。我就在那個飯館和一個電 yǐngyuàn 的中 jiān。電 yǐngyuàn 在我的 zuǒbian，飯館在 yòubian。

小謝： 好。你就在車 zhàn 的西門。你從車 zhàn wǎng běi 走。

小張： Guò 馬路嗎？

小謝： 對，你得 xiān guò 馬路，再 wǎng běi 走。在 Gōngyuán 路 wǎng zuǒ guǎi。

to be continued...

Vocabulary

biéde	bié 的	noun description	*other*
bù hǎo yìsi	不好 yìsi	conversational expression	*embarrassed*
chēzhàn	車 zhàn	noun	*station*
dào	到	verb	*arrive*
Dōngjīng	東京	city name	*Tokyo*
gàosu		verb	*inform, tell*
guǎi		verb	*turn*
guò		verb	*cross, pass*
jiù	就	adverb	*precisely*
kànjian	看見	verb	*see*
kèrén [gè]	kè 人	noun	*guest*
lǐ		*	*inside*

lǐbiān		noun	*inside*
mǎlù	馬路	noun	*road (local road), street (literally: horse road)*
méi guānxi	沒 guānxi	conversational expression	*not be important, (it) doesn't matter*
néng		modal verb	*able*
nín		pronoun	*you (polite)*
shàng	上	*	*on, above*
shàngbiān	上 biān	noun	*on, above*
wài		*	*outside*
wàibiān		noun	*outside*
wéi, wèi		conversational expression	*(greeting used when answering the telephone)*
wèi		classifier	*(polite classifier for people)*
xià	下	*	*under, below*
xiàbiān	下 biān	noun	*under, below*
xiān		adverb	*first*
yòu		*	*right*
yòubiān		noun	*right side*
zài	再	adverb	*afterward*
zhǎo	找	verb	*look for (here: find)*
zhēn		intensifier	*really (L3 zhēn 的)*
zhōngjiān	中 jiān	noun	*between, in between*
zuǒ		*	*left*
zuǒbiān		noun	*left side*

Characters

車	chē	*car*	**qì** 車 (**qìchē**) *vehicle that rides on the ground and has an engine*
			gōnggòng qì 車 (**gōnggòng qìchē**) *bus*
			huǒ 車 (**huǒchē**) *train*
			車 **zhàn** (**chēzhàn**) *bus or train station*
從	cóng	*from*	
到	dào	*to (preposition)* *arrive (verb)*	
得	děi	*must*	
	de	*	**jué** 得 (**juéde**) *think, hold an opinion*
			說得快 (**shuō de kuài**) *speak quickly*
東	dōng	*east*	東 **biān** (**dōngbian**) *east*
			東京 (**Dōngjīng**) *Tokyo*
和	hé	*and*	
京	jīng	*	東京 (**Dōngjīng**) *Tokyo*
			Běi 京 (**Běijīng**) *Beijing*
經	jīng	*	已經 (**yǐjing**) *already*
路	lù	*road*	馬路 (**mǎlù**) *(local) road*
馬	mǎ	*horse, (family name)*	馬路 (**mǎlù**) *(local) road*
門	mén	*door, gate*	門口 (**ménkǒu**) *doorway, gateway*
容	róng	*	容易 (**róngyì**) *easy*
問	wèn	*ask*	請問 (**qǐng wèn**) *may I ask*
西	xī	*west*	西 **biān** (**xībiān**) *west*
			東西 (**dōngxi**) *thing*

現	xiàn	*	現在 (**xiànzài**) *now*
已	yǐ	*already*	已經 (**yǐjing**) *already*
易	yì	*	容易 (**róngyì**) *easy*
找	zhǎo	*look for*	
		give change	找錢 (**zhǎo qián**) *give money in change*
走	zǒu	*go*	

Stroke Order Flow Chart

character:	strokes:											total strokes:
車	一	厂	斤	亘	亘	車						7
從	丿	彳	彳	彳	社	衸	衸	従	従	從		11
到	一	云	云	至	至	到	到					8
得	丿	彳	彳	彳	律	律	律	得	得	得		11
東	一	厂	斤	亘	亘	車	東	東				8
和	丿	二	千	禾	禾	和	和	和				8
京	丶	亠	宀	古	古	宁	京	京				8
經	乚	乡	幺	糸	糸	糸	絅	經	經	經	經	13
路	丶	口	口	尸	尸	卫	足	趵	趵	政	路	13
馬	一	厂	斤	斤	斤	馬	馬	馬	馬	馬		10
門	丨	尸	尸	尸	尸	門	門	門				8
容	丶	丷	宀	宀	宀	突	突	容	容			10
問	丨	尸	尸	尸	尸	門	門	門	問	問	問	11
西	一	一	口	西	西	西						6

現	一	二	干	王	珇	玑	玥	珇	珇	現				11
已	乛	冯	已											3
易	丶	冂	日	日	尸	弓	昮	易						8
找	一	十	扌	扌	找	找	找							7
走	一	十	土	丰	卡	走	走							7

Dialogue practice

Do these activities in class after mastering the dialogue for this lesson. Change partners so that you practice each part several times.

Dialogue 13A: Work with a classmate, taking turns calling each other on the phone. Each conversation should include asking for the person you wish to speak to and asking who the caller is. If you are the person who the caller seeks, identify yourself. You can also say that you are not the person who the caller seeks. You may then explain that the person is not here.

Dialogue 13B: Work with a classmate, and apologize for something that you cannot do for him or her. Your classmate should say that it's not important and should suggest an alternative.

Dialogue 13C: *Twenty questions.* Prepare a street map with the names of several streets and locations. Working with a classmate, pick a location on the map as your location, and have your classmate identify your location by asking yes-no questions and 還是 questions.

Use and structure

13.1. Telephone etiquette: **Wéi** or **wèi**

Wéi and its variation in fourth tone, **wèi**, are used at the beginning of a telephone conversation. You can translate **wéi/wèi** as *hello*, but it is much more restricted in use than *hello* is in English, and it is only used in telephone conversations. **Wèi** (in fourth tone) is relatively abrupt and conveys the sense of impatience.

When answering a telephone, say **wéi** (in second tone). The person who places the call may respond by saying **wéi** or **wèi** before asking to speak with the person he is calling, or before identifying himself. Alternatively, the person who is calling may say 請問 *may I ask*, before asking to speak with the person he is calling. In the dialogue in this lesson, 小張 introduces his question with 請問:

請問，小謝在嗎？　*May I ask, is Xiao Xie there?*

He could have introduced it with **wéi** or **wèi**:

Wéi，小謝在嗎？　*Hello. Is Xiao Xie there?*

Nowadays, people may answer the telephone by saying **Wéi**, 你好, especially in business contexts.

13.2.　Indicating exact identification with 就

In Lesson 9 we learned to use the adverb 就 to indicate that an action occurs sooner than expected (Use and Structure note 9.10), and in Lesson 11 we learned that 就 may also mean *only* (Use and Structure note 11.1). In this lesson we see 就 used to indicate exact identification. In the dialogue, when Xiao Zhang asks for Xiao Xie, Xiao Xie replies that he is Xiao Xie with the sentence:

我就是。
That's me.

就 occurs in the sentence to emphasize that the identification is exactly correct. In Part C of the dialogue, Xiao Xie uses 就 for the same purpose, to indicate a precise location. When used to identify locations, 就 can sometimes be translated as *right* as in the expression *right there*:

你就在車 **zhàn** 的西門。
You are at the west gate of the station.

13.3.　A polite way to refer to people: **Nín** 是哪 **wèi**？

To politely ask for someone's identity, say:

Nín 是哪 **wèi**？　*Who are you?*

Nín is the polite form of 你 and it indicates respect toward the addressee.

Wèi is a classifer for people, and it is used when referring to people politely and with deference. For example, in a restaurant, a waiter may ask you how many people are in your group with the question:

幾 **wèi**？　　　*How many people are you?*

Wèi is typically not followed by a noun.

13.4.　**Néng**, 會, and 可以: Three ways to say *can*

Néng, 會, and 可以 are all modal verbs that can be translated into English as *can*. The words sometimes overlap in use, but the basic meanings of these three words are as follows:

會 refers to innate or learned ability (Use and Structure note 3.4). To say that you can speak Chinese or that you can sing, use 會:

> 我會說中文。
> *I can speak Chinese.*

> 我會 **chàng gē**。
> *I can sing.*

可以 refers to permission (Use and Structure note 5.12). To say that you have permission to go dancing, or to ask someone for permission to do something, use 可以.

> **Māma** 說我可以去 **tiào wǔ**。
> *Mom says I can go dancing.*

> 我可以說 **Yīng** 文嗎?
> *Can I speak English? (Is it okay to speak English?)*

Néng refers to physical or circumstantial ability. When saying that you are physically able to do something (for example, *I can pick up that big box*), or that circumstances make it possible for you to do something (*I can go to your house on Thursday*), use **néng**. To say that you are physically unable to do something or that circumstances make it impossible to do something, say 不 **néng**:

> 我不 **néng** 去 **jiē** 你。
> *I can't go and get you.*

13.5.　Making an apology and accepting an apology

To apologize about not being able to do something for someone, say:

> **Zhēn** 不好 **yìsi**。
> *I'm really embarrassed.*

To acknowledge an apology by saying that the situation was not important (or not one that warrants an apology), say:

> 沒 **guānxi**。
> *It's not important. (Forget it.)*

The expression 對不起 can also be used as an apology, but it is a little different from 不好 **yìsi**. 不好 **yìsi** is used when you are unable to do something for someone who you would not ordinarily refuse, a good friend, a relative, a teacher, a boss, etc. 對不起 can be used with a broader range of people.

13.6.　容易 + V *easy to do*, and **nán** + V *hard to do*

When talking about a specific task being easy to do or hard to do, say:

O 容易 **V**

or

O nán V

我家很容易找。

My home is easy to find.

那個 **zì** 很 **nán xiě**。

That character is difficult to write.

When talking <u>generally</u> about a type of task being easy to do or hard to do, say:

VP 很容易。

or

VP 很 **nán**。

Chàng kǎlā OK 很容易。

Karaoke is easy to sing.

Kāi 車很 **nán**。

Cars are difficult to drive.

13.7. Stating location with respect to some reference point: 車 **zhàn** 的 **lǐbiān** *inside the station*

To indicate a location with respect to some reference point, for example, *inside the station, to the right of the movie theater,* or *behind the coffee shop,* say:

reference point (的) **direction**
車 **zhàn**   (的) **lǐbiān**
inside (of) the station

In the following phrases from the dialogue, the reference point is underlined. Notice that in Mandarin, the reference point is always stated first and the direction is stated last. 的 may often be omitted.

車 **zhàn** 的 **lǐbiān**   *inside of <u>the station</u>*
車 **zhàn** 的 **wàibiān**   *outside of <u>the station</u>*
我的 **zuǒbiān**   *to <u>my</u> left*

The following diagram illustrates *inside the station, outside the station, to the left of the station,* and *to the right of the station.*

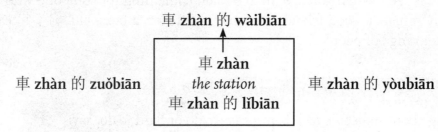

Reference point (的) direction is a <u>location phrase</u>.

Some directions with respect to a location can be expressed with a shorter structure. See Use and Structure note 13.9.

13.8.   Using a location phrase with 有 and 在

As we learned in Lesson 11, 在 is used in the following structure when stating that some person, place, or thing is located at a place (Use and Structure note 11.11):

N 在 location

The location phrase described in Use and Structure note 13.7 often occurs as the "location" in this structure:

學 **xiào** 在圖書館的西 **biān**。
The school is to the west of the library.

你在車 **zhàn** 的 **lǐbiān** 還是在車 **zhàn** 的 **wàibiān**?
Are you inside the train station or outside the train station?

As we learned in Lesson 12, the word 有 *there is, there are*, is used in the following structure to indicate that something exists at a location (Use and Structure note 12.9):

有 **N** 在 **location**   or   在 **location** 有 **N**
有人在 **wàibian**。   在 **wàibian** 有人。
There is a person outside.

The location phrase described in Use and Structure note 13.7 often occurs as the "location" in this structure:

(在)圖書館的西 **biān** 有一個學 **xiào**。
To the west of the library there is a school.

or

有一個學 **xiào** 在圖書館的西 **biān**。
There is a school to the west of the library.

13.9.   The short form of direction expressions: 門上 *on the door* and 車 **zhàn** **wài** *outside of the station*

When talking about *inside, outside, below,* or *on or above* some reference point, you can use the structure described in Use and Structure note 13.7, or you can often use the following short form of direction expressions in which a direction particle alone, without a suffix, follows the reference point

reference point + direction particle
門上
on the door

車 **zhàn wài**
outside of the station

The correspondence between the long form and the short form of direction expressions with respect to a reference point is illustrated here. Speakers in different regions of China differ in their acceptance of the short form for various nouns. The directions *left* and *right*, and the compass directions *east*, *south*, *west*, and *north*, do not occur in the short form.

	short form	long form
reference point **lǐ** *inside the reference point*	**gōngyuán lǐ** *inside the park*	**gōngyuán** 的 **lǐbiān** *inside the park*
reference point **wài** *outside the reference point*	車 **zhàn wài** *outside the station*	車 **zhàn** 的 **wàibiān** *outside the station*
reference point 上 *above or on the reference point*	**chuáng** 上 *on the bed*	**chuáng** 的 上 **biān** *on the bed*
reference point 下 *below or under the reference point*	**chuáng** 下 *under the bed*	**chuáng** 的 下 **biān** *under the bed*

13.10.   Indicating sequence with **xiān** + ActV₁ 再 + ActV₂ *first do ActV₁ then do ActV₂*

To say that you do something <u>first</u> and then something <u>afterwards</u>, use **xiān** *first* and 再 *again, then* and say:

(S) xiān VP₁ 再 **VP₂**
你得 **xiān guò** 馬路，再 **wǎng běi** 走。
First cross the street, then go north.

Xiān and 再 are adverbs and can only occur before a verb phrase. They never occur before a noun.

Sentence pyramids

The sentence pyramids illustrate the use of each new vocabulary item and structure introduced in the lesson. Use them to help you learn how to form phrases and sentences in Mandarin. Supply the English translation for the last line where indicated.

I. 在嗎？ 小謝在嗎？ 請問，小謝在嗎？	*at (location)?* *Is Xiao Xie there?* *May I ask, is Xiao Xie there?*

2.	
是	*am*
就是	*(precisely) am*
我就是。	*That's me.*

3.	
wèi	*(polite classifier for people)*
哪 **wèi**?	*which person?*
Nín 是哪 **wèi**?	*Who are you?*

4.	
到	*arrive*
到了	*arrived*
已經到了。	*already arrived*
Kè 人已經到了。	*The guests have already arrived.*
Bié 的 **kè** 人已經到了。	*The other guests have already arrived.*

5.	
mài 這本書	*sell this book*
不 **mài** 這本書	*do not sell this book*
書 **diàn** 不 **mài** 這本書	*bookstores do not sell this book*
Bié 的書 **diàn** 不 **mài** 這書。	

6.	
jiē 你	*pick you up (get you)*
去 **jiē** 你	*go pick you up (get you)*
néng 去 **jiē** 你	*able to go pick you up*
不 **néng** 去 **jiē** 你	*can't go pick you up*
我不 **néng** 去 **jiē** 你。	*I can't go pick you up.*
我不 **néng** 去 **jiē** 你了。	*I can't go pick you up anymore.*

7.	
不好 **yìsi**	*embarrassing, embarrassed*
Zhēn 不好 **yìsi**。	*It's really embarrassing. (I'm really sorry.)*

8.	
小謝：對不起。	*Xiao Xie: Sorry.*
小張：沒 **guānxi**。	*Xiao Zhang: Don't worry about it.*

9.	
找	*look for, find*
容易找	*easy to find*
我家很容易找。	*My home is very easy to find.*

10. **nán xiě** 很 **nán xiě** 中文很 **nán xiě**。	*difficult to write* *very difficult to write* ————————————
11. 走 怎麼走 **gàosu** 你怎麼走 我 **gàosu** 你怎麼走。	*go* *how to go* *tell you how to go* ————————————
12. **wàibiān** 在 **wàibiān** 我在 **wàibiān**。	*outside* *located outside* ————————————
13. **wàibiān** 車 **zhàn** 的 **wàibiān** 我在車 **zhàn** 的 **wàibiān**。	*outside* *outside of the station* *I am outside of the station.*
14. **wàibiān** 車 **zhàn** 的 **wàibiān** 在車 **zhàn** 的 **wàibiān** 在車 **zhàn** 的 **lǐbiān** 還是在車 **zhàn** 的 **wàibiān**？ 你在車 **zhàn** 的 **lǐbiān** 還是在車 **zhàn** 的 **wàibiān**？	*outside* *outside of the station* *located outside of the station* *located inside the station or outside the station?* ————————————
15. 門 **wài** 在門 **wài** 我在門 **wài**。	*outside the door* *located outside the door* *I'm outside the door.*
16. 中 **jiān** 飯館的中 **jiān** 在電 **yǐngyuàn** 和飯館的中 **jiān** 我在電 **yǐngyuàn** 和飯館的中 **jiān**。	*between* *between the restaurants* *between the restaurant and the movie theater* ————————————
17. **yòubiān** 我的 **yòubiān** 在我的 **yòubiān** 飯館在我的 **yòubiān**。	*right hand side* *my right hand side* *on my right* *The restaurant is on my right.*

18.	
zhǐ	*paper*
一張 **zhǐ**	*a piece of paper*
有一張 **zhǐ**	*there is a piece of paper*
門上有一張 **zhǐ**。	*On the door there is a piece of paper.*

19.	
zuǒbiān	*left hand side*
我的 **zuǒbiān**	*my left hand side*
在我的 **zuǒbiān**	*on my left*
電 **yǐngyuàn** 在我的 **zuǒbiān**。	*The movie theater is to my left.*
有一個電 **yǐngyuàn** 在我的 **zuǒbiān**。	*There is a movie theater to my left.*

20.	
很多人	*a lot of people*
有很多人	*there are a lot of people*
飯館 **lǐ** 有很多人。	*In the restaurant there are a lot of people.*

21.	
走	*go, walk*
wǎng běi 走	*go north, walk north*
從車 **zhàn wǎng běi** 走	*from the station walk north*
你從車 **zhàn wǎng běi** 走。	_____

22.	
馬路	*street*
guò 馬路	*cross the street*
你得 **guò** 馬路。	*You have to cross the street.*

23.	
wǎng běi 走	*go north*
再 **wǎng běi** 走	*then go north*
xiān guò 馬路，再 **wǎng běi** 走	*first cross the street, then go north*
你得 **xiān guò** 馬路，再 **wǎng běi** 走。	_____

24.	
guǎi	*turn*
wǎng zuǒ guǎi	*turn left*
在 **Gōngyuán** 路 **wǎng zuǒ guǎi**。	*Turn left at Park Road.*

Language FAQs

Two pronunciations and two meanings for 得

Most characters have only one pronunciation, but some characters have more than one pronunciation. The character 得 introduced in this lesson is one of them.

得 is pronounced **de** when it is used to indicate the way that actions are performed:

> **ActV + 得 (de) + AdjV phrase**
> 我 **xiě** 得太慢。 *I write too slowly.*
> 他吃得很多。 *He eats a lot.*

得 is pronounced **de** when it occurs in the word **jué** 得 (**juéde**) *think*.

得 is pronounced **děi** when it indicates an obligation and means *must, have to,* or *should*. When 得 indicates an obligation it occurs right before an action verb or verb phrase.

> **得 (děi) + ActV**
> 你得 **guò** 馬路。 *You have to cross the street.*

Notes on Chinese culture

Evolving telephone culture

Many Chinese homes have never had a landline, but more than one-third of Chinese people have a cell phone. When answering a cell phone call, you say **Wéi**? But since cell phones typically display caller information, there is often no need to ask for the caller's identity. Text messaging is widely used in China, and everything from personal messages to news, traffic, and weather reports, and even advertisements, are sent by text message. Text messages can be sent in Chinese characters or in English.

Lesson 13 Dialogue in English

Part A

Xiao Xie: Hello?
Xiao Zhang: Excuse me, is Xiao Xie there?
Xiao Xie: That's me. Who are you (*polite*)?
Xiao Zhang: It's me, Xiao Zhang. I'm now at the Zhonghua Road Station.

Part B

Xiao Xie: I'm sorry. The other guests have already arrived. I can't go and get you.
                     I'm really sorry.
Xiao Zhang: No problem.
Xiao Xie: I'll tell you how to go. My home is easy to find.
Xiao Zhang: Okay.

Part C

Xiao Xie: Are you inside the station or outside the station?
Xiao Zhang: I'm outside.
Xiao Xie: Outside of the station there is a Japanese restaurant. On the door there are
                     the two characters "Dong Jing" (*Tokyo*). Do you see it?
Xiao Zhang: I see it. I am in between that restaurant and a movie theater. The movie
                     theater is on my left, the restaurant is on my right.
Xiao Xie: Okay. You are at the west gate of the station. Head north from the station.
Xiao Zhang: Do I cross the street?
Xiao Xie: Yes, first you have to cross the street, then go north. At Park Avenue turn left.

Lesson 14 我家的 hòubiān 有一個很 piàoliang 的公園

There is a very pretty park behind my house

Communication goals
- Give and follow street directions
- Paraphrase information
- Tell someone not to do something

Key structures
indicating how an action with an object is performed:

    V + O V 得 AdjV

after situation₁, situation₂:

    V₁ 了 O 以 **hòu** 就 V₂

first, second, third:

    dì + number: **dì** 一, **dì** 二, **dì** 三

也就是說 *that is to say*

一 **zhí** + ActV *continue doing an action*

bié + ActV *don't do the action*

Dialogue

The Situation: Xiao Xie and Xiao Zhang continue their telephone conversation. Xiao Xie is telling Xiao Zhang how to walk from the subway station to his home. Xiao Zhang finds that following directions in Chinese is a little challenging.

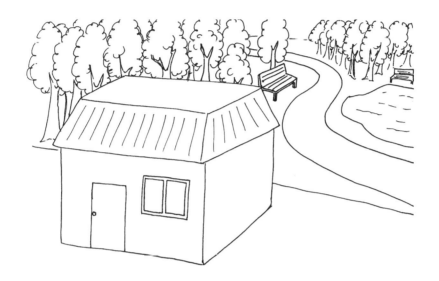

Part A

小張： 小謝，你說話說得太快。請你說慢一點。

小謝： 好。車站的對 miàn 有一個書店，賣 jiù 書，你看見了嗎？

小張： 看見了。你昨天就 gàosu 我了。

小謝： 你過馬路到書店去。過了馬路以 hòu 往北走。在 dì 三個路口有一個 hóng-lù dēng。那 tiáo 路是公園路。在那兒往西 guǎi。

小張： 往西 guǎi 也就是說往 zuǒ guǎi，對不對？

小謝： 對。一 zhí 往西走。Qiánbiān 有一個十字路口。

小張： 還要過馬路嗎？

小謝： Bié 過馬路。在那兒往南 guǎi。也就是說，往 zuǒ guǎi。

小張： 好。

小謝： 你會看見一個 yínháng。我家在 yínháng 的 pángbiān。我家的 hòubiān 有一個很 piàoliang 的公園。

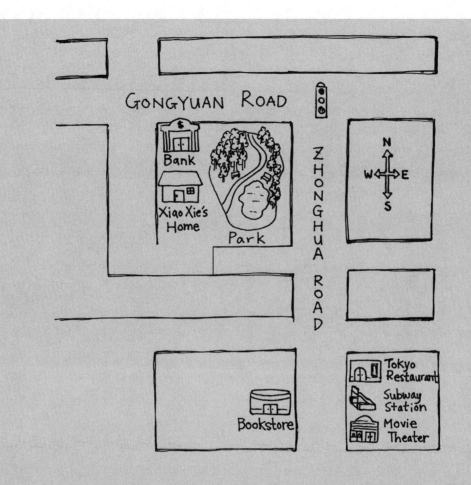

Part B

小張：　好。知道了。不會很難找。從車站到你家走路要走多 **jiǔ**？

小謝：　差不多十分 **zhōng** 就可以到。

小張：　那，我現在就往你家走。

小謝：　好，一會兒見。

小張：　再見。

Vocabulary

bié		negation	*don't*
dēng [gè]		noun	*lamp, light*
dì		prefix	*(ordinal prefix)*
duō jiǔ	多 **jiǔ**	question phrase	*how long (duration)*
duìmiàn	對 **miàn**	noun	*across from*
hóng		adjectival verb	*red*
hóng-lù dēng [gè]		noun phrase	*traffic light (red-green light)*
hòu		*	*behind, after*
hòubiān		noun	*behind, in back (of)*
huì	會	modal verb	*will (can, able to)*
jiù		adjectival verb	*old (for describing objects)*
lù		adjectival verb	*green*
lùkǒu [gè]	路口	noun	*intersection*
pángbiān		noun	*beside, alongside*
piàoliang		adjectival verb	*beautiful*
qián		*	*front, in front*
qiánbiān		noun	*front, in front (of)*
shízì lùkǒu [gè]	十字路口	noun phrase	*four-way intersection*
tiáo		classifier	*(classifier for streets)*
yě jiù shì shuō	也就是說	conversational expression	*in other words*
yǐhòu	以 **hòu**	noun	*after, afterward*
yīhuìr	一會兒	time phrase	*a short period of time*

yīhuìr jiàn	一會兒見	conversational expression	*see you soon*
yínháng		noun	*bank*
yīzhí	一 zhí	adverb	*continuously, keep (doing V)*
zǒu	走	verb	*walk (L12 go)*
zǒu lù	走路	verb + object	*walk*

Spatial directions

qiánbiān	*in front*	**hòubiān**	*behind*
lǐbiān	*inside*	**wàibiān**	*outside*
上 **biān**	*on top of, above*	下 **biān**	*below*
zuǒbiān	*to the left*	**yòubiān**	*to the right*
pángbiān	*beside, alongside*	對 **miàn**	*across from*
中 **jiān**	*between, in between*		

Expressing locations with respect to the station

The following map illustrates locations with respect to the 車站 *station*. Each location is specified with a location noun (*inside, outside, next to, behind, in front of*, etc.).

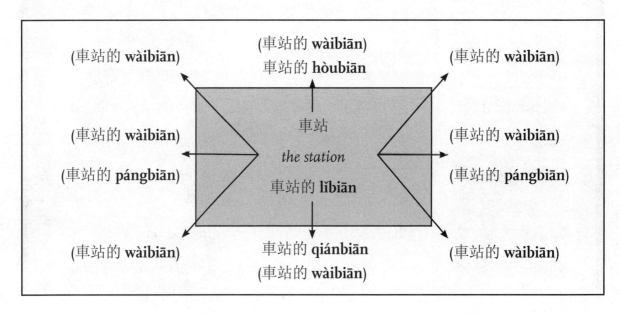

Characters

北	běi	*north*	北 **biān** (**běibiān**) *north*
差	chà	*	差不多 (**chàbuduō**) *almost*
道	dào	*	知道 (**zhīdào**) *know*
店	diàn	*store*	書店 (**shūdiàn**) *bookstore*
公	gōng	*	公園 (**gōngyuán**) *park*
			公 **gòng qì** 車 (**gōnggòng qìchē**) *bus*
過	guò	*cross, pass*	
口	kǒu	*mouth*	路口 (**lùkǒu**) *intersection*
			門口 (**ménkǒu**) *doorway*
快	kuài	*fast, quickly*	
賣	mài	*sell*	
慢	màn	*slow, slowly*	
南	nán	*south*	南 **biān** (**nánbiān**) *south*
難	nán	*difficult*	
往	wǎng	*toward*	
要	yào	*will, want*	
園	yuán	*	公園 (**gōngyuán**) *park*
站	zhàn	*station*	
知	zhī	*	知道 (**zhīdào**) *know*
字	zì	*character*	十字路口 (**shízì lùkǒu**) *four-way intersection*
			Hàn 字 (**Hàn zì**) *Chinese character*
			xiě 字 (**xiě zì**) *write, write characters*
昨	zuó	*	昨天 (**zuótiān**) *yesterday*

Stroke Order Flow Chart

character:	strokes:												total strokes:
北	丨	十	扌	北	北								5
差	丶	丷	丷	半	羊	羊	差	差	差				10
道	丶	丷	丷	丷	产	屵	首	首	首	道	道	道	13
店	丶	宀	广	庁	庁	店	店	店					8
公	丿	八	公	公									4
過	丨	冂	冎	冎	冎	丹	咼	咼	咼	渦	渦	過	13
口	丨	冂	口										3
快	丨	忄	忄	忄	忄	快	快						7
賣	一	十	士	吉	声	声	壱	壱	声	壱	賣	賣	
賣	賣												15
慢	丨	忄	忄	忄	忄	忄	忄	忄	慢	慢	慢	慢	14
南	一	十	十	冇	内	内	南	南	南				9
難	一	十	艹	艹	艹	苂	苗	莒	菫	菓	菓	蓳	蓳
難	蓳	蓳	難	難									19
往	丿	彳	彳	彳	彳	行	往	往					8
要	一	一	冂	襾	襾	西	覀	要	要				9
園	丨	冂	冂	冂	閂	閂	周	周	閽	園	園	園	13
站	丶	宀	立	立	立	刘	站	站	站				10
知	丿	上	上	矢	矢	知	知	知					8
字	丶	宀	宀	宁	字	字							6
昨	丨	冂	日	日	旷	旷	昨	昨	昨				9

Dialogue practice

Do these activities in class after mastering the dialogue for this lesson. Change partners so that you practice each part several times.

Dialogue 14A: Share a street map with a partner and give each other directions from one location to another.

Dialogue 14B: *Activity 1.* Using the map of a city that you are familiar with, find out how long it takes to go from one location to another on foot, by car, by bus, and by train.

Activity 2. Using the internet, find out how long it takes to go from one world location to another.

Use and structure

14.1. Indicating how an action with an object is performed

In Lesson 10 we learned how to indicate how actions are performed when the verb does not take an object (Use and Structure note 10.5).

ActV 得 **AdjV**
xiě 得(很) 慢
write slowly

In this lesson, we learn to describe how actions are performed when the verb takes an object. When the verb takes an object, the verb is repeated twice, once followed by the object and once followed by 得 + **AdjV**:

V + O V 得 **AdjV**
你說話說得太快。
You speak too quickly.

我 **xiě Hàn** 字 **xiě** 得很慢。
I write Chinese characters very slowly.

他吃飯吃得太多。
He eats too much.

Notice that in this pattern, the particle **de** is written as 得. Notice also that the object of the verb is not always translated into English. See Use and Structure notes 8.13 and 9.11 for more about the objects of action verbs.

14.2.   V + AdjV + 一點 *do the action a little more AdjV*

In Lesson 7 (Use and Structure note 7.2) we learned how to use the phrase <u>AdjV + 一點</u> to say *a little more AdjV*: 你可以 **piányi** 一點嗎？ *Can you make it a little cheaper?* In this lesson we learn to use the structure <u>V + AdjV + 一點</u> to say *do the action a little more AdjV*.

請你說慢一點。   *Please speak a little slower.*
請你 **xiě** 快一點。   *Please write a little faster.*

14.3.   V₁ 了 (O) 以 **hòu**, 就 V₂ *after one action happens, another action happens*

Actions are expressed as verbs. To say *after an action happens, another action happens*, use the verb suffix 了, the adverb 就, and the word 以 **hòu** *after* and say:

(S) V₁ 了 (O) 以 hòu 就 V₂
過<u>了</u>馬路<u>以 **hòu**</u> 就往北走。
After you cross the street go north.

她買<u>了</u>書<u>以 **hòu**</u> 就 **huí** 家。
After she buys the book she will return home.

When used in sequence sentences like these, 了 always occurs immediately after the verb:

過<u>了</u>馬路以 **hòu**   *after crossing the road*
買<u>了</u>書以 **hòu**   *after buying the book*
吃<u>了</u>飯以 **hòu**   *after eating*

就 occurs right before the second verb phrase:

過了馬路以 **hòu** <u>就往北走</u>。
After crossing the road, go north.

There is no need to translate 就 into English in sequence sentences, but if you want a translation to help you understand its function in these sentences, think of it as adding the meaning *then*.

過了馬路以 **hòu** 就往北走。
Cross the road <u>and then</u> go north.

以 **hòu** *after* occurs at the end of the first clause, after the object of the first verb if there is an object, or after the first verb if there is no object. Notice that in English, the word *after* occurs at the beginning of the first clause.

To help you to understand the relationship of 以 **hòu** to the first clause of sequence sentences like these, we have put square brackets around the first clause in the following examples.

[過了馬路以 **hòu**] 就往北走。
[After you cross the street,] go north.

[我吃了晚飯以 **hòu**] 就給你打電話。
[After I eat dinner,] I will phone you.

Inclusion and omission of 了, 以 **hòu**, and 就

Sequence sentences do not have to include all three sequence markers 了, 就 and 以 **hòu**. A sentence may contain all three of them, two of them, or only one of them.

V₁ 了 **O** 以 **hòu** 就 V₂	過了馬路以 **hòu** 就 **wǎng** 北走。
V₁ 了 **O** 以 **hòu** V₂	過了馬路以 **hòu** **wǎng** 北走。
V₁ 了 **O** V₂	過了馬路 **wǎng** 北走。
V₁ **O** 就 V₂	過馬路就 **wǎng** 北走。
V₁ **O** 以 **hòu** V₂	過馬路以 **hòu** **wǎng** 北走。

After you cross the street, go north.

Talking about sequence in the future, sequence in general time, and sequence in the past

Sequence is indicated in the same way whether the sentence refers to future events, events that generally occur, or completed, past events. The sentences above all refer to events that generally occur or that will occur in the future. To indicate that a sequence <u>occurred in the past</u>, add 了 after the <u>last verb</u> (V₂) or after the object of the last verb.

V₁ 了 **O** 以 **hòu**, 就 V₂ **O** 了
[我吃了晚飯以 **hòu**] 就給她打電話了。
[After I ate dinner,] I phoned her.

她買了書以 **hòu** 就 **huí** 家了。
After she bought the books, she returned home.

我下了課以 **hòu** 就吃 **wǔ** 飯了。
After I got out of class, I ate lunch.

14.4. Ordinal numbers: *First, second, third*

To turn a number into an <u>ordinal</u> number (*first, second, third,* etc.) add the prefix **dì** before the number:

dì 一 *first,* **dì** 二 *second,* **dì** 三 *third*
在 **dì** 三個十字路口 *at the third four-way intersection*
在 **dì** 三個路口有一個 **hóng-lù dēng**。
At the third intersection there is a traffic light.

After **dì**, the number *two* is always 二:

dì 二個人	*the second person*
dì 二 **běn** 書	*the second book*

14.5. Introducing a paraphrase: 也就是說 *in other words*

To introduce another way of saying the same thing, use the expression 也就是說 *in other words*.

往西 **guǎi** 也就是說往 **zuǒ guǎi**，對不對？
Turn west means turn left, is that correct?

在 **dì** 三個十字路口往西 **guǎi**，也就是說往 **yòu guǎi**。
Turn west at the third intersection. In other words, turn right.

14.6. 一 **zhí** + ActV *continue to do an action*

To say to continue doing an action, use the adverb 一 **zhí** before the verb phrase that presents the action. 一 **zhí** is a very useful phrase when giving directions.

一 **zhí** 往西走。
Keep going west. (Keep walking west.)

一 **zhí** is also used to say that a situation is continuous.

我昨天一 **zhí** 很 **máng**。
I was busy all day yesterday.

14.7. **bié** + ActV *don't do the action*

To tell someone not to do something, say:

bié + ActV
Bié 過馬路。
Don't cross the street.

Bié 說話。學生在 **kǎo shì** 呢。
Don't talk. The students are taking a test.

Bié 在中 **huá** 路下車。
Don't get off (the bus, train) at Zhonghua Road.

14.8. 會 *will* and future situations

In Lesson 3 we learned to use 會 to indicate learned or innate ability (Use and Structure note 3.4). In this lesson we learn that 會 can also be used when talking about a future situation. In this use it can be translated into English as *will*.

你會看見一個 **yínháng**。
You will see a bank.

14.9.　多 jiǔ and 多 cháng shíjiān *how long?*

The expression 多 **jiǔ**, like the expression 多 **cháng shíjiān** introduced in Lesson 12, means *how long*, and is used to ask about the duration of a situation. As we learned in Use and Structure note 12.10, duration expressions go <u>after</u> the verb.

從車站到你家要走多 **jiǔ**？
How long do you have to walk from the station to your house?

If the verb is followed by an object, you must first state the verb and the object, and then state the verb and the duration expression:

V + O V + 多 **jiǔ**
從車站到你家走路要走多 **jiǔ**？
How long do you have to walk from the station to your house?

To say that you are doing an action for a long period of time, you can say 很 **jiǔ** *a long time*.

我 **děng** 了很 **jiǔ**。
I waited for a long time.

When asking about duration, the question phrase 多 **cháng shíjiān** is more commonly used in Beijing and northern China. The expression 多 **jiǔ** is more commonly used in Taiwan.

14.10.　一會兒見 *see you soon*

The phrase 一會兒 means *a short period of time*. It can be used directly following a verb as a duration expression:

請 **děng** 一會兒。
Please wait for a few minutes.

It can also be used in a variation of the expression 再見 *goodbye*:

一會兒見　　*See you soon.*

The expression 再見 can be varied by replacing 再 with other phrases as well. Here are some examples:

明天見	*See you tomorrow.*
下 **wǔ** 見	*See you in the afternoon.*
三點 **zhōng** 見	*See you at 3 o'clock.*

Sentence pyramids

The sentence pyramids illustrate the use of each new vocabulary item and structure introduced in the lesson. Use them to help you learn how to form phrases and sentences in Mandarin. Supply the English translation for the last line where indicated.

1.
快   *fast*
太快   *too fast*
說得太快   *speak too fast*
說話說得太快   *speak too fast*
你說話說得太快。   *You speak too fast.*

2.
慢   *slow*
fēicháng 慢   *extremely slow*
走得 **fēicháng** 慢   *walk extremely slowly*
走路走得 **fēicháng** 慢   *walk extremely slowly*
他走路走得 **fēicháng** 慢。   _____

3.
zhēn 好   *really well*
xiě 得 **zhēn** 好   *writes really well*
xiě Hàn 字 **xiě** 得 **zhēn** 好   *writes Chinese characters really well*
她 **xiě Hàn** 字 **xiě** 得 **zhēn** 好。   *She writes Chinese characters really well.*

4.
多 **jiǔ**?   *how long?*
走多 **jiǔ**?   *walk how long?*
走路走多 **jiǔ**?   *walk how long?*
我們走路走多 **jiǔ**?   *How long did we walk? (How long have we been walking?)*

5.
一點   *a little*
慢一點   *a little slower*
說慢一點   *speak a little slower*
請你說慢一點。   _____

6.
快一點   *a little faster*
走快一點   *walk a little faster*
請你走快一點。   _____

7. 對 **miàn** 車站的對 **miàn**	*across* *across from the station*
8. 書店 有一個書店 對 **miàn** 有一個書店 車站的對 **miàn** 有一個書店。	*bookstore* *there is a bookstore* *across there is a bookstore* *Across from the station there is a bookstore.*
9. **pángbiān** **yínháng** 的 **pángbiān** 我家在 **yínháng** 的 **pángbiān**。	*beside, next to* *next to the bank* *My house is next to the bank.*

10.
公園
piàoliang 的公園
有一個很 **piàoliang** 的公園
hòubiān 有一個很 **piàoliang** 的公園
我家的 **hòubiān** 有一個很 **piàoliang**
   的公園。
	park
	beautiful park
	there is a beautiful park
	behind there is a beautiful park
	*Behind my house there is a beautiful
	    park.*

11. **jiù** 書 賣 **jiù** 書 那個書店賣 **jiù** 書。	*old books* *sells old books*
12. **jiù** 東西 很多 **jiù** 東西 他家的 **wàibiān** 有很多 **jiù** 東西。	*old things* *a lot of old things* *Behind his house there are a lot of old things.*

13.
dēng
hóng-lù dēng
有一個 **hóng-lù dēng**
Qiánbiān 有一個 **hóng-lù dēng**。
Qiánbiān 有一個 **hóng-lù dēng**。
   你看見了嗎?
	light
	traffic light
	there is a traffic light
	Ahead there is a traffic light.
	Ahead there is a traffic light.
	    Do you see it?

14. 中 **jiān** 兩個公園的中 **jiān** 在兩個公園的中 **jiān** 學 **xiào** 在兩個公園的中 **jiān**。 他們的學 **xiào** 在兩個公園的中 **jiān**。	*between* *between two parks* *(located) between two parks* *The school is between two parks.* _____
15. 往北走 一 **zhí** 往北走。	*go north* *Keep going north.*
16. 往北走 過了馬路以 **hòu** 往北走。	*go north* *After you cross the street, go north.*
17. **huí** 家 下了 **kè** 以 **hòu** 就 **huí** 家 我 **měi** 天下了 **kè** 以 **hòu** 就 **huí** 家。	*return home, go home* *after getting out of class go home* *Every day after I get out of class,* *I go home.*
18. **huí** 家了 下了 **kè** 以 **hòu** 就 **huí** 家了 我 **měi** 天下了 **kè** 以 **hòu** 就 **huí** 家了。	*returned home, went home* *after getting out of class went home* *Every day after I got out of class,* *I went home.*
19. 吃飯了 就吃飯了 我們就吃飯了 **lái** 了以 **hòu** 我們就吃飯了 **Kè** 人 **lái** 了以 **hòu** 我們就吃飯了。	*ate* *ate* *we ate* *after arriving we ate* *After the guests arrived, we ate.*
20. 公園路 是公園路 那 **tiáo** 路是公園路。	*Park Street* *is Park Street* *That street is Park Street.*
21. 往南 **guǎi** 到了公園路就往南 **guǎi**。	*turn south* *After arriving at Park Street, turn south.*

22.	
路口	*intersection*
十字路口	*four-way intersection*
dì 一個十字路口	*the first four-way intersection*

23.	
往 **zuǒ guǎi**	*turn left*
在十字路口往 **zuǒ guǎi**	*at the four-way intersection turn left*
在 **dì** 一個十字路口往 **zuǒ guǎi**。	*At the first four-way intersection turn left.*

24.	
往東 **guǎi**	*turn east*
也就是說往東 **guǎi**。	*In other words, turn east.*
往 **zuǒ guǎi**。也就是說往東 **guǎi**。	*Turn left. In other words, turn east.*

25.	
過馬路	*cross the road*
Bié 過馬路。	*Don't cross the road.*

26.	
買東西	*buy things*
給我買東西	*buy things for me*
Bié 給我買東西。	*Don't buy things for me.*

27.	
bié 的學生	*other students*
gàosu bié 的學生	*tell other students*
Bié gàosu bié 的學生。	*Don't tell other students.*

28.	
見	*see*
一會兒見。	*See you soon.*

29.	
一會兒	*a short amount of time*
děng 一會兒	*wait for a little while*
請 **děng** 一會兒。	*Please wait for little while.*

Language FAQs

What is the difference between 的 (de) and 得 (de)?

We have now learned two characters pronounced **de**: 的 and 得.

的 is used when you are describing a noun. The <u>description + 的</u> occurs right before the noun:

我的 **péngyou**	*my friend*
小張的 **tóngwū**	*Xiao Zhang's roommate*
xīn 的 **kāfēi** 館	*a new coffee shop*

得 is used when you are describing the way that an action is performed. The <u>action verb + 得</u> occurs before the adjectival verb or adjectival verb phrase.

我 **xiě** 得太慢。	*I write too slowly.*
他吃得很多。	*He eats a lot.*
你說話說得太快。	*You speak too quickly.*
她 **chàng gē chàng** 得很好。	*She sings very well.*

Notes on Chinese culture

Using compass directions in China

In China, many cities are oriented around the compass directions north, south, east, and west. Therefore, people commonly give directions and express locations using compass direction words, saying things like "go north" and "to the east of the station". When you visit a city in China, be sure to get your bearings by identifying landmarks that are in the north, south, east, and west of the city.

Lesson 14 Dialogue in English

Part A

Xiao Zhang: Xiao Xie, you are speaking too fast. Please speak a little slower.

Xiao Xie: Okay. Across from the station there is a bookstore, it sells old books. Do you see it?

Xiao Zhang: I see it. You mentioned it yesterday.

Xiao Xie: Cross the street and go to the bookstore. After you cross the street, go north. At the third intersection there is a traffic light. That street is Park Road. Turn west there.

Xiao Zhang: Turn west means turn left, is that correct?

Xiao Xie: Yes. Keep going west. Ahead of you there will be a four-way intersection.

Xiao Zhang: Do I have to cross the street again?

Xiao Xie: Don't cross the street. Turn south there. That is to say, turn left.

Xiao Zhang: Okay.

Xiao Xie: You will see a bank. My house is next to the bank. Behind my house is a very pretty park.

Part B

Xiao Zhang: Okay. I understand. It won't be hard to find. How far do I have to walk from the station to your house?

Xiao Xie: You can get here in about 10 minutes.

Xiao Zhang: Well then, I'm heading to your house now.

Xiao Xie: Okay. See you soon.

Xiao Zhang: Goodbye.

Lesson 15 請 kè
Entertaining guests

Communication goals
- Behave as a guest and host in a semi-formal gathering
- Give and respond to compliments

Key structures
V-過

situation₁ 以前 situation₂

多 V 一點

Dialogue

The Situation: Xiao Zhang has arrived at Xiao Xie's home from the subway station. When he enters Xiao Xie's home, Xiao Xie introduces him to his parents, who he has not met before. Xiao Wang, Xiao Ye, and Xiao Gao, the other dinner guests, have already arrived. Xiao Wang and Xiao Gao are Xiao Zhang's classmates, Xiao Ye is Xiao Gao's roommate and also Xiao Zhang's girlfriend.

Part A

小謝： 小張，請 jìn，請 jìn。我給你們 jièshào 一下。這是我爸爸，這是我媽媽。這是我的 tóngwū，張大 wéi。

謝先生： Huānyíng 你到我們家來。很 gāoxìng néng rènshi 國 qiáng 的朋友。

小張： 謝先生，謝太太，謝謝你們請我到你們家來吃飯。我買了一 xiē 水 guǒ sòng 給你們。

謝太太： Bié 那麼 kèqi。叫 shūshu āyí 吧。你來中國已經快一年了。早就 yīnggāi 請你來家坐坐。

小張： Āyí，你們家 zhēn piàoliang。

謝太太： 哪 li，這個 fáng 子很 jiù 了。沒甚麼。

Part B

小王：	大 **wéi** 你好。
小張：	高美 **lì**，**Yǒu** 文，王 **Màikè**，你們早就到了嗎？
小 **Yè**：	我們也 **gāng** 到。
謝太太：	飯快好了。吃飯 以前 我們先 **zhào** 一張 **zhàopiàn** 吧。
謝先生：	好，我 來 **zhào**。大家說 "**qié** 子。" *(see Language FAQs)*

Part C

謝先生：	來。吃飯吧。**Suíbiàn** 坐。**Bié kèqi**。
謝太太：	不好 **yìsi**，今天 沒甚麼 **cài**。我就做了三個：**hóngshāo jī**，回 **guō ròu**，和 **chǎo báicài**，都是家 **cháng cài**，沒甚麼，還有 **jiǎo** 子。你們 吃過 **jiǎo** 子嗎？
小謝：	媽，他們去年八月就來中國了，在中國已經 **zhù** 了差不多一年了，當然吃過 **jiǎo** 子了。
小高：	我很 **xǐhuan** 吃 **jiǎo** 子。來中國以前我 沒吃過，可是來中國以後我 **cháng** 吃。您的 **jiǎo** 子 **fēicháng** 好吃。
謝太太：	那太好了，來，多吃一點。小高，你 **yòng kuài** 子 **yòng** 得 **zhēn** 好。
小高：	我會 **yòng**，可是 **yòng** 得不好。

…to be continued.

Vocabulary

āyí [gè]	noun	*aunt*
báicài	noun	*cabbage*
cài [gè]	noun	*dishes (food)*
cháng	adverb	*often*
chǎo	verb	*stir-fry*

chǎo báicài		noun phrase	stir-fried cabbage
dàjiā	大家	noun phrase	everyone
fángzi [gè]	**fáng** 子	noun	house
guò	過	verb suffix	(experienced doing the action)
hǎo chī	好吃	adjectival verb phrase	delicious
hóngshāo		noun description	red-simmered, red-cooked
hóngshāo jī		noun phrase	red-simmered chicken
huānyíng		verb	welcome
huí guō ròu	回 **guō ròu**	noun phrase	twice-cooked pork (returned-to-the-pot meat)
jī		noun	chicken
jiā cháng cài	家 **cháng cài**	noun phrase	home-style food, simple food
jiǎozi [gè]	**jiǎo** 子	noun	Chinese dumplings, "jiaozi"
jièshào		verb	introduce
kèqi		adjectival verb	polite
kuàizi	**kuài** 子	noun	chopsticks
mā	媽	noun	mom
méi shénme cài	沒甚麼 **cài**	conversational expression	there aren't any special dishes
nǎlǐ	哪 **lǐ**	conversational expression	(used for deflecting compliments)
nàme	那麼	intensifier	so
qiézi [gè]	**qié** 子	noun	eggplant

qùnián	去年	noun	*last year*
ròu		noun	*meat*
shāo		verb	*simmer*
shuǐguǒ	水 **guǒ**	noun	*fruit*
shūshu		noun	*uncle*
sònggěi	**sòng** 給	verb	*give as a present*
suíbiàn		adverb	*as you please*
tàitai [gè, wèi]	太太	title	*Mrs.*
xiānsheng [gè, wèi]	先生	title	*Mr.*
xiē		classifier	*several*
yīnggāi		modal verb	*should*
yǐqián	以前	noun	*before*
yī xià	一下	verb suffix	*(do an action for a short duration)*
yòng		verb	*use*
zǎo jiù	早就	adverb	*long before now, long ago*
zhào		verb	*photograph, take (a photograph)*
zhù		verb	*live/reside in a place*
zuò	做	verb	*cook (L9 做 do)*

Time words: past, present, future

	past	present	future
days	昨天	今天	明天
	yesterday	*today*	*tomorrow*
weeks	上個星期	這個星期	下個星期
	last week	*this week*	*next week*
months	上個 **yuè**	這個 **yuè**	下個 **yuè**
	last month	*this month*	*next month*
years	去年	今年	明年
	last year	*this year*	*next year*

Characters

爸	bà	*dad*	爸爸 (**bàba**) *dad*
吧	ba	*(indicates suggestions and supposition)*	
高	Gāo	*(family name)*	高**xìng** (**gāoxìng**) *happy*
國	guó	*country*	中國 (**Zhōngguó**) *China*
			美國 (**Měiguó**) *America*
後	hòu	*	以後 (**yǐhòu**) *after, afterward*
回	huí	*return*	回家 (**huí jiā**) *go home (return home)*
			回 **guō ròu** (**huí guō ròu**) *twice-cooked pork (returned-to-the-pot meat)*

叫	jiào	call	你叫甚麼？ (**Nǐ jiào shénme**？) *What are you called?*
今	jīn	*	今天 (**jīntiān**) *today* 今年 (**jīnnián**) *this year*
來	lái	come	
媽	mā	*ma, mom*	媽媽 (**māma**) *mom*
美	měi	*beautiful*	美國 (**Měiguó**) *America* 美 **lì** (**Měilì**) *given name (female)*
年	nián	year	今年 (**jīnnián**) *this year* 去年 (**qùnián**) *last year*
您	nín	*you (polite)*	
朋	péng	*	朋友 (**péngyou**) *friend*
前	qián	*front* *	以前 (**yǐqián**) *before* 前 **biān** (**qiánbiān**) *in front*
水	shuǐ	*water*	一 **píng** 水 (**yī píng shuǐ**) *one bottle of water* 水 **guǒ** (**shuǐguǒ**) *fruit*
先	xiān	*first*	先生 (**xiānsheng**) *Mr.*
友	yǒu	*	朋友 (**péngyou**) *friend*
子	zi	*	**hái** 子 (**háizi**) *child* **jiǎo** 子 (**jiǎozi**) *dumplings*
坐	zuò	sit	

Stroke Order Flow Chart

character:	total strokes:
爸	8
吧	7
高	10
國	11
後	9
回	6
叫	5
今	4
來	8
媽	13
美	9
年	6
您	11
朋	8
前	9
水	4
先	6
友	4
子	3
坐	7

Dialogue practice

Do these activities in class after mastering the dialogue for this lesson. Change partners so that you practice each part several times.

Dialogue 15A and 15B: Work with two or three other classmates and take turns introducing one of your classmates to your "parents" when they visit your home. Hosts should try to use as many polite expressions as possible to make the guest feel welcome. Guests should express gratitude and praise. Someone should suggest that they take a picture.

Dialogue 15C: Continue playing the role of guest and host through dinner. Hosts: be humble about your food offerings and curious about what your guests have eaten before. Guests: be generous in your praise of the food and your hosts' home.

Use and structure

15.1. 給 (people) **jièshào** *introduce (people)*

To introduce people, say:

給 **(people) jièshào** 一下
我給你們 **jièshào** 一下。
Let me introduce you.

or

給 **(person A** 和 **person B) jièshào** 一下
請給小張和小高 **jièshào** 一下。
Please introduce Xiao Zhang and Xiao Gao (to each other).

When giving introductions in this way, the verb **jièshào** *introduce* is generally followed by 一下 or is repeated: **jièshào jièshào**. The following sentences with **jièshào jièshào** are equivalent to the sentences above with 一下.

我給你們 **jièshào jièshào**。
Let me introduce you.

請給小張和小高 **jièshào jièshào**。
Please introduce Xiao Zhang and Xiao Gao (to each other).

See also Use and Structure note 15.2.

15.2. V 一下: Do an action for a short period of time

V 一下 indicates that the action continues for a short period of time.

我給你們 **jièshào** 一下。
Let me introduce you.

Another verb that we have learned that is often followed by 一下 is **děng** *wait*.

請 **děng** 一下。
Please wait a moment.

As indicated in Use and Structure note 15.1, when making introductions, you can say **jièshào** 一下 or you can repeat the verb and say **jièshào jièshào**. That is because verb repetition, like V 一下, indicates that the action happens for a short period of time (Use and Structure note 11.2).

15.3. 一 xiē (+ N) *several (nouns), some (nouns)*

The phrase 一 **xiē** (+ N) means *several (nouns)* or *some (nouns)*. It is used when you want to indicate that there is more than one noun, but you do not want to indicate a precise number.

我買了一 **xiē** 水 **guǒ**。
I bought some fruit.

In Lesson 10 we learned the expression 有的, which is also translated into English as *some* (Use and Structure note 10.9).

有的 **yǔfǎ** 我不 **dǒng**，有的字我不會 **xiě**。
I didn't understand some of the grammar, I couldn't write some of the characters.

Although 有的 and 一 **xiē** can both be translated with the English word *some* they are not used in the same way. 有的 + N must occur before the verb, either as the subject or as the topic of the sentence. In addition, 有的 + N implies some comparison with other nouns. When Xiao Gao says 有的字我不會 **xiě** in the dialogue in Lesson 10 she is implying that there were characters that she <u>was</u> able to write. 一 **xiē** + N can occur before or after the verb, and it does not imply any comparison with other nouns.

15.4. Sòng 給 *give as a gift*

Sòng 給 means *give as a gift* and is always followed by the recipient of the gift.

我買了一 **xiē** 水 **guǒ sòng** 給你們。
I bought some fruit to give you as a gift.

15.5.   那麼 + AdjV *so AdjV*

那麼 and 這麼 are intensifiers that can occur before adjectival verbs.

> 那麼/這麼 **+ AdjV**
> **Bié** 那麼 **kèqi**。
> *Don't be so polite.*

這麼 is used when describing things that are very close to the speaker. For example, if you were shopping, and you picked up an item and looked at the price tag, you could say:

> 這麼 **guì**！我不想買。
> *So expensive! I do not want to buy it.*

那麼 is used when describing things that are at some distance from the speaker. For example, if the library was far from your home you could say:

> 圖書館 **lí** 我家那麼 **yuǎn**，我不 **yào** 去。
> *The library is so far from my house, I don't want to go.*

Sometimes, either 那麼 or 這麼 can be used. For example, in the dialogue, Mrs. Xie could have said to Xiao Zhang:

> **Bié** 這麼 **kèqi**。
> *Don't be this polite.*

15.6.   早就 *long ago*

早就 *long ago* is an adverb and always occurs at the beginning of a verb phrase, before the verb and any prepositional phrases. It is used to indicate that some action happened a long time before the moment of speaking, or a long time before some other action.

> 高美 **lì**，友文，王 **Màikè**，你們早就到了嗎？
> *Gao Meili, Youwen, Wang Maike, did you get here a long time ago?*

早就 is also used as part of polite expressions when saying that you should have done something long ago:

> 早就 **yīnggāi** 請你來家坐坐。
> *We should have invited you to our home long ago.*

This is one of several polite conversational expressions that are often used in the "ritual" of guest and host in Mandarin. The structure of the phrases in ritual expressions need not follow the regular rules of grammar. For example, in regular conversation, you would probably say 來我們家 *come to <u>our</u> home* instead of 來家.

15.7.   Deflecting a compliment: 哪 lǐ (nǎlǐ)

In traditional Chinese culture, you do not respond to a compliment by saying 謝謝 *thank you* or some other expression that implies that you accept the compliment. Instead, you <u>deflect</u> the compliment by using some expression that either indicates that the compliment is not accurate or that asks if it could really be accurate. The expression 哪 lǐ (nǎlǐ) is often used to deflect a compliment. 哪 lǐ literally means *where?*, and in response to a compliment it means something like *how could that be true?* Another expression that we have learned which can be used to deflect a compliment is 是嗎? *really?*

15.8.   沒甚麼 *it's nothing special* and 沒甚麼 cài *there aren't any special dishes*

沒甚麼 *it's nothing special* and 沒甚麼 cài *there aren't any special dishes* are polite expressions or kèqi 話 *polite talk*. Like the expression 哪 lǐ discussed in Use and Structure note 15.7, 沒甚麼 *it's nothing special* is used to deflect a compliment. 沒甚麼 cài *there aren't any special dishes* is used as part of the ritual of guest and host. It expresses modesty on the part of the host, suggesting that the host is not completely fulfilling his or her obligation to treat the guests in a special manner. Whether or not the host has prepared special dishes for the guests, it is appropriate for the host to apologize to the guests for a lack of special food by saying:

今天沒甚麼 cài。
There aren't any special dishes today.

15.9.   Sequence with 以前 *before*

To indicate that some situation occurs before another situation, say:

situation₁ 以前 (先) **situation₂**
吃飯以前我們先 zhào 一張 zhàopiàn 吧。
Before we eat, let's first take a picture.

The word 以前 *before* occurs at the end of situation₁ and it is grouped with situation₁. In writing, a comma may be placed after 以前. In speaking, there is often a pause after 以前. Notice that in English, the word *before* occurs at the <u>beginning</u> of situation₁.

[你 kǎo shì 以前] 得先 fùxí gōngkè。
[Before you take a test,] you should review the lesson.

In Mandarin, the clause that ends with 以前 is stated first in the sentence. Notice that in English, the *before* clause can occur either as the first or the second clause in the sentence.

[我 shuì jiào 以前] 都 xǐ zǎo。
I always take a shower [before I go to sleep].
or
[Before I go to sleep,] I always take a shower.

15.10.   (我)來 (VP) *I'll take charge (of the action)*

<u>我來</u> VP is a conversational expression that means you take the responsibility of doing some action. In the dialogue, Mr. Xie takes on the responsibility of taking the picture by saying:

我來 **zhào**。
I'll take the picture.

To say that you will take charge of some action, say

我來做。   or   我來。
I'll do it.

To ask who will take charge of some action, ask:

誰來做?
Who will do it? (Who will take on this responsibility?)

15.11.   **Suíbiàn** + ActV: Do the action informally, without ceremony

The expression **suíbiàn** 坐 means *sit wherever you want; there is no formal seating plan.*

At formal dinners, there is a ritual way of assigning seats according to rank and importance at the dinner. But at informal dinner parties such as the one that the Xie family is hosting, it is common to tell the guests **suíbiàn** 坐.

By itself, the word **suíbiàn** means *casual* or *informal*, or *as you wish.* If you ask someone how something should be done and she replies "**suíbiàn**," that means you can do it however you wish. The word **suíbiàn** can sometimes carry negative overtones. If you describe someone as being 太 **suíbiàn** you are saying that he or she is *careless, sloppy,* or *too familiar.*

15.12.   **V**-過: Talking about actions experienced some time in the past

Stating that someone has had the experience of doing an action in the past

To state that someone has had the experience of doing some action in the past, follow the action verb with the verb suffix 過 and say:

(S) V-過 **(O)**
他們當然吃過 **jiǎo** 子了。
Of course they have eaten Chinese dumplings before.

Notice that the object occurs after <u>verb</u>-過. Nothing comes between the verb and the suffix 過.

她去過中國。
She has been to China before.

V-過 is used when talking about an action that someone has experienced sometime in the past. The action itself has to be repeatable, but it cannot be something that the subject does on a regular basis. For example, it is appropriate for Xiao Xie, a Chinese person, to use V-過 to say that he has eaten French food before, since eating French food is not an everyday experience for a Chinese person in China:

小謝：　　我吃過 **Fǎ** 國飯。
Xiao Xie:　*I have eaten French food before.*

But the same sentence would be strange if spoken by Xiao Gao, a French person, since she probably eats French food on a regular basis. Similarly, it would be strange for Xiao Xie to say:

我吃過中國飯。
I have eaten Chinese food before.

The sentence itself is fine, but it is inappropriate for Xiao Xie to use verb suffix 過 when talking about eating Chinese food, since he probably eats it on a regular basis.

Stating that someone has *not* had the experience of doing an action in the past

To state that someone has <u>not</u> had the experience of doing some action in the past, negate <u>verb-過</u> with the negation word 沒 and say:

(S) 沒 **V-**過 **(O)**
我沒吃過 **jiǎo** 子。
I have not eaten Chinese dumplings before.

來中國以前我沒吃過 **jiǎo** 子。
Before I came to China, I had not eaten Chinese dumplings.

我沒做過中國飯。
I haven't ever cooked Chinese food before.

To say that someone has <u>not yet</u> had the experience of doing something, say:

(S) 還沒 **V-**過 **(O)**
我還沒 **chàng** 過 **kǎlā OK**。
I haven't yet sung karaoke.

我還沒看過那個電 **yǐng**。
I haven't seen that movie yet.

Asking if someone has had the experience of doing an action in the past

To ask if someone has done some action before, ask:

(S) V-過 **(O)** 嗎？
or

(S) V-過 (O) 沒有？

你們吃過 **jiǎo** 子嗎？
Have you eaten Chinese dumplings before?

你們吃過 **jiǎo** 子沒有？
Have you eaten Chinese dumplings before?

你 **yòng** 過 **kuài** 子嗎？
Have you used chopsticks before?

你坐過 **fēijī** 沒有？
Have you ridden on an airplane before?

15.13.   The duration of actions that continue to the present time: 已經 V 了 duration 了

In Lesson 12 we learned to indicate the duration of a situation by following the verb with the duration expression:

V + duration
我 **shuì** 了八個 **zhōngtóu**。
I slept for eight hours.

To indicate the duration of an action that began in the past and is still going on, add 了 to the end of the sentence and say:

V 了 duration 了

The adverb 已經 (**yǐjing**) *already* often occurs in the sentence, before the verb phrase.

他在中國已經住了一年了。
He has already been living in China for a year.

我學中文已經學了一年半了。
I have already been studying Chinese for a year and a half.

15.14.   多 V 一點 *do the action a little more*, 少 V 一點 *do the action a little less*

In Lesson 14 (Use and Structure note 14.2) we learned to use the pattern V + AdjV + 一點 to say *do the action a little more AdjV*: 請你說慢一點 *Please speak a little slower*. In this lesson we see that when the AdjV is 多 *more* or 少 *less* the order of information is:

多 V 一點   *do an action a little more*
少 V 一點   *do an action a little less*

(S) 多 V 一點 (O)
請你多說一點。
Please say a little more.

你得多 **fùxí** 一點。
You should review a little more.

多 **hē** 一點水。
Drink a little more water.

(S) 少 **V** 一點 **(O)**
你得少 **hē** 一點 **kāfēi**。
You should drink a little less coffee.

請你少 **tīng** 一點 **yīnyuè**。
Please listen to music a little less.

Sentence pyramids

The sentence pyramids illustrate the use of each new vocabulary item and structure introduced in the lesson. Use them to help you learn how to form phrases and sentences in Mandarin. Supply the English translation for the last line where indicated.

1. 一下 **jièshào** 一下 給你們 **jièshào** 一下 我給你們 **jièshào** 一下。	*(for a bit, briefly)* *introduce (briefly)* *introduce you* *Let me introduce you.*
2. 一下 **děng** 一下 請 **děng** 一下。	*(for a bit, briefly)* *wait a minute* *Please wait a minute.*
3. 朋友 好朋友 我們是好朋友。	*friend* *good friend* *We are good friends.*
4. 到我們家來 **Huānyíng** 你到我們家來。	*come to our home* *Welcome to our home.*
5. 先生 謝先生	*Mr.* *Mr. Xie*

6.	
太太	*Mrs.*
王太太	*Mrs. Wang*

7.	
到你們家來	*come to your home*
請我到你們家來	*invite me to come to your home*
謝謝你們請我到你們家來。	_____

8.	
kèqi	*polite*
那麼 **kèqi**	*so polite*
Bié 那麼 **kèqi**。	_____

9.	
shūshu	*uncle*
我 **shūshu**	*my uncle*
是我 **shūshu**	*is my uncle*
我爸爸的 **dìdi** 是我 **shūshu**。	*My dad's younger brother is my uncle.*

10.	
āyí	*aunt*
我的 **āyí**	*my aunt*
是我的 **āyí**	*is my aunt*
我媽媽的 **jiějie**，**mèimei** 是我的 **āyí**。	*My mom's older sisters and younger sisters are my aunts.*

11.	
shūshu āyí	*uncle and aunt*
叫 **shūshu āyí**	*call (us) uncle and aunt*
叫 **shūshu āyí** 吧。	*Call (us) uncle and aunt.*

12.	
到我們家來	*come to our home*
請你到我們家來	*invite you to come to our home*
yīnggāi 請你到我們家來	*should invite you to come to our home*
早就 **yīnggāi** 請你到我們家來	*long before now should have invited you to come to our home*
我們早就 **yīnggāi** 請你到我們家來。	_____

13. 吃飯 回家吃飯 **yīnggāi** 回家吃飯 我 **yīnggāi** 回家吃飯。 快六點了。我 **yīnggāi** 回家吃飯。	*eat* *go home to eat* *should go home to eat* *I should go home to eat.* _____
14. 水 **guǒ** 一 **xiē** 水 **guǒ** 買了一 **xiē** 水 **guǒ** 我買了一 **xiē** 水 **guǒ**。	*fruit* *some fruit* *bought some fruit* _____
15. **sòng** 給你們 買了一 **xiē** 水 **guǒ sòng** 給你們 我買了一 **xiē** 水 **guǒ sòng** 給你們。	*give you as a present* *bought some fruit to give you as a present* _____
16. **piàoliang** **zhēn piàoliang** **fáng** 子 **zhēn piàoliang** 您的 **fáng** 子 **zhēn piàoliang**。 小張：您的 **fáng** 子 **zhēn piàoliang**。 謝太太：哪 **lǐ**。	*beautiful* *really beautiful* *house really beautiful* *Your house is really beautiful.* *Xiao Zhang:* _____ *Mrs. Xie:* _____
17. 好吃 很好吃 **cài** 很好吃 今天的 **cài** 很好吃。	*delicious* *very delicious* *the food is very delicious* *Today's food is very delicious.*
18. 好吃 **fēicháng** 好吃 這個 **hóngshāo jī fēicháng** 好吃。	*delicious* *extremely delicious* *This red-simmered chicken is extremely delicious.*
19. **cài** 沒甚麼 **cài** 今天沒甚麼 **cài**。	*food* *not much food* _____

20.	
家 **cháng cài**	*home-style food*
是家 **cháng cài**	*is home-style food*
都是家 **cháng cài**	*is all home-style food*
今天的 **cài** 都是家 **cháng cài**。	_____

21.	
cài	*dishes*
三個 **cài**	*three dishes*
做了三個 **cài**	*cooked three dishes*
就做了三個 **cài**	*only cooked three dishes*
我就做了三個 **cài**。	_____

22.	
báicài	*cabbage*
chǎo báicài	*stir-fried cabbage*
做了 **chǎo báicài**	*cooked stir-fried cabbage*
就做了 **chǎo báicài**	*only cooked stir-fried cabbage*
我今天就做了 **chǎo báicài**。	_____

23.	
家 **cháng cài**	*home-style food*
Hóngshāo jī 是家 **cháng cài**。	*Red-simmered chicken is home-style food.*
回 **guō ròu** 和 **hóngshāo jī** 是家 **cháng cài**。	*Twice-cooked pork and red-simmered chicken are home-style food.*

24.	
kuài 子	*chopsticks*
yòng kuài 子	*use chopsticks*
會 **yòng kuài** 子	*know how to use chopsticks*
會不會 **yòng kuài** 子？	*know how to use chopsticks?*
你們會不會 **yòng kuài** 子？	_____

25.	
jiǎo 子	*Chinese dumplings*
吃過 **jiǎo** 子	*eaten Chinese dumplings before*
吃過 **jiǎo** 子嗎？	*eaten Chinese dumplings before?*
你們吃過 **jiǎo** 子嗎？	*Have you eaten Chinese dumplings before?*

26. 一年 一年了 差不多一年了 **zhù** 了差不多一年了 已經 **zhù** 了差不多一年了 他們在中國已經 **zhù** 了差不多一年了。	*one year* *one year (new information)* *almost one year* *lived almost one year* *already lived almost one year* _____
27. 吃過 **jiǎo** 子 當然吃過 **jiǎo** 子 他們當然吃過 **jiǎo** 子。	*eaten Chinese dumplings before* *of course eaten Chinese dumplings before* _____
28. 吃過 **jiǎo** 子 沒吃過 **jiǎo** 子 我沒吃過 **jiǎo** 子。	*eaten Chinese dumplings before* *haven't eaten Chinese dumplings before* _____

29.
沒吃過 **jiǎo** 子
來中國以前沒吃過 **jiǎo** 子
 	
我來中國以前沒吃過 **jiǎo** 子。
	haven't eaten Chinese dumplings
	before coming to China had not eaten
	    Chinese dumplings
	Before I came to China I had not eaten
	    Chinese dumplings.

30. 美國 去過美國嗎? 你去過美國嗎?	*America* *gone to America before?* _____
31. 美國人 中國人還是美國人? 您是中國人還是美國人?	*American person* *Chinese person or American person?* _____
32. **Fǎ** 國人 是 **Fǎ** 國人 小高是 **Fǎ** 國人。	*French person* *be a French person*

33. **hē chá** 先 **hē chá** 吃飯以前先 **hē chá**。	*drink tea* *first drink tea* *Before we eat, we'll first drink tea.*
34. **zhào** **zhào zhàopiàn** **zhào** 一張 **zhàopiàn** 先 **zhào** 一張 **zhàopiàn** 吃飯以前先 **zhào** 一張 **zhàopiàn** 我們吃飯以前先 **zhào** 一張 **zhàopiàn** 　吧。	*take (a photograph)* *take a photograph* *take one photograph* *first take a photograph* *before eating, take a photograph* _____ _____
35. **zhào** 我來 **zhào**。	*take (a photograph)* *I'll take the picture.*
36. **qié** 子 說 "**qié** 子" 大家說 "**qié** 子。"	*eggplant* *say "eggplant"* _____
37. 吃 **jiǎo** 子 **cháng** 吃 **jiǎo** 子 來中國以後 **cháng** 吃 **jiǎo** 子 我來中國以後 **cháng** 吃 **jiǎo** 子。	*eat dumplings* *often eat dumplings* *after coming to China, often eat Chinese* 　*dumplings* _____
38. 坐 **suíbiàn** 坐。	*sit* *Sit anywhere.*
39. **kèqi** **Bié kèqi**。 **Suíbiàn** 吃。 **Bié kèqi**。	*polite* *Don't be polite.* *Eat whatever you want. Don't be polite.*
40. 一點 吃一點 多吃一點。 多吃一點。 **Bié kèqi**。	*a little* *eat a little* *eat a little more* _____

Language FAQs

Everyone say "cheese" (or "eggplant")

In the USA, people say "cheese" when they are being photographed, but in China, they often say "**qiézi**" *eggplant*. The reason for a "camera" expression is to get everyone to smile, and in Mandarin, the word **qiézi** *eggplant* accomplishes that goal. You know that you are pronouncing the word **qiézi** correctly if you are smiling while you say **qié**.

What kind of meat is ròu?

Ròu means *meat*, and you can specify the kind of meat by saying, for example, **jī ròu** *chicken meat* (*chicken*). But when no description is added before the word **ròu** it is understood to mean *pork*. If the type of meat is not specified, as in the dish 回 **guō ròu**, you can assume that the meat is pork. What do you say if you don't eat pork?

What is the difference between fáng 子 and 家?

Fáng 子 *house* refers to the building. Mrs. Xie uses the word in this sense when she says:

這個 **fángzi** 很 **jiù** 了。
This house is old.

家 refers to *family* and also the place where a family lives: a *home*. In China, when people talk about where they live, they use the word 家 and not **fáng** 子. When you ask someone where they live, ask:

你家在哪兒？
Where is your home?

Do not ask:

⊗ 你的 **fáng** 子在哪兒？
Where is your house?

The question 你家在哪兒？also means *Where is your ancestral home?*, that is, where (in China) does your family come from?

Notes on Chinese culture

The rituals of guest and host in Chinese culture

All cultures have certain "ritual" behavior that people follow in certain situations. In Chinese culture, there are rituals associated with being a guest and a host, and we see some of them in the dialogue in this lesson. In Chinese culture, the host always offers the guest something to eat and/or drink, even when the event does not focus on food. As in Western countries, the guest must compliment the host on the food. But unlike in the West, the host does not accept the compliment, and does not reply by saying 謝謝 *thank you* or an equivalent expression. Instead, the host deflects the compliment, saying instead that the food was not special, or that there was not enough, or that it was not cooked that well. At the end of a visit, the host is expected to see the guests off. We will learn more about the ritual of seeing guests off in Lesson 16.

先生 *Mr.* and 太太 *Mrs.*

The titles 先生 *Mr.* and 太太 *Mrs.* are used differently in different parts of the Chinese speaking world. In Taiwan, they are used as titles much the way they are in English speaking countries, except that they <u>follow</u> the family name: 謝先生 *Mr. Xie*, 謝太太 *Mrs. Xie*. That is, they are used as terms of address when speaking to a man or a married woman, and they are used when referring to one's spouse (我的先生 *my husband*, 我的太太 *my wife*). In mainland China, however, in the early decades of the People's Republic of China, the words 先生 and 太太 were replaced by other words that carried a more revolutionary flavor. Today, the revolutionary words that replaced 先生 and 太太 are no longer used. But no neutral words have emerged to take their place. In informal settings, people use kinship terms like aunt and uncle to address others (see the following note), and there are a number of very informal expressions that people use when referring to their husband or wife. The titles 先生 and 太太 are considered polite but formal, and they are too formal for Xiao Zhang to use when addressing the parents of his good friend Xiao Xie.

叫 shūshu āyí 吧 *call us uncle and aunt*

In Chinese culture, it is common to use the terms **shūshu** *uncle* and **āyí** *aunt* as friendly, informal ways to address men and women unrelated to you who are about the same age as your parents. The terms are usually used among close acquaintances, and they are also used as a friendly way to address strangers whose status is equal to or lower than your own. Since Mr. and Mrs. Xie's son is the roommate and friend of Xiao Zhang, it is appropriate for Xiao Zhang to address Mr. and Mrs. Xie as **shūshu** *uncle* and **āyí** *aunt*.

家 cháng cài *home-style food*

家 **cháng cài** is the kind of food that people cook at home and eat in restaurants on an everyday basis. Home-style dishes differ from banquet dishes, which are prepared with expensive, sometimes exotic ingredients. Home-style food is different in different regions of the country. In Beijing, home-style food includes dishes from northern China and also Sichuan.

Main dishes and side dishes: Jiǎo 子 vs. cài

Chinese food is categorized in terms of **zhǔshí** *main dishes* and **cài** *side dishes*. **Cài** *side dishes* are made with vegetables or meat. The **zhǔshí** *main dish* is a grain or starch, that is, rice or noodles. Dumplings, which are made with flour, are also categorized as a **zhǔshí**. Therefore, Mrs. Xie describes her dinner as including three **cài** *dishes* and also **jiǎo** 子 *dumplings*. A Chinese meal always includes a **zhǔshí**, but it need not include any **cài**. Traditionally, Chinese people consumed much more **zhǔshí** than **cài**, since grains and starch are less expensive than vegetables or meat.

Lesson 15 Dialogue in English

Part A

Xiao Xie: Xiao Zhang, come in, come in. Let me introduce you. This is my dad, this is my mom. This is my roommate Zhang Dawei.

Mr. Xie: Welcome to our home. I'm glad to be able to meet Guoqiang's friends.

Xiao Zhang: Mr. Xie, Mrs. Xie, thanks for inviting me to your home for dinner. I've bought some fruit to give you.

Mrs. Xie: Don't be so polite. Call (us) uncle and aunt! You have already been in China for almost a year. We should have invited you here long before now.

Xiao Zhang: Aunt, your home is really beautiful.

Mrs. Xie: How could that be? This house is old. It isn't anything special.

Part B

Xiao Wang: Hi Dawei.

Xiao Zhang: Gao Meili, Youwen. Wang Maike, have you been here a long time? (literally: *Did you get here a long time ago?*)

Xiao Ye: We also just got here.

Mrs. Xie: The food is almost ready. Before we eat, let's take a picture.

Mr. Xie: Okay, I'll take it. Everyone say "eggplant."

Part C

Mr. Xie: Come. Let's eat. Sit anywhere. Don't be polite.

Mrs. Xie: I'm so embarrassed. Today there aren't any special dishes. I only made three: red-simmered chicken, twice-cooked pork, and stir-fried cabbage. They are all home-style food, nothing special. There's also jiaozi (*dumplings*). Have you eaten jiaozi before?

Xiao Xie: Mom, they came to China last August. They've been living in China for almost a year. Of course they have eaten jiaozi before.

Xiao Gao: I really like to eat jiaozi. Before I came to China I hadn't ever eaten them, but after coming to China I eat them often. Your jiaozi are extremely delicious.

Mrs. Xie: That's great. Come on, eat some more. Xiao Gao, you use chopsticks really well.

Xiao Gao: I can use them, but I don't use them well.

Lesson 16 Tán xià 天的 jìhuà
Talking about summer plans

Communication goals
- Evaluate past experiences and current situations
- Talk about future plans

Key structures
situation₁ 的時候 situation₂
suī 然 situation₁ 可是 situation₂
慢慢地 + VP

Dialogue

The Situation: Xiao Xie's parents have invited Xiao Zhang, Xiao Wang, Xiao Gao, and Xiao Ye to dinner and are chatting after the meal. Mr. and Mrs. Xie are interested in learning about their guests' impressions of China, and they also want to know what plans they have for the summer.

Part A

謝先生： 你們在中國學中文已經學了快一年了，覺得怎麼樣？

小高： 我覺得這一年過得真快。開 **shǐ**，我不習 **guàn** 住在中國，慢慢地習 **guàn** 了，也覺得在中國生 **huó** 很有 **yìsi**。

小張： 我剛來的時候，覺得中文非常難，可是現在我覺得不太難了。**Suī** 然我說中國話說得很慢，漢字也寫得很不好看，可是我非常喜歡學中文。

小王： 我們學了很多。現在可以跟中國人說話，還會寫一 **xiē** 漢字。

小 **Yè**： 你們的中文 **jìnbù** 得很快。

小謝： 小張 **měi** 天都跟小 **Yè** 說中文，中文當然 **jìnbù** 得很快了。

Part B

謝先生： 你們 xià 天有甚麼 jìhuà？

小張： 我打 suan 先在中國 lǚyóu 一個月，再回國看 fùmǔ。

小王： 我要跟幾個朋友一起去 Táiwān 看看，再從 Táiwān 回美國。你呢，
小高？

小高： <mark>Fàng 了 shǔjià</mark>，我就回法國。我得找一個 shǔ 期的 gōngzuò，
zhèng 一點錢。

謝太太： 你們九月還都回北京學中文嗎？

小張，小高，小王： 當然了。

Part C

小 Yè： 現在已經很晚了。我們得回 sùshè 了。

謝先生： <mark>再坐一會兒</mark>。<mark>一會兒</mark>我們開車 sòng 你們回 sùshè。

小 Yè： 太 máfan 你們了。真不好 yìsi。

謝先生： Bié kèqi。

Vocabulary

Běijīng	北京	city name	*Beijing*
dǎsuan	打 suan	noun, verb	*plan*
fàng jià		verb + object	*begin vacation*
fùmǔ		noun phrase	*mother and father*
gōngzuò		noun, [verb]	*job, work*
hǎo kàn	好看	adjectival verb phrase	*pretty, nice looking*
huí guó	回國	verb + object	*return to one's home country*

jìhuà [gè]		noun, verb	*plan*
jìnbù		verb	*advance, progress, improve*
		noun	*improvement, progress*
kāishǐ	开 **shǐ**	verb	*begin*
lǚyóu		verb	*travel*
máfan		verb, adjectival verb	*inconvenience, bother*
mànmān de	慢慢地	adverb	*gradually, little by little*
shēnghuó	生 **huó**	noun	*life*
		verb	*live*
shǔjià [gè]		noun phrase	*summer vacation*
shǔqī	**shǔ** 期	noun phrase	*summertime (the time period of the summer)*
sòng		verb	*see a guest off*
suīrán	**suī** 然	conjunction	*although*
Táiwān		proper noun	*Taiwan*
tán		verb	*talk, chat*
xiàtiān	**xià** 天	noun	*summer*
xíguàn	习 **guàn**	verb	*be accustomed to*
yǒu yìsi	有 **yìsi**	adjectival verb phrase	*be interesting*
zhèng		verb	*earn*

Characters

常	cháng	*often*	非常 (**fēicháng**) *extremely*
地	de, dì	*particle*	地圖 (**dìtú**) *map*
			慢慢地 (**mànmān de**) *gradually, little by little*
法	fǎ	*	法國 (**Fǎguó**) *France*
非	fēi	*	非常 (**fēicháng**) *extremely*
剛	gāng	*just now*	
跟	gēn	*with*	
漢	Hàn	*	漢字 (**Hàn zì**) *Chinese characters*
候	hòu		時候 (**shíhou**) *time*
			甚麼時候？ (**shénme shíhòu?**) *what time?*
			的時候 (**de shíhou**) *when, while*
歡	huān	*	喜歡 (**xǐhuan**) *like*
覺	jué	*	覺得 (**juéde**) *think, have an opinion*
	jiào		**shuì** 覺 (**shuì jiào**) *sleep*
開	kāi	*	開 **shǐ** (**kāishǐ**) *begin*
			開車 (**kāi chē**) *drive a car*
時	shí	*	時候 (**shíhou**) *time*
			甚麼時候？ (**shénme shíhòu?**) *what time?*
			的時候 (**de shíhou**) *when, while*

習	xí	*	習 guàn (xíguàn) *accustomed to, used to* liàn 習 (liànxí) *practice* fù 習 (fùxí) *review*
喜	xǐ	*	喜歡 (xǐhuān) *like*
寫	xiě	*write*	寫字 (xiě zì) *write (characters, letters)*
月	yuè	*month*	一月 (yīyuè) *January* 一個月 (yī gè yuè) *one month*
真	zhēn	*really*	真的 (zhēn de) *really*
住	zhù	*reside (in a location)* *live (in a location)*	

Stroke Order Flow Chart

character:	strokes:											total strokes:
常	⺌	⺌	⺌	⺌	当	学	常	常	常	常		11
地	一	十	土	圠	坩	地						6
法	丶	冫	氵	沪	汁	泆	法	法				8
非	丿	丿	扌	扌	非	非	非					8
剛	丨	冂	冂	罓	罔	用	岡	岡	剧	剛		10

跟	丶	口	口	甲	甲	昆	足	趵	跟	趵	跟	跟	跟	13
漢	丶	冫	氵	汁	汸	汻	汻	灌	漢	漢	漢	漢	漢	14
候	丿	亻	亻	仁	佗	佗	佗	候	候					10
歡	丶	丷	丬	艹	莊	莊	莊	莊	苗	莭	莭	華	華	
	華	萑	萑	雚	雚	雚	歡	歡						22
覺	丶	丷	彡	彣	俗	俗	臽	臽	臼	臼	臼	學	學	
	學	學	覺	覺	覺	覺								20
開	丨	冂	冂	冂	門	門	門	門	門	開	開			12
時	丨	冂	日	日	旷	旪	昡	昄	時	時				10
習	フ	ヲ	ヲ	习	羽	羽	羽	羿	習	習	習			11
喜	一	十	士	吉	吉	吉	吉	吉	壴	壴	喜	喜		12
寫	丶	宀	宀	宀	宀	宀	宀	宁	宵	宵	寫	寫	寫	
	寫													15
月	丿	刀	月	月										4
真	一	十	广	市	市	直	直	直	真	真				10
住	丿	亻	亻	广	住	住	住							7

Dialogue practice

Do these activities in class after mastering the dialogue for this lesson. Change partners so that you practice each part several times.

Dialogue 16A: Work with a partner and share your thoughts about studying Chinese this year and your progress in the language.

Dialogue 16B: Work with a partner and ask each other about your plans for the summer and your thoughts about continuing Chinese next semester.

Use and structure

16.1. 住在 location *live in a location*

We have already learned that in Mandarin, prepositional phrases usually occur before the verb. However, when talking about living in a place, especially when you are not focusing on the length of time that you have lived there, the prepositional phrase (在 location *at the location*) typically <u>follows</u> the verb:

開 **shǐ**，我不習 **guàn** 住在中國。
At first, I was not used to living in China.

Notice that when duration is included, the preposition phrase <u>在 location</u> occurs <u>before</u> the verb.

他們在中國已經住了差不多一年了。
They have already lived in China for almost a year.

16.2. 慢慢地 + VP

To say that a situation comes about gradually, say:

慢慢地 **VP**
開 **shǐ**，我不習 **guàn** 住在中國，慢慢地都習 **guàn** 了。
At first, I wasn't used to living in China, (but) gradually I got used to it.

Notice that in the phrase 慢慢地, the second syllable is pronounced in first tone: **mànmān de**. Notice also that in this expression, the character 地 is pronounced **de**. When the character 地 occurs in the word 地圖 *map* it is pronounced **dì**.

開 **shǐ**，我不會說中文，慢慢地會說了。
At first I couldn't speak Chinese, but then gradually I was able to speak it.

你慢慢地吃，我們還有時 **jiān**.
Take your time eating. We have plenty of time.

我們吃了晚飯以後，就慢慢地開車回 **sùshè** 了。
After we ate dinner, we took our time driving back to the dorm.

16.3. Situation₁ 的時候 situation₂

To indicate that two situations overlap in time, say:

situation₁ 的時候 **situation₂**
我剛來的時候，覺得中文非常難。
When I first arrived, I thought that Chinese was extremely difficult.

Notice that 的時候 occurs <u>at the end of the first situation</u>, while its English translation *when* occurs at the <u>beginning</u> of the first situation.

[**Kǎo shì** 的時候] **bié** 說話。
[When you take a test,] don't talk.

[吃中國飯的時候] **yīnggāi yòng kuài** 子。
[When you eat Chinese food,] you should use chopsticks.

的時候 *when, while*, and 甚麼時候? *when? what time?*

We have now learned two expressions that can be translated with the English word *when*, both of which involve the word 時候 *time*: 的時候 *when, while*, and 甚麼時候? *when, what time*. These expressions have very different functions and are never interchangeable.

甚麼時候 *when, what time* is used to ask <u>when</u> some situation occurs, or to say that <u>you don't know when</u> some action occurs.

你甚麼時候 **fàng shǔjià**?
When do you begin summer vacation?

我不知道你甚麼時候 **fàng shǔjià**。
I don't know when you begin summer vacation.

我們甚麼時候 **kǎo shì**?
When do we take the test?

我不知道我們甚麼時候 **kǎo shì**。
I don't know when we take the test.

When answering questions with 甚麼時候, always replace the question phrase with the answer. The question phrase and the answer occur in the same place in the sentence.

你<u>甚麼時候</u> **fàng shǔjià**?
When do you begin summer vacation?

我<u>五月</u>就 **fàng shǔjià**。
I begin summer vacation in May. (and that is early from the perspective of the speaker)

的時候 *when, while* indicates that two situations overlap in time. Its use always involves two situations.

我回 **sùshè** 的時候我的 **tóngwū** 已經 **shuì** 覺了。
When I returned to the dorm, my roommate was already asleep.

我做中國飯的時候都做家常 **cài**。
When I cook Chinese food, I always cook home-style food.

16.4. Suī 然 situation₁ 可是 situation₂

To indicate contrast between two situations, say:

Suī 然 **situation₁**, 可是 **situation₂**
<u>Suī</u> 然我說中國話說得很慢，漢字也寫得很不好看，<u>可是</u>我非常喜歡學中文。

We have already learned how to use the word 可是 *but* in Lesson 10. In Mandarin, when indicating contrast, a sentence may include both of the words **suī** 然 and 可是, or it may include only one of the words by itself.

> **Suī** 然今天只 **kǎo** 十個漢字，可是 **měi** 個字都很難寫。
> *Although we are only having a test on 10 characters today, every character is hard to write.*

Suī 然 may occur before or after the subject.

> 他 **suī** 然 **fù**習 **gōngkè** 了，可是還 **wàng** 了幾個字。
> *Although he studied the lesson, he still forgot some of the characters.*

16.5.   Fàng jià *begin vacation* and fàng shǔjià *begin summer vacation*

Fàng jià is a verb + object phrase that means *begin a period of vacation*.

> 你們學 **xiào fàng jià** 了嗎?
> *Has your school started vacation yet?*

To indicate a specific vacation, for example, <u>summer</u> vacation, replace the general object **jià** with the more specific object: **fàng shǔjià** *begin summer vacation*.

> 我五月就 **fàng shǔjià**。
> *I begin summer vacation in May.*

When Xiao Gao says **fàng** 了 **shǔjià** she is using the sequence structure that we learned in Lesson 14 to say *after the period of summer vacation begins*.

> **Fàng** 了 **shǔjià**，我就回法國。
> *After the start of summer vacation, I will return to France.*

To review sequence with 以後, see Use and Structure note 14.3.

16.6.   再 + ActV *continue doing the action*

To tell someone to continue doing some action, use the adverb 再 and say <u>再 + ActV</u>:

> 再坐一會兒。
> *Sit for a little while longer.*

16.7.   一會兒 used in two different ways

Mr. Xie uses the expression 一會兒 *a short period of time* in two different ways in Part C of the dialogue. In his first sentence, he says it after the verb 坐. Therefore, 一會兒 indicates <u>duration</u> (that is, how long the "sitting" will occur).

> 再坐一會兒。
> *Sit for a little while longer.*

In his second sentence, he says 一會兒 at the beginning of the sentence. In this sentence, 一會兒 indicates the <u>time when</u> the action will take place, and can be translated into English as *in a little while*.

一會兒我們開車 **sòng** 你們回 **sùshè**。
In a little while we will drive you back to the dormitory.

Sentence pyramids

The sentence pyramids illustrate the use of each new vocabulary item and structure introduced in the lesson. Use them to help you learn how to form phrases and sentences in Mandarin. Supply the English translation for the last line where indicated.

1. 快 真快 過得真快 一年過得真快。	*fast* *really fast* *passed really quickly* *One year passed really quickly.*
2. 有 **yìsi** 真有 **yìsi** 那個電 **yǐng** 真有 **yìsi**。	*interesting* *really interesting* *That movie is really interesting.*
3. 很有 **yìsi** 生 **huó** 很有 **yìsi** 在中國生 **huó** 很有 **yìsi** 我覺得在中國生 **huó** 很有 **yìsi**。	*very interesting* *living (passing one's days) is very interesting* *living in China is very interesting* *I think that living in China is very interesting.*
4. 有 **yìsi** 沒有 **yìsi** 那本書沒有 **yìsi** 我覺得那本書沒有 **yìsi**。	*interesting* *not interesting* *that book is not interesting* _____
5. 住在中國 習 **guàn** 住在中國 不習 **guàn** 住在中國 我不習 **guàn** 住在中國。 開 **shǐ**，我不習 **guàn** 住在中國。	*live (reside) in China* *be used to living in China* *not used to living in China* *I am not used to living in China.* *In the beginning, I was not used to living in China.*

6. 吃飯 **yòng kuài** 子吃飯 習 **guàn yòng kuài** 子吃飯 你習 **guàn yòng kuài** 子吃飯嗎？	*eat* *use chopsticks to eat* *used to using chopsticks to eat* *Are you used to using chopsticks to eat?*
7. 習 **guàn** 了 慢慢地習 **guàn** 了 我慢慢地習 **guàn** 了。	*became used to (it)* *gradually became used to (it)* _____
8. 難 非常難 中文非常難 我覺得中文非常難 剛來的時候，我覺得中文非常難。	*difficult* *extremely difficult* *Chinese is extremely difficult* *I think that Chinese is extremely difficult* *When I first arrived, I thought that Chinese was extremely difficult.*
9. **yòng kuài** 子 吃中國飯的時候 **yòng kuài** 子 我吃中國飯的時候 **yòng kuài** 子。	*use chopsticks* *use chopsticks when eating Chinese food* *I use chopsticks when eating Chinese food.*
10. 喜歡學中文 我非常喜歡學中文 可是我非常喜歡學中文 我說得很慢，可是我非常喜歡學中文 **Suī** 然我說話說得很慢，可是我非常 喜歡學中文。	*like to study Chinese* *I like to study Chinese a lot* *but I like to study Chinese a lot* *I speak slowly, but I like to study Chinese a lot* *Although I speak slowly, I like to study Chinese a lot.*
11. 說中文 她不會說中文 可是她不會說中文 她的 **fùmǔ** 是中國人可是她不會說中文。 **Suī** 然她的 **fùmǔ** 是中國人，可是她不會說中文。	*speak Chinese* *she cannot speak Chinese* *but she cannot speak Chinese* *Her parents are Chinese but she cannot speak Chinese.* _____ _____

12.	
yòng kuài 子	*use chopsticks*
會 **yòng kuài** 子	*able to use chopsticks*
可是他不會 **yòng kuài** 子	*but he cannot use chopsticks*
他常吃中國飯可是他不會 **yòng kuài** 子。	*He often eats Chinese food but he cannot use chopsticks.*
Suī 然他常吃中國飯可是他不會 **yòng kuài** 子。	*Although he eats Chinese food a lot, he cannot use chopsticks.*

13.	
jìnbù	*progress*
很大的 **jìnbù**	*very big progress, improvement*
你的中文有很大的 **jìnbù**。	*Your Chinese has had a very big improvement. (Your Chinese has improved a lot.)*

14.	
很快	*very quick*
jìnbù 得很快	*progressed very quickly*
中文 **jìnbù** 得很快	*Chinese progressed very quickly*
你的中文 **jìnbù** 得很快	_____

15.	
說話	*speak*
跟中國人說話	*speak with Chinese people*
可以跟中國人說話	*can speak with Chinese people*
我現在可以跟中國人說話。	_____

16.	
漢字	*Chinese characters*
一 **xiē** 漢字	*some Chinese characters*
寫一 **xiē** 漢字	*write some Chinese characters*
會寫一 **xiē** 漢字	*able to write some Chinese characters*
我還會寫一 **xiē** 漢字。	*I am also able to write some Chinese characters.*

17.	
jìhuà	*plan*
甚麼 **jìhuà**？	*what plan?*
有甚麼 **jìhuà**？	*have what plan?*
xià 天有甚麼 **jìhuà**？	*have what plan for the summer?*
你們 **xià** 天有甚麼 **jìhuà**？	_____

18. **lǚyóu** 在中國 **lǚyóu** 我打 suan 在中國 **lǚyóu**。	*travel* *travel in China* _____
19. 一個月 **lǚyóu** 一個月 在中國 **lǚyóu** 一個月 我打 suan 在中國 **lǚyóu** 一個月。	*one month* *travel for one month* *travel in China for one month* _____
20. 回國 甚麼時候回國? 你甚麼時候回國?	*return to one's home country* *return home when?* _____
21. 回國 就回國 **fàng** 了 **jià** 以後就回國 我打 suan **fàng** 了 **jià** 以後就回國。	*return to one's home country* *return to one's home country* *return home after (when) we start vacation* *I plan to return home after we start vacation.*
22. 看 **fùmǔ** 回國看 **fùmǔ** 我就回國看 **fùmǔ**。 **Fàng** 了 **shǔjià**，我就回國看 **fùmǔ**。	*see parents* *return home and see parents* *I will return home and see my parents.* *After summer vacation begins, I will return home and see my parents.*
23. **gōngzuò** **shǔ** 期 **gōngzuò** 找一個 **shǔ** 期 **gōngzuò** 我得找一個 **shǔ** 期 **gōngzuò**。	*work, job* *summer job* *look for a summer job* *I have to look for a summer job.*
24. 錢 一點錢 **zhèng** 一點錢 我找一個 **shǔ** 期 **gōngzuò zhèng** 　一點錢。	*money* *a little money* *earn a little money* _____

25. 學中文	study Chinese
學中文嗎？	study Chinese?
回北京學中文嗎？	return to Beijing to study Chinese?
你打 **suan** 回北京學中文嗎？	Do you plan to return to Beijing to study Chinese?
26. 回 **sùshè**	return to the dormitory
sòng 你們回 **sùshè**	take you back to the dormitory
開車 **sòng** 你們回 **sùshè**	drive you back to the dormitory
我們開車 **sòng** 你們回 **sùshè**。	We will drive you back to the dormitory.
再坐一會兒，我們開車 **sòng** 你們回**sùshè**.	Sit a little longer and then we'll drive you back to the dormitory.
27. **máfan** 你們	bother you
太 **máfan** 你們了。	(That is) too much trouble for you.
28. Guest：太 **máfan** 你們了。	Guest: That's too much trouble for you.
Host：**Bié kèqi**。	Host: Don't be polite.

Language FAQs

Noun or verb or both?

住 *live* and 生 **huó** *live*

住 and 生 **huó** can both be translated as *live*, but they do not mean the same thing.

住 can only be used as a verb. It means *to reside or live (in a location)*. It is used when talking about where you live:

你住在哪兒？
Where do you live?

or how long you have lived somewhere:

你在法國住了多 **cháng** 時 **jiān**？
How long did you live in France?

It can be used when talking about "staying" or "residing" in a location for a short period of time. For example, it can be used when saying that you are "staying" in a hotel or at someone's house for a few days, or "living" some place for a short period of time.

> 我去北京的時候會住在小張家。
> *When I go to Beijing I will stay at Xiao Zhang's house.*

生 **huó** can be used as verb or as a noun. As a verb it means *to live* or *to pass one's days* in some location:

> 我很喜歡在中國生 **huó**。
> *I really like experiencing life in China; I like spending time in China.*

As a noun 生 **huó** means *life*:

> 我很喜歡中國的生 **huó**。
> *I really like life in China. (I really like Chinese life.)*

Jìhuà *plan* and 打 **suan** *plan*

Jìhuà and 打 **suan**, like the English word *plan*, can function as nouns or as verbs.

Jìhuà usually refers to a more formal, detailed plan.

> 你們 **xià** 天有甚麼 **jìhuà**?
> *What plans do you have for the summer?*

打 **suan** often suggests an intention, similar to *thinking about* (doing something).

> 我打 **suan** 在中國 **lǔyóu** 一個月。
> *I plan to travel in China for a month.*

Gōngzuò *job, work*

Gōngzuò can be used as either a noun or a verb.

As a noun it is usually translated as *job*, though it can also sometimes be translated as *work*.

> 我得找一個 **shǔ** 期的 **gōngzuò**, **zhèng** 一點錢。
> *I have to look for a summer job and earn a little money.*

> 他做甚麼 **gōngzuò**。
> *What kind of work does he do?*

As a verb, it is translated as *work*.

她 **xià** 天在法國 **gōngzuò**。
In the summer she works in France.

Jìnbù *improve, improvement*

Jìnbù can be used as a noun or as a verb.

As a noun, **jìnbù** means *progress*, *improvement*, or *advancement*.

你的中文有很大的 **jìnbù**。
Your Chinese has made a lot of progress.

As a verb, **jìnbù** means *progress*, *improve*, or *advance*:

你的中文 **jìnbù** 得很快。
Your Chinese has progressed quickly.

Two pronunciations and meanings for the character 覺

Most characters have only a single pronunciation, but a small number have more than one. In this lesson we learn the character 覺 and its two very different pronunciations.

In the word 覺得 (**juéde**) 覺 is pronounced **jué**.
In the word 睡覺 (**shuì jiào**) 覺 is pronounced **jiào**.

Recall that the character 得 also has two pronunciations. **De** is one of them. What is the other one, and what is the meaning of 得 in the other pronunciation?

Notes on Chinese culture

Seeing guests off

Seeing guests off is part of the ritual of guest and host. At the end of a gathering, the host is required to **sòng** the guests, or see them off. To **sòng** the guests does not necessarily require taking the guests home, but it does require seeing the guests out of the house (or meeting place), and watching (and usually waving) as they depart. In the USA, at the end of a visit, the polite host will see the guests to the door, often closing it as soon as the guests are outside. In China, the host often exits with the guests and walks them to their car, or at least part way to their bus, subway, or home. The polite host does not turn her back on the guests or go inside until the guests are out of sight.

Lesson 16 Dialogue in English

Part A

Mr. Xie: You've been studying Chinese in China for almost a year already. What do you think about your experience?

Xiao Gao: I think this year passed really quickly. At the beginning, I wasn't used to living in China, but I gradually got used to it, and (began to) think that living in China is very interesting.

Xiao Zhang: When I first got here, I thought that Chinese was extremely difficult, but now I think that it isn't difficult. Although I speak Chinese very slowly and my Chinese characters don't look too good, I really like studying Chinese.

Xiao Wang: We've learned a lot. We can speak with Chinese people now and we can write a bit in Chinese.

Xiao Ye: Your Chinese has progressed very quickly.

Xiao Xie: Xiao Zhang speaks Chinese with Xiao Ye every day. Of course his Chinese has improved quickly.

Part B

Mr. Xie: What plans do you have for the summer?

Xiao Zhang: I plan first to travel in China for a month, and then return home to see my parents.

Xiao Wang: I'm going to Taiwan with a few friends to look around, and then I'll return to the USA from Taiwan. What about you, Xiao Gao?

Xiao Gao: Once vacation begins, I'll go back to France. I have to find a summer job and earn a little money.

Mrs. Xie: Will you all come back to Beijing in September to study Chinese?

Xiao Zhang, Xiao Gao, Xiao Wang: Of course!

Part C

Xiao Ye: It's already very late. We should go back to the dorm.

Mr. Xie: Sit for a little bit longer. In a while we'll drive you back to the dorm.

Xiao Ye: That's too much trouble for you. So embarrassing!

Mr. Xie: Don't be polite.

Vocabulary: English to Mandarin Pinyin

The lesson number indicates the lesson in which the vocabulary item is introduced. The last column of each row shows each word written using the characters introduced through lesson 16. To find the lesson where a character is first introduced, see the Chinese Character Indices.

A

				Traditional	Simplified
able	**néng**	modal verb	L13		
able to, can, will	**huì**	modal verb	L3, 14	會	会
accustomed to	**xíguàn**	verb	L16	習 **guàn**	习 **guàn**
across from	**duìmiàn**	noun	L14	對 **miàn**	对 **miàn**
action in progress	**zài**	adverb	L9	在	在
after, afterwards	**yǐhòu**	noun	L14	以後	以后
afternoon	**xiàwǔ**	noun	L9	下 **wǔ**	下 **wǔ**
afterward	**zài**	adverb	L13	再	再
airplane	**fēijī**	noun	L11		
airport	**fēijīchǎng**	noun	L11		
all, both	**dōu**	adverb	L2	都	都
almost	**chàbuduō**	adverb	L12	差不多	差不多
already	**yǐjing**	adverb	L10	已經	已经
also	**yě**	adverb	L1	也	也
although	**suīrán**	conjunction	L16	**suī** 然	**suī** 然
altogether	**yígòng**	adverb	L7	一 **gòng**	一 **gòng**
America (USA)	**Měiguó**	country name	L2	美國	美国
American	**Měiguó rén**	noun phrase	L2	美國人	美国人
American English	**Měiguó huà**	noun phrase	L3	美國話	美国话
and	**hé**	conjunction	L3	和	和
arrive	**dào**	verb	L13	到	到
as you please	**suíbiàn**	adverb	L15		
ask	**wèn**	verb	L11	問	问
at, in, on	**zài**	preposition	L12	在	在
attend; go up, get on	**shàng**	verb	L9	上	上
aunt	**āyí**	noun	L15		

B

bank	**yínháng**	noun	L14		
bathe	**xǐ zǎo**	verb + object	L9		
be	**shì**	stative verb	L1	是	是
beautiful	**piàoliang**	adjectival verb	L14		
bed	**chuáng**	noun	L9		
beer	**píjiǔ**	noun	L8		
before	**yǐqián**	noun	L15	以前	以前
begin	**kāishǐ**	verb	L16	開 **shǐ**	开 **shǐ**
begin vacation	**fàng jià**	verb + object	L16		
behind, after	**hòu**	*	L14	後	后
behind, in back (of)	**hòubiān**	noun	L14	後 **biān**	后 **biān**
Beijing	**Běijīng**	city name	L16	北京	北京
beside, alongside	**pángbiān**	noun	L14		

between, in between	zhōngjiān	noun	L13	中 jiān	中 jiān
big	dà	adjectival verb	L6	大	大
birthday	shēngri	noun	L8	生日	生日
book	shū	noun	L7	書	书
bookstore	shūdiàn	noun	L11	書店	书店
bottle	píng	classifier	L6		
boy (male child)	nán háizi	noun phrase	L5	男 hái 子	男 hái 子
breakfast	zǎofàn	noun	L9	早飯	早饭
Britain	Yīngguó	country name	L2	Yīng 國	Yīng 国
British	Yīngguó rén	noun phrase	L2	Yīng 國人	Yīng 国人
British English	Yīngguó huà	noun phrase	L3	Yīng 國話	Yīng 国话
bus (public bus)	gōnggòng qìchē	noun	L12	公 gòng qì 車	公 gòng qì 车
busy	máng	adjectival verb	L11		
but	kěshì	conjunction	L10	可是	可是
buy	mǎi	verb	L6	買	买
by the way	duì le	conversational expression	L11	對了	对了

C

cabbage	báicài	noun	L15		
call, be called	jiào	verb	L3	叫	叫
can (permission)	kěyǐ	modal verb	L5	可以	可以
car (with an engine)	qìchē	noun	L12	qì 車	qì 车
car, vehicle	chē	noun	L12	車	车
cell phone, mobile phone	shǒujī	noun	L5		
center	zhōngxīn	noun	L11	中 xīn	中 xīn
change (one thing for another)	huàn	verb	L12		
character (Chinese character)	zì	noun	L7	字	字
cheap	piányi	adjectival verb	L6		
chicken	jī	noun	L15		
child	háizi	noun	L5	hái 子	hái 子
China	Zhōnghuá	country name	L12	中 huá	中 huá
China	Zhōngguó	country name	L2	中國	中国
Chinese character	Hàn zì	noun phrase	L7	漢字	汉字
Chinese dumplings	jiǎozi	noun	L15	jiǎo 子	jiǎo 子
Chinese language	Zhōngwén	noun	L4	中文	中文
Chinese language	Zhōngguó huà	noun phrase	L3	中國話	中国话
Chinese mile	lǐ	classifier	L11		
Chinese person	Zhōngguó rén	noun	L2	中國人	中国人
chopsticks	kuàizi	noun	L15	kuài 子	kuài 子
city	shì	*	L11		
city center, center of the city, downtown	shì zhōngxīn	noun phrase	L11	shì 中 xīn	shì 中 xīn
class	kè	noun	L9		
class work	gōngkè	noun	L9		
(classifier for books)	běn	classifier	L7	本	本
(classifier for flat rectangular and square objects)	zhāng	classifier	L6	張	张
(classifier for people and some other nouns)	gè (ge)	classifier	L5	個	个
(classifier for streets)	tiáo	classifier	L14		

(classifier (polite) for people)	**wèi**	classifier	*L13*	位	位
(classifier for writing implements)	**zhī**	classifier	*L6*		
classmate	**tóngxué**	noun	*L4*	**tóng** 學	**tóng** 学
clerk, service person	**fúwùyuán**	noun	*L6*		
coffee	**kāfēi**	noun	*L10*		
coffee shop	**kāfēiguǎn**	noun	*L10*	**kāfēi** 館	**kāfēi** 馆
cola	**kělè**	noun	*L6*	可 **lè**	可 **lè**
college	**dàxué**	noun	*L12*	大學	大学
come	**lái**	verb	*L11*	來	来
computer	**diànnǎo**	noun	*L9*	電 **nǎo**	电 **nǎo**
continuously, keep (doing verb)	**yīzhí**	adverb	*L14*	一 **zhí**	一 **zhí**
correct	**duì**	adjectival verb	*L2*	對	对
country	**guó**	noun	*L2*	國	国
cross, pass	**guò**	verb	*L13*	過	过
cup	**bēi**	classifier	*L10*		
D					
dad	**bàba**	noun	*L4*	爸爸	爸爸
dance	**tiào wǔ**	verb + object	*L8*		
date of the month	**hào**	classifier	*L8*	號	号
David	**Dàwéi**	given name	*L3*	大 **wéi**	大 **wéi**
day	**tiān**	classifier	*L8*	天	天
delicious	**hǎo chī**	adjectival verb phrase	*L15*	好吃	好吃
difficult	**nán**	adjectival verb	*L10*	難	难
dime	**máo**	classifier	*L6*	毛	毛
dinner	**wǎnfàn**	noun	*L8*	晚飯	晚饭
dishes (food)	**cài**	noun	*L15*		
(do an action for a short duration)	**yīxià**	verb suffix	*L15*	一下	一下
do, cook	**zuò**	verb	*L9, 15*	做	做
dollar	**kuài**	classifier	*L6*	塊	块
don't	**bié**	negation	*L14*		
door, gate	**mén**	noun	*L12*	門	门
doorway	**ménkǒu**	noun	*L12*	門口	门口
dormitory	**sùshè**	noun	*L9*		
dot, o'clock	**diǎn**	classifier	*L9*	點	点
draw	**huà**	verb	*L11*		
drink	**hē**	verb	*L8*		
drink alcohol	**hē jiǔ**	verb + object	*L8*		
drive	**kāi**	verb	*L12*	開	开
drive a car	**kāi chē**	verb + object	*L12*	開車	开车
E					
early; *good morning*	**zǎo**	adjectival verb; greeting	*L6*	早	早
earn	**zhèng**	verb	*L16*		
east	**dōng**	*	*L11*	東	东
east side	**dōngbiān**	noun	*L11*	東 **biān**	东 **biān**
easy	**róngyì**	adjectival verb	*L10*	容易	容易
eat	**chī**	verb	*L8*	吃	吃

eat (food)	chī fàn	verb + object	L8	吃飯	吃饭
eggplant	qiézi	noun	L15	qié 子	qié 子
eight	bā	number	L5	八	八
embarrassed	bù hǎo yìsi	conversational expression	L13	不好 yìsi	不好 yìsi
evening, night	wǎnshang	noun	L8	晚上	晚上
every	měi	quantifier	L11		
everyone	dàjiā	noun phrase	L15	大家	大家
excuse me	duìbuqǐ	conversational expression	L3	對不起	对不起
excuse me	qǐng wèn	conversational expression	L2	請問	请问
expensive	guì	adjectival verb	L6		
(experienced doing an action)	guò	verb suffix	L15	過	过
extremely	fēicháng	intensifier	L10	非常	非常
F					
family, home	jiā	noun	L5	家	家
(family name)	Chén	family name	L2		
(family name)	Gāo	family name	L1	高	高
(family name)	Lǐ	family name	L1		
(family name)	Mǎ	family name	L8	馬	马
(family name)	Wáng	family name	L2	王	王
(family name)	Xiè	family name	L4	謝	谢
(family name)	Yè	family name	L8		
(family name)	Zhāng	family name	L1	張	张
(family name prefix)	xiǎo	family name prefix	L1	小	小
family name, be family named	xìng	noun, verb	L3		
far	yuǎn	adjectival verb	L11		
fast, soon	kuài	adjectival verb	L10	快	快
female	nǚ	adjective	L5	女	女
fetch someone	jiē	verb	L12		
few, little in number	shǎo	adjectival verb	L10	少	少
first	xiān	adverb	L13	先	先
first-year level	yī niánjí	noun phrase	L7	一年 jí	一年 jí
five	wǔ	number	L5	五	五
for, to	gěi	preposition	L11	給	给
forget	wàng	verb	L10		
(forms follow-up questions)	ne	final particle	L2	呢	呢
(forms yes-no questions)	ma	final particle	L1	嗎	吗
four	sì	number	L5	四	四
four-way intersection	shízì lùkǒu	noun phrase	L14	十字路口	十字路口
France	Fǎguó	country name	L2	法國	法国
French language	Fǎguó huà	noun phrase	L3	法國話	法国话
French person	Fǎguó rén	noun phrase	L2	法國人	法国人
Friday	xīngqīwǔ	noun	L8	星期五	星期五
friend	péngyou	noun	L5	朋友	朋友
from	cóng	preposition	L12	從	从
front, in front	qián	*	L14	前	前

| front, in front (of) | qiánbiān | noun | L14 | 前 biān | 前 biān |
| fruit | shuǐguǒ | noun | L15 | 水 guǒ | 水 guǒ |

G

German language	Déguó huà	noun phrase	L3	Dé 國話	Dé 国话
German person	Déguó rén	noun phrase	L2	Dé 國人	Dé 国人
Germany	Déguó	country name	L2	Dé 國	Dé 国
get out of bed	qǐ chuáng	verb + object	L9	起 chuáng	起 chuáng
get out of class	xià kè	verb + object	L9	下 kè	下 kè
get up, rise up	qǐ	verb	L9	起	起
girl (female child)	nǚ háizi	noun phrase	L5	女 hái 子	女 hái 子
give	gěi	verb	L7	給	给
give as a present	sònggěi	verb	L15	sòng 給	sòng 给
go	qù	verb	L8	去	去
go down, get off	xià	verb	L12	下	下
go to class	shàng kè	verb + object	L9	上 kè	上 kè
go;	zǒu	verb	L12	走	走
walk			L14		
good	hǎo	adjectival verb	L1	好	好
goodbye	zài jiàn	conversational expression	L1	再見	再见
gradually	mànmān de	adverb	L10	慢慢地	慢慢地
grammar	yǔfǎ	noun	L10		
great, terrific	tài hǎo le	conversational expression	L8	太好了	太好了
green	lǜ	adjectival verb	L14		
guest	kèrén	noun	L13	kè 人	kè 人

H

half	bàn	number	L9	半	半
happy	gāoxìng	adjectival verb	L4	高 xìng	高 xìng
happy	kuàilè	adjectival verb	L8	快 lè	快 lè
happy birthday	shēngri kuàilè	conversational expression	L8	生日快 lè	生日快 lè
have	yǒu	stative verb	L4	有	有
have something to do, be busy	yǒu shì	verb phrase	L9	有 shì	有 shì
he/him, she/her, it	tā	pronoun	L1	他，她	他，她
hello (formal greeting)	nǐ hǎo	greeting	L1	你好	你好
help	bāng	verb	L11		
here	zhèr	noun	L11	這兒	这儿
hit	dǎ	verb	L5	打	打
home-style food, simple food	jiā cháng cài	noun phrase	L15	家常 cài	家常 cài
hour	zhōngtóu	noun	L12		
house	fángzi	noun	L15	fáng 子	fáng 子
how	zěnme	question word	L5	怎麼	怎么
how about it, okay?	zěnmeyàng	question phrase	L8	怎麼樣?	怎么样?
how far	duō yuǎn	question phrase	L11	多 yuǎn	多 yuǎn
how long (duration)	duō jiǔ	question phrase	L14	多 jiǔ	多 jiǔ
how many	jǐ	question word	L5	幾	几
how much, how many	duōshao	question word	L5, 6	多少	多少

how much time, how long	**duō cháng shíjiān**	question phrase	*L12*	多 **cháng** 時 **jiān**	多 **cháng** 时 **jiān**
how old	**duō dà**	question phrase	*L8*	多大	多大
hundred	**bǎi**	number	*L7*		
husband	**xiānsheng**	noun	*L15*	先生	先生

I

I/me	**wǒ**	pronoun	*L1*	我	我
improve, improvement	**jìnbù**	verb, noun	*L16*		
in addition	**hái**	adverb	*L6*	還	还
in addition, furthermore	**hái yǒu**	adverb	*L10*	還有	还有
in other words	**yě jiù shì shuō**	conversational expression	*L14*	也就是說	也就是说
in this way, how about this	**zhè yàng**	noun phrase	*L8*	這樣	这样
inconvenience, bother	**máfan**	verb, adjectival verb	*L16*		
(indicates noun description)	**de**	particle	*L4*	的	的
(indicates speaker's supposition, suggestions)	**ba**	final particle	*L4, L8*	吧	吧
(indicates verb description)	**de**	particle	*L10*	得	得
inform	**gàosu**	verb	*L13*		
inside	**lǐ**	*	*L13*		
inside	**lǐbiān**	noun	*L13*		
interesting	**yǒu yìsi**	adjectival verb phrase	*L16*	有 **yìsi**	有 **yìsi**
intersection	**lùkǒu**	noun	*L14*	路口	路口
introduce	**jièshào**	verb	*L15*		
invite	**qǐng**	verb	*L8*	請	请

J

Japan	**Rìběn**	country name	*L3*	日本	日本
Japanese language	**Rìběn huà**	noun phrase	*L3*	日本話	日本话
job, work	**gōngzuò**	noun, verb	*L16*		
jump, dance	**tiào**	verb	*L8*		
just now	**gāng**	adverb	*L10*	剛	刚

K

karaoke	**kǎlā OK**	noun	*L8*		
know	**zhīdào**	verb	*L5*	知道	知道

L

lake	**hú**	noun	*L11*		
lamp, light	**dēng**	noun	*L14*		
last year	**qùnián**	noun	*L15*	去年	去年
late	**wǎn**	adjectival verb	*L9*	晚	晚
left	**zuǒ**	*	*L13*		
left side	**zuǒbiān**	noun	*L13*		
library	**túshūguǎn**	noun	*L9*	圖書館	图书馆
like	**xǐhuan**	stative verb	*L8*	喜歡	喜欢
line (train line, subway line)	**xiàn**	noun	*L12*		
listen (to)	**tīng**	verb	*L8*		
listen to music	**tīng yīnyuè**	verb + object	*L8*		

little (a little)	**yīdiǎn**	quantifier	*L7*	一點	一点
little by little	**mànmān de**	adverb	*L10*	慢慢地	慢慢地
live, life	**shēnghuó**	verb, noun	*L16*	生 **huó**	生 **huó**
live/reside in a place	**zhù**	verb	*L15*	住	住
located at	**zài**	verb	*L11*	在	在
long before now, long ago,	**zǎo jiù**	adverb	*L15*	早就	早就
look for, find	**zhǎo**	verb	*L13*	找	找
lunch	**wǔfàn**	noun	*L10*	**wǔ** 飯	**wǔ** 饭

M

make (change)	**zhǎo (qián)**	verb	*L7*	找錢	找钱
male	**nán**	adjective	*L5*	男	男
many, a lot	**duō**	adjectival verb	*L10*	多	多
map	**dìtú**	noun	*L6*	地圖	地图
Marie, Mary	**Měilì**	given name	*L3*	美 **lì**	美 **lì**
may I ask	**qǐng wèn**	conversational expression	*L2*	請問	请问
meat	**ròu**	noun	*L15*		
meet, know	**rènshi**	verb	*L4*		
middle	**zhōng**	*	*L9*	中	中
mom	**mā**	noun	*L15*	媽	妈
mom	**māma**	noun	*L4*	媽媽	妈妈
money	**qián**	noun	*L6*	錢	钱
month	**yuè**	noun	*L8*	月	月
morning	**shàngwǔ**	noun	*L9*	上 **wǔ**	上 **wǔ**
morning	**zǎoshang**	noun	*L9*	早上	早上
mother and father	**fùmǔ**	noun phrase	*L16*		
mountain	**shān**	noun	*L11*		
mouth	**kǒu**	noun	*L12*	口	口
movie	**diànyǐng**	noun	*L12*	電 **yǐng**	电 **yǐng**
movie theater	**diànyǐng yuàn**	noun	*L12*	電 **yǐng yuàn**	电 **yǐng yuàn**
Mr.	**xiānsheng**	title	*L15*	先生	先生
Mrs.	**tàitai**	title	*L15*	太太	太太
music	**yīnyuè**	noun	*L8*		
must	**děi**	modal verb	*L9*	得	得

N

name	**míngzi**	noun	*L3*		
near, close by	**jìn**	adjectival verb	*L11*		
new	**xīn**	adjectival verb	*L10*		
(new information, change, completion)	**le**	particle	*L6, 9, 10*	了	了
next (used with certain time expressions)	**xià**	specifier	*L8*	下	下
next year	**míngnián**	noun	*L8*	明年	明年
nine	**jiǔ**	number	*L5*	九	九
no, not	**bù**	negation	*L1*	不	不
*no, not (negation for **yǒu** have)*	**méi**	negation	*L4*	沒	没
noon	**zhōngwǔ**	noun	*L9*	中 **wǔ**	中 **wǔ**
north	**běi**	*	*L11*	北	北
north side	**běibiān**	noun	*L11*	北 **biān**	北 **biān**
northwest (side)	**xīběi (biān)**	noun	*L11*	西北 **(biān)**	西北 **(biān)**

not be important, (it) doesn't matter	**méi guānxi**	conversational expression	*L13*	沒 **guānxi**	没 **guānxi**
not until, (later than expected)	**cái**	adverb	*L8*		
notebook	**běnzi**	noun	*L7*	本子	本子
notebook	**liànxí běn**	noun	*L7*	**liàn** 習本	**liàn** 习本
November	**shíyī yuè**	noun	*L8*	十一月	十一月
now	**xiànzài**	time word	*L9*	現在	现在
number	**hàomǎ**	noun	*L5*	號 **mǎ**	号 **mǎ**
number (for buses and trains)	**hào**	classifier	*L12*	號	号

O

of course	**dāngrán**	adverb	*L2*	當然	当然
often	**cháng**	adverb	*L15*	常	常
oh no!	**zāogāo**	conversational expression	*L8*		
okay, acceptable	**xíng**	adjectival verb	*L8*		
old (objects)	**jiù**	adjectival verb	*L14*		
older brother	**gēge**	noun	*L4*		
older sister	**jiějie**	noun	*L4*		
on, above	**shàng**	*	*L13*	上	上
on, above	**shàngbiān**	noun	*L13*	上 **biān**	上 **biān**
one	**yāo**	number	*L5*		
one	**yī**	number	*L5*	一	一
only	**zhǐ**	adverb	*L3*	只	只
only, precisely, sooner than expected	**jiù**	adverb	*L9, 11, 13*	就	就
or	**háishi**	conjunction	*L12*	還是	还是
(ordinal prefix)	**dì**	prefix	*L14*		
other	**biéde**	noun description	*L13*	**bié** 的	**bié** 的
outside	**wài**	*	*L13*		
outside	**wàibiān**	noun	*L13*		

P

paper	**zhǐ**	noun	*L6*		
park	**gōngyuán**	noun	*L11*	公園	公园
pen, writing implement	**bǐ**	noun	*L6*		
pencil	**qiānbǐ**	noun	*L6*		
penny, cent;	**fēn**	classifier	*L6*	分	分
minute			*L9*		
person	**wèi**	classifier	*L13*		
person	**rén**	noun	*L2*	人	人
photograph	**zhàopiàn**	noun	*L4*		
photograph, take (a photograph)	**zhào**	verb	*L15*		
plan	**jìhuà**	noun, verb	*L16*		
plan	**dǎsuan**	noun, verb	*L16*	打 **suan**	打 **suan**
please come in	**qǐng jìn**	conversational expression	*L4*	請 **jìn**	请 **jìn**
polite	**kèqi**	adjectival verb	*L15*		
practice	**liànxí**	verb	*L7*	**liàn** 習	**liàn** 习
pretty, nice looking	**hǎo kàn**	adjectival verb phrase	*L16*	好看	好看

Q

quarter	**kè**	classifier	*L9*		

R

read	**kàn shū**	verb + object	*L9*	看書	看书
read, see, look at	**kàn**	verb	*L9*	看	看
really	**zhēn**	intensifier	*L13*	真	真
really?	**zhēnde ma?**	conversational expression	*L3*	真的嗎？	真的吗？
red	**hóng**	adjectival verb	*L14*		
red-simmered	**hóngshāo**	noun description	*L15*		
red-simmered chicken	**hóngshāo jī**	noun phrase	*L15*		
(response to compliments)	**nǎlǐ**	conversational expression	*L15*	哪 **lǐ**	哪 **lǐ**
restaurant	**fànguǎn**	noun	*L12*	飯館	饭馆
return to a location	**huí**	verb	*L9*	回	回
return to one's home country	**huí guó**	verb + object	*L16*	回國	回国
review	**fùxí**	verb	*L9*	**fù** 習	**fù** 习
rice, food	**fàn**	noun	*L8*	飯	饭
right	**yòu**	*	*L13*		
right side	**yòubiān**	noun	*L13*		
road, street	**lù; mǎlù**	noun	*L11; L13*	路，馬路	路，马路
roommate	**tóngwū**	noun	*L4*		

S

say it again	**zài shuō yī cì**	conversational expression	*L6*	再說一 **cì**	再说一 **cì**
school	**xuéxiào**	noun	*L11*	學 **xiào**	学 **xiào**
see	**kànjian**	verb	*L13*	看見	看见
see a guest off	**sòng**	verb	*L16*		
see you soon	**yīhuìr jiàn**	conversational expression	*L14*	一會兒見	一会儿见
sell	**mài**	verb	*L6*	賣	卖
separated from	**lí**	preposition	*L11*		
seven	**qī**	number	*L5*	七	七
several	**xiē**	classifier	*L15*		
several	**jǐ**	quantifier	*L10*	幾	几
short period of time	**yīhuìr**	time phrase	*L14*	一會兒	一会儿
should	**yīnggāi**	modal verb	*L15*		
simmer	**shāo**	verb	*L15*		
sing	**chàng**	verb	*L8*		
sing songs	**chàng gē**	verb + object	*L8*		
sit, ride, or "take" a form of transportation	**zuò**	verb	*L12*	坐	坐
six	**liù**	number	*L5*	六	六
sleep	**shuì**	verb	*L9*		
sleep	**shuì jiào**	verb + object	*L9*	**shuì** 覺	**shuì** 觉
slow, slowly	**màn**	adjectival verb	*L10*	慢	慢
small	**xiǎo**	adjectival verb	*L6*	小	小
so	**nàme**	intensifier	*L15*	那麼	那么

some	yǒu de	noun description phrase	L10	有的	有的
song	gē	noun	L8		
south	nán	*	L11	南	南
south side	nánbiān	noun	L11	南 **biān**	南 **biān**
speak, talk	shuō huà	verb + object	L3	說話	说话
speak, talk, say	shuō	verb	L3	說	说
speech, language	huà	noun	L3	話	话
station, (bus or train) stop	zhàn,	noun	L11	站	站
	chēzhàn		L13	車站	车站
stir-fried cabbage	chǎo báicài	noun phrase	L15		
stir-fry	chǎo	verb	L15		
street	lù, mǎlù	noun	L11, L13	路，馬路	路，马路
student	xuésheng	noun	L1	學生	学生
study	xué	verb	L4	學	学
study	xuéxí	verb	L9	學習	学习
subway	dìtiě	noun	L12	地 **tiě**	地 **tiě**
summer	xiàtiān	noun	L16	**xià** 天	**xià** 天
summer vacation	shǔjià	noun phrase	L16		
summertime (the time period of the summer)	shǔqī	noun phrase	L16	**shǔ** 期	**shǔ** 期
Sun Yatsen	Zhōngshān	given name	L11	中 **shān**	中 **shān**
Sunday	xīngqītiān	noun	L8	星期天	星期天
surf the web, go online	shàng wǎng	verb + object	L11	上 **wǎng**	上 **wǎng**

T

take (a test)	kǎo	verb	L9		
take a test	kǎo shì	verb + object	L9		
talk, chat	tán	verb	L16		
tea	chá	noun	L10		
teach	jiāo	verb	L8		
teacher, professor	lǎoshī	noun	L1	老師	老师
telephone	diànhuà	noun	L5	電話	电话
(telephone greeting)	wéi, wèi	conversational expression	L13		
television	diànshì	noun	L11	電 **shì**	电 **shì**
tell	gàosu	verb	L13		
ten	shí	number	L5	十	十
test	kǎoshì	noun	L8		
thank you	xièxie	conversational expression	L1	謝謝	谢谢
that	nà	demonstrative	L4	那	那
that	nà, nèi	specifier	L6	那	那
there	nàr	noun	L11	那兒	那儿
there aren't any special dishes	méi shénme cài	conversational expression	L15	沒什麼 **cài**	没什么 **cài**
they/them	tāmen	pronoun	L2	他們	他们
thing (concrete object)	dōngxi	noun	L6	東西	东西
think (about), plan (to), want (to)	xiǎng	verb	L7	想	想
think, hold an opinion	juéde	verb	L10	覺得	觉得

this	**zhè**	demonstrative	*L4*	這	这
this	**zhè, zhèi**	specifier	*L6*	這	这
this year	**jīnnián**	noun	*L8*	今年	今年
three	**sān**	number	*L5*	三	三
Thursday	**xīngqīsì**	noun	*L8*	星期四	星期四
ticket	**piào**	noun	*L12*		
time	**shíhou**	noun	*L11*	時候	时候
time	**shíjiān**	noun	*L12*	時 **jiān**	时 **jiān**
to	**dào**	preposition	*L12*	到	到
today	**jīntiān**	noun	*L8*	今天	今天
together with NP	**gēn** NP **yīqǐ**	prepositional phrase	*L10*	跟 NP 一起	跟 NP 一起
Tokyo	**Dōngjīng**	city name	*L13*	東京	东京
tomorrow	**míngtiān**	noun	*L8*	明天	明天
too	**tài**	intensifier	*L6*	太	太
toward	**wǎng**	preposition	*L12*	往	往
traffic light	**hóng-lù dēng**	noun phrase	*L14*		
train	**huǒchē**	noun	*L11*	**huǒ** 車	**huǒ** 车
train station	**huǒchē zhàn**	noun phrase	*L11*	**huǒ** 車站	**huǒ** 车站
travel	**lǚyóu**	verb	*L16*		
turn	**guǎi**	verb	*L13*		
twice-cooked pork	**huí guō ròu**	noun phrase	*L15*	回 **guō ròu**	回 **guō ròu**
two	**èr**	number	*L5*	二	二
two	**liǎng**	number	*L5*	兩	两

U

uncle	**shūshu**	noun	*L15*		
under, below	**xià**	*	*L13*	下	下
under, below	**xiàbiān**	noun	*L13*	下 **biān**	下 **biān**
understand	**dǒng**	verb	*L10*		
use	**yòng**	verb	*L15*		
use internet, go online	**shàng wǎng**	verb + object	*L11*	上 **wǎng**	上 **wǎng**

V

very	**hěn**	intensifier	*L1*	很	很

W

wait	**děng**	verb	*L12*		
walk	**zǒu lù**	verb + object	*L14*	走路	走路
want	**yào**	verb	*L6*	要	要
wash	**xǐ**	verb	*L9*		
water	**shuǐ**	noun	*L6*	水	水
we/us	**wǒmen**	pronoun	*L2*	我們	我们
web, internet	**wǎng**	noun	*L11*		
week	**xīngqī**	noun	*L8*	星期	星期
welcome	**huānyíng**	verb	*L15*		
well then	**nà**	pause particle	*L5*	那	那
west	**xī**	*	*L11*	西	西
west side	**xībiān**	noun	*L11*	西 **biān**	西 **biān**
what	**shénme**	question word	*L3*	甚麼	什么

what time	**shénme shíhou?**	question phrase	*L11*	甚麼時候	什么时候
What's up?	**yǒu shì ma?**	conversational expression	*L9*	有 **shì** 嗎？	有 **shì** 吗？
where	**nǎr?**	question word	*L11*	哪兒	哪儿
which country	**nǎguó, něiguó**	question phrase	*L2*	哪國	哪国
who	**shéi?**	question word	*L4*	誰	谁
wife	**tàitai**	title	*L15*	太太	太太
wine, alcohol	**jiǔ**	noun	*L8*		
with; and	**gēn**	preposition; conjunction	*L10*	跟	跟
work (see 有 **shì**)	**shì**	*	*L9*		
write	**xiě**	verb	*L10*	寫	写

Y

year	**nián**	classifier	*L8*	年	年
year in school, grade	**niánjí**	noun	*L7*	年 **jí**	年 **jí**
years of age	**suì**	classifier	*L8*		
yesterday	**zuótiān**	noun	*L10*	昨天	昨天
you	**nǐ**	pronoun	*L1*	你	你
you (plural)	**nǐmen**	pronoun	*L2*	你們	你们
you (polite)	**nín**	pronoun	*L13*	您	您
younger brother	**dìdi**	noun	*L4*		
younger sister	**mèimei**	noun	*L4*		

Z

zero	**líng**	number	*L5*		

Vocabulary: Mandarin (Pinyin) to English

The lesson number indicates the lesson in which the vocabulary item is introduced. The last column of each row shows each word written using the characters introduced through Lesson 16. To find the lesson where a character is first introduced, see the Chinese Character Indices.

				Traditional	Simplified
A					
āyí	noun	*aunt*	L15		
B					
ba	particle	*(indicates speaker's supposition; suggestions)*	L4 L8	吧	吧
bā	number	*eight*	L5	八	八
bàba	noun	*dad*	L4	爸爸	爸爸
bǎi	number	*hundred*	L7		
báicài	noun	*cabbage*	L15		
bàn	number	*half*	L9	半	半
bāng	verb	*help*	L11		
bēi	classifier	*cup*	L10		
běi	*	*north*	L11	北	北
běibiān	noun	*north side*	L11	北 **biān**	北 **biān**
Běijīng	city name	*Beijing*	L16	北京	北京
běn	classifier	*(classifier for books)*	L7	本	本
běnzi	noun	*notebook*	L7	本子	本子
bǐ	noun	*pen, writing implement*	L6		
bié	negation	*don't*	L14		
biéde	noun description	*other*	L13		
bù	negation	*no, not*	L1	不	不
bù hǎo yìsi	conversational expression	*be embarrassed*	L13	不好 **yìsi**	不好 **yìsi**
C					
cái	adverb	*not until, (later than expected)*	L8		
cài	noun	*dishes (food)*	L15		
chá	noun	*tea*	L10		
chàbuduō	adverb	*almost*	L12	差不多	差不多
cháng	adverb	*often*	L15	常	常
chàng	verb	*sing*	L8		
chàng gē	verb + object	*sing songs*	L8		
chǎo	verb	*stir-fry*	L15		
chǎo báicài	noun phrase	*stir-fried cabbage*	L15		
chē	noun	*car, vehicle*	L12	車	车
chēzhàn	noun	*station*	L13	車站	车站
Chén	family name	*(family name)*	L2		
chī	verb	*eat*	L8	吃	吃
chī fàn	verb + object	*eat (food)*	L8	吃飯	吃饭
chuáng	noun	*bed*	L9		
cóng	preposition	*from*	L12	從	从

D

dǎ	verb	hit	L5	打	打
dà	adjectival verb	big	L6	大	大
dàjiā	noun phrase	everyone	L15	大家	大家
dāngrán	adverb	of course	L2	當然	当然
dào	preposition	to	L12	到	到
dào	verb	arrive	L13	到	到
dǎsuan	noun, verb	plan	L16	打 suan	打 suan
Dàwéi	given name	David	L3	大 wéi	大 wéi
dàxué	noun	college	L12	大學	大学
de	particle	(indicates noun description)	L4	的	的
de	particle	(indicates verb description)	L10	得	得
Déguó	country name	Germany	L2	**Dé** 國	**Dé** 国
Déguó huà	noun phrase	German language	L3	**Dé** 國話	**Dé** 国话
Déguó rén	noun phrase	German person	L2	**Dé** 國人	**Dé** 国人
děi	modal verb	must	L9	得	得
dēng	noun	lamp, light	L14		
děng	verb	wait	L12		
dì	prefix	(ordinal prefix)	L14		
diǎn	classifier	dot, o'clock	L9	點	点
diànhuà	noun	telephone	L5	電話	电话
diànnǎo	noun	computer	L9	電 **nǎo**	电 **nǎo**
diànshì	noun	television	L11	電 **shì**	电 **shì**
diànyǐng	noun	movie	L12	電 **yǐng**	电 **yǐng**
diànyǐng yuàn	noun	movie theater	L12	電 **yǐng yuàn**	电 **yǐng yuàn**
dìdi	noun	younger brother	L4		
dìtiě	noun	subway	L12	地 **tiě**	地 **tiě**
dìtú	noun	map	L6	地圖	地图
dōng	*	east	L11	東	东
dǒng	verb	understand	L10		
dōngbiān	noun	east side	L11	東 **biān**	东 **biān**
Dōngjīng	city name	Tokyo	L13	東京	东京
dōngxi	noun	thing (concrete object)	L6	東西	东西
dōu	adverb	all, both	L2	都	都
duì	adjectival verb	correct	L2	對	对
duì le	conversational expression	by the way	L11	對了	对了
duìbuqǐ	conversational expression	excuse me	L3	對不起	对不起
duìmiàn	noun	across from	L14	對 **miàn**	对 **miàn**
duō	adjectival verb	many, a lot	L10	多	多
duō cháng shíjiān	question phrase	how much time, how long	L12	多 **cháng** 時 **jiān**	多 **cháng** 时 **jiān**
duō dà	question phrase	how old	L8	多大	多大
duō jiǔ	question phrase	how long (duration)	L14	多 **jiǔ**	多 **jiǔ**
duōshao	question word	how much, how many	L5, 6	多少	多少
duō yuǎn	question phrase	how far	L11	多 **yuǎn**	多 **yuǎn**

E

èr	number	two	L5	二	二

F

Fǎguó	country name	*France*	*L2*	法國	法国
Fǎguó huà	noun phrase	*French language*	*L3*	法國話	法国话
Fǎguó rén	noun phrase	*French person*	*L2*	法國人	法国人
fàn	noun	*rice, food*	*L8*	飯	饭
fàng jià	verb + object	*begin vacation*	*L16*		
fànguǎn	noun	*restaurant*	*L12*	飯館	饭馆
fángzi	noun	*house*	*L15*	**fáng** 子	**fáng** 子
fēicháng	intensifier	*extremely*	*L10*	非常	非常
fēijī	noun	*airplane*	*L11*		
fēijīchǎng	noun	*airport*	*L11*		
fēn	classifier	*penny, cent, minute*	*L6, 9*	分	分
fùmǔ	noun phrase	*mother and father*	*L16*		
fúwùyuán	noun	*clerk, service person*	*L6*		
fùxí	verb	*review*	*L9*	**fù** 習	**fù** 习

G

gāng	adverb	*just now*	*L10*	剛	刚
Gāo	family name	*(family name)*	*L1*	高	高
gàosu	verb	*inform, tell*	*L13*		
gāoxìng	adjectival verb	*happy*	*L4*	高 **xìng**	高 **xìng**
gē	noun	*song*	*L8*		
gè (ge)	classifier	*(classifier for people and some other nouns)*	*L5*	個	个
gēge	noun	*older brother*	*L4*		
gěi	verb; preposition	*give;* *to, for*	*L7* *L11*	給	给
gěi (someone) dǎ diànhuà	prepositional phrase	*phone (someone)*	*L5*	給 (someone) 打電話	给 (someone) 打电话
gēn	preposition; conjunction	*with;* *and*	*L10*	跟	跟
gēn NP yīqǐ	prepositional phrase	*together with NP*	*L10*	跟 NP 一起	跟 NP 一起
gōnggòng qìchē	noun	*(public) bus*	*L12*	公 **gòng qì** 車	公 **gòng qì** 车
gōngkè	noun	*class work*	*L9*		
gōngyuán	noun	*park*	*L11*	公園	公园
gōngzuò	noun, verb	*job, work*	*L16*		
guǎi	verb	*turn*	*L13*		
guì	adjectival verb	*expensive*	*L6*		
guó	noun	*country*	*L2*	國	国
guò	verb; verb suffix	*cross, pass;* *(experienced doing the action)*	*L13* *L15*	過	过

H

hái	adverb	*in addition*	*L6*	還	还
hái yǒu	adverb	*in addition, furthermore*	*L10*	還有	还有
háishi	conjunction	*or*	*L12*	還是	还是
háizi	noun	*child*	*L5*	**hái** 子	**hái** 子
Hàn zì	noun phrase	*Chinese character*	*L7*	漢字	汉字

hǎo	adjectival verb	*good*	*L1*	好	好
hào	classifier	*date of the month*	*L8*	號	号
hào	classifier	*number (for buses and trains)*	*L12*	號	号
hǎo chī	adjectival verb phrase	*delicious*	*L15*	好吃	好吃
hǎo kàn	adjectival verb phrase	*pretty, nice looking*	*L16*	好看	好看
hàomǎ	noun	*number*	*L5*	號 **mǎ**	号 **mǎ**
hē	verb	*drink*	*L8*		
hé	conjunction	*and*	*L3*	和	和
hē jiǔ	verb + object	*drink alcohol*	*L8*		
hěn	intensifier	*very*	*L1*	很	很
hóng	adjectival verb	*red*	*L14*		
hóng-lǜ dēng	noun phrase	*traffic light*	*L14*		
hóngshāo	noun description	*red-simmered*	*L15*		
hóngshāo jī	noun phrase	*red-simmered chicken*	*L15*		
hòu	*	*behind, after*	*L14*	後	后
hòubiān	noun	*behind, in back (of)*	*L14*	後 **biān**	后 **biān**
hú	noun	*lake*	*L11*		
huà	noun	*speech, language*	*L3*	話	话
huà	verb	*draw*	*L11*		
huàn	verb	*change (one thing for another)*	*L12*		
huānyíng	verb	*welcome*	*L15*		
huí	verb	*return to a location*	*L9*	回	回
huì	modal verb	*able to, can, will*	*L3, 14*	會	会
huí guó	verb + object	*return to one's home country*	*L16*	回國	回国
huí guō ròu	noun phrase	*twice-cooked pork*	*L15*	回 **guō ròu**	回 **guō ròu**
huǒchē	noun	*train*	*L11*	**huǒ** 車	**huǒ** 车
huǒchē zhàn	noun phrase	*train station*	*L11*	**huǒ** 車站	**huǒ** 车站

J

jǐ	question word	*how many*	*L5*	幾	几
jǐ	quantifier	*several*	*L10*	幾	几
jī	noun	*chicken*	*L15*		
jiā	noun	*family, home*	*L5*	家	家
jiā cháng cài	noun phrase	*home-style food, simple food*	*L15*	家常 **cài**	家常 **cài**
jiào	verb	*be called, call*	*L3*	叫	叫
jiāo	verb	*teach*	*L8*		
jiǎozi	noun	*Chinese dumplings*	*L15*	**jiǎo** 子	**jiǎo** 子
jiē	verb	*fetch a person*	*L12*		
jiějie	noun	*older sister*	*L4*		
jièshào	verb	*introduce*	*L15*		
jìhuà	noun, verb	*plan*	*L16*		
jìn	adjectival verb	*near, close by*	*L11*		
jìnbù	verb, noun	*improve, improvement*	*L16*		
jīnnián	noun	*this year*	*L8*	今年	今年
jīntiān	noun	*today*	*L8*	今天	今天
jiǔ	number	*nine*	*L5*	九	九
jiǔ	noun	*wine, alcohol*	*L8*		

jiù	adverb	only, precisely, sooner than expected	L9, 11, 13	就	就
jiù	adjectival verb	old (objects)	L14		
juéde	verb	think, hold an opinion	L10	覺得	觉得

K

kāfēi	noun	coffee	L10		
kāfēiguǎn	noun	coffee shop	L10	kāfēi 館	kāfēi 馆
kāi	verb	drive	L12	開	开
kāi chē	verb + object	drive a car	L12	開車	开车
kāishǐ	verb	begin	L16	開 shǐ	开 shǐ
kǎlā OK	noun	karaoke	L8		
kàn	verb	read, see, look at	L9	看	看
kàn shū	verb + object	read	L9	看書	看书
kànjian	verb	see	L13	看見	看见
kǎo	verb	take (a test)	L9		
kǎo shì	verb + object	take a test	L9		
kǎoshì	noun	test	L8		
kè	noun	class	L9		
kè	classifier	quarter	L9		
kělè	noun	cola	L6	可 lè	可 lè
kèqi	adjectival verb	polite	L15		
kèrén	noun	guest	L13	kè 人	kè 人
kěshì	conjunction	but	L10	可是	可是
kěyǐ	modal verb	can (permission)	L5	可以	可以
kǒu	noun	mouth	L12	口	口
kuài	classifier	dollar	L6	塊	块
kuài	adjectival verb	fast, soon	L10	快	快
kuàilè	adjectival verb	happy	L8	快 lè	快 lè
kuàizi	noun	chopsticks	L15	kuài 子	kuài 子

L

lái	verb	come	L11	来	来
lǎoshī	noun	teacher, professor	L1	老師	老师
le	particle	(new information, change, completion)	L6, 9, 10	了	了
lí	preposition	separated from	L11		
Lǐ	family name	(family name)	L1		
lǐ	classifier	Chinese mile	L11		
lǐ	*	inside	L13		
lǐbiān	noun	inside	L13		
liǎng	number	two	L5	兩	两
liànxí	verb	practice	L7	liàn 習	liàn 习
liànxí běn	noun	notebook	L7	liàn 習本	liàn 习本
líng	number	zero	L5		
liù	number	six	L5	六	六
lù	noun	road	L11	路	路
lǜ	adjectival verb	green	L14		
lùkǒu	noun	intersection	L14	路口	路口
lǚyóu	verb	travel	L16		

M

ma	final particle	*(forms yes-no questions)*	*L1*	嗎	吗
mā	noun	*mom*	*L15*	媽	妈
Mǎ	family name	*(family name)*	*L8*	馬	马
mǎlù	noun	*road (local road)*	*L13*	馬路	马路
máfan	verb, adjectival verb	*inconvenience, bother*	*L16*		
mǎi	verb	*buy*	*L6*	買	买
mài	verb	*sell*	*L6*	賣	卖
māma	noun	*mom*	*L4*	媽媽	妈妈
màn	adjectival verb	*slow*	*L10*	慢	慢
máng	adjectival verb	*busy*	*L11*		
mànmān de	adverb	*gradually, little by little*	*L16*	慢慢地	慢慢地
máo	classifier	*dime*	*L6*	毛	毛
méi	negation adverb	*no, not (negation for **yǒu** have)*	*L4*	沒	没
měi	quantifier	*every*	*L11*		
méi guānxi	conversational expression	*not be important, (it) doesn't matter*	*L13*	沒 **guānxi**	没 **guānxi**
méi shénme cài	conversational expression	*there aren't any special dishes*	*L15*	沒甚麼 **cài**	没什么 **cài**
Měiguó	country name	*America (USA)*	*L2*	美國	美国
Měiguó huà	noun phrase	*American English*	*L3*	美國話	美国话
Měiguó rén	noun phrase	*American*	*L2*	美國人	美国人
Měilì	given name	*Marie, Mary*	*L3*	美 **lì**	美 **lì**
mèimei	noun	*younger sister*	*L4*		
mén	noun	*door, gate*	*L12*	門	门
ménkǒu	noun	*doorway*	*L12*	門口	门口
míngnián	noun	*next year*	*L8*	明年	明年
míngtiān	noun	*tomorrow*	*L8*	明天	明天
míngzi	noun	*name*	*L3*		

N

nà	demonstrative	*that*	*L4*	那	那
nà	pause particle	*well then*	*L5*	那	那
nà, nèi	specifier	*that*	*L6*	那	那
nǎguó, něiguó	question phrase	*which country*	*L2*	哪國	哪国
nǎlǐ	conversational expression	*(used for deflecting compliments)*	*L15*	哪 **lǐ**	哪 **lǐ**
nàme	intensifier	*so*	*L15*	那麼	那么
nán	adjectival verb	*difficult*	*L10*	難	难
nán	*	*south*	*L11*	南	南
nàn	adjective	*male*	*L5*	男	男
nánbiān	noun	*south side*	*L11*	南 **biān**	南 **biān**
nán háizi	noun phrase	*boy (male child)*	*L5*	男 **hái** 子	男 **hái** 子
nǎr	question word	*where*	*L11*	哪兒	哪儿
nàr	noun	*there*	*L11*	那兒	那儿
ne	final particle	*(forms follow-up questions)*	*L2*	呢	呢
néng	modal verb	*able*	*L13*		
nǐ	pronoun	*you*	*L1*	你	你
nǐ hǎo	greeting	*hello (formal greeting)*	*L1*	你好	你好

nián	classifier	*year*	L8	年	年
niánjí	noun	*year in school, grade*	L7	年 jí	年 jí
nǐmen	pronoun	*you (plural)*	L2	你們	你们
nín	pronoun	*you (polite)*	L13	您	您
nǔ	adjective	*female*	L5	女	女
nǔ háizi	noun phrase	*girl (female child)*	L5	女 hái 子	女 hái 子

P

pángbiān	noun	*beside, alongside*	L14		
péngyou	noun	*friend*	L5	朋友	朋友
piányi	adjectival verb	*cheap*	L6		
piào	noun	*ticket*	L12		
piàoliang	adjectival verb	*beautiful*	L14		
píjiǔ	noun	*beer*	L8		
píng	classifier	*bottle*	L6		

Q

qī	number	*seven*	L5	七	七
qǐ	verb	*get up, rise up*	L9	起	起
qǐ chuáng	verb + object	*get out of bed*	L9	起 chuáng	起 chuáng
qián	noun	*money*	L6	錢	钱
qián	*	*front, in front*	L14	前	前
qiānbǐ	noun	*pencil*	L6		
qiánbiān	noun	*front, in front (of)*	L14	前 biān	前 biān
qìchē	noun	*car (with an engine)*	L12	qì 車	qì 车
qiézi	noun	*eggplant*	L15	qié 子	qié 子
qǐng	verb	*invite*	L8	請	请
qǐng jìn	conversational expression	*please come in*	L4	請 jìn	请 jìn
qǐng wèn	conversational expression	*may I ask, excuse me*	L2	請問	请问
qù	verb	*go*	L8	去	去
qùnián	noun	*last year*	L15	去年	去年

R

rén	noun	*person*	L2	人	人
rènshi	verb	*meet, know*	L4		
Rìběn	country name	*Japan*	L3	日本	日本
Rìběn huà	noun phrase	*Japanese language*	L3	日本話	日本话
róngyì	adjectival verb	*easy*	L10	容易	容易
ròu	noun	*meat*	L15		

S

sān	number	*three*	L5	三	三
shān	noun	*mountain*	L11		
shàng	verb	*attend;*	L9	上	上
		go up, get on	L12		
shàng	*	*on, above*	L13	上	上
shàngbiān	noun	*on, above*	L13	上 biān	上 biān
shàng kè	verb + object	*go to class*	L9	上 kè	上 kè

shàng wǎng	verb + object	use the internet, go online	L11	上 **wǎng**	上 **wǎng**
shàngwǔ	noun	morning	L9	上 **wǔ**	上 **wǔ**
shǎo	adjectival verb	few, little in number	L10	少	少
shāo	verb	simmer	L15		
shéi?	question word	who	L4	誰	谁
shēnghuó	noun, verb	life, live	L16	生 **huó**	生 **huó**
shēngri	noun	birthday	L8	生日	生日
shēngri kuàilè	conversational expression	happy birthday	L8	生日快 **lè**	生日快 **lè**
shénme	question word	what	L3	甚麼	什么
shénme shíhou?	question phrase	what time	L11	甚麼時候	什么时候
shí	number	ten	L5	十	十
shì	stative verb	be	L1	是	是
shì	noun	work (see 有 **shì**)	L9		
shì	*	city	L11		
shì zhōngxīn	noun phrase	city center, center of the city, downtown	L11	**shì** 中 **xīn**	**shì** 中 **xīn**
shíhou	noun	time	L11	時候	时候
shíjiān	noun	time	L12	時 **jiān**	时 **jiān**
shíyī yuè	noun	November	L8	十一月	十一月
shízì lùkǒu	noun phrase	four-way intersection	L14	十字路口	十字路口
shǒujī	noun	cell phone, mobile phone	L5		
shū	noun	book	L7	書	书
shūdiàn	noun	bookstore	L11	書店	书店
shuǐ	noun	water	L6	水	水
shuì	verb	sleep	L9		
shuì jiào	verb + object	sleep	L9	**shuì** 覺	**shuì** 觉
shuǐguǒ	noun	fruit	L15	水 **guǒ**	水 **guǒ**
shǔjià	noun phrase	summer vacation	L16		
shuō	verb	speak, talk, say	L3	說	说
shuō huà	verb + object	speak, talk	L3	說話	说话
shǔqī	noun phrase	summertime (the time period of the summer)	L16	**shǔ** 期	**shǔ** 期
shūshu	noun	uncle	L15		
sì	number	four	L5	四	四
sòng	verb	see a guest off	L16		
sònggěi	verb	give as a present	L15	**sòng** 给	**sòng** 给
suì	classifier	years of age	L8		
suíbiàn	adverb	as you please	L15		
suīrán	conjunction	although	L16	**suī** 然	**suī** 然
sùshè	noun	dormitory	L9		

T

tā	pronoun	he/him, she/her, it	L1	他，她	他，她
tài	intensifier	too	L6	太	太
tài hǎo le	conversational expression	great	L8	太好了	太好了
tàitai	title	Mrs., wife	L15	太太	太太
tāmen	pronoun	they/them	L2	他們	他们
tán	verb	talk, chat	L16		

tiān	classifier	*day*	L8	天	天
tiáo	classifier	*(classifier for streets)*	L14		
tiào	verb	*jump, dance*	L8		
tiào wǔ	verb + object	*dance*	L8		
tīng	verb	*listen (to)*	L8		
tīng yīnyuè	verb + object	*listen to music*	L8		
tóngwū	noun	*roommate*	L4		
tóngxué	noun	*classmate*	L4	tóng 學	tóng 学
túshūguǎn	noun	*library*	L9	圖書館	图书馆

W

wài	*	*outside*	L13		
wàibiān	noun	*outside*	L13		
wǎn	adjectival verb	*late*	L9	晚	晚
wǎnfàn	noun	*dinner*	L8	晚飯	晚饭
Wáng	family name	*(family name)*	L2	王	王
wǎng	noun	*web, internet*	L11		
wǎng	preposition	*toward*	L12	往	往
wàng	verb	*forget*	L10		
wǎnshang	noun	*evening, night*	L8	晚上	晚上
wèi	classifier	*person*	L13		
wéi, wèi	conversational expression	*(greeting used when answering the telephone)*	L13		
wèn	verb	*ask*	L11	問	问
wǒ	pronoun	*I/me*	L1	我	我
wǒmen	pronoun	*we/us*	L2	我們	我们
wǔ	number	*five*	L5	五	五
wǔfàn	noun	*lunch*	L10	wǔ 飯	wǔ 饭

X

xǐ	verb	*wash*	L9		
xī	*	*west*	L11	西	西
xībiān	noun	*west side*	L11	西 biān	西 biān
xǐ zǎo	verb + object	*bathe*	L9		
xià	specifier	*next (used with certain time expressions)*	L8	下	下
xià	verb	*go down, get off*	L12	下	下
xià	*	*under, below*	L13	下	下
xiàbiān	noun	*under, below*	L13	下 biān	下 biān
xià kè	verb + object	*get out of class*	L9	下 kè	下 kè
xiàn	noun	*line (train line, subway line)*	L12		
xiān	adverb	*first*	L13	先	先
xiǎng	verb	*think (about), plan (to), want (to)*	L7	想	想
xiānsheng	title	*Mr., husband*	L15	先生	先生
xiànzài	time word	*now*	L9	現在	现在
xiǎo	family name prefix, adjectival verb	*small*	L1	小	小

xiàtiān	noun	*summer*	*L16*	xià 天	xià 天
xiàwǔ	noun	*afternoon*	*L9*	下 **wǔ**	下 **wǔ**
xīběi (biān)	*	*northwest (side)*	*L11*	西北 **(biān)**	西北 **(biān)**
xībiān	noun	*west side*	*L11*	西 **(biān)**	西 **(biān)**
xiē	classifier	*several*	*L15*		
xiě	verb	*write*	*L10*	寫	写
Xiè	family name	*(family name)*	*L4*	謝	谢
xièxie	conversational expression	*thank you*	*L1*	謝謝	谢谢
xíguàn	verb	*be accustomed to*	*L16*	習 **guàn**	习 **guàn**
xǐhuan	stative verb	*like*	*L8*	喜歡	喜欢
xīn	adjectival verb	*new*	*L10*		
xíng	adjectival verb	*okay, acceptable*	*L8*		
xìng	verb, noun	*be family-named, be surnamed; family name, surname*	*L3*		
xīngqī	noun	*week*	*L8*	星期	星期
xīngqīsì	noun	*Thursday*	*L8*	星期四	星期四
xīngqītiān	noun	*Sunday*	*L8*	星期天	星期天
xīngqīwǔ	noun	*Friday*	*L8*	星期五	星期五
xué	verb	*study*	*L4*	學	学
xuésheng	noun	*student*	*L1*	學生	学生
xuéxí	verb	*study*	*L9*	學習	学习
xuéxiào	noun	*school*	*L11*	學 **xiào**	学 **xiào**
Y					
yào	verb	*want*	*L6*	要	要
yāo	number	*one*	*L5*		
Yè	family name	*(family name)*	*L8*		
yě	adverb	*also*	*L1*	也	也
yě jiù shì shuō	conversational expression	*in other words*	*L14*	也就是說	也就是说
yī	number	*one*	*L5*	一	一
yī niánjí	noun phrase	*first-year level*	*L7*	一年 **jí**	一年 **jí**
yī xià	verb suffix	*(do an action for a short duration)*	*L15*	一下	一下
yīdiǎn	quantifier	*a little*	*L7*	一點	一点
yīgòng	adverb	*altogether*	*L7*	一 **gòng**	一 **gòng**
yǐhòu	noun	*after, afterward*	*L14*	以後	以后
yīhuìr	time phrase	*a short period of time*	*L14*	一會兒	一会儿
yīhuìr jiàn	conversational expression	*see you soon*	*L14*	一會兒見	一会儿见
yǐjing	adverb	*already*	*L10*	已經	已经
yīnggāi	modal verb	*should*	*L15*		
Yīngguó	country name	*Britain*	*L2*	**Yīng** 國	**Yīng** 国
Yīngguó huà	noun phrase	*British English*	*L3*	**Yīng** 國話	**Yīng** 国话
Yīngguó rén	noun phrase	*British person*	*L2*	**Yīng** 國人	**Yīng** 国人
yínháng	noun	*bank*	*L14*		
yīnyuè	noun	*music*	*L8*		
yǐqián	noun	*before*	*L15*	以前	以前
yīzhí	adverb	*continuously, keep (doing verb)*	*L14*	一 **zhí**	一 **zhí**

yòng	verb	*use*	L15		
yǒu	stative verb	*have*	L4	有	有
yòu	*	*right*	L13		
yòubiān	noun	*right side*	L13		
yǒu de	noun description phrase	*some*	L10	有的	有的
yǒu shì	verb phrase	*have something to do, be busy*	L9	有 **shì**	有 **shì**
yǒu shì ma?	conversational expression	*What's up?*	L9	有 **shì** 嗎?	有 **shì** 吗?
yǒu yìsi	adjectival verb phrase	*be interesting*	L16	有 **yìsi**	有 **yìsi**
yòubiān	noun	*right side*	L13		
Yǒuwén	given name	*(given name)*	L11	友文	友文
yuǎn	adjectival verb	*far*	L11		
yuè	noun	*month*	L8	月	月
yǔfǎ	noun	*grammar*	L10		

Z

zài	adverb;	*(action in progress);*	L9	在	在
	verb;	*be located at;*	L11		
	preposition	*at, in, on*	L12		
zài	adverb	*afterward*	L13	再	再
zài jiàn	conversational expression	*goodbye*	L1	再見	再见
zài shuō yī cì	conversational expression	*say it again*	L6	再說一 **cì**	再说一 **cì**
zǎo	adjectival verb; greeting	*early; good morning*	L6	早	早
zǎo jiù	adverb	*long before now, long ago,*	L15	早就	早就
zǎofàn	noun	*breakfast*	L9	早飯	早饭
zāogāo	conversational expression	*oh no!*	L8		
zǎoshang	noun	*morning*	L9	早上	早上
zěnme	question word	*how*	L5	怎麼	怎么
zěnmeyàng	question phrase	*how about it? okay?*	L8	怎麼樣?	怎么样?
zhàn	noun	*station, (bus or train) stop*	L11	站	站
Zhāng	family name	*(family name)*	L1	張	张
zhāng	classifier	*(classifier for flat rectangular and square objects)*	L6	張	张
zhǎo	verb	*look for, find*	L13	找	找
zhào	verb	*photograph, take (a photograph)*	L15		
zhàopiàn	noun	*photograph*	L4		
zhǎo (qián)	verb	*make (change)*	L7	找錢	找钱
zhè	demonstrative	*this*	L4	這	这
zhè, zhèi	specifier	*this*	L6	這	这
zhè yàng	noun phrase	*in this way, how about this*	L8	這樣	这样
zhēn	intensifier	*really*	L13	真	真
zhēnde ma?	conversational expression	*really?*	L3	真的嗎?	真的吗?
zhèng	verb	*earn*	L16		

zhèr	noun	*here*	L11	這兒	这儿
zhī	classifier	*(classifier for writing implements, e.g. pencils, pens)*	L6		
zhǐ	adverb	*only*	L3	只	只
zhǐ	noun	*paper*	L6		
zhīdào	verb	*know*	L5	知道	知道
zhōng	*	*middle*	L9	中	中
Zhōngguó	country name	*China*	L2	中國	中国
Zhōngguó huà	noun phrase	*Chinese language*	L3	中國話	中国话
Zhōngguó rén	noun	*Chinese person*	L2	中國人	中国人
Zhōnghuá	country name	*China*	L12	中 **huá**	中 **huá**
zhōngjiān	noun	*between, in between*	L13	中 **jiān**	中 **jiān**
Zhōngshān	given name	*Sun Yatsen*	L11	中 **shān**	中 **shān**
zhōngtóu	noun	*hour*	L12		
Zhōngwén	noun	*Chinese language*	L4	中文	中文
zhōngwǔ	noun	*noon*	L9	中 **wǔ**	中 **wǔ**
zhōngxīn	noun	*center*	L11	中 **xīn**	中 **xīn**
zhù	verb	*live/reside in a place*	L15	住	住
zì	noun	*character (Chinese character)*	L7	字	字
zǒu	verb	*go, walk*	L12, 14	走	走
zǒu lù	verb + object	*walk*	L14	走路	走路
zuǒ	*	*left*	L13		
zuò	verb	*do;*	L9	做	做
		cook	L15		
zuò	verb	*sit, ride, or "take" a form of transportation*	L12	坐	坐
zuǒbiān	noun	*left side*	L13		
zuótiān	noun	*yesterday*	L10	昨天	昨天

Chinese character index alphabetically arranged

B		Meaning		Illustrative words	Simplified
bā	八	eight	L6		八
bà	爸	dad	L15	爸爸 (bàba) dad	爸
ba	吧	(indicates speaker's supposition and suggestions)	L15		吧
bàn	半	half	L11		半
běi	北	north	L14	北 biān (běibiān) north side	北
běn	本	(volume of books)	L12	一本書 (yī běn shū) one book 日本 (Rìběn) Japan	本
bù	不	no (negation)	L8		不

C					
chà	差	*	L14	差不多 (chàbuduō) almost	差
cháng	常	often	L16	非常 (fēicháng) extremely	常
chē	車	car	L13	huǒ 車 (huǒchē) train 公 gòng qì 車 (gōnggòng qìchē) bus 下車 (xià chē) get off the vehicle	车
chī	吃	eat	L10	吃飯 (chī fàn) eat	吃
cóng	從	from	L13		从

D					
dǎ	打	hit	L12	打 suàn (dǎsuàn) plan (to) 打電話 (dǎ diànhuà) make a phonecall	打
dà	大	big	L12	大學 (dàxué) college	大
dāng	當	*	L10	當然 (dāngrán) of course	当
dào	到	to (prep.), arrive (V)	L13		到
dào	道	*	L14	知道 (zhīdào) know	道
de	的	(indicates noun description)	L7		的
de, dì	地	particle	L16	地圖 (dìtú) map 地 tiě (dìtiě) subway	地
děi, de	得	must, (particle)	L13		得
diǎn	點	dot	L11	一點 (yīdiǎn) a little 一點 zhōng (yīdiǎn zhōng) one o'clock	点
diàn	電	electricity	L12	電話 (diànhuà) telephone 電 yǐng (diànyǐng) movie 電 yǐng yuàn (diànyǐng yuàn) movie theater	电
diàn	店	store	L14	書店 (shūdiàn) bookstore	店
dōng	東	east	L13	東 biān (dōngbiān) east 東西 (dōngxi) thing	东
dōu	都	all, both	L10		都
duì	對	correct	L9	對不起 (duìbuqǐ) excuse me	对
duō	多	many, more	L10		多

E					
ér / r	兒	*	L11		儿
èr	二	two	L6		二

F

fǎ	法	*	L16	法國 (**Fǎguó**) France	法
fàn	飯	rice	L10	吃飯 (**chī fàn**) eat	饭
fēi	非	*	L16	非常 (**fēicháng**) extremely	非
fēn	分	minute, cent, penny	L9		分

G

gāng	剛	just now	L16		刚
Gāo	高	(family name)	L15	高 xìng (**gāoxìng**) happy	高
gè	個	(classifier for people and some other nouns)	L7		个
gěi	給	give, for, to	L12	給 (someone) 打電話 (**gěi** (someone) **dǎ diànhuà**) phone (someone)	给
gēn	跟	with	L16		跟
gōng	公	*	L14	公園 (**gōngyuán**) park 公 gòng qì 車 (**gōnggòng qìchē**) (public) bus	公
guǎn	館	*	L12	圖書館 (**túshuguǎn**) library kāfēi 館 (**kāfēiguǎn**) coffee shop	馆
guó	國	country	L15	中國 (**Zhōngguó**) China 美國 (**Měiguó**) USA 法國 (**Fǎguó**) France Dé 國 (**Déguó**) Germany Yīng 國 (**Yīngguó**) Britain	国
guò	過	cross, pass	L14		过

H

hái	還	in addition	L11		还
Hàn	漢	*	L16	漢字 (**Hàn zì**) Chinese character	汉
hǎo	好	good, well	L8		好
hào	號	number	L12	電話號 mǎ (**diànhuà hàomǎ**) telephone number 幾月幾號 (**jǐ yuè jǐ hào**) what month and date is it?	号
hé	和	and	L13		和
hěn	很	very	L8		很
hòu	後	*	L15	以後 (**yǐhòu**) after 後 biān (**hòubiān**) behind	后
hòu	候	*	L16	時候 (**shíhou**) time	候
huà	話	speech, language	L9	說話 (**shuō huà**) speak, 中國話 (**Zhōngguó huà**) Chinese language	话
huān	歡	*	L16	喜歡 (**xǐhuan**) like	欢
huí	回	return	L15	回家 (**huí jiā**) return home 回國 (**huí guó**) return to one's home country 回 guō ròu (**huíguō ròu**) twice-cooked pork	回
huì	會	can, able to	L10		会

J

jǐ	幾	how many, how much	L7		几
jiā	家	family, home	L11		家
jiàn	見	see	L9	再見 (**zài jiàn**) goodbye	见
jiào	叫	call	L15		叫

jīn	今	*	L15	今天 (jīntiān) today	今
jīng	京	*	L13	東京 (Dōngjīng) Tokyo	京
				北京 (Běijīng) Beijing	
jīng	經	*	L13	已經 (yǐjing) already	经
jiù	就	only, precisely, sooner than expected	L12		就
jiǔ	九	nine	L6		九
jué, jiào	覺	*	L16	覺得 (juéde) think	觉
				shuì 覺 (shuì jiào) sleep	

K

kāi	開	*	L16	開 shǐ (kāishǐ) begin	开
				開車 (kāi chē) drive a car	
kàn	看	look at, see, read	L11	看見 (kànjian) see	看
				看書 (kàn shū) read (books)	
				看朋友 (kàn péngyou) see friends	
kě	可	*	L9	可以 (kěyǐ) can	可
kǒu	口	mouth	L14	門口 (ménkǒu) doorway	口
				路口 (lùkǒu) intersection	
				十字路口 (shízì lùkǒu) four-way intersection	
kuài	塊	dollar	L12	一塊錢 (yī kuài qián) one dollar	块
kuài	快	fast, quickly	L14		快

L

lái	來	come	L15		来
lǎo	老	old	L10	老師 (lǎoshī) teacher	老
le	了	(completion, new situation)	L10		了
liǎng	兩	two (of something)	L7		两
liù	六	six	L6		六
lù	路	road	L13	馬路 (mǎlù) road	路
				路口 (lùkǒu) intersection	
				十字路口 (shízì lùkǒu) four-way intersection	
				走路 (zǒu lù) walk	

M

mā	媽	mom	L15	媽媽 (māma) mom, mama	妈
mǎ	馬	(family name), horse	L13	馬路 (mǎlù) road	马
ma	嗎	(yes no questions)	L7		吗
mǎi	買	buy	L12		买
mài	賣	sell	L14		卖
màn	慢	slow, slowly	L14	慢慢地 (mànmān de) gradually, little by little	慢
máo	毛	dime	L12	一毛錢 (yī máo qián) one dime	毛
me	麼	*	L7	甚麼 (shénme) what?	么
méi	沒	no, not (negation)	L10		没
měi	美	beautiful	L15	美國 (Měiguó) USA	美
mén	門	door, gate	L13	門口 (ménkǒu) doorway	门
men	們	(plural suffix for pronouns)	L8	我們 (wǒmen) we, us;	们
				你們 (nǐmen) you;	
				他們 (tāmen) they, them	
míng	明	*	L9	明天 (míngtiān) tomorrow	明
				明年 (míngnián) next year	

N

nǎ	哪	which	L7		哪
nà, nèi	那	that	L7		那
nán	男	male	L11	男 **hái** 子 (**nán háizi**) *boy* 男朋友 (**nán péngyou**) *boyfriend*	男
nán	南	south	L14	南 **biān** (**nánbiān**) *south side*	南
nán	難	difficult	L14		难
ne	呢	(final particle/ follow-up questions)	L8		呢
nǐ	你	you	L8	你們 (**nǐmen**) *you (plural)*	你
nián	年	year	L15	今年 (**jīnnián**) *this year* 明年 (**míngnián**) *next year* 去年 (**qùnián**) *last year* 一年 **jí** (**yī niánjí**) *first-year level*	年
nín	您	you (polite)	L15		您
nǔ	女	female	L11	女 **hái** 子 (**nǔ háizi**) *girl* 女朋友 (**nǔ péngyou**) *girlfriend*	女

P

péng	朋	*	L15	朋友 (**péngyou**) *friend*	朋

Q

qī	七	seven	L6		七
qī	期	*	L11	星期 (**xīngqī**) *week* shǔ 期 (**shǔqī**) *summer duration*	期
qǐ	起	get up, rise	L9	對不起 (**duìbuqǐ**) *excuse me*	起
qián	錢	money	L12	多少錢 (**duōshao qián**) *how much money?* 一塊錢 (**yī kuài qián**) *one dollar*	钱
qián	前	*	L15	以前 (**yǐqián**) *before* 前 **biān** (**qiánbiān**) *in front of*	前
qǐng	請	invite	L11	請問 (**qǐng wèn**) *may I ask*	请
qù	去	go	L10		去

R

rán	然	*	L10	當然 (**dāngrán**) *of course*	然
rén	人	person	L7		人
rì	日	*	L12	日本 (**Rìběn**) *Japan*	日
róng	容	*	L13	容易 (**róngyì**) *easy*	容

S

sān	三	three	L6		三
shàng	上	last (week, month), above	L11	上 **wǔ** (**shàngwǔ**) *morning*	上
shǎo	少	few, less	L10	多少 (**duōshao**) *how many, how much*	少
shéi	誰	who	L11		谁
shén	甚	*	L7	甚麼 (**shénme**) *what?*	什
shēng	生	be born	L10	學生 (**xuésheng**) *student* 生活 (**shēnghuó**) *live, life*	生
shī	師	*	L10	老師 (**lǎoshī**) *teacher*	师

shí	十	ten	L6		十
shí	時	*	L16	時候 (shíhou) time	时
				時 jiān (shíjiān) time	
shì	是	be	L8		是
shū	書	book	L12	圖書館 (túshūguǎn) library	书
				看書 (kàn shū) read (books)	
shuǐ	水	water	L15	水 guǒ (shuǐguǒ) fruit	水
shuō	說	speak, talk	L9	說話 (shuō huà) speak	说
sì	四	four	L6		四

T

tā	他	he	L8	他們 (tāmen) they, them	他
tā	她	she	L8	她們 (tāmen) they, them (female)	她
tài	太	too	L11	人太 (tàitai) Mrs., wife	太
tiān	天	day, heaven	L11	今天 (jīntiān) today	天
				星期天 (xīngqītiān) Sunday	
tú	圖	*	L12	圖書館 (túshūguǎn) library	图
				地圖 (dìtú) map	

W

wǎn	晚	late	L10	晚上 (wǎnshang) evening	晚
				晚飯 (wǎnfàn) dinner	
Wáng	王	(family name)	L11		王
wǎng	往	toward	L14		往
wén	文	*	L9	中文 (Zhōngwén) Chinese language	文
wèn	問	ask	L13	請問 (qǐng wèn) please may I ask	问
wǒ	我	I, me	L8	我們 (wǒmen) we, us	我
wǔ	五	five	L6		五

X

xī	西	west	L13	西 biān (xībiān) west	西
				東西 (dōngxi) thing	
xí	習	*	L16	liàn 習 (liànxí) practice	习
				fù 習 (fùxí) review	
				習 guàn (xíguàn) be accustomed to	
xǐ	喜	*	L16	喜歡 (xǐhuan) like	喜
xià	下	below, down	L12	下 biān (xiàbiān) below	下
				下 kè (xià kè) get out of class	
				下車 (xià chē) get off the vehicle	
				下个星期 (xià gè xīngqī) next week	
xiàn	現	*	L13	現在 (xiànzài) now	现
xiān	先	first	L15	先生 (xiānsheng) Mr., husband	先
xiǎng	想	think, want, plan to	L12		想
xiǎo	小	little, small, (family name prefix)	L9	小張 (Xiǎo Zhāng) Xiao Zhang	小
xiě	寫	write	L16	寫字 (xiě zì) write (characters, letters)	写
xiè	謝	thank (family name)	L9	謝謝 (xièxie) thank you	谢
xīng	星	star	L11	星期 (xīngqī) week	星
xué	學	study	L10	學生 (xuésheng) student	学

Y

yàng	樣	*	L11	怎麼樣 (**zěnmeyàng**) *what about it?* *how about it?* 這樣 (**zhèyàng**) *this way*		样
yào	要	*will, want*	L14			要
yě	也	*also*	L8			也
yī	一	*one*	L6			一
yǐ	以	*	L9	可以 (**kěyǐ**) *can*		以
yǐ	已	*	L13	已經 (**yǐjing**) *already*		已
yì	易	*	L13	容易 (**róngyì**) *easy*		易
yǒu	有	*have, there is/there are*	L9			有
yǒu	友	*	L15	朋友 (**péngyou**) *friend*		友
yuán	園	*	L14	公園 (**gōngyuán**) *park*		园
yuè	月	*month*	L16	一月 (**yīyuè**) *January*		月

Z

zài	再	*again*	L9	再見 (**zài jiàn**) *goodbye*		再
zài	在	*located at; (ongoing action)*	L11			在
zǎo	早	*early*	L9	早飯 (**zǎofàn**) *breakfast*		早
zěn	怎	*	L10	怎麼 (**zěnme**) *how*		怎
zhàn	站	*station*	L14	車站 (**chēzhàn**) *station* 地 tiě 站 (**dìtiězhàn**) *subway station*		站
zhāng	張	*sheet (classifier), (family name)*	L9			张
zhǎo	找	*look for*	L13	找錢 (**zhǎo qián**) *give change*		找
zhè, zhèi	這	*this*	L7			这
zhēn	真	*really*	L16			真
zhī	知	*	L14	知道 (**zhīdào**) *know*		知
zhǐ	只	*only*	L11			只
zhōng	中	*middle, (part of the word for China, Chinese language, etc.)*	L9	中文 (**Zhōngwén**) *Chinese language* 中國 (**Zhōngguó**) *China* 中 huá (**Zhōnghuá**) *China*		中
zhù	住	*reside (in a location)*	L16			住
zì	字	*(Chinese) character*	L14	漢字 (**Hàn zì**) *Chinese character*		字
zi	子	*	L15	hái 子 (**háizi**) *child* jiǎo 子 (**jiǎozi**) *dumpling* fáng 子 (**fángzi**) *house*		子
zǒu	走	*go*	L13	走路 (**zǒu lù**) *walk*		走
zuó	昨	*yesterday*	L14	昨天 (**zuótiān**) *yesterday*		昨
zuò	做	*do*	L11			做
zuò	坐	*sit*	L15			坐

Chinese character index by lesson

Lesson 6	Pinyin	Meaning	Illustrative words	Simplified
一	yī	one		一
二	èr	two		二
三	sān	three		三
四	sì	four		四
五	wǔ	five		五
六	liù	six		六
七	qī	seven		七
八	bā	eight		八
九	jiǔ	nine		九
十	shí	ten		十

Lesson 7				
的	de	*(indicates noun description)*		的
個	gè	*(classifier for people and some other nouns)*		个
幾	jǐ	*how many, how much*		几
兩	liǎng	*two (of something)*		两
嗎	ma	*(yes-no questions)*		吗
麼	me	*	甚麼 (**shénme**) *what?*	么
哪	nǎ	*which*		哪
那	nà, nèi	*that*		那
人	rén	*person*		人
甚	shén	*	甚麼 (**shénme**) *what?*	什
這	zhè, zhèi	*this*		这

Lesson 8				
不	bù	*no (negation)*		不
好	hǎo	*good, well*		好
很	hěn	*very*		很
們	men	*(plural suffix for pronouns)*	我們 (**wǒmen**) *we, us;* 你們 (**nǐmen**) *you;* 他們 (**tāmen**) *they, them*	们
呢	ne	*(final particle/ follow-up questions)*		呢
你	nǐ	*you*	你們 (**nǐmen**) *you (plural)*	你
是	shì	*be*		是
她	tā	*she*	她們 (**tāmen**) *they, them (female)*	她
他	tā	*he*	他們 (**tāmen**) *they, them*	他
我	wǒ	*I, me*	我們 (**wǒmen**) *we, us*	我
也	yě	*also*		也

Lesson 9				
對	duì	*correct*	對不起 (**duìbuqǐ**) *excuse me*	对
分	fēn	*minute, cent, penny*		分
話	huà	*speech, language*	說話 (**shuō huà**) *speak* 中國話 (**Zhōngguó huà**) *Chinese language*	话
見	jiàn	*see*	再見 (**zài jiàn**) *goodbye*	见

可	**kě**	*	可以 (**kěyǐ**) *can*	可
明	**míng**	*	明天 (**míngtiān**) *tomorrow*	明
			明年 (**míngnián**) *next year*	
起	**qǐ**	*get up, rise*	對不起 (**duìbuqǐ**) *excuse me*	起
說	**shuō**	*speak, talk*	說話 (**shuō huà**) *speak*	说
文	**wén**	*	中文 (**Zhōngwén**) *Chinese language*	文
小	**xiǎo**	*little, small, (family name prefix)*	小張 (**Xiǎo Zhāng**) *Xiao Zhang*	小
謝	**xiè**	*thank, thank you, (family name)*	謝謝 (**xièxie**) *thank you*	谢
以	**yǐ**	*	可以 (**kěyǐ**) *can*	以
有	**yǒu**	*have, there is/there are*		有
再	**zài**	*again*	再見 (**zài jiàn**) *goodbye*	再
早	**zǎo**	*early*	早飯 (**zǎofàn**) *breakfast*	早
張	**zhāng**	*sheet (classifier), (family name)*		张
中	**zhōng**	*middle, (part of the word for China, Chinese language, etc.)*	中文 (**Zhōngwén**) *Chinese language* 中國 (**Zhōngguó**) *China* 中 huá (**Zhōnghuá**) *China*	中

Lesson 10

吃	**chī**	*eat*	吃飯 (**chī fàn**) *eat*	吃
當	**dāng**	*	當然 (**dāngrán**) *of course*	当
都	**dōu**	*all, both*		都
多	**duō**	*many, more*		多
飯	**fàn**	*rice*	吃飯 (**chī fàn**) *eat*	饭
會	**huì**	*can, able to*		会
老	**lǎo**	*old*	老師 (**lǎoshī**) *teacher*	老
了	**le**	*completion, new situation*		了
沒	**méi**	*no, not (negation)*		没
去	**qù**	*go*		去
然	**rán**	*	當然 (**dāngrán**) *of course*	然
少	**shǎo**	*few, less*	多少 (**duōshao**) *how many, how much*	少
生	**shēng**	*be born*	學生 (**xuésheng**) *student* 生活 (**shēnghuó**) *live, life*	生
師	**shī**	*	老師 (**lǎoshī**) *teacher*	师
晚	**wǎn**	*late*	晚上 (**wǎnshang**) *evening* 晚飯 (**wǎnfàn**) *dinner*	晚
學	**xué**	*study*	學生 (**xuésheng**) *student*	学
怎	**zěn**	*	怎麼 (**zěnme**) *how*	怎

Lesson 11

半	**bàn**	*half*		半
點	**diǎn**	*dot*	一點 (**yīdiǎn**) *a little* 一點 zhōng (**yīdiǎn zhōng**) *one o'clock*	点
兒	**ér / r**	*		儿
還	**hái**	*in addition*		还
家	**jiā**	*family, home*		家

看	kàn	look at, see, read	看見 (kànjian) see	看
			看書 (kàn shū) read (books)	
			看朋友 (kàn péngyou) see friends	
男	nán	male	男孩子 (nán háizi) boy	男
			男朋友 (nán péngyou) boyfriend	
女	nǔ	female	女孩子 (nǔ háizi) girl	女
			女朋友 (nǔ péngyou) girlfriend	
期	qī	*	星期 (xīngqī) week	期
			暑期 (shǔqī) summer duration	
請	qǐng	invite	請問 (qǐng wèn) may I ask	请
上	shàng	last (week, month), above	上午 (shàngwǔ) morning	上
誰	shéi	who		谁
太	tài	too	太太 (tàitai) Mrs., wife	太
天	tiān	day, heaven	今天 (jīntiān) today	天
			星期天 (xīngqītiān) Sunday	
王	Wáng	(family name)		王
星	xīng	star	星期 (xīngqī) week	星
樣	yàng	*	怎麼樣 (zěnmeyàng) what about it? how about it?	样
			這樣 (zhèyàng) this way	
在	zài	located at		在
只	zhǐ	only		只
做	zuò	do		做

Lesson 12

本	běn	(classifier: volume)	一本書 (yī běn shū) one book	本
			日本 (Rìběn) Japan	
打	dǎ	hit	打算 (dǎsuàn) plan (to)	打
			打電話 (dǎ diànhuà) make a phonecall	
大	dà	big	大學 (dàxué) college	大
電	diàn	electricity	電話 (diànhuà) telephone	电
			電影 (diànyǐng) movie	
			電影院 (diànyǐng yuàn) movie theater	
給	gěi	give, for, to	給 (someone) 打電話 (gěi (someone) dǎ diànhuà) phone (someone)	给
館	guǎn	*	圖書館 (túshūguǎn) library	馆
			咖啡館 (kāfēiguǎn) coffee shop	
號	hào	number	電話號碼 (diànhuà hàomǎ) telephone number	号
			幾月幾號 (jǐ yuè jǐ hào) what month and date is it?	
就	jiù	only, precisely, sooner than expected		就
塊	kuài	dollar	一塊錢 (yī kuài qián) one dollar	块
買	mǎi	buy		买
毛	máo	dime	一毛錢 (yī máo qián) one dime	毛
錢	qián	money	多少錢 (duōshao qián) how much money?	钱
			一塊錢 (yī kuài qián) one dollar	

日	rì	*	日本 (Rìběn) *Japan*	日
書	shū	*book*	圖書館 (túshūguǎn) *library*	书
			看書 (kàn shū) *read (books)*	
圖	tú	*	圖書館 (túshūguǎn) *library*	图
			地圖 (dìtú) *map*	
下	xià	*next, go down,*	下 biān (xiàbiān) *below*	下
		get off, below	下 kè (xià kè) *get out of class*	
			下車 (xià chē) *get off the vehicle*	
			下個星期 (xià gè xīngqī) *next week*	
想	xiǎng	*think, want, plan to*		想

Lesson 13

車	chē	*car*	huǒ 車 (huǒchē) *train*	车
			公 gòng qì 車 (gōnggòng qìchē) *bus*	
			下車 (xià chē) *get off the vehicle*	
從	cóng	*from*		从
到	dào	*to (prep.), arrive (V)*		到
得	děi, de	*must, (particle)*		得
東	dōng	*east*	東 biān (dōngbiān) *east*	东
			東西 (dōngxi) *thing*	
和	hé	*and*		和
京	jīng	*	東京 (Dōngjīng) *Tokyo*	京
			北京 (Běijīng) *Beijing*	
經	jīng	*	已經 (yǐjing) *already*	经
路	lù	*road*	馬路 (mǎlù) *road*	路
			路口 (lùkǒu) *intersection*	
			十字路口 (shízì lùkǒu)	
			four-way intersection	
			走路 (zǒu lù) *walk*	
馬	mǎ	*(family name); horse*	馬路 (mǎlù) *road*	马
門	mén	*door, gate*	門口 (ménkǒu) *doorway*	门
容	róng	*	容易 (róngyì) *easy*	容
問	wèn	*ask*	請問 (qǐng wèn) *please may I ask*	问
西	xī	*west*	西 biān (xībiān) *west*	西
			東西 (dōngxi) *thing*	
現	xiàn	*	現在 (xiànzài) *now*	现
已	yǐ	*	已經 (yǐjing) *already*	已
易	yì	*	容易 (róngyì) *easy*	易
找	zhǎo	*look for*	找錢 (zhǎo qián) *give change*	找
走	zǒu	*go*	走路 (zǒu lù) *walk*	走

Lesson 14

北	běi	*north*	北 biān (běi biān) *north side*	北
差	chà	*	差不多 (chàbuduō) *almost*	差
道	dào	*	知道 (zhīdào) *know*	道
店	diàn	*store*	書店 (shūdiàn) *bookstore*	店
公	gōng	*	公園 (gōngyuán) *park*	公
			公 gòng qì 車 (gōnggòng qìchē) *bus*	
過	guò	*cross, pass*		过

口	kǒu	mouth	門口 (ménkǒu) doorway	口
			路口 (lùkǒu) intersection	
			十字路口 (shízì lùkǒu) four-way intersection	
快	kuài	fast, quickly		快
賣	mài	sell		卖
慢	màn	slow, slowly	慢慢地 (mànmān de) gradually, little by little	慢
南	nán	south	南 biān (nánbiān) south side	南
難	nán	difficult		难
往	wǎng	towards		往
要	yào	will, want		要
園	yuán	*	公園 (gōngyuán) park	园
站	zhàn	station	車站 (chēzhàn) station	站
			地 tiě 站 (dìtiězhàn) subway station	
知	zhī	*	知道 (zhīdào) know	知
字	zì	(Chinese) character	漢字 (Hàn zì) Chinese character	字
昨	zuó	yesterday	昨天 (zuótiān) yesterday	昨

Lesson 15

爸	bà	dad	爸爸 (bàba) dad	爸
吧	ba	(indicates speaker's suppositions and suggestions)		吧
高	Gāo	(family name)	高 xìng (gāoxìng) happy	高
國	guó	country	中國 (Zhōngguó) China	国
			美國 (Měiguó) USA	
			法國 (Fǎguó) France	
			Dé 國 (Déguó) Germany	
			Yīng 國 (Yīngguó) Britain	
後	hòu	*	以後 (yǐhòu) after	后
			後 biān (hòubiān) behind	
回	huí	return	回家 (huí jiā) return home	回
			回國 (huí guó) return to one's home country	
			回 guō ròu (huí guō ròu) twice-cooked pork	
叫	jiào	call		叫
今	jīn	*	今天 (jīntiān) today	今
來	lái	come		来
媽	mā	mom	媽媽 (māma) mom, mama	妈
美	měi	beautiful	美國 (Měiguó) USA	美
年	nián	year	今年 (jīnnián) this year	年
			明年 (míngnián) next year	
			去年 (qùnián) last year	
			一年 jí (yī niánjí) first-year level	
您	nín	you (polite)		您
朋	péng	*	朋友 (péngyou) friend	朋
前	qián	*	以前 (yǐqián) before	前
			前 biān (qiánbiān) in front of	
水	shuǐ	water	水 guǒ (shuǐguǒ) fruit	水
先	xiān	first	先生 (xiānsheng) Mr., husband	先
友	yǒu	*	朋友 (péngyou) friend	友

子	zi	*	hái 子 (**háizi**) *child*	子
			jiǎo 子 (**jiǎozi**) *dumpling*	
			fáng 子 (**fángzi**) *house*	
坐	zuò	*sit*		坐

Lesson 16

常	cháng	*often*	非常 (**fēicháng**) *extremely*	常
地	de, dì	*particle*	地圖 (**dìtú**) *map*	地
			地 tiě (**dìtiě**) *subway*	
法	fǎ	*	法國 (**Fǎguó**) *France*	法
非	fēi	*	非常 (**fēicháng**) *extremely*	非
剛	gāng	*just now*		剛
跟	gēn	*with*		跟
漢	Hàn	*	漢字 (**Hàn zì**) *Chinese character*	汉
候	hòu	*	時候 (**shíhou**) *time*	候
歡	huān	*	喜歡 (**xǐhuan**) *like*	欢
覺	jué, jiào	*	覺得 (**juéde**) *think*	觉
			shuì 覺 (**shuì jiào**) *sleep*	
開	kāi	*	開 shǐ (**kāishǐ**) *begin*	开
			開車 (**kāi chē**) *drive a car*	
時	shí	*	時候 (**shíhou**) *time*	时
			時 jiān (**shíjiān**) *time*	
習	xí	*	liàn 習 (**liànxí**) *practice*	习
			fù 習 (**fùxí**) *review*	
			習 guàn (**xíguàn**) *be accustomed to*	
喜	xǐ	*	喜歡 (**xǐhuan**) *like*	喜
寫	xiě	*write*	寫字 (**xiě zì**) *write (characters, letters)*	写
月	yuè	*month*	一月 (**yīyuè**) *January*	月
真	zhēn	*really*		真
住	zhù	*reside (in a location)*		住

Index of Use and Structure

MOVEMENT: *go* to a location with **qù** (去) 10.16, 12.2, *come* to a location with **lái** (來) 11.3, 12.2, *move toward* a location with **wǎng** (往) 12.1, move *from* one place *to* another 12.2, open-ended movement with **zǒu** (走) *go* L12 Language FAQs

NAMES: family names and addressing friends 1.1, names and titles 1.10, Chinese names 3.1, asking for someone's name 3.3

ne (呢) questions: *see* QUESTIONS

NEGATION: **bù** (不) 1.9, **méi** (沒) 4.9, 10.14, **bù** (不) and **méi** (沒) compared 10.15

NEW INFORMATION: with sentence-final **le** (了) 9.6

NOUNS: linking nouns and noun phrases with **shì** (是) *be* 1.4, counting nouns and saying *this noun* and *that noun* 5.3, 6.2, 7.6, joining nouns with *and* 3.5, *see also* DESCRIBING NOUNS, PRONOUNS

NUMBERS: 1–10 and *zero* L5, 11–99 7.3, 100–999 7.9, ordinal numbers: *first, second, third* 14.4

OBLIGATION: **děi** (得) *must* 9.7

one **yāo** (一) and **yī** (一) 5.10

OPINIONS: **juéde** (覺得) *in (my) opinion* 10.1

PARAPHRASE: **yě jiù shì shuō** (也就是說) *in other words* 14.5

PAST ACTIONS: *see* COMPLETED ACTION, ACTIONS

PAST EXPERIENCE: **V-guò** (過) 15.12

PERMISSION: **kěyǐ** (可以) *can* 5.12

PHYSICAL ABILITY: **néng** 13.4

POSSESSION: with **de** (的) 4.4, with **yǒu** (有) *have* 5.2

PREPOSITIONS: **gēn** (跟) *with* and **gēn** (跟) NP **yīqǐ** (一起) *with NP* 10.19, **gěi** (給) *to, for* 11.8, **cóng** (從) *from* 12.1, **lí** *separated from* 11.6, **dào** (到) *to* 12.1, **zài** (在) *at, in, on* 11.11, **wǎng** (往) *toward* 12.1

PRICES AND SHOPPING: 6.4, money phrase 6.6, asking how something is sold 6.8, cost per item 6.9, negotiating prices L7 Notes on Chinese Culture

PROHIBITIONS: **bù kěyǐ** (不可以) *cannot* 9.7, **bié** *don't* 14.7

PRONOUNS: 1.3, plural form 2.2

QUESTIONS

Content questions: location of content question words in the sentence 3.2, **shénme** (甚麼) *what* 3.2, **shéi** (誰) *who* 4.1, **jǐ** (幾) *how much, how many?* 5.4, **zěnme** (怎麼) *how?* 5.9, **duōshao** (多少) *how much? how many?* 6.3, **duōshao** (多少) and **jǐ** (幾) compared 6.5, **nǎ** 哪 *which?* 7.1, **nǎr?** (哪兒?) *where?* 11.7

ne (呢) questions 2.3

Yes-no questions: with **ma** (嗎) 1.6, V-not-V yes-no questions 3.7, answering *yes* 1.7, answering *no* and saying *no* 1.9

RELATIVE CLAUSES: see DESCRIBING NOUNS

RETROFLEX SUFFIX **–r**: 8.18

SEE A GUEST OFF AND FETCH A GUEST: L13, L16 Notes on Chinese Culture

Related titles from Routledge

The Routledge Course in Modern Mandarin Chinese

Textbook Level 2
(forthcoming)

Claudia Ross, Baozhang He, Pei-Chia Chen, Meng Yeh

The Routledge Course in Mandarin Chinese is a two-year undergraduate course for students with no prior background in Chinese study. Designed to build a strong foundation in both spoken and written forms of the language, it develops all the basic skills such as pronunciation, character writing, word use and structures, while placing strong emphasis on the development of communicative skills.

The Routledge Course in Modern Mandarin Chinese: Textbook Level 2 incorporates the innovative features of *Textbook Level 1* including the separation of vocabulary from characters, a "basic to complex" introduction of grammatical structures, and a separate comprehensive workbook with extensive exercises to practice all language skills and functions. An accompanying teacher's manual is also available.

Textbook Level 2 also adds a "narrative" component that helps learners with the transition from spoken Mandarin to formal written Chinese and from the comprehension and production of short sentences to paragraphs and essays.

Key features of the narrative component include:

- Model narratives that introduce formal written Chinese with *explanations* of the features of each narrative
- Focus on narrative *function* including description, comparison, explanation, persuasion, and hypothesis
- Reading and writing assignments that guide students to internalize model structures, to read for information, and to compose original essays for specific purposes.

The Routledge Course in Modern Mandarin Chinese: Textbook Level 2 bridges the gap that characterizes the transition between basic level Chinese courses and more advanced work.

Pb: 978-0-415-47246-3 (Traditional)
Pb: 978-0-415-47250-0 (Simplified)

Related titles from Routledge

The Routledge Course in Modern Mandarin Chinese

Workbook Level 2
(forthcoming)

Claudia Ross, Baozhang He, Pei-Chia Chen, Meng Yeh

The Routledge Course in Mandarin Chinese is a two-year undergraduate course for students with no prior background in Chinese study. Designed to build a strong foundation in both spoken and written forms of the language, it develops all the basic skills such as pronunciation, character writing, word use, and structures, while placing strong emphasis on the development of communicative skills.

Workbook level 2 is designed to accompany *Textbook level 2* lesson by lesson, and offers exercises for homework, independent study and classroom use. The activities in the workbook are cross-referenced with the Use and Structure points in the textbook so that students are directed to review material as they work through the exercises.

Each lesson focuses on the skills of listening and speaking as well as reading and writing. The book contains pronunciation practice, structure drills, listening exercises, and practice of characters, structures and communication. All the necessary audio materials, recorded by native speakers, are included on the enclosed CD.

Pb: 978-0-415-47253-1 (Traditional)
Pb: 978-0-415-47247-0 (Simplified)

Available at all good bookshops
For ordering and further information please visit:
www.routledge.com